DATE DUE

DISCARD

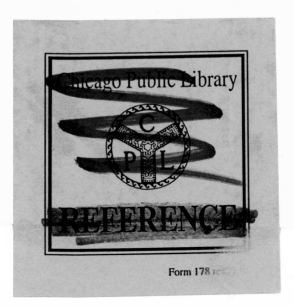

The Post-NAFTA
Political Economy

The Post-NAFTA Political Economy

Mexico and the Western Hemisphere

Edited by Carol Wise

The Pennsylvania State University Press
University Park, Pennsylvania

Library of Congress Cataloging-in-Publication Data

The post-NAFTA political economy : Mexico and the Western Hemisphere /
edited by Carol Wise.
   p.   cm.
   Includes bibliographical references and index.
   ISBN 0-271-01822-4 (cloth : alk. paper)
   ISBN 0-271-01823-2 (pbk. : alk. paper)
   1. Mexico—Economic conditions—1994– 2. North America—Economic
integration. 3. America—Economic integration. 4. Canada.
Treaties, etc. 1992 Oct. 7. I. Wise, Carol.
HC135.P715 1998
330.972'0836—dc21   98-16941
                                                   CIP

Printed in the United States of America
Published by The Pennsylvania State University Press,
University Park, PA 16802-1003

It is the policy of The Pennsylvania State University Press to use acid-free paper for
the first printing of all clothbound books. Publications on uncoated stock satisfy the
minimum requirements of American National Standard for Information Sciences—
Permanence of Paper for Printed Library Materials, ANSI Z39.48–1992.

Contents

For Glen

Preface

Partly by design, but also by luck, the publication of this collection of essays coincides with the very point at which long-stated goals of western hemispheric integration finally appear to be on track. It is now nearly a decade since former President George Bush proposed the creation of a hemispheric free trade zone as part of his 1990 Enterprise for the Americas Initiative. Despite the considerable political conflict that has surrounded domestic debates about economic integration in Canada and the United States, and the prolonged adjustment stress that Latin America has weathered in the wake of massive financial crises in Mexico (1994) and Asia (1997–1998), the integration process has continued to move forward: A North American Free Trade Agreement (NAFTA) joining Canada, Mexico and the United States was implemented on January 1, 1994; the Southern Cone Common Market (MERCOSUR) was launched exactly a year later with the initial participation of Argentina, Brazil, Paraguay, and Uruguay; and, three other sub-regional integration schemes are now underway in the Caribbean Basin, Central American, and Andean blocs.

In tandem with the integration inroads being made within these sub-regional schemes, two hemispheric summits held in Miami (December 1994) and Santiago (April 1998) have sought to advance the broader hemispheric integration initiative that was originally articulated by U.S. policy makers in 1990. The financial press has been less than optimistic about both summits, declaring each more or less "dead on arrival" because stated economic integration goals were forced to compete with a multitude of other non-economic issues like corruption, drug trafficking, judicial reform and human rights. The fact that Clinton administration officials arrived at both summits without the fast-track authority necessary to negotiate and submit foreign trade agreements to the U.S. Congress for an up-or-down vote without further meddling has also fueled pessimism about the prospects for a hemisphere-wide integration agreement. In short, for some critics, the road from Miami to Santiago has been one long detour.

But, as the essays in this collection will reveal, much has also happened along the way. For starters, the Miami Summit of the Americas was convened unilaterally by the United States, whereas the Santiago meeting was a truly multilateral event hosted by the Organization of American States in conjunction with the Inter-American Development Bank and the United Nations Economic Commission for Latin America and the Caribbean. Underpinning the Santiago meeting of all 34 democratically elected governments in the western hemisphere was the multilateral Free Trade Area of the Americas (FTAA) initiative that had been launched in Miami. Since 1994, the FTAA's various working groups have tackled tough issues in such areas as rules of origin, market access, intellectual property rights, and customs procedures; and, they have advanced on some of the issues mentioned above which, although non-economic, have been essential for building the kind of collegiality and cooperation that are also essential for bringing the FTAA to fruition. Progress on all of these matters has been such that in the "Second Summit of the Americas Plan of Action," all parties committed themselves to convening the FTAA negotiations commitee no later than June 30, 1998, to achieving "concrete progress in the negotiations by the year 2000," and to completing the full negotiations by the year 2005. While the FTAA is perhaps not barrelling ahead at the speed some would prefer, and U.S. leadership has all but stalled, the negotiations themselves have clearly entered second gear and will remain there for some time.

In essence, the essays in this collection represent a third wave of scholarship, and one which attempts to summarize and critique the various dimensions of this current holding pattern in the western hemisphere. Prior to the implementation of NAFTA, the early 1990's saw a flurry of published monographs which projected the future costs and benefits of integration mainly from the standpoint of NAFTA. Once NAFTA was a *fait accompli*, many of these same analysts turned their attention to questions of compliance, implementation and the expansion of NAFTA southward. Now, with the FTAA negotiations on the starting block, and the formation of a hemispheric accord a political economic reality proper, attention has turned to analyses which tackle the dynamics of integration both from the advantage of hindsight, and from a broader comparative standpoint. Thanks to a number of institutions and individuals, this joint effort at updating and synthesizing the track record on hemispheric integration has been made possible. Since 1992, funding has been provided by the American Area Republics Fulbright Grant, the Carnegie Endowment for International Peace, the William and Flora Hewlett Foundation, the John D. and Catherine T. MacArthur

Foundation, the North-South Center at the University of Miami, and the U.S. Institute of Peace.

Warm thanks are also due to four colleagues in particular—Jeff Frieden, Steph Haggard, Bob Kaufman, and Moises Naim—for their support and incredible patience in writing the many letters of recommendation necessary to secure this research funding. Manuel Pastor was also instrumental in the fundraising, planning, and completion of this project. At Penn State Press, Sandy Thatcher and Cherene Holland were a dream to work with: reliable, straightforward, and always collegial. The manuscript also benefitted from the thoughtful review and editorial comments offered by Max Cameron, Michelle Miller-Adams, and Chandler Stolp. Finally, my home department, the Program on Western Hemisphere Studies at Johns Hopkins University's School of Advanced International Studies (SAIS), supported the two conferences and numerous overhead expenses that accrued in the course of completing this book. Guadalupe Paz, the director of our Mexico Program, and two SAIS research assistants, Maria Barboza and Walter Weaver, provided invaluable backup. I am especially grateful to my department chair, Riordan Roett, for his encouragement and generosity in seeing this edited collection all the way through to the end.

Carol Wise
Washington, D.C.
April 1998

Introduction

NAFTA, Mexico, and the Western Hemisphere

Carol Wise

The past decade has seen the proliferation of regional and subregional agreements that explicitly promote liberalization and higher levels of trade and investment. By 1995, for example, rough estimates show that some 53 percent of world trade was conducted within the context of regional trade agreements.[1] In the Western Hemisphere, which is the subject of this edited collection, there are now five principal subregional agreements[2]

---

1. Jaime Serra et al., *Reflections on Regionalism: Report of the Study Group on International Trade* (Washington, D.C.: Carnegie Endowment for International Peace, 1997), 5–8. This report notes that between 1990 and 1994 more than thirty new regional agreements were notified to the General Agreement on Tariffs and Trade (GATT); moreover, of the some 120 countries that have now joined the GATT, approximately 90 percent belong to a regional grouping of one kind or another.

2. The North American Free Trade Agreement (NAFTA, 1/1/94), the Southern Cone Common Market (Mercosur, 1/1/95), the Andean Group (12/94), the Caribbean Common Market (CARICOM, 1973), and the Central American

and four major preferential trade schemes,[3] and in the 1990s alone, more than twenty bilateral trade accords have thus far been negotiated between states within the hemisphere. These accords, such as the Bolivia-Peru bilateral agreement that was signed in 1992, have included former foes and, like the Argentina-Ecuador agreement that was signed that same year, some rather unexpected bedfellows. With regard to the Western Hemisphere, two points can be made with certainty about these trends.

First, in the case of Latin America, the embrace of regional agreements geared toward liberalizing trade and investment flows in the 1990s represents a radical departure from past agreements based on import substitution and heavy protectionism. Second, although world trade has increased twelvefold since the mid-1940s,[4] multilateral rule making within the General Agreement on Tariffs and Trade (GATT) and now the World Trade Organization (WTO) has simply not moved quickly enough to secure broader market access, particularly for middle-income developing countries like Mexico. As an ever-increasing number of developing states clamor to secure access to industrial markets and to attract international investment in the post–Cold War era, regional and subregional agreements offer the more immediate possibility of capturing greater trade and capital flows.[5]

Apart from these general observations, political economists remain divided when it comes to identifying those more specific contingencies that have prompted policy makers to pursue regional and subregional agreements. On one side of the debate are those who define regionalism as the adoption of discriminatory trade and investment policies by a group of geographically proximate states.[6] In other words, participants

Common Market (1961). These regional groupings are elaborated on in Richard L. Bernal, "Paths to the Free Trade Area of the Americas" (Policy Papers on the Americas, Center for Strategic and International Studies, Washington, D.C., January 15, 1997), app. 2.

3. The Caribbean Basin Initiative (CBI, 1984), the Andean Trade Preference Act (ATPA, 12/91), the Venezuela/CARICOM Agreement (7/91), and the Colombia/CARICOM Agreement (1/95). See ibid.

4. Serra et al., *Reflections on Regionalism,* ix.

5. See Magnus Blomstrom and Ari Kokko, "Regional Integration and Foreign Direct Investment: A Conceptual Framework" (Policy Research Working Paper 1750, World Bank, Washington, D.C., 1997).

6. Comments made by Helen Milner at a workshop, "APEC in the International Affairs Curriculum" (Graduate School of International Relations and Pacific Studies, University of California at San Diego, February 22, 1997). A broader definition of regionalism is that put forth by Andrew Hurrell, "Latin America in the New World Order: A Regional Bloc of the Americas?" *International Affairs* 68, no. 1 (1992): 123: "A set of policies by one or more states designed to promote the emergence of

in regional trade agreements strive to benefit through the diversion of trade and investment away from outsiders that may be more competitive but that are edged out by preferences afforded only to the members of the regional scheme. Regional insiders are also able to increase their bargaining power by dealing with nonmembers from the strength of a regional bloc, and there is more latitude for shaping—or, if the need be, constraining—the economic and political behavior of neighboring states that are members of the same regional agreement. From this standpoint, it is difficult to imagine regionalism as complementary to the long-standing goals of multilateralism and nondiscrimination as they were originally articulated within the GATT.

An alternative view of regionalism is based on a definition of inclusion and openness: participants in a regional agreement need not necessarily be geographic neighbors, and there is a joint commitment to low entry barriers. "Open regionalism" is seen as a process that bolsters the efforts of each member to increase its links with the world economy and to promote the international competitiveness of those goods and services that each country has to offer.[7] By definition, preferential regional schemes will foster some diversion of trade and investment away from more efficient producers who are nonmembers. However, the net welfare gains can still be positive. This is because many of the recent regional integration schemes go much further than the reduction of tariff and nontariff trade barriers, for example, by incorporating measures to liberalize foreign investment and services and guaranteeing intellectual-property rights. Thus, the dynamic benefits can extend beyond trade creation in rendering a group of states more efficient and competitive. When interpreted from this angle, regionalism has been cast as a strategy that is compatible with and reinforces the long-standing multilateral goals of the GATT/WTO.

Debates concerning the open or closed nature of specific regional and subregional agreements and the actual economic consequences of regionalism are also far from settled. Although economists unanimously agree that multilateral liberalization is the optimal (albeit slow and politi-

---

a cohesive unit, which dominates the patterns of relations between states of that region and the rest of the world, and which forms the organizing basis for policy within the region across a range of issues."

7. United Nations Economic Commission for Latin America and the Caribbean (ECLAC), "Open Regionalism in Latin America and the Caribbean" (paper prepared for the nineteenth session, Committee of High-Level Government Experts, Santiago, Chile, March 1994).

cally cumbersome) strategy for maximizing the gains from trade and investment, there is much less consensus over the economic costs and benefits of regional approaches to liberalization. Obviously, the likelihood that a regional scheme will enhance world efficiency through the creation of new trade and investment depends on the kinds of trade patterns that have been established between all of the participants, and on the way in which the agreement is designed.[8] In the real world of political expedience and policy implementation, the launching of a regional scheme that is welfare-maximizing for the entire international community also depends on the political motives of participant states and on the capacity to enact such an agreement in a nondiscriminatory manner. Since numerous states simultaneously pursue their goals of trade and investment liberalization in both a regional and a multilateral context, it is not surprising that trade theory and empirical analysis have been unable to rule decisively on the costs and benefits of regionalism. As Robert Lawrence has observed, "various models suggest that forces are operating in both directions."[9]

While it will clearly take more time to resolve these numerous debates surrounding the wave of regional initiatives launched during the past decade, this book seeks to advance our understanding of these issues as they relate to the premiere regional agreement of the 1990s—the North American Free Trade Agreement (NAFTA), implemented between Canada, Mexico, and the United States on January 1, 1994. When compared with its main regional counterpart, the fifteen-member European Union (EU), NAFTA differs considerably. First, whereas the EU is a customs union (members establish a common external tariff, while trading freely within the union), NAFTA is a free-trade area (FTA), which eliminates internal barriers between members, while each maintains its own external tariff.[10] Second, although the closer integration of the three signatory countries created a regional grouping on a par with the EU in terms of gross domestic product (GDP), NAFTA was unusual in that it brought together two highly developed countries with a middle-income developing country.[11]

---

8. Serra et al., *Reflections on Regionalism*, ix–x.

9. Robert Z. Lawrence, *Regionalism, Multilateralism, and Deeper Integration* (Washington, D.C.: Brookings Institution, 1996), 5.

10. Ibid., 7.

11. At its outset, NAFTA united a population of approximately 372 million, with a combined GNP of more than U.S.$7 trillion; of this, Mexico accounted for about 87 million people and a GNP of about U.S.$325 billion. See Bernal, "Paths to the Free Trade Area of the Americas," app. 4.

Finally, there are several ways in which NAFTA goes beyond the accomplishments of the EU and the GATT/WTO in liberalizing trade and investment. For example, NAFTA offers a broader treatment of trade in services and intellectual-property rights, and the agreement spells out more comprehensive procedures for settling disputes between governments and investors.[12] However, NAFTA's designers have displayed little ambition to extend this agreement along the same institutional lines as those of the EU, as the latter now advances toward a common currency and perhaps even political union—all underpinned by long-standing institutions such as the European Parliament and a formidable legislative bureaucracy in Brussels.

The essays in this collection explore two main themes that have increasingly come to dominate discussions about NAFTA since the launching of the initiative in January 1994. First is the complicated question of how Mexico has fared, both economically and politically, as a NAFTA participant. Economic theory tells us that Mexico, as the smaller and less developed country, stands to gain the most from entering into a NAFTA-style arrangement with Canada and the United States. As closer integration triggers dynamic changes in terms of scale economies, the less developed participant is expected to benefit disproportionately through an acceleration in the rate of productivity growth and an increase in the rate of capital formation.[13] Overall, the net welfare gains in terms of production, employment, and consumption are predicted to outweigh the losses.

Before NAFTA's passage, there was certainly no shortage of computable-general-equilibrium (CGE) models to bolster the economic case for Mexico's entry into the agreement. And, of course, the Mexican government financed a massive public-relations campaign to convince the U.S. Congress and the Mexican people of NAFTA's merits. While the field has become increasingly crowded with analyses that project Mexico's future under NAFTA, this book approaches the subject with the benefit of hindsight. Four of the essays (by Pastor and Wise, Pastor, Heath, and Dresser) in this collection examine the Mexican political economy in the NAFTA era by way of detailed case and data analysis, the data generated since the implementation of the agreement just now becoming available. On

---

12. Lawrence, *Regionalism, Multilateralism, and Deeper Integration*, 70–72.

13. Roberto Bouzas and Jaime Ros, "The North-South Variety of Economic Integration: Issues and Prospects for Latin America," in *Economic Integration in the Western Hemisphere*, ed. Roberto Bouzas and Jaime Ros (Notre Dame, Ind.: University of Notre Dame Press, 1994), 7–12.

balance, the essays confirm the success of NAFTA in producing many of
the dynamic benefits suggested by integration theory. However, it turns
out that the failure of Mexican policy makers to factor in credible social
mechanisms for compensating the losers in the adjustment process, and
their premature discounting of the possibility of volatile political protest
in response to a major reallocation of domestic resources, have been
costly and serious oversights.[14]

The second theme explored here is the prospect for expanding the
kind of economic integration represented by NAFTA into a full-blown
hemispheric initiative. After committing itself at the December 1994
Miami Summit of the Americas to the negotiation of a Free Trade Area
of the Americas (FTAA) by the year 2005, the United States promptly
took a three-year holiday as far as hemispheric trade policy is concerned.[15] What happened? Admittedly, although the economic news for
all three partners has basically been favorable, including Mexico's
faster-than-expected recovery from the December 1994 peso crisis, the
political news has been shocking: reports of drug trafficking, money
laundering, violent guerrilla insurgencies, assassinations, massacres, and
kidnappings that garner seven-figure ransoms now dominate the front-
page news on Mexican politics.[16]

Has the earlier commitment to hemispheric integration waned because of these adverse political trends? Or, when all is said and done, is
the economic logic for an FTAA simply not compelling enough? Perhaps
diplomatic gestures like President Bush's 1990 Enterprise for the Americas Initiative (EAI) and the 1994 Miami Summit catapulted NAFTA prema-
turely onto a hemispheric track,[17] before all of the economic
technicalities had been clearly thought through. The remaining five essays (by Maxfield and Shapiro, Woods, Andreas, Wise, and Haggard) in
this collection explore these questions, first, from the angle of U.S.-Mexi-
can relations and, second, from a broader hemispheric standpoint. De-

14. See Victor Bulmer-Thomas et al., "Mexico and NAFTA: Who Will Benefit?" in *Mexico and the
North American Free Trade Agreement: Who Will Benefit?* ed. Victor Bulmer-Thomas, Nikki Craske,
and Mónica Serrano (New York: St. Martin's Press, 1994), 204–10.

15. I. M. Destler, "American Trade Politics in the Wake of the Uruguay Round," in *The World
Trading System: Challenges Ahead,* ed. Jeffrey J. Schott (Washington, D.C.: Institute for International
Economics, 1996), 115–16.

16. Alma Guillermoprieto, "Mexico: Murder Without Justice," *New York Review of Books,* October 3, 1996, 31–36.

17. For more detail on the EAI and the Miami Summit, see the chapter by Stephan Haggard in
this collection.

spite the dominant tendency for optimistic projections concerning the prospects of hemispheric integration, these essays, taken together, suggest that although the FTAA process is still on track, the timing, content, and outcomes will be quite different from the vision that was originally articulated at the Miami Summit.

The remainder of this introduction consists of the following: The second section provides a brief background summary of NAFTA, including its origins, the debate that preceded NAFTA's passage by the U.S. Congress in November 1993, and the nature of the actual agreement that was finally ratified by all three countries. The remaining sections highlight the two themes taken up by the essays in this collection. A third section touches on the main arguments and trends that have surrounded the performance of the Mexican political economy in the NAFTA era. The final section explores how NAFTA has, and has not, fared thus far as a hemispheric initiative. While Canada is surely just as important a player in any discussion of the political economy of NAFTA, this book focuses mainly on the two countries on which NAFTA's passage ultimately hinged: Mexico and the United States, and the evolving U.S.-Mexican relationship.

NAFTA in Retrospect

NAFTA's Origins

Although bipartisan proposals for a trilateral economic partnership between Canada, Mexico, and the United States first surfaced in 1979 within the U.S. Congress and the National Governors Association, it was presidential candidate Ronald Reagan who drew attention to this issue by making the pursuit of a "North American Accord" a centerpiece of his foreign-policy platform during the 1979–80 electoral campaign.[18] At the time, neither Canada nor Mexico responded with any enthusiasm, citing historical concerns about heavy U.S. influence over both countries, and a fear of being swallowed up by powerful U.S. competitors. When the negotiations for NAFTA did finally materialize, it was Mexico—which had objected most vigorously to the U.S. offer for a similar arrangement a decade earlier—that approached the Bush administration

18. Donald Barry, "The Road to NAFTA," in *Toward a North American Community? Canada, the United States, and Mexico,* ed. Donald Barry (Boulder, Colo.: Westview Press, 1995), 3–9.

in 1990 about the possibility of its entry into the Canadian-U.S. Free Trade Agreement (CUSFTA) that had just been ratified.

Canada's change of heart had come about in 1983–84, when Canadian policy makers could no longer ignore the country's lagging productivity and declining trade position within European markets.[19] As Canadian exporters encountered increasing levels of protectionism in the United States, the necessity for a more formal agreement to guarantee market access had gradually become clear. Canada's shift in favor of stronger U.S. economic ties represented a fundamental change of attitude, especially within the domestic political arena. But given the highly homogeneous nature of the two countries, including similar factor endowments and levels of development, and the dominant role that each country played in the other's trade and investment portfolio, the pursuit of the CUSFTA was still mainly an evolutionary phenomenon. In contrast, Mexico's full turnabout—from high protectionism and a determination to maintain its national sovereignty to a more open stance that embraced free trade and close ties with the United States—represented an outright revolution. What kinds of international and domestic factors worked to favor the creation of a NAFTA-style relationship, which had been extremely difficult to fathom just a decade ago, mainly because of the pronounced disparities between Mexico and the CUSFTA signatories?

At first glance, international-level explanations take us a long way in answering these questions. For example, in the parlance of international-relations theory, both structural realism and regime analysis offer important insights into the origins of NAFTA.[20] The former approach explains the extent to which all three parties sought an FTA as a means to maximize their economic power and advance their respective national interest. Indeed, several challenges that arose at the level of the international political economy during the 1980s led all three participants to undertake a sober assessment of where things stood. These challenges varied,

19. Ibid., 7–11. See also Maxwell A. Cameron and Brian W. Tomlin, "Canada and Latin America in the Shadow of U.S. Power: Toward an Expanding Hemispheric Agreement?" in *Toward a North American Community?* ed. Donald Barry.

20. For elaboration on these theories, see the essays in *Neorealism and Its Critics*, ed. Robert O. Keohane (New York: Columbia University Press, 1986) and *International Regimes*, ed. Stephen D. Krasner (Ithaca, N.Y.: Cornell University Press, 1983). For an application of these theories to NAFTA, see Frederick W. Mayer, *Interpreting NAFTA: The Art and Science of Political Analysis* (New York: Columbia University Press, forthcoming), draft chap. 3A.

however, according to which side of the industrial divide one came down on.

For the United States, there was increasing economic uncertainty as the country slipped into net-debtor status in the mid-1980s, and the monthly trade balance registered unprecedented multibillion-dollar deficits. Concern mounted over the declining competitiveness of U.S. goods in foreign markets and the increasing tendency for trade relations to be dominated by a regional-bloc mentality, led by Europe and to a lesser extent Asia. The slowness with which the GATT's Uruguay Round negotiations moved forward in the late 1980s also did little to assuage policy makers' fears that multilateral bargaining over trade was no longer the most effective means for furthering U.S. commercial interests. Not surprisingly, U.S. policy makers responded somewhat aggressively to these perceived economic threats: first, by providing the highest level of import relief to domestic industry that the country had seen in the entire postwar period;[21] second, by seeking out bilateral deals like the CUSFTA, which offered more immediate prospects for guaranteed market access.

Canada's interest in bilateralism in the 1980s was a reaction to these same competitive trends that had emerged at the level of the international economy and to the ways in which they were already affecting U.S.-Canadian economic ties.[22] Despite their joint membership in the industrial world's two foremost insider clubs (the G-7 and the OECD) and their shared roots in Anglo-Saxon democratic capitalism, it was the combination of large economic disparities between the United States and Canada and the latter's disproportionate dependence on the United States that eventually brought it to the CUSFTA negotiating table. The CUSFTA did not necessarily represent a departure from Canada's long-standing preferences for multilateralism and diversification of its trade and investment ties. Rather, the decision to accept U.S. overtures toward bilateralism was based on self-interest—the pragmatic realization that

21. Destler, "American Trade Politics in the Wake of the Uruguay Round," 120.
22. For further analysis of the Canadian political economy in the 1980s, see the following two articles by Denis Stairs: "Change in the Management of Canada–United States Relations in the Post-War Era," in *Toward a North American Community? Canada, the United States, and Mexico*, ed. Donald Barry (Boulder, Colo.: Westview Press, 1995), and "The Canadian Dilemma in North America," in *NAFTA and Sovereignty: Trade-offs for Canada, Mexico, and the United States*, ed. Joyce Hoebing et al. (Washington, D.C.: Center for Strategic and International Studies, 1996).

"Canada might as well put all of its Grade A eggs in the American basket because the other baskets were either too small, beyond repair, or out of reach. Canadians, in short, lived in North America, and had nowhere else to go."[23]

South of the industrial divide, Mexico faced different but equally difficult international challenges. By the late 1980s, it had become clear that the damage wreaked by the 1982 debt crisis was not just transitory and that policy makers still had their work cut out for them in designing a credible framework that would entice desperately needed investment—both direct and portfolio—back into the economy. As the de la Madrid administration (1982–88) moved forward with its ambitious unilateral opening of the economy in 1985, efforts to improve Mexico's international economic position were bolstered by the signing of a series of trade and investment framework accords with the United States between 1985 and 1989, and by the country's accession to the GATT in 1986. By 1990, the Salinas administration (1988–94) had successfully promoted Mexico as the first country to secure a reduction of its U.S.$48 billion commercial debt under the Brady Plan, which cut about U.S.$1 billion off the country's annual debt-service payment.[24]

Structural realism holds that states will act rationally in defending their economic interests and shoring up market power, but stops short of predicting the timing and nature of state action. This approach is also vague when it comes to explaining the kinds of fallback positions that might be adopted when states have failed to achieve their designated goals. NAFTA, in essence, was a fallback position for all three partners. It is no secret that Canada entered the NAFTA negotiations with reluctance.[25] Given the volatile national debate that had preceded the ratification of the CUSFTA, and continued political infighting over the extent to which the country's high unemployment rate could be attributed to that agreement, Mexico's request to negotiate a new FTA with the United States was not a welcome turn for Ottawa. The decision to enter the trilateral negotiations was based on the goal of preserving Canada's foothold in U.S. markets, given that a U.S.-Mexican FTA would put Canada at a distinct disadvantage vis-à-vis Mexican exports to the U.S. market.[26]

23. Stairs, "Change in the Management of Canada-U.S. Relations in the Post-War Era," 68.
24. William A. Orme, *Understanding NAFTA* (Austin: University of Texas Press, 1996), 30–32.
25. Cameron and Tomlin, "Canada and Latin America in the Shadow of U.S. Power," 132–36.
26. Leonard Waverman, "The NAFTA Agreement: A Canadian Perspective," in *Assessing NAFTA: A Trilateral Analysis,* ed. Steven Globerman and Michael Walker (Vancouver: Fraser Institute, 1992), 32–33.

Canada also sought to avoid a diversion of foreign investment toward the United States, since the United States would become the main investment gateway to the continental market under a U.S.-Mexican FTA that did not include Canada.

On the U.S. side, the joint strategy of negotiating a bilateral accord with Canada while maintaining a stance of selective protectionism toward various other trade partners did little to alleviate the economic stresses or the foot-dragging within the Uruguay Round that had inspired these policies in the first place. Although the negotiation of an FTA with Mexico held obvious risks, the latter's advances with market reform suggested that the United States could also benefit handsomely by integrating more closely with the Mexican economy. In the grand scheme of things, the huge disparities between the two economies meant that NAFTA entry was enormously more important for Mexico; however, the prospect of a more economically stable and successful neighbor to the south held strong appeal in terms of U.S. security interests,[27] as did the formation of a North American bloc that could counter the stiff competition emanating from Europe and Asia.

Similarly, for Mexico, the failure of domestic and international investment to come forth in any magnitude, despite the significant strides that had been made in opening markets, indicated by 1990 that a more binding commitment to economic reform would be necessary. Thus, as the competition to attract foreign capital became more fierce in the new post–Cold War context, President Salinas grew more willing to tread where his predecessor had feared to go: despite decades of diplomatic acrimony and mutual suspicion between Mexico and the United States, Salinas buried the hatchet and aggressively pursued an FTA with the Bush administration. In other words, when unilateral gestures failed to accomplish the investment and trade goals that Salinas had deemed crucial for answering his country's pressing economic needs, and the prospect of multilateral gains seemed too distant, bilateralism prevailed.

Regime theory sheds some light on why Canada, Mexico, and the United States, as self-interested actors, sought to institutionalize respective political-economic ties that had long been in place but had thus far been managed in an ad hoc manner.[28] Without going into the various

27. Joe Foweraker, "From NAFTA to WHFTA? Prospects for Hemispheric Free Trade," in *Cooperation or Rivalry? Regional Integration in the Americas and the Pacific Rim,* ed. Shoji Nishijima and Peter H. Smith (Boulder, Colo.: Westview Press, 1996), 162–63.

28. This discussion of regime theory applied to NAFTA borrows from Mayer, *Interpreting NAFTA,* draft chap. 3A.

debates that have divided regime theorists, suffice it to say that by 1990 both Canada and Mexico saw NAFTA as an opportunity to secure access to the U.S. market and to establish clearly defined rules and procedures for resolving trade and investment disputes. The United States, while also concerned with promoting and rationalizing economic ties within the North American bloc, primarily sought to bolster the rules and norms that constituted the international trade regime codified within the GATT. Apart from the slow progress on the Uruguay Round negotiations, the creation of a new NAFTA regime within the larger GATT/WTO framework was warranted on two grounds: first, because a NAFTA-style FTA technically conforms with the criteria set forth in Article 24 of the GATT/WTO;[29] second, because the CUSFTA had generally been perceived as "shallow" in its commitment to greater liberalization[30] and the NAFTA negotiations afforded an opportunity to push further on this front.[31]

In the process of negotiating a revised set of rules to facilitate the consolidation and deeper liberalization of a North American bloc proper, each participant was clearly looking to reduce transaction costs while simultaneously increasing the benefits of cooperation.[32] Although international-level explanations are helpful for understanding how each state came to perceive a new round of rule making under NAFTA as the most efficient way for overcoming barriers to economic advancement, there remains the question why the debate over NAFTA's ratification became so contentious. Furthermore, it is still unclear why the agreement took the final shape that it did. The answers to these questions lie more in the realm of domestic politics, to which the analysis now turns.

The Debate over NAFTA

From the launching of the negotiations in September 1991 to the ratification vote in the U.S. House of Representatives on November 17, 1993, the tone of the NAFTA debate was counterintuitive. Economic integration

---

29. Serra et al., *Reflections on Regionalism*, 30–33. Although vague, GATT's Article 24 has always permitted the formation of regional and subregional schemes, on the condition that "substantially all" trade is free among participants and where the remaining barriers against outsiders are not raised.

30. Lawrence, *Regionalism, Multilateralism, and Deeper Integration*, 66.

31. As Cameron and Tomlin ("Canada and Latin America in the Shadow of U.S. Power," 135–36) point out, Canada came to see the NAFTA negotiations as an opportunity to improve on the CUSFTA's weaknesses in the areas of government procurement, rules of origin, and financial services, and in settling disputes over the application of antidumping and countervailing duties.

32. Mayer, *Interpreting NAFTA*, draft chap. 3A.

theory suggests that both the United States and Canada, as the larger, wealthier, and more open economies, should expect marginal adjustments, at worse. In turn, Mexico, as the smaller, poorer, and more highly protected economy, should expect to undergo a more sweeping and costly adjustment in the short term, but to realize considerable dynamic gains in the medium to long term.[33] From this theory it should follow that the debate over whether to pursue an FTA would be more heated in Mexico, the country that had the most at stake. Conversely, given that the United States and Canada had much less on the line, one would expect a fairly tame discussion about whether to negotiate an FTA that included Mexico. Paradoxically, the opposite pattern emerged. Before the implementation of the agreement, a full-scale national debate over NAFTA never picked up momentum in Mexico, whereas in the United States the prospect of NAFTA inspired a heated public discussion on a par with the controversy that surrounded the passage of the Smoot-Hawley Tariff in 1930. Similarly, for Canada, the government's announcement of its intentions to join the NAFTA negotiations reignited the bitter exchanges over politics, economics, and U.S.-Canadian relations that had surrounded the earlier CUSFTA negotiations.

In Mexico, the apparently lackadaisical attitude toward NAFTA also defied long-standing notions concerning the domestic politics of trade. For example, according to the traditional literature on the political economy of trade, Mexico, as a capital-scarce developing country with an abundant supply of labor, should expect aggressive private-sector lobbying against trade liberalization.[34] Although this is exactly what happened when President Lopez Portillo (1976–82) came close to signing Mexico into the GATT back in 1980, just a decade later the private sector declared itself ready to face new unprecedented levels of external competition. The essays here by Pastor and Wise, Heath, Dresser, and Wise address the underlying political and economic dynamics that gave rise to this sea change, which, in turn, helps explain why the domestic debate over NAFTA in Mexico was basically a nonstarter.[35]

---

33. Bouzas and Ros, "The North-South Variety of Economic Integration."

34. See, for example, Ronald Rogowski, *Commerce and Coalitions: How Trade Affects Domestic Political Alignments* (Princeton: Princeton University Press, 1989), and Mancur Olson, *The Logic of Collective Action: Public Goods and the Theory of Groups* (New York: Schocken Books, 1968).

35. Although the NAFTA negotiations were not officially launched until September 1991, Juan Gallardo, the leader of the Mexican Business Coordinating Council for Free Trade (COECE), pronounced during an August 1991 interview that, as far as the Mexican business community was

In a nutshell, the Mexican economy had been adjusting since the debt shocks of 1982, and unilateral trade liberalization had been under way since 1985. With GATT accession in 1986 and another deep round of tariff cuts in 1988, it had gradually become clear to the domestic private sector that there was no going back to the old protectionist way of doing things. Three trends worked to foster a new coalition in Mexico that favored NAFTA entry.[36] First was the quiet explosion in intra-industry trade and cross-border production between the United States and Mexico that occurred throughout the 1980s. Closer U.S.-Mexican integration was initially spurred by the joining of U.S. capital and inputs with Mexico's cheap labor supply and lax regulatory standards—a relationship that was cemented within the *maquila* export-processing zones that had been established in the 1960s along the U.S.-Mexican border. Over the past decade, however, joint investment strategies among North American firms have become increasingly sophisticated, as scale economies and intra-industry specialization have fostered a much more dynamic pattern of export-led growth. The guarantee of permanently low trade barriers held special appeal for this select group of cross-border producers, who predictably led the charge for Mexico's entry into NAFTA.

But the pro-NAFTA contingent in Mexico reflected much more than the preferences of those engaged in intra-industry trade and specialization. A second trend was the coalitional dynamics that came to life in the context of the Economic Solidarity Pact that was first launched in December 1987 to combat inflation and was renewed throughout the six-year Salinas administration. In essence, the pact brought the main representatives of business and labor together with the government's powerful technocratic elite, toward the goal of jointly negotiating a viable stabilization strategy. By combining price administration and import liberalization with a tight fiscal and monetary policy, this approach succeeded in reducing inflation from an annual high of 160 percent in 1987 to 19 percent in 1991.

Although many of those operating within Mexico's small and medium-sized business sector still opposed NAFTA—producers as well as workers—the successful linking of trade liberalization with macroeco-

---

concerned, NAFTA was already "locked up!" Author's interview with Juan Gallardo, Mexico City, August 1991.

36. For more detail on these arguments, see Manuel Pastor Jr. and Carol Wise, "The Origins and Sustainability of Mexico's Free Trade Policy," *International Organization* 48, no. 3 (1994): 477–84.

nomic stabilization helped gradually to persuade those who had held out for protectionism that, as painful as the medicine of increased competition might be, it was in their best long-term economic interest. As big business, co-opted representatives of organized labor, and an impressive corps of highly trained government technocrats quickly came to dominate the pact, those who remained doubtful about their prospects under NAFTA were subjected to the same bullying tactics (e.g., tax harassment, credit rationing) upon which the country's ruling party (Revolutionary Institutional Party, or PRI) has traditionally based its "legitimacy."[37]

A third trend that accounts for the comparative ease with which Mexico's leaders ushered the country into NAFTA has to do with Salinas's brilliant manipulation of political symbols. By linking some of the main ideals of the Mexican Revolution, such as distributional equity and social justice, with the neoliberal rhetoric embodied in NAFTA, Salinas and his cohort managed to convince the population at large that NAFTA was simply another phase in the realization of the country's long-term revolutionary goals. Given his party's extremely weak showing in the 1988 presidential elections, Salinas was also willing to put up the necessary political capital to back his aspirations for joining NAFTA. By launching his National Solidarity Program, or PRONASOL (which amounted to less than 1 percent of yearly GDP spent on a wide range of social capital projects), Salinas succeeded in bringing the PRI's disillusioned base back into the fold. By the time the NAFTA negotiations were firmly under way, these tactics had left NAFTA's potential winners in Mexico with an exaggerated sense of their future gains; similarly, NAFTA's obvious losers had been encouraged to underestimate their probable losses. Looking back, this overblown expectation that the winners' circle in Mexico could only widen under NAFTA helps to explain the political and social upheaval that has occurred in the face of the opposite scenario.

Whereas Mexican political leaders were masterful at confining the debate over NAFTA to vague generalities while at the same time embellishing it with nationalistic symbols, the debate on the U.S. side bogged down in grueling detail. The first sign that the proposed NAFTA negotiations would not be met with the same disinterest in the United States that had characterized the CUSFTA negotiations came in the spring of

---

37. This statement is based on a survey, conducted by the author, of Mexico's small and medium-sized business representatives between 1991 and 1993. See Pastor and Wise, "The Origins and Sustainability of Mexico's Free Trade Policy," 467–68.

1991, when President Bush sought congressional approval for an extension of the "fast-track" authority necessary to bring the agreement to an up-or-down vote in the U.S. House of Representatives. Under fast track, Congress would vote on the original trade bill as it was submitted, without the opportunity to amend it. As the deadline for securing the fast-track extension approached late that spring, NAFTA's champions on both sides of the congressional aisle were clearly caught off guard by the scope and intensity of the debate that ensued.

At its most economistic, the NAFTA debate in the United States focused on three main indicators: the U.S.-Mexican trade balance, the number of U.S. jobs that would correlate with this trade balance, and the impact that NAFTA would have on investment decisions in the North American economy.[38] Those who favored NAFTA on economic grounds insisted that one must be mindful of the fact that the global economy is increasingly driven by strategic corporate alliances, massive investment flows, and highly specialized cross-border trade and production. Thus, the argument went, NAFTA would simply codify and institutionalize a similar pattern of production and investment at the regional level, while also providing strong incentives for the expansion of market access and the deepening of transborder integration into higher-skilled sectors and labor markets. For NAFTA's defenders, although the risks of trade and investment diversion were real (e.g., in the auto sector), these would be more than offset by higher levels of direct investment, dynamic productivity gains, and job expansion under NAFTA.

NAFTA's detractors in the United States focused more immediately on the indicators mentioned above. On economic grounds alone, the opposition, led by organized labor and a loose coalition of nonunion workers in threatened sectors, clearly did not like what it saw. Although the Bush administration made much of the trade surplus that the United States had run with Mexico during the 1990s, and used this as justification for the economic desirability of NAFTA, the opposition (backed by some sympathetic think-tank economists in Washington) pointed out that this surplus was a historical anomaly: it did not appear until 1991, and was driven by the combination of Mexico's unilateral trade opening

38. For a good review of these debates, see Office of Technology Assessment (OTA), *U.S.-Mexico Trade: Pulling Together or Pulling Apart?* (Washington, D.C.: U.S. Congress, 1992); Sidney Weintraub, "U.S.-Mexico Trade: Implications for the United States," in *Assessments of the North American Free Trade Agreement*, ed. Ambler H. Moss (Miami, Fla.: North-South Center, University of Miami, 1993); and Orme, *Understanding NAFTA*, chap. 1.

and an increasingly overvalued peso, which spurred domestic demand in Mexico for cheap U.S. imports.[39] Should the Mexicans devalue, wouldn't the reverse logic take hold—that is, wouldn't cheap imports flood from Mexico into the United States, thus provoking widespread U.S. job losses?

The NAFTA opposition in the United States was similarly suspicious of the Bush administration's promises that the expansion of U.S. exports to Mexico under NAFTA would generate a net increase in jobs at home. Although there was substantial consensus among U.S. economists that NAFTA would have a modest net positive impact of 100,000–200,000 jobs over its first ten years, the long-term trend toward corporate downsizing and wage stagnation in the United States gave understandable cause for concern.[40] As for NAFTA's potential impact on investment decisions in the United States, the opposition envisioned a bleak scenario whereby U.S. corporations could have it both ways; they could farm out the lower end of their production lines to Mexico, taking advantage of dirt-cheap wages and low regulatory barriers, while also using the threat of relocation south to hold down wage-and-benefit packages for their higher-skilled workforce back home.

Clearly, there was more at stake here than the negotiation of another FTA. The NAFTA debate elicited contrasting views about what we should expect from government, the role of markets, and strategies for economic development. In between the two main views that had crystallized around these issues—one positive-sum, the other negative-sum—lay the crucial question of how economic integration would ultimately be managed. The hard truth is that U.S.-Mexican integration has thus far proceeded haphazardly, although NAFTA does represent an opportunity to begin managing this process more constructively. As Dani Rodrik has recently observed, "[S]ince trade policy almost always has redistributive consequences . . . one cannot produce a principled defense of free trade without confronting the fairness and legitimacy of the practices that generate these consequences . . . however, international economic inte-

---

39. There was some justification for this suspicion: according to data from the U.S. Department of Commerce, the U.S. trade balance with Mexico was negative through the 1980s, then shifted to a surplus in 1991, but quickly moved back to a deficit position in 1995, after the peso's dramatic devaluation.

40. Indeed, from 1980 to 1989, based on a family size of four, the percentage of full-time U.S. workers with annual incomes below the poverty level rose from 12 percent to 18 percent. See OTA, *U.S.-Mexico Trade: Pulling Together or Pulling Apart?* 3.

gration is taking place against the background of receding governments and diminished social obligations."[41] In other words, whether NAFTA results in a more favorable growth path based on higher skills, productivity, and wage gains will depend largely on the extent to which its member governments are committed to devising the kinds of public policies and market incentives that would foster such an outcome—a point to which I return below.

The remainder of the domestic debate over NAFTA in the United States fastened onto what the public perceived as the government's two main social obligations under an expanded FTA:[42] (1) the need to uphold labor standards and worker rights within the entire NAFTA community and (2) the need to tighten guidelines and enforce compliance procedures that would guarantee stronger environmental protection within the North American bloc. Interestingly, and contrary to traditional thinking on the political economy of trade, it was not those U.S. producers most vulnerable to increased competition from Mexican imports who objected most strongly to NAFTA (e.g., apparel and glassmakers in manufacturing, and producers of citrus fruits, sugar, and winter vegetables in the agricultural sector). These weaker producers did indeed lobby to defend their economic interests; but the core opposition was composed of a new "blue-green" coalition of grassroots labor and environmental activists that came to life during the spring of 1991.

From the standpoint of the Bush administration, these grassroots groups seemed to come out of nowhere. Not only did they succeed in politicizing the congressional decision over whether to extend fast-track negotiating authority to the president—a decision that heretofore had been confined to dry committee debates—but the raucous debate over worker rights and trade-related environmental degradation also served to link these concerns inextricably to the pending NAFTA negotiations. This merging of labor and environmental concerns with an international trade agreement was unprecedented in the United States, and it put trade-policy makers on an entirely new political plane. Yet, although NAFTA was the catalyst for the increasing power wielded by this blue-green coalition, this power cannot be fully explained by international

41. Dani Rodrik, *Has Globalization Gone Too Far?* (Washington, D.C.: Institute for International Economics, 1997), 6.

42. See Robert A. Pastor, "NAFTA as the Center of the Integration Process: The Nontrade Issues," in *North American Free Trade: Assessing the Impact,* ed. Nora Lustig et al. (Washington, D.C.: Brookings Institution, 1992).

variables. In fact, the commanding presence of the grassroots opposition in the United States, as well as the ability of these groups to put their own spin on the NAFTA ratification process, was largely a result of domestic politics.

Up until the final vote on NAFTA in November 1993, the grassroots opposition gathered steam on two fronts. First was a realistic reaction to the miserable working conditions and badly polluted *maquila* production sites that lined the U.S.-Mexican border. If NAFTA signified a free flow of goods, services, and capital between all three countries, what was to stop the flow northward of environmental pollution and substandard working conditions—or, for that matter, the flow of illegal immigrants willing to work under any circumstances and for just a fraction of the legal minimum wage? Why risk the lowering of wages and standards that workers and consumers in the United States had fought to achieve since the 1930s?

Second was more of a gut response, akin to that witnessed in Canada,[43] whereby NAFTA came to symbolize all that was cumulatively wrong with the U.S. political economy at the outset of the 1990s. Thus, what had started out as an issue-oriented blue-green coalition in 1990 blossomed into a full-blown anti-NAFTA movement that included everyone—from job-seeking college grads to downsized business executives and laid-off factory workers and even welfare mothers. Regardless of the actual effect that NAFTA would have on any of these constituents, they were united in their perception that they had somehow been excluded from the prosperity that marked the long post–World War II boom in the United States, and they were understandably angry about it. The steep economic recession that prevailed until late 1993 only fueled fears that NAFTA would put the average U.S. citizen even further behind.

While there was little that either the Bush or subsequent Clinton administration could do in the short term to assuage these free-floating economic anxieties, U.S. policy makers did move to address the concrete and immediate concerns that had been raised about labor standards, the environment, and possible surges of import competition under NAFTA. The Bush administration moved timidly, but succeeded in winning the fast-track battle—against a NAFTA opposition led largely by the House Democratic majority—with promises of an environmental clean-up fund on the border and adjustment assistance for displaced workers. As the

---

43. Stairs, "The Canadian Dilemma in North America," 31.

NAFTA torch was passed to the Clinton trade-policy team in early 1993, it became clear that the bill's passage would require more smoothing of the feathers of the anti-NAFTA forces in Congress, which included a sizable portion of the Democratic leadership.

Because the NAFTA negotiations had been completed before Clinton's election, the incoming Democratic administration initiated a second round of bargaining with Canada and Mexico over side agreements addressing the contentious issues that threatened to kill the NAFTA bill altogether. In August 1993, the NAFTA signatories finally hammered out three separate side agreements that covered labor standards (e.g., occupational safety and health, job training, labor law and worker rights, protection against child labor, and productivity and workforce quality), environmental protection (e.g., the establishment of a Border Environment Financing Facility to provide funding and technical assistance for projects that combat pollution along the border), and import surges.[44] The agreements, for example, created various bilateral and trilateral institutions to monitor compliance in these areas and administer dispute-settlement procedures. With the side agreements in place, the Clinton team was able to gain enough leverage to win the NAFTA vote in the House by a comfortable margin (234 to 200). Yet, not surprisingly, the glass still came up half empty for all of the main NAFTA protagonists— both pro and con.

On the one hand, the opposition was embittered by the fact that the labor and environmental side agreements provided for enforcement of national legislation that already existed, but stopped short of strengthening and harmonizing North American standards in these issue areas.[45] On the other hand, for NAFTA's supporters in the private sector, the side agreements went much too far. In particular, business interests with an eye toward expanding aggressively into the Mexican market saw the side agreements as an unnecessary intrusion into their business practices. Because these agreements have not been in place long enough to evaluate their impact, they are not addressed in this volume; however,

44. See Mayer, *Interpreting NAFTA*, draft chap. 6, for a fascinating insider's account of these side-agreement negotiations.

45. Although the enforcement of each nation's own laws will be monitored under NAFTA, and although a nation will be subjected to trade sanctions when these laws are violated, Lawrence (*Regionalism, Multilateralism, and Deeper Integration,* 70–71) notes that "countries remain free to avoid such sanctions by changing rules that they are not found to enforce."

even at this early stage, it appears that private-sector fears have been exaggerated, in the sense that the labor and environmental side agreements actually impinge very little on national sovereignty.

In hindsight, while the side agreements turned out to be an effective negotiating tactic for securing the NAFTA vote, these lingering grudges have made it difficult for the Clinton administration to make good on its earlier promises to expand NAFTA southward. The private sector in the United States continues to lobby for the elimination of additional side agreements for countries still seeking to join NAFTA, and since 1994 has succeeded in blocking congressional approval of the fast-track authority that would be necessary for expanding the agreement. At the same time, the blue-green opposition continues to lobby in favor of attaching similar side agreements for all future entrants to NAFTA, and has also opposed the granting of fast-track negotiating authority to the president until these conditions are met. Thus, well into the second Clinton term, congressional members who have little else in common—business-backed Republicans versus Democrats beholden to labor and environmental grassroots constituencies—have found themselves united in opposing fast-track and NAFTA expansion on the grounds that the side agreements go either too far or not far enough.[46]

NAFTA Summarized

Since the launching of the formal negotiations in September 1991, NAFTA has remained controversial.[47] To this day, both the anti-NAFTA coalition in the United States and its counterparts in Canada and Mexico have cast the agreement as an exploitative multicorporate plot.[48] Apart from the private sector's animosity toward the labor and environmental side

46. John F. Harris and Peter Baker, "Clinton Neglected to Sell 'Fast Track' to U.S. Public," *Washington Post,* November 12, 1997, A4, and Michael Shifter, "United States–Latin American Relations: Shunted to the Slow Track," *Current History* 97, no. 616 (1998): 49–54.

47. The following summary draws from Gary C. Hufbauer and Jeffrey J. Schott, *North American Free Trade: Issues and Recommendations* (Washington, D.C.: Institute for International Economics, 1992), chap. 1; ECLAC, *NAFTA Implementation in the United States: The First Two Years* (Santiago: ECLAC, 1996); Peter Smith, "The United States, Regional Integration, and the Reshaping of the International Order," in *Cooperation or Rivalry?* ed. Nishijima and Smith; and Lawrence, *Regionalism, Multilateralism, and Deeper Integration,* chap. 6.

48. This was the tone of a report entitled "The Failed Experiment: NAFTA at Three Years," issued on June 26, 1997, by six groups—including the Sierra Club, Public Citizen's Global Trade Watch, and the International Labor Rights Fund.

agreements, business interests on both sides of the border would also have preferred fewer concessions on their part and a longer liberalization timeline for the more trade-sensitive sectors. Although the ratification of the NAFTA bill was considered a victory for free-trade advocates, some liberal economists were still alarmed by the extent to which special interests had prevailed in writing blatantly protectionist rules of origin into the final agreement.[49] On balance, NAFTA may reflect the efforts of all parties to cope with the pressures of globalization, not by shirking from external competition but by strengthening their international ties through policies that promote exports and foreign investment. Yet, the agreement also reveals the extent to which the term "open regionalism" has become a moving target. NAFTA classifies as open in the sense that it is multilateral and thus meets the conditions for exemption under Article 24 of the GATT; it would, however, be very difficult to defend this subregional arrangement as nondiscriminatory.

Apart from the side agreements on labor standards, environmental protection, and import surges, NAFTA promotes the free flow of goods, investment, and services within the new North American bloc over a period of fifteen years. Within the first five years, tariffs and nontariff barriers will be eliminated on 65 percent of all U.S. goods shipped to Mexico; tariff reductions on automobiles will occur over a ten-year period, with the rules-of-origin stipulation that such vehicles must meet a 62.5 percent local-content requirement in order to qualify; a fifteen-year timeline has been set for just a handful of agricultural products, for which a shorter liberalization schedule could not be agreed upon (e.g., corn and dry beans in Mexico; sugar, peanuts, and frozen concentrated orange juice in the United States). Two years into the agreement, the average Mexican tariff on U.S. products was reduced from 10 percent to 4.9 percent, while the average U.S. tariff on Mexican products was brought down from 4 percent to 2.3 percent.

As for the liberalization of investment and trade in services, NAFTA adopts the principle of national treatment for member countries, removes performance requirements, protects intellectual property, and provides investors the opportunity to settle disputes through binding international arbitration. For Mexico, in particular, this willingness to

---

49. To qualify for NAFTA's preferences, goods must (1) be produced entirely within the NAFTA bloc, (2) incorporate only those non-NAFTA materials that are sufficiently processed in North America to qualify for a tariff reclassification, (3) satisfy a minimum-content rule.

allow national treatment for all NAFTA investors, as well as external over-sight of foreign-investment disputes, represents a major reversal of past practices; it also reflects the extent to which Mexico's pursuit of NAFTA was driven by concerns over attracting foreign investment. The private sector within the NAFTA bloc has responded swiftly: during NAFTA's first two years, over half of the total investments made by NAFTA members in Mexico's industrial sector went toward activities that had been liberal-ized under the agreement. Similarly, the opening up of Mexico's service sector is expected to create lucrative opportunities for NAFTA investors, for example, in banking, insurance, and data processing. The liberaliza-tion of services has proceeded more slowly than envisioned, but will eventually cover all services that are not specifically listed as exceptions by the member countries.

While NAFTA reaches beyond the CUSFTA and the Uruguay Round agreement in protecting intellectual-property rights, liberalizing trade in investment and services, and adopting a norm of national treatment for NAFTA members, the agreement still falls short in some significant ways. Perhaps the most pressing problem is the persistence of adminis-tered protection under NAFTA. This is evident, first, in the setting of hefty percentages for local content under NAFTA's rules of origin in such sectors as autos, textiles and apparel, and high-technology products. Nor was substantial progress made toward the elimination of antidumping policies and countervailing duties. Finally, domestic political constraints on both sides of the border prohibited the inclusion of key topics such as the liberalization of Mexico's oil sector, and the establishment of a more rational and humane policy to manage the massive flow of illegal immigrants from Mexico into the United States. Despite the ability of special interests to assert themselves in securing specific protectionist concessions, NAFTA's bigger picture still reflects an overriding commit-ment to liberalization and international economic integration on the part of its member countries.

Mexico in the NAFTA Era

Assessments of the performance of the Mexican political economy in the NAFTA era have varied wildly. On the upside, when the Mexico-NAFTA relationship is judged on its own terms, that is, from the standpoint of the specific economic benefits that an agreement of this kind potentially offers a middle-income developing country like Mexico, the assessments have been favorable. Positive views of Mexico in the NAFTA era have been shaped by the country's ability to attract greater FDI (foreign direct investment) flows, which have surpassed U.S.$50 billion since the announcement of the NAFTA negotiations in 1990 (compared to approximately U.S.$23 billion in FDI for the entire decade that began in 1980). Similarly, Mexico's total trade (exports plus imports) since 1990 is around 60 percent higher than it was for all of the 1980s, while its trade with the United States jumped by more than 400 percent between 1986 and 1996. The country now has the highest U.S. content among major trading partners in coproduced imports in the United States, and it is rapidly joining step with Canada and Japan as the United States' largest trading partner. These figures suggest that Mexico is well on its way to consolidating the foreign investment and export-led development model originally sought by Presidents de la Madrid and Salinas, and that NAFTA membership has been instrumental in achieving these goals.[50]

Underpinning these favorable trade and investment trends are some fundamental institutional transformations that have clearly been beneficial for Mexico.[51] First, NAFTA membership has enabled Mexican policy makers effectively to "lock in" their commitment to market reform. The December 1994 peso crisis posed the first major test to this commitment, and the fact that the Zedillo administration honored the country's NAFTA obligations sent a strong, confidence-enhancing signal to international investors concerning the irreversibility of the market-reform process. Second, Mexico has now secured greater access to the U.S. market, which, despite its low tariff levels, still imposes tough restrictions in the form of nontariff barriers. Third, U.S.-Mexican trade ties are becoming increasingly more dynamic. Although a more sophisticated pattern of production based on Mexico's importing of intermediate goods for use in manufactured exports back to the United States was well under way by the mid-1980s, NAFTA has further institutionalized this relationship. Moreover, transborder production is now moving into more advanced

---

50. World Bank data show that between 1994 and 1996 Mexico accumulated U.S.$31.5 billion in FDI, based on equity investment, earnings reinvested, and investments or loans to foreign subsidiaries. Much of this FDI activity is due to cross-border mergers and acquisitions and postprivatization investment in infrastructure.

51. See Nora Lustig, "NAFTA: Potential Impact on Mexico's Economy and Beyond," in *Economic Integration in the Western Hemisphere*, ed. Bouzas and Ros, 56–66.

sectors (e.g., semiconductors, medical devices, aerospace equipment) that represent a higher-skill, higher-productivity track.

On the downside, even though the economic news on NAFTA has been predominantly favorable, NAFTA's opponents in the United States and Mexico have blamed the agreement for an impressive array of Mexican ills.[52] This is true of everything from the Zapatista uprising, which was staged in the southern state of Chiapas on the first day of NAFTA's implementation, to the December 1994 peso crisis, to the country's recent displacement of Colombia as the locus of Latin America's most powerful drug cartels.[53] Through a detailed analysis of the economic and political trends that have accompanied Mexico's ambitious program of market reform, the essays in this collection examine the stark contrast between economic progress and political backlash that has characterized Mexico in the NAFTA era. Given that Mexico launched its liberalization strategy in the mid-1980s, before NAFTA was even on the drawing board, the analyses here focus on NAFTA as an intervening variable and explore how the liberalization measures have interacted with long-term cumulative problems in the Mexican political economy.

The chapters by Pastor and Wise and by Heath capture the extent to which the market strategy embodied by NAFTA has triggered impressive growth and productivity gains in the globalized sectors of the Mexican economy. At the same time, however, the adjustment costs in terms of job displacement, wage compression, and the haphazard restructuring of small and medium-sized firms have been extremely harsh for the population at large. In both the urban-industrial and the rural-agricultural sectors of the Mexican economy, the data show an increasing polarization of income distribution and asset holdings over the past decade, and a worsening of these patterns since the 1994 peso debacle. Yet, these two chapters suggest that, as much as NAFTA may have accelerated the adjustment process and aggravated Mexico's dismal distributional trends, the blame for today's hardship is more appropriately traced to the reckless management errors of the country's rulers. The Salinas team was especially disingenuous in packaging NAFTA as a painless solution to the country's long-standing economic woes, all the while taking few

---

52. Sergio Sarmiento, "A U.S. Senator Teams up with Anti-NAFTA Mexicans," *Wall Street Journal*, March 28, 1997, A17.

53. Douglas Farah and Molly Moore, "Mexican Drug Traffickers Eclipse Colombian Cartels," *Washington Post*, March 30, 1997, A1.

precautions to ensure that the gains from heightened economic integration would be more widely dispersed.

In fact, Mexican-style market reform has confirmed that when a highly unequal set of income and asset holdings are churned through the "free market"—without properly providing for the kinds of antitrust guidelines and human-capital investments that typically complement market management in the OECD countries—this can result in an even more abysmal distribution of national wealth. By world standards, Mexico's is the sixteenth largest economy, but in 1996 the country had the fifth largest collection of billionaires. Meanwhile, 70 percent of the population accounts for just 30 percent of total household income. The fact that Mexico now looks less like a recent member of the OECD, and more like a caricature of a developing country, has prompted NAFTA analysts, pro and con alike, to search deeper for causal explanations. Respectively, the chapters by Pastor and by Maxfield and Shapiro address two main claims that have been made with regard to these adverse trends. First is the notion that the implementation of NAFTA triggered the 1994 peso crisis, which in turn forced a massive contraction in per capita GDP; second is the impression that, because of Mexico's weak bargaining position at the NAFTA negotiating table, the Salinas administration made far too many concessions to the United States and Canada in order to secure Mexico's entry into the agreement.

Pastor's chapter argues that the roots of Mexico's dramatic currency crisis actually date back to the fixing of the exchange rate as an anti-inflationary tool within the context of the 1987 Economic Solidarity Pact. As Mexico's trade deficit rapidly expanded under the thrust of unilateral liberalization and an increasingly overvalued exchange rate, the government relied heavily on volatile short-term portfolio capital to finance the deficit. At the margins, NAFTA is perhaps responsible for setting in motion the chain of events that ultimately led to the peso's crash: portfolio investors, who were drawn like magnets to the large profit margins that Mexico's entry into NAFTA came to symbolize, purchased some U.S.$70 billion in Mexican stocks and bonds from 1990 to 1994; this, in turn, persuaded Mexican consumers that prosperity was finally within grasp, and hence, the country went on a massive spending binge; finally, these huge portfolio flows deluded PRI policy makers into thinking that quicksilver capital would back them to the end, regardless of their egregious management errors. As convenient as it may be to blame NAFTA for the subsequent economic fallout, Pastor suggests that this "causal chain" was not structurally predetermined. Instead, the Salinas team could have intervened at any point, since more viable policy options were readily available at each step along the way.

In probing the question whether Mexico paid exceedingly high entry fees for its NAFTA membership, the chapter by Maxfield and Shapiro further substantiates that each country went into the negotiations seeking to promote an explicit set of economic interests. In the process of lowering transaction costs and institutionalizing a new regime to govern trade in the North American bloc, Mexico received no special breaks for its developing-country status. But nor did Mexican negotiators simply cave in to the demands of their U.S. and Canadian counterparts. Rather, the liberalization timeline and content of the final NAFTA agreement reflects *both* the asymmetries between Mexico and the United States *and* the preconceived goals that shaped the bargaining strategy of each country. Having entered the negotiations at an early stage in its own trade opening, Mexico was primarily interested in market access and bargaining over crucial sectoral concerns (e.g., autos, energy, agriculture). The United States, on the other hand, was more intent on securing legal trade norms that had proved extremely challenging to negotiate multilaterally within the Uruguay Round (e.g., intellectual-property rights, investment, government procurement). If anything, Mexican negotiators largely accomplished what they had set out to do, including the design of a liberalization timeline geared toward mitigating adjustment-related economic stress.

In the end, the explanation for today's exceedingly high levels of conflict in Mexico leads back to domestic variables. The Salinas administration oversold NAFTA to the Mexican people, not only by exaggerating the rapidity and magnitude of real-income gains that the agreement would deliver, but also by packaging the PRONASOL safety net program as an adjustment mechanism that would soften the landing for those most vulnerable to external competition. Unfortunately, not only were PRONASOL's resources too limited and short-term, but the program quickly eclipsed a more serious debate over the kinds of productive investments in infrastructure and human capital that would be essential for Mexico fully to realize its growth and income goals under NAFTA. In short, the Salinas team counted too heavily on market forces to fulfill its tremendous social obligations in the 1990s, and it erred in assuming that a passive and downtrodden populace would be willing to bear the adjustment costs of market restructuring indefinitely. Prior to NAFTA's ratification, the PRI's savvy public-relations campaign effectively short-circuited the emergence of a national debate on a par with the one that erupted in the United States from 1991 to 1993.

Instead, Mexico's status as a NAFTA member has become highly politicized since the implementation of the agreement, and much of the turbulence since 1994 can be attributed to the adverse ways in which NAFTA has interacted with long-term political problems intrinsic to six decades of single-party rule. Although PRI leaders initially prided themselves on having avoided the "Gorbachev syndrome" of liberalizing the economy only to lose a grip on domestic politics, this is exactly what is happening in Mexico today. The chapter by Dresser explores the main political transformations that have occurred in Mexico during the NAFTA era. On the one hand has been the decline of presidential authority and the increasing decentralization of power to the regions; on the other hand has been the rise of nongovernmental organized movements that have challenged single-party rule, and the growing importance of political-party competition and electoral contestation of the PRI. The latter trend is reflected in the ruling party's loss of its historical majority hold on Mexico's lower house of Congress in the July 1997 midterm elections, as well as the first-ever election of an opposition candidate, Cuauhtémoc Cárdenas, to be mayor of Mexico City.[54] This emergence of a more competitive political regime is just what PRI leaders had promised, as part of the country's market transformation; but because the ruling-party faithful have repeatedly proved themselves incapable of gracefully managing this transition, it appears that political modernization in post-NAFTA Mexico will entail a fight until the PRI's bitter end.[55]

NAFTA as a Hemispheric Initiative?

Until late 1997, debates concerning Western Hemispheric integration centered on different scenarios for expanding NAFTA. But with the repeated failures of the Clinton administration to obtain the necessary fast-track negotiating authority from the U.S. Congress,[56] and the rapid ap-

54. Armand B. Peschard-Sverdrup, "The 1997 Mexican Midterm Elections: Post-Election Report" (Western Hemisphere Election Study Series, Center for Strategic and International Studies, Washington, D.C., August 30, 1997).

55. Sam Dillon, "Viva Mexican Democracy—In Theory," *New York Times*, July 13, 1997, 18.

56. See I. M. Destler, "Renewing Fast-Track Legislation" (Policy Analyses in International Economics, Institute for International Economics, Washington, D.C., September 1997).

proach of the planned April 1998 summit to launch the FTAA negotiations in Santiago, Chile, the debate shifted from possible NAFTA expansion to negotiation of an FTAA through alternative means. On the eve of the Santiago Summit, the two dominant options were negotiation of an FTAA based on the twelve working groups created in the wake of the Miami Summit,[57] or negotiation based on representation from the five subregional schemes mentioned at the outset of this Introduction. Ultimately, however, given the uncertainties surrounding U.S. commitment and leadership with respect to the FTAA, the blueprint for a Western Hemispheric accord will most likely rely on the multilateral negotiating and dispute-resolution mechanisms established within the GATT/WTO. How is it that the United States, which triggered the FTAA initiative with President Bush's announcement of the EAI in 1990 and advanced it at President Clinton's 1994 Miami Summit, has not been able to sustain leadership in this area? What were the political and economic dynamics that worked to render NAFTA expansion a foreclosed option by 1998?

Apart from the political standoff over whether to negotiate labor and environmental side agreements for future NAFTA members, the integration debate in the United States also bogged down in procedural disputes over how best to move forward. For example, NAFTA's accession clause (embodied in Article 2204) establishes a general framework for bringing new members into the agreement, but it does not specify the procedures to be followed. Other political factors, such as the dominance, since 1994, of a conservative Republican congressional majority that views the idea of further market opening with some suspicion, and the relentless tales of violence and corruption emanating from Mexico, also muddied the prospects for expanding NAFTA. Nevertheless, as formidable as these political obstacles appear to be, it should be remembered that a business-government alliance in all three NAFTA countries triumphed over similarly difficult obstacles prior to securing that agreement in late 1993. Furthermore, while economic analysts remain divided over the costs and

---

57. Since 1995, the twelve FTAA working groups have tackled the following issues: market access; customs procedures and rules of origin; investment; standards and technical barriers to trade; sanitary and phytosanitary measures; subsidies, antidumping and countervailing duties; smaller economies; government procurement; intellectual-property rights; services; competition policy; and dispute settlement. See "Trade Liberalization: Western Hemisphere Trade Issues Confronting the United States" (National Security and International Affairs Division, U.S. General Accounting Office, Washington, D.C., July, 1997), 8–13.

benefits of subregional arrangements,[58] even the most cautious assessments of NAFTA show favorable returns. Yet, the respective governments and the domestic private sector in the NAFTA countries have not shown the same determination for pursuing the FTAA. Why?

In principle, NAFTA was designed as an inclusive arrangement; in practice, the structural logic of intra-industry specialization and cross-border production that propelled the North American private sector toward NAFTA is simply weaker when it comes to fighting for an FTAA. Obviously, as the industrial anchor and hegemonic state in the region, the United States will have to bear most responsibility for initiative and leadership in both the public and the private sectors if the full-fledged expansion of hemispheric integration is to be realized. While Canada has shifted from the mainly defensive and reactive role that it played in the NAFTA negotiations, and has gradually come to see the benefit of forging stronger trade and investment ties with other countries in Latin America—for example, with the signing in 1996 of a Canada-Chile FTA modeled on the NAFTA format—Canada has also made it clear that it will continue to take its cues from the United States.[59] Mexico, which is still struggling with the double challenges of industrial restructuring and economic adjustment in the wake of the 1994 peso crisis, has yet to display any convincing enthusiasm for the rapid extension of the FTAA.

In the NAFTA era, Mexico's buoyant trade and investment trends bear testimony to the fact that domestic firms have actively identified strategic foreign partners, expanded their operations, and created new markets. However, current estimates also show that some 80 percent of Mexico's smaller and medium-sized firms have yet to adapt to a more competitive environment, a situation that has been exacerbated by rising financial costs and tightly contracted markets since the 1994–95 crisis. At this point, Mexican trade policy remains committed to multilateral liberalization within the GATT/WTO framework and collegial toward other Latin states (since 1994, Mexico has signed FTA's with Costa Rica, Bolivia, Nicaragua, and Peru). But Mexico's official stance, both public

---

58. Ronald Wonnacott, "Free-Trade Agreements: For Better or Worse?" *American Economic Review* 86, no. 2 (1996): 62–65, and Jagdish Bhagwati and Arvind Panagariya, "The Theory of Preferential Trade Agreements: Historical Evolution and Current Trends," *American Economic Review* 86, no. 2 (1996): 82–87.

59. Hal Klepak, "What's in It for us? Canada's Relationship with Latin America" (FOCAL Papers, Canadian Foundation for the Americas, Ottawa, 1994), and Cameron and Tomlin, "Canada and Latin America in the Shadow of U.S. Power."

and private, toward further integration endeavors has been neutral, since PRI policy makers would prefer "to consolidate what already exists rather than to accelerate a process that would be politically and economically unattractive—if not outright dangerous—for its current members."[60]

Along with the U.S. private sector's noncommittal attitude toward the FTAA, and the need to tread carefully with regard to Mexico's post–peso crisis economic recovery, the Clinton administration has been increasingly restrained by the negative reaction that Mexico's domestic turmoil has provoked within Congress and the U.S. public. Anti-NAFTA sentiments prevail, despite the fact that NAFTA's economic impact on the United States has thus far been positive. In the long run, NAFTA's success lies in the extent to which transborder production has spawned a sophisticated pattern of industrial restructuring and a more buoyant demand for services in the North American economic bloc. The accompanying trade and employment trends are just part of the larger NAFTA story, which is one of increasingly dynamic productivity and welfare gains. But even if NAFTA is judged by these partial indicators alone, the impact on the United States has been advantageous.

On average, U.S. exports to Canada and Mexico have grown steadily in the 1990s; these countries respectively now represent the number-one and number-three markets for U.S. goods.[61] Between 1993 and 1996, total U.S. exports to these two countries grew by 34.5 percent, or from U.S.$49 billion in 1993 to U.S.$191 billion in 1996. Similarly, two-way trade between the United States and these NAFTA partners grew by some 44 percent over this same time period. By 1996, U.S. two-way trade with Canada and Mexico accounted for nearly one-third of total U.S. two-way trade, or U.S.$421 billion. This boom in two-way trade reflects the extent to which North American producers have shifted to trading scale economies within a much more complex and dynamic intra-industry context.[62]

---

60. Luis Rubio, "Mexico, NAFTA, and the Pacific Basin," in *Cooperation or Rivalry?* ed. Nishijima and Smith, 88.

61. The figures cited here are taken from Raul Hinojosa-Ojeda et al., "North American Integration Three Years After NAFTA: A Framework for Tracking, Modeling, and Internet Accessing the National and Regional Labor Market Impacts" (School of Public Policy and Social Research, University of California at Los Angeles, 1996); "Study on the Operation and Effects of the North American Free Trade Agreement" (Office of the U.S. Trade Representative, Washington, D.C., July 1997); and Sidney Weintraub, *NAFTA at Three: A Progress Report* (Washington, D.C.: Center for Strategic and International Studies, 1997).

62. Marc L. Busch and Helen V. Milner, "The Future of the International Trading System," in

As for jobs, contrary to the dire estimates of anti-NAFTA opponents like Ross Perot and Pat Choate, U.S. employment data show that net job losses related to NAFTA have basically been zero. Thus far, increased import competition has displaced U.S. workers in old-fashioned sectors like apparel, textiles, and leather goods. But because organized labor in the United States lobbied successfully for government-sponsored programs (e.g., the NAFTA Transitional Adjustment Assistance Program and the North American Development Bank) to help cushion these losses, workers displaced by NAFTA-related competition are eligible for employment retraining, income assistance, and job-placement services. Moreover, in a recent influential report, Raul Hinojosa-Ojeda argues that, to date, these job losses have been more than offset by jobs created directly through U.S. exports and indirectly through the deepening of the process of economic integration under NAFTA.[63] For example, with the liberalization of services in Mexico, which account for more than 60 percent of domestic GDP, indirect job creation is booming on both sides of the border in such service activities as transportation, communications, finance, insurance, and real estate. In the end, however, because North American trade is increasingly dominated by a two-way exchange of intermediate goods, whereby both Canadian and Mexican imports have become predominantly linked to export production for the U.S. market, the tallying up of jobs won versus jobs lost, or exports minus imports, captures just part of how NAFTA is progressing.

In sum, while most of the economic news related to NAFTA has been good, it is the continuous flow of bad political news from Mexico that has dominated the debate over the expansion of hemispheric trade in the United States. The chapter by Andreas explores this theme with regard to the influx of undocumented migrant labor and illicit drugs (cocaine, heroin, marijuana) from Mexico, two issues the U.S. public has consistently ranked as top concerns in national opinion polls. According to Andreas, the removal of barriers to the free flow of goods, services, and capital under NAFTA has unwittingly intensified illegal flows across the U.S.-Mexican border. The primary U.S. response—curbing the supply and targeting the source of demand for these black-market endeavors— reflects a main contradiction embodied in NAFTA: the quest to promote

---

Political Economy and the Changing Global Order, ed. Richard Stubbs and Geoffrey Underhill (Toronto: McClelland & Stewart, 1994), 270–71.

63. Hinojosa-Ojeda, "North American Integration Three Years After NAFTA."

free trade and open markets in North America while simultaneously policing the borders and enforcing strict market prohibitions. Illegal migrant workers and illicit drugs are now two of Mexico's leading exports
to the United States, despite unprecedented efforts to halt these flows.[64]

The Andreas chapter suggests that, until U.S. policy makers devise
an approach to these clandestine economic activities that recognizes they
are part and parcel of the integration process, the contradictions will
continue to multiply. In the case of drug flows, for example, diplomatic
exigencies in the NAFTA era have compelled the Clinton administration
to "certify" Mexico as a fully cooperating partner in the war on drugs,
even though the country's top former drug-enforcement officer had been
accused of being on the payroll of drug traffickers![65] In the case of illegal
immigration, in refusing to address this controversial issue at the NAFTA
negotiating table, the United States opted for a costly punitive approach
to illegal immigration that has virtually nothing to show for itself. While
these policies may have been generated in the spirit of promoting NAFTA,
all outward signs show that they have backfired.

As illicit entrepreneurs continue to thrive on the same comparative
advantages and laws of supply and demand as everyone else, the failure
of policy makers to incorporate new rules and norms that more effectively address these weaknesses within NAFTA has clearly been undermining the NAFTA regime itself. It seems that, at the very least, the
NAFTA regime will require modifications that explicitly take into account
these escalating black-market transactions not simply as negative exter-
nalities but as intrinsic to the very process of North American integration. As clandestine economic activities continue to move upward in
tandem with U.S. expenditures on policing and enforcement, previously
unthinkable options may become more appealing. With regard to illegal
immigration, in light of recent research findings that suggest immigrant

---

64. Approximately 150 million Mexicans continue to enter the United States illegally each year,
despite a 72 percent increase between 1993 and 1996 in the Clinton administration's budget requests
for enforcement funding for the Immigration and Naturalization Service (INS). The illicit-drug figures show a 70 percent rise in the percentage of cocaine entering the U.S. market through Mexico
between the mid-1980s and the mid-1990s, and a fiscal-year 1997 budget request for federal drug-
control spending of U.S.$15 billion, compared to U.S.$1 billion in 1981.

65. See Joe Davidson and Helene Cooper, "U.S. Congress Bucks Clinton on Mexico," *Wall Street
Journal,* March 14, 1997, A14. The authors note that "decertification" of Mexico by the U.S. Congress would result in a 50 percent cut in official U.S. aid to Mexico, bar project financing from the
U.S. Export-Import Bank, and require that the United States vote against loans to Mexico by the
leading multilateral institutions.

workers provide net fiscal benefits over time,[66] this might mean the incorporation into NAFTA of laws that monitor and rationalize the flow of people into the United States. With regard to illicit drug flows, some form of controlled legalization, although still anathema to the majority of citizens and policy makers in the United States, may be the only way to rupture the lucrative supply and high U.S. demand that has rendered the Latin drug trade one of the most successful commodity-export businesses in the world.

The chapter by Woods explores another major political sore point since NAFTA's implementation: the 1995 bailout of Mexico's economy with some U.S.$50 billion in loans, U.S.$12.5 billion of which was provided by the United States and the remainder by international financial institutions (IFIS). Woods takes an essentially functionalist position by asserting that the increase in economic interaction within NAFTA should motivate participating governments to devise regional institutions that would replace IFIS in the management of economic crises. Instead, as Woods points out, the 1994 peso crisis triggered a very different institutional scenario. The United States intervened in traditional G-1 fashion, first, by requesting emergency support for Mexico from the U.S. Congress and, when that effort failed, by drawing on an emergency fund within the U.S. Treasury. Second, the Clinton administration aggressively appealed to the IFIS for additional loans to Mexico, on the grounds that Mexico's peso crisis represented a threat to the international financial system.

In hindsight, the U.S. ability to "internationalize" the peso crisis may have been a Pyrrhic victory. This is not to deny the success of the loan package in enabling Mexico to stabilize its exchange rate and adjust accordingly. But the executive branch's reliance on highly autonomous decision making to push the massive loan package through has created tensions within the U.S. Congress that further distract from the FTAA process, even though Mexico has already repaid its loan from the United States in full. For example, despite the string of currency collapses that began to spread across Asia in mid-1997, and the clear need for IFI assistance to support economic adjustment in these Asian countries, the U.S. Congress has been extremely reluctant to commit further funds to a key

66. Robert Pear, "Academy's Report Says Immigration Benefits the U.S.," *New York Times,* May 18, 1997, A1.

IFI such as the International Monetary Fund (IMF).[67] Yet, the longer the Asian crisis lingers as an international threat, the less time U.S. policy makers have to devote to the FTAA process. Another complication has been the resistance of the United States to the creation of Western Hemispheric institutions that could more appropriately manage crises like Mexico's in 1994. This does not bode well for the continued cooperation of other countries, or the IFIs—all of whom expressed dismay at having to share the financial burden for a currency crisis that was distinctly North American and for which they have yet to be repaid.

The final two chapters in this collection approach the question of hemispheric integration by analyzing both the domestic dynamics of trade reform in other Latin countries and the patterns of subregional integration that have emerged in the 1990s. The chapter by Wise suggests that, as necessary as U.S. leadership will be for the transformation of NAFTA into a broader hemispheric initiative, the fruition of the FTAA project will depend as much on the readiness and ability of prospective Latin participants to rise to the occasion. In this respect, the very economic disparities that have made additional access to the U.S. market such an appealing prospect for other Latin reformers have also made it difficult for these countries to present themselves as credible and viable candidates for FTAA membership.

Wise argues that trade liberalization was initially embraced as a way of stabilizing domestic prices and signaling to foreign investors that a serious commitment to reform was finally in place. The anchoring of these liberal policy commitments within subregional schemes like Mercosur and the Andean Group has helped to bolster intra-bloc trade and investor confidence, although growth, investment, and total-factor productivity rates still fall short of projected gains. The one exception to these trends is Chile, now into its third decade of an open-trade regime that has been driven largely by microeconomic concerns. Yet, even Chile, having made the U.S. shortlist for NAFTA entry at the 1994 Miami Summit, has been left on hold indefinitely—hence Chile's signing of an FTA with the Mercosur bloc in 1996 and its increased focus on strengthening trade and investment ties with its Southern Cone neighbors.

The slowness of the FTAA process, and the erratic pattern of growth

---

67. Joanne Thornton, "Congressional Spotlight on the IMF," *International Watch* (Schwab Washington Research Group, Washington, D.C.), January 30, 1998, 1.

and investment outside of NAFTA, raise the possibility that the economic and political rationale for deepening and quickening the pace of hemispheric integration may simply be too weak at this point in time. Outside of Mexico, for example, the intra-industry trade and investment links that were instrumental for forging NAFTA are considerably weaker between the United States and other states in the region. Indeed, in reviewing the findings of a number of researchers who have modeled the effects of NAFTA expansion to the rest of the region, Albert Fishlow concludes, "There is simply no significant static gain from the extension of free trade."[68] However, the dynamic gains in terms of increased investment could range from 0.3 to 2 percent of a given country's GDP. The fact that other Latin reformers are trading scale economies among themselves, as in the case of Mercosur, helps explain why business-government coalitions in the United States and in countries like Argentina and Brazil have not pushed harder for a broad regional initiative.[69] These trends suggest that the efforts of non-NAFTA countries in the region to consolidate a dynamic investment-led economic model based on freer trade would best be pursued via multilateral bargaining and subregional schemes that reinforce multilateralism while also deepening investment guarantees.

Finally, Haggard's chapter approaches the hemispheric question through a detailed analysis of the various subregional integration schemes that have either been created or revived during the 1990s. In examining the track record thus far, as well as the various options for future integration that have been debated since the 1994 summit, Haggard argues that (1) regardless of the actual route that is chosen for the creation of an FTAA, any future hemispheric initiative will necessarily entail the resolution of numerous issues that have increasingly divided the NAFTA and Mercosur blocs; (2) without a "big push" on the part of the United States, the FTAA process will continue to move forward at the hands of the functional committees that were part of the original FTAA Summit design. These points do not preclude the advancement of the FTAA process in crucial areas such as intellectual property, dispute settlement, and trade in services and investment. But the Clinton adminis-

68. Albert Fishlow, "From NAFTA to a WHFTA? The Summit May Tell," in *Integrating the Americas: Shaping Future Trade Policy*, ed. Sidney Weintraub (Miami, Fla.: North-South Center, University of Miami, 1994), 125.

69. For an elaboration of this point, see Helen Milner, "Industries, Governments, and the Creation of Regional Trade Blocs," in *The Political Economy of Regionalism*, ed. Edward Mansfield and Helen Milner (New York: Columbia University Press, 1997).

tration's continued lack of fast-track authority, combined with the inability of regional political leaders at the mid-1997 FTAA trade ministerial in Brazil to decide on the "objectives, approaches, structure and venue" for the FTAA negotiations planned for 1998,[70] amounts to a more watered down approach to hemispheric integration than that proposed on the heels of NAFTA's implementation.

70. Geoff Dyer, "Americas Free Trade Talks Get Green Light," *Financial Times*, May 19, 1997, 4.

Part I   From the NAFTA Negotiations to the Peso Crisis

1 Mexican-Style Neoliberalism

State Policy and Distributional Stress

Manuel Pastor Jr. and Carol Wise

Arguments in favor of neoliberal reform have long held that an economic strategy based on liberalization, privatization, and deregulation is the surest recipe for triggering higher levels of growth, efficiency, and productivity.[1] While neoliberal theorists have been less explicit about the relationship between market reform and improved income distribution, the implicit assumption is that, as the size of the economic pie expands under a market-based strategy, so too will the economic opportunities for the population at large.[2] Yet, despite the am-

An earlier version of this chapter appeared in the *Journal of Latin American Studies* 29, no. 2 (1997).

1. See, for example, Bela Balassa et al., *Development Strategies in Semi-Industrial Economies* (Baltimore: Johns Hopkins University Press, 1982), and Pedro Bustelo, "Neoliberalismo y nuevos países industriales," *Revista de Economía* (Madrid), no. 727 (1994): 77–93.

2. We thank Chandler Stolp for his clarification of this point.

bitious programs of market restructuring undertaken in Latin America since the mid to late 1980s, the evidence to support these assumptions is still ambiguous. The region's annual growth rates averaged just 3–4 percent during the 1990s—well below the estimated 6 percent rate that would be required for a significant improvement in employment and social welfare.[3] Indeed, only a handful of countries have seen an increase in per capita gross domestic product (GDP) since 1991, and while total-factor productivity has improved during the 1990s, Latin America has still not caught up to its position on this indicator in 1980.

In this chapter, we explore the gap between expectation and reality with regard to the gains forecast from neoliberal reform in Mexico. Given that Mexico first liberalized in 1985 and ranks second only to Chile in the length of time that the reforms have been in place, we argue that disappointing returns on the equity and efficiency fronts represent more than a longer-than-expected adjustment lag; rather, as policy makers have disproportionately harnessed their neoliberal reform program to the tasks of macroeconomic stabilization, the tendency has been both to overemphasize the benefits from economic opening and to ignore the accompanying microeconomic stresses—all in the name of market management. Even as the Mexican economy stages an impressive comeback in the wake of the 1994–95 peso crisis, the domestic distribution of income worsens, the country's labor markets remain problematic, and real wages are still 25 percent below the level achieved before the crash.

This suggests the need for an explicit and innovative set of public policies to help bridge the gap between macroeconomic stabilization and microeconomic adjustment. In this regard, we emphasize that Chile, which posted the highest growth and productivity rates in the 1990s, did not realize such growth and productivity gains until neoliberal nostrums were set aside in favor of a more pragmatic set of market-supporting policies in the wake of the 1982 debt crisis.[4] Although Chile's long-standing authoritarian regime (1973–90) was also able to quell adjust-

3. These figures on growth, income shares, and productivity are cited from "Increased Productivity, Key to Development," CEPAL News 16, no. 6 (1996): 1–3, and "Poverty in Latin America and the Caribbean Is Greater Now Than in the 1980's," CEPAL News 16, no. 7 (1996): 1–3.

4. This is a main theme of the essays in The Chilean Economy: Policy Lessons and Challenges, ed. Barry Bosworth, Rudiger Dornbusch, and Raúl Labán (Washington, D.C.: Brookings Institution, 1994). Despite the Chilean record of impressive growth, problems for income distribution remain. See Dagmar Raczynski and Pilar Romaguera, "Chile: Poverty, Adjustment, and Social Policies in the 1980's," in Coping with Austerity: Poverty and Inequality in Latin America, ed. Nora Lustig (Washington, D.C.: Brookings Institution, 1995), 286–90.

ment-related social protest until growth finally took root, Mexican policy makers do not enjoy this same "luxury": crime, violence, and other
assorted distributional conflicts have escalated since the peso crisis and
show no signs of abating.[5] Thus, the problems of distribution, and a
widening of the winners' circle from reform, must assume a higher priority in the coming years.

We begin with a brief overview of economic performance and house-
hold-income trends since the implementation of Mexico's neoliberal
model in the mid-1980s. We then examine neoliberal policy directives
and accompanying distributional trends within the urban-industrial and
rural-agricultural sectors of the economy, as well as the government's
responses to resulting sectoral pressures. A final section reviews the
country's general approach to social policy, taking into account the numerous new social demands that have arisen within the context of a
market-based development model. We conclude by suggesting that, despite the claims of neoliberal theorists with regard to the growth and
income gains that can be derived from a market-oriented development
approach, a bigger economic pie has meant very little for the majority of
the population. Finally, we suggest that the prospects for better income
equality and stronger economic growth would be greatly enhanced
through the implementation of a cohesive set of market-supporting policies that more explicitly address these goals.

An Overview of Recent Mexican Economic Performance and Household Income

The Mexican debt crisis that began in 1982 marked the end of an era of
state-led development based on import-substitution industrialization
(ISI). Since then, Mexico has joined step with the rest of the region by
embracing a neoliberal economic model based on liberalization, privatization, and deregulation. Immediately following the debt crisis, the administration of President Miguel de la Madrid (1982–88) had little choice
but to focus its efforts on macroeconomic stabilization.[6] The basic goal
was to ameliorate the external debt problem through a reduction of gov-

5. See Mark Fineman, "Zedillo Address Touts 'New Era,' Targets Rebels," *Los Angeles Times*,
September 2, 1996, A1, and Molly Moore and John Ward Anderson, "New Mayor Ties His Future
to Taming Mexico City," *Washington Post*, December 5, 1997, A43.

6. For more detail on the macroeconomic history, see Pastor's chapter in this volume.

ernment spending and a large one-time devaluation of the peso. In hindsight, the recessionary impact of this initial strategy was more severe than originally anticipated, and much of the task of economic adjustment was left to de la Madrid's successor.

The program adopted by President Carlos Salinas (1988–94) was more comprehensive in its efforts to privatize state enterprises and the banks and to liberalize domestic prices, foreign trade, and investment. Of most significance, however, was the decision to stabilize the macroeconomy by combining (1) an incomes policy (i.e., wage and price guidelines), which was codified in a series of tripartite pacts including government, business, and labor;[7] (2) fiscal restraint, which removed the underlying inflationary impetus; and (3) a commitment to a stable peso and a more liberal trading regime.

Despite some initial skepticism on the part of outside policy makers and domestic agents,[8] the strategy was successful in accomplishing its immediate goals of lowering inflation and resurrecting growth. However, when these returns began to diminish halfway into the Salinas *sexenio*, policy makers were reluctant to shift tracks and abandon the pact. First, their credibility on both the domestic and the international fronts came to hinge on their ability to produce the most favorable indicators that the Mexican economy had seen in nearly a decade. Second, as the Salinas team entered into negotiations with the United States and Canada over Mexico's entry into the North American Free Trade Agreement (NAFTA) in late 1991, the series of tripartite pacts emerged as one important venue for organizing domestic support for NAFTA, particularly among those members of the business community that still doubted the decision to quicken the pace of trade liberalization.[9]

The trends in Table 1.1 reflect the ways in which the pact both achieved its initial stabilization goals and overstayed its welcome as an effective institutional mechanism for managing Mexico's rapidly chang-

---

7. For more detail on these pacts, see Robert R. Kaufman, Carlos Bazdresch, and Blanca Heredia, "Mexico: Radical Reform in a Dominant Party System," in *Voting for Reform: Democracy, Political Liberalization, and Economic Adjustment,* ed. Stephan Haggard and Steven B. Webb (New York: Oxford University Press, 1994), 361–410.

8. Ibid., 381–83.

9. Authors' confidential interviews conducted in Mexico City during 1991 and 1992 with a broad sample from within the Mexican business community concerning those factors which most influenced their support for NAFTA. As trade opening became positively linked with inflation reduction, the losers from external competition were gradually persuaded of the overall merits of the program.

Table 1.1. Mexican macroeconomic indicators since 1980

	1980	1981	1982	1983	1984	1985	1986	1987	1988	1989	1990	1991	1992	1993	1994	1995
GDP growth (annual percent)	8.4%	8.8%	-0.7%	-4.1%	3.7%	2.7%	-3.9%	1.9%	1.3%	3.5%	4.3%	3.9%	2.8%	0.4%	3.8%	-6.2%
Inflation rate (Dec.–Dec.)	29.8%	28.7%	98.9%	80.8%	59.2%	63.7%	105.7%	159.2%	51.7%	19.7%	29.9%	18.8%	11.9%	8.0%	7.1%	52.0%
Trade ($US mil.)																
Exports	18,031	23,307	24,056	25,953	29,101	26,758	21,803	27,599	30,692	35,171	40,711	42,687	46,196	51,885	60,879	79,543
Imports	21,087	27,184	17,009	11,848	15,915	18,359	16,784	18,813	28,081	34,766	41,592	49,966	62,130	65,366	79,346	72,454
Trade balance	(3,056)	(3,877)	7,047	14,105	13,186	8,399	5,019	8,786	2,611	405	(881)	(7,279)	(15,934)	(13,481)	(18,467)	7,089
Investment flows ($US mil.)																
Foreign direct investment	2,090	3,078	1,901	2,192	1,542	1,984	2,036	1,184	2,011	2,785	2,549	4,742	4,393	4,389	10,972	6,963
Portfolio investment	60	996	645	(519)	(435)	(595)	(517)	(1,002)	1,001	354	3,369	12,741	18,041	28,919	8,185	(10,140)
Total reserves less gold (millions of US$)	2,960	4,074	834	3,913	7,272	4,906	5,670	12,464	5,279	6,329	9,863	17,726	18,942	25,110	6,278	16,847
Real exchange rate (1980=100), controlled rate	100.0	91.1	134.6	143.8	124.3	120.0	149.0	148.6	119.1	112.8	105.4	92.4	82.5	77.5	79.5	115.2

SOURCES: WORLD BANK's *World Data, 1995*; and the IMF, *International Financial Statistics*, December 1995, March 1996, September 1996 (CD-ROM versions); CEPAL's *Economic Panorama of Latin America, 1996*; and author estimates. Following the new IMF practice, trade figures include *maquila* exports and imports and so may differ from other historical tables that treated the net earnings of the *maquila* sector as part of the current balance in services.

ing position within foreign trade and financial markets. Although growth averaged 2.6 percent during the Salinas *sexenio* and inflation dropped from 159 percent in 1987 to 7.1 percent in 1994, one of the pact's main tenets—the use of a fixed exchange rate as a price "anchor"—led to an increasingly overvalued real peso. As a result, the trade balance turned from a surplus of $8.8 billion in 1987 to a deficit of $18.5 billion by 1994, with rising import demand driven in part by the government's decision to aggressively increase personal credit. To finance the trade imbalance, Mexico turned to foreign investment, the bulk of which consisted of highly mobile portfolio capital.

When these buoyant portfolio-capital flows began to dry up in 1994, a combination of poor economic decision making and bad political luck converged to cause the December 1994 peso crisis.[10] The government having lost the public's confidence, an incomes-policy–*cum*–social-pact approach to disinflation had been ruled out; instead, the government, as reflected in the stabilization plan implemented in March 1995, fell back on the traditional orthodox cure of severe cuts in public spending as well as a clearly regressive increase in the value-added tax. Meanwhile, real wages continued to fall well into 1997.

Today's adjustment, however, has been superimposed on a social landscape scarred by long-standing inequities and the more recent hardship wrought by the economic turmoil of the 1980s and the neoliberal restructuring of the Mexican economy. Between 1984 and 1994, for example, the wealthiest 10 percent of Mexicans saw their share of national income rise from around 34 percent to more than 41 percent, while every other income decile suffered a decline (see Table 1.2).[11] The pattern over various subperiods is quite revealing: note that while much of the regressive redistribution did occur during the initial shocks of macroeco-

---

10. For more political and economic analysis concerning the peso crash, see the chapters by Denise Dresser and Manuel Pastor Jr., respectively, in this volume.

11. Our figures on the distribution of household income are taken from the household surveys of income and spending undertaken by Mexico's National Institute of Statistics (INEGI). The national results are available for 1984, 1989, and 1992 as both raw data and a series of comparative tables on CD-ROM; the most recent survey (1994) has been in general release only as a "hard-copy" book that includes summary but not comparative (multiyear) tables. We readily acknowledge the difficulty with which reliable and comparable household income surveys are obtained; our hope is that the use of the same source at least allows for the over-time comparisons drawn in the text. For an analysis and critique of the INEGI household survey with specific regard to its measurement of poverty, see J. Boltvinik, "La pobreza en México 1984–1992 según INEGI-CEPAL," *Economía Informe*, no. 237 (1995).

Table 1.2. Distribution of current monetary income by household deciles

Household Deciles[a]	Percentage of Total Income to Household Decile			
	1984	1989	1992	1994
Total	100.00	100.00	100.00	100.00
I	1.19	1.14	1.00	1.01
II	2.66	2.48	2.27	2.27
III	3.86	3.52	3.36	3.27
IV	5.01	4.56	4.38	4.26
V	6.26	5.76	5.45	5.35
VI	7.66	7.21	6.77	6.67
VII	9.68	9.02	8.62	8.43
VIII	12.42	11.42	11.22	11.19
IX	17.00	15.92	16.09	16.30
X	34.26	38.97	40.84	41.24
Gini Coefficient[b]	0.46	0.49	0.51	0.51

SOURCE: Instituto Nacional de Estadística, Geografía e Informática, *Encuesta Nacional de ingresos y gastos de los hogares,* Third Quarter, 1984, 1989 Y 1992 (CD-ROM); 1994 hard copy.

[a]Households are ordered in terms of income (the first decile includes the poorest, the last deciles the richest).
[b]The Gini coefficient is an aggregate measure of income inequality that ranges from zero in a completely equal society to 1 in a completely unequal society.

nomic adjustment (1984–89), the drift upward continued in a moderated but steady fashion over the Salinas period as well (1989–92 and 1992–94).

Such a deteriorating distribution of income does not preclude welfare improvements for the poor if overall levels of income for those individuals are rising. In Table 1.3, we look at the annual rate of growth of real monetary income for household deciles between 1984 and 1992. Note that while all income deciles saw some gain between 1984 and 1989, several deciles, including the two poorest, experienced a decline over the period 1989–92.[12] Data problems preclude an exact estimate of the evolution over 1992–94, but our best guess is that real income held more or less steady for the lower deciles, declined slightly in the middle, and improved marginally in the top two deciles.[13]

12. If one focuses on the income earned solely by the head of household, the distributional picture under Salinas worsens; specifically, the four lowest deciles showed markedly negative growth from 1989 to 1992, suggesting that the more favorable picture reflected in the data may be largely due to the increased workforce participation of women, youths, and other nontraditional wage earners.
13. The 1984–89 and 1989–92 growth figures are taken directly from the comparative tables

Table 1.3. Annual rate of growth of real monetary income for household deciles, 1984–1989 and 1989–1992

Household Deciles[a]	1984–89	1989–92
Total	2.3	1.7
I	1.4	−2.6
II	0.9	−1.2
III	0.4	0.1
IV	0.4	0.4
V	0.6	−0.1
VI	1.1	−0.4
VII	0.9	0.2
VIII	0.6	1.2
IX	1.0	2.1
X	5.0	3.3

SOURCE: Instituto Nacional de Estadística, Geografía e Informática, *Encuesta nacional de ingresos y gastos de los hogares tercer,* Third Quarter, 1984, 1989 Y 1992 (CD-ROM).

NOTE: Real monetary income is calculated with the monthly average consumer price index of the Bank of Mexico for the same period as the household income survey.

[a]Households are ordered in terms of income (the first decile includes the poorest, the last deciles the richest).

The usual adverse political effects of such distributional deterioration appear to have been offset by the overvaluation of the Mexican currency. While real gross national product (GNP) per capita grew at a modest annual rate of 1 percent between 1988 and 1994, dollar GNP per capita increased at an average annual rate of 12.5 percent over the same time period (see Table 1.4). Such large annual increases in dollar GNP per capita encouraged a precarious pattern of overspending. This consumer binge was particularly sharp among those middle-class Mexicans en-

---

offered in Instituto Nacional de Estadística, Geografía e Informática (INEGI), *Encuesta nacional de ingresos y gastos de los hogares* (1994 CD-ROM). A similar figure for 1992–94 is not available directly and must be calculated by "splicing" two different samples. The method suggested by INEGI, combining reported household income and the CPI, yielded an estimate, but when we tried to check the calculation procedure against the directly reported INEGI figures for the earlier time period, there were significant discrepancies. Our "best" alternative method of linking the time periods was via the growth in real per capita GDP, which was 1.64 percent over 1989–92 as against a reported 1.7 percent increase in real monetary income for households over the same period. This standard gives the pattern reported in the text but does not use the same method and hence is not strictly comparable to the other growth figures; moreover, it may understate gains in consumer welfare, since the concurrent overvaluation of the peso tended to enhance purchasing power at every level of income. Of course, as we stress below, this overvaluation prop is now gone, and lower-income groups are now experiencing the full pain of the earlier redistribution.

Table 1.4. Comparison of real GNP and dollar value GNP, 1982–1994

Mexico	GNP in $ per capita	Real GNP per capita index	Percentage change $GNP per capita	Percentage change real GNP per capita
1982	2,840	100.0		
1983	2,280	94.6	−19.7	−5.4
1984	2,100	96.3	−7.9	1.7
1985	2,180	97.4	3.8	1.1
1986	1,980	90.5	−9.2	−7.0
1987	1,950	91.7	−1.5	1.3
1988	1,990	91.2	2.1	−0.5
1989	2,210	92.5	11.1	1.4
1990	2,570	94.3	16.3	1.9
1991	2,990	96.7	16.3	2.6
1992	3,440	97.3	15.1	0.7
1993	3,730	95.7	8.4	−1.6
1994	4,010	96.9	7.5	1.2

SOURCE: World Bank, *World Tables, 1995* (CD-ROM).

joying their first real access to personal credit, due largely to the government's explicit encouragement of this new form of financial intermediation (Fig. 1.1).[14] This overextension of short-term credit—which was facilitated by financial liberalization, massive capital inflows, and low nominal interest rates in the early 1990s—now poses enormous problems, since volatile interest rates have made it extremely difficult for individual debtors to meet their servicing obligations on credit cards, mortgages, and car loans. The Salinas government's reprivatization of the domestic banking system has turned out to be another exacerbating factor, since it is now clear that the new owners of these banks have been less than prudent in their lending decisions.

The current scenario is complicated politically by the fact that the pre-1995 expectations for prosperity had been so high, mainly because neoliberal reform had been oversold by the Salinas team as the route to sustained and rapid growth. We turn now to a more disaggregated analysis of Mexico's neoliberal reform model, with a focus on the main policies that have prevailed in the urban-industrial and rural-agricultural sectors, the general impacts of these policies, and government efforts to address structural distortions and the social tensions triggered by reform.

---

14. These insights were confirmed in June 1995 during the authors' fieldwork interviews with two professional members of Mexico City's banking community: Jorge Arreola, Banco Nacional de Obras y Servicios Públicos, and Gerardo Vargas, Banco Nacional de México.

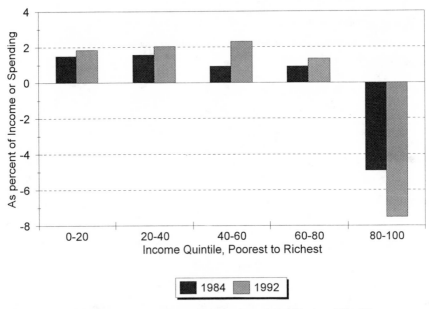

Fig. 1.1. Share of spending less share of income by quintile, Mexico, 1984–92

SOURCE: Instituto Nacional de Estadística, Geografía e Informática, *Encuesta nacional de ingresos y gastos de los hogares,* Third Quarter, 1984 and 1992 (CD-ROM).

NOTE: The figure measures the difference between each quintile's share of spending and its share of income in the two years considered. It is not unexpected that the poorer quintiles would have a larger share of spending than income, primarily because some households may fall in these categories due to falls in temporary and not permanent income. What is significant is that this "excess" spending rose in all the lower quintiles but especially in the middle, a pattern which is consistent with overspending due to an increase in credit card and other consumer credit.

Distributional Stresses in Mexico: A Sectoral Analysis

The Urban Sector: Industrial Restructuring, Employment, and Informality

With the advent of the Salinas administration in 1988, the overriding policy objective became the consolidation of an export-led industrial model, driven by private investment and cheap labor inputs, which would deliver the higher growth, productivity, and income gains that had eluded Mexico since 1980.[15] Thus, the urban-industrial strategy centered mainly on the modernization of the manufacturing sector; the Salinas team combined liberalization of trade with an aggressive privatization drive—phasing out most government supports for industry and selling off nearly $24 billion in state assets from 1989 to 1993—and a series of legal reforms that substantially deregulated Mexico's rules concerning foreign investment.

The extent to which Mexico was actually able to improve the export orientation of industry is shown in Table 1.5. As the data indicate, all but four subsectors of manufacturing (tobacco, leather goods, miscellaneous petroleum and coal products, and basic nonferrous metals) have increased their export ratios since the early 1980s. Overall, non-oil exports grew by 38 percent from 1989 to 1992 and now constitute about 80 percent of Mexico's total exports. The historical concentration of manufacturing activity in the country's old industrial heartland (Mexico City, Jalisco, and Nuevo León) has also given way to a more geographically dispersed pattern (see Table 1.6). Since the early 1980s, the central states of Guanajuato, Hidalgo, Michoacán, Oaxaca, Puebla, and Tlaxcala have increased their industrial profile, as have the border states of Chihuahua, Coahuila, Sonora, and Tamaulipas. While incentives for industrial decentralization into the former group of states have been provided to help alleviate environmental and infrastructure stresses, particularly in Mexico City, the increasing industrialization of the border states is a reflection of the boom that has occurred in the *maquiladora* sector over the past decade.

From the standpoint of job creation, food processing, textiles, metals,

---

15. This section is based on the following sources: Carlos Alba Vega, "La microindustria ante la liberalización económica y el Tratado de Libre Comercio," *Foro Internacional* 23, no. 3 (1993): 453–83; Centro de Estudios Económicos del Sector Privado, "Evolución y problemática de las empresas en 1994," *Actividad Económica*, no. 183 (1995): 1–23; Clemente Ruiz Durán, "México: Crecimiento e innovación en las micro y pequeñas empresas," *Comercio Exterior* 43, no. 6 (1993): 525–29; United Nations Industrial Development Organization (UNIDO), *Mexico: The Promise of NAFTA* (Vienna: UNIDO, 1994); Enrique Dussel Peters, "From Export-Oriented to Import-Oriented Industrialization: Changes in Mexico's Manufacturing Sector, 1988–1994," in *Neoliberalism Revisited: Economic Restructuring and Mexico's Political Future*, ed. Gerardo Otero (Boulder, Colo.: Westview Press, 1996), 63–83; and confidential fieldwork interviews conducted by the authors within Mexico's small-enterprise sector from 1991 to 1994. On the policy objectives of the Salinas administration, see Jaime Zabludovsky, "Trade and Industrial Policy for Structural Adjustment in Mexico," in *Perspectives on the Pacific Basin Economy*, ed. Takao Fukuchi and Mitsuhiro Kagami (Tokyo: Asia Club Foundation, 1989), 439–69.

Table 1.5. Ratio of exports to output by subsector of manufacturing, 1975, 1980, and 1990 (percentage)

Manufacturing Subsector	1975	1980	1990
Total manufacturing	3.5	3.9	23.9
Food	3.7	5.2	17.9
Beverages	1.1	1.5	6.5
Tobacco	1.1	0.6	0.7
Textiles	3.2	1.3	22.9
Clothing	2.0	1.7	23.9
Leather and substitutes	1.3	1.4	0.8
Leather footwear	1.5	1.8	19.2
Wood and cork	1.1	1.2	27.7
Furniture and fixtures	0.5	0.7	36.1
Paper and products	0.3	0.2	4.9
Printing, publishing, and allied industries	3.5	3.4	12.4
Industrial chemicals	5.5	7.6	23.3
Other chemicals	3.5	2.7	8.8
Petroleum refineries	1.4	6.2	20.5
Miscellaneous petroleum and coal products	0.6	3.0	0.1
Rubber products	0.6	0.2	4.0
Plastic products	0.8	1.0	50.7
Pottery, china, earthenware	2.2	2.4	18.5
Glass and glass products	5.8	4.1	23.8
Nonmetallic mineral products	1.9	1.8	10.3
Basic iron and steel	1.8	0.9	16.5
Basic nonferrous metal industries	51.4	38.9	40.0
Metal products, excluding machinery	2.2	2.1	18.6
Nonelectrical machinery	7.0	18.4	—
Electrical machinery	3.7	3.7	32.1
Transport equipment	2.8	4.4	29.2
Professional and scientific equipment	2.4	3.9	—
Other	4.9	3.7	78.0

SOURCE: UNIDO, Regional Database. Reproduced from UNIDO, *Mexico: The Promise of NAFTA* (Vienna: UNIDO, 1994), 42.

machinery, equipment, and chemicals are now the most important industries in terms of labor absorption, accounting jointly for about 75 percent of total manufacturing employment. Unfortunately, the manufacturing sector as a whole accounts for just 22 percent of Mexican employment, and while the subsectors noted above have been high performers with regard to exports, their ability to generate new jobs has been lackluster. Indeed, overall manufacturing employment actually began to decline as of mid-1991, well before the recent recession took its

Table 1.6. Distribution of industry by state and establishment size, 1989 (percentage)

State	Total	Micro[a] (1–15 Employees)	Small (16–100 Employees)	Medium (101–250 Employees)	Large (>251 Employees)
Federal District	15.78	13.33	2.08	0.23	0.14
México	8.67	7.17	1.07	0.25	0.18
Puebla	8.00	7.57	0.33	0.07	0.03
Jalisco	7.37	6.52	0.75	0.06	0.03
Veracruz	6.15	6.05	0.08	0.00	0.02
Guanajuato	5.00	4.89	0.10	0.01	0.00
Michoacán	5.54	5.06	0.41	0.05	0.02
Nuevo León	4.30	3.43	0.71	0.09	0.07
Oaxaca	3.65	3.62	0.02	0.00	0.00
Chiapas	2.92	2.89	0.03	0.00	0.00
Chihuahua	2.73	2.37	0.22	0.04	0.09
Yucatán	2.57	2.44	0.12	0.01	0.00
Guerrero	2.49	2.48	0.01	0.00	0.00
San Luis Potos	2.42	2.30	0.10	0.01	0.01
Coahuila	2.28	2.02	0.22	0.02	0.02
Tamaulipas	2.27	2.14	0.09	0.02	0.02
Sonora	1.72	1.57	0.12	0.02	0.02
Hidalgo	1.63	1.55	0.07	0.01	0.00
Sinaloa	1.60	1.52	0.06	0.01	0.01
Baja California	1.48	1.16	0.23	0.05	0.03
Durango	1.45	1.26	0.15	0.03	0.01
Morelos	1.37	1.32	0.04	0.00	0.00
Zacatecas	1.34	1.33	0.01	0.00	0.00
Nayarit	1.19	1.18	0.02	0.00	0.00
Tlaxcala	1.15	1.09	0.04	0.02	0.01
Aguascalientes	1.13	1.02	0.08	0.01	0.01
Querétaro	1.03	0.93	0.07	0.01	0.01
Tabasco	0.93	0.91	0.00	0.01	0.00
Campeche	0.61	0.59	0.02	0.00	0.00
Colima	0.47	0.46	0.01	0.00	0.00
Quintana Roo	0.39	0.38	0.01	0.00	0.00
Baja California Sur	0.39	0.38	0.01	0.00	0.00
Total	100.00	90.95	7.27	1.03	0.76

Source: Instituto Nacional de Estadística, Geografía e Informática, Censos Económicos 1989. Reproduced from UNIDO, *Mexico: The Promise of NAFTA* (Vienna: UNIDO, 1994), 76.

[a]Includes "unspecified" companies.

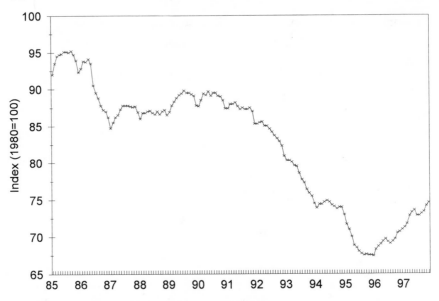

Fig. 1.2. Index of manufacturing employment, 1985–97

toll (see Fig. 1.2). Underpinning this trend were two factors. The first was an impressive increase in manufacturing productivity, or output per labor unit, of 6.6 percent annually between 1988 and 1993;[16] while this is certainly positive, it does imply a reduction in labor demanded unless sales volumes are increasing at an equally rapid pace. The second trend was a drop in the number of small and medium-sized firms registered in the manufacturing sector, from 871 in 1988 to only 401 in 1993; since such firms are usually quite labor-intensive, this meant a loss of some 43,000 jobs over the same five-year period.[17] This combination of productivity gains in the manufacturing sector, on the one hand, and the "shakeout" of smaller firms, on the other hand, goes to the heart of Mexico's distributional challenge in the urban-industrial sector: there is no indication that the current model will generate badly needed employment opportunities anytime soon.

Real-wage trends since 1982 provide another angle on distributional stress within this sector. From 1982 to 1987, both the real minimum wage and the real industrial wage fell by more than 30 percent, reflecting the government's desire to leave wage setting to the market. By stabilizing

16. See Jonathan Heath's chapter in this volume.
17. Ibid.

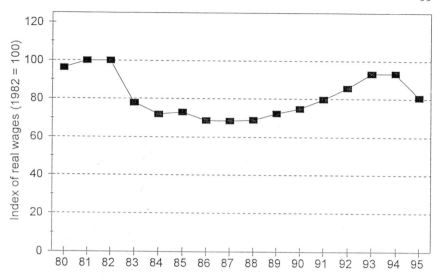

Fig. 1.3. Evolution of real wages in Mexico

Real wages in manufacturing: data taken from Sebastian Edwards, *Crisis and Reform in Latin America* (Washington, D.C.: Oxford University Press, 1995), CEPAL's *Estudio economico de America Latina y el Caribe, 1994–1995,* and INEGI's database at http://dgcnesyp.iniegi.job.mx.

prices and wages simultaneously, the incomes policy instituted in late 1987 helped to moderate the downward spiral of real wages. While the real minimum wage fell 18.5 percent between 1988 and 1991, average real wages began rising after 1988 and were within 10 percent of their pre-debt-crisis levels by 1993 (see Fig. 1.3). However, we should recall that manufacturing was steadily shrinking over this period, implying that the wage was accruing to a smaller group. Overall, there seems to have been growing discrepancies between the wages earned by skilled and unskilled workers, a phenomenon that has exacerbated inequality and is consistent with recent theories about the differential effects of trade liberalization on skilled and unskilled labor.[18] Meanwhile, the

18. For a theoretical explanation of why liberalization might induce a widening of wage differentials within Mexico, see Edward Leamer, "Wage Effects of a US-Mexican Free Trade Agreement" (NBER Working Paper 3391, National Bureau of Economic Research, Cambridge, Mass., 1992). Indirect evidence for the wage-dispersion effect also comes from comparing household distribution data with household income by sources; wages, salaries, and overtime actually improved slowly but steadily between 1984 and 1992 even as distribution by household decile worsened, a pattern that is consistent with rising inequality *within* labor markets.

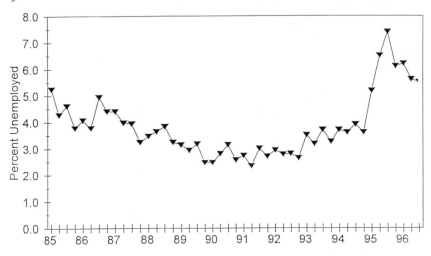

Fig. 1.4. Rate of open unemployment in Mexico by quarter, 1985–96

sharp increase of unemployment in the postcrash Mexican economy (see Fig. 1.4) negatively impacted all wages; as Figure 1.3 indicates, the 1995 recession forced real manufacturing wages back to their 1991 levels, and 1996 brought a further drop even though economic activity recovered. In 1997, real wages finally began to drift upward but remained nearly 25 percent below their 1994 level.

With regard to employment, one exception to disappointing trends of the 1990s has been the *maquila,* or in-bond, industry.[19] Once restricted to the border states, foreign investors (80 percent of whom are U.S. majority holders) can now establish a *maquila* anywhere within Mexico, can own up to a 100 percent share, and under NAFTA will be able to sell a gradually increasing share of production to the local Mexican market.[20] Now comprising over two thousand firms, which account for about half a million manufacturing jobs in Mexico, the *maquila* sector

19. Originally launched in 1965, Mexico's *maquila* program allows duty-free imports of capital equipment for use in manufacturing and assembly, with the stipulation that investors pay duty only on the value added within Mexico and that 80 percent of a plant's output be exported. For more detail on the *maquila* industry, see Leslie Sklair, *Assembling for Development: The Maquila Industry in Mexico and the United States* (La Jolla: Center for U.S.-Mexican Studies, University of California at San Diego, 1993).

20. Gary C. Hufbauer and Jeffrey J. Schott, *NAFTA: An Assessment,* rev. ed. (Washington, D.C.: Institute for International Economics, 1993), 152.

has seen strong employment growth, and *maquila* exports have accounted for more than 50 percent of the expansion of industrial exports that appears in Table 1.5.[21] At the same time, it is important not to exaggerate the potential of the *maquila* industries to resolve the distributional shortcomings identified here: the very logic of production in the key manufacturing subsectors (e.g., electronic components, transportation equipment, and electrical machinery) still hinges on combining foreign investment from capital-abundant nations like the United States with Mexico's abundant supply of cheap unskilled labor. Moreover, average real wages and benefits in the *maquiladoras,* while holding their value better than the average wage-benefit package in manufacturing as a whole, still remain at only half of the manufacturing average; thus, a shift toward *maquila* production may be regressive, at least until employment in that sector finally drives wages upward.[22]

Another aspect of distribution in urban industry is the concentration of assets in this sector. Despite the ambitious program of liberalization, privatization, and deregulation that has been implemented since the late 1980s, the traditionally oligopolistic ownership structure within Mexican industry has changed very little. By the end of the 1980s, the country's top ten industrial conglomerates still produced 20 percent of total manufacturing output, and the aforementioned export growth has been strongest in those tradable subsectors that are dominated by large-scale producers with strong ties to international markets (e.g., passenger vehicles and auto parts).[23] Although these large globally integrated companies (officially defined as having more than 250 employees) constitute just 2 percent of all manufacturing establishments in Mexico, together they account for half of manufacturing production and employment. In

---

21. UNIDO, *Mexico: The Promise of NAFTA,* 36.

22. A comparison of the average values of the wage-benefit package in manufacturing with those of the *maquiladoras* is reported in Fred Rosen, "Is Inflation the Enemy?" *El Financiero Internacional,* March 14–20, 1996, 1, 8. The article is based on data supplied by the Ministry of Labor and INEGI; the manufacturing figures square with what we report in Figure 3.

23. For example, Cementos Mexicanos (CEMEX) accounts for almost 70 percent of national cement production, and Vitro accounts for 90 percent of glass output; three companies still control 75 percent of the country's petrochemicals market, and Grupo Industrial Maseca controls over 70 percent of the maize-flour market. See UNIDO, *Mexico: The Promise of NAFTA,* 67; Maria de los Angeles Pozas, *Industrial Restructuring in Mexico* (La Jolla: Center for U.S.-Mexican Studies, University of California at San Diego, 1993); and Peters, "From Export-Oriented to Import-Oriented Industrialization," 72–78.

the post-peso-crisis era of even tighter credit and stiffer competition, just 2.8 percent of the 27,000 firms involved in exporting in 1995 accounted for 80 percent of all sales.[24]

The remaining 50 percent of manufacturing production and employment is accounted for by some 125,000 firms that have been categorized by the Mexican government according to size as micro (1–15 employees), small (16–100 employees) or medium (101–250 employees). Although the number of these small and medium-sized enterprises (SMEs) has increased by approximately 60 percent since 1982, manufacturing output and wages within this sector have stagnated. There are various explanations for the SME sector's poor performance. First, the bulk of these enterprises (about 100,000) are microfirms clustered in low value-added manufacturing branches such as printing, clay products, metal tanks, dairy, and tortilla production. These micro-level firms employed 21 percent of the workforce in 1993, up from 14 percent in 1988, but this increase seems to be partly due to stagnant productivity and hence a higher (albeit inefficient) absorption of labor within the country's nontradable sectors.[25] Second, privatization has eradicated the government contracts and support that had been so plentiful for these smaller companies during the ISI era. Third, even in those SME industries which have been able to weather import competition, employment has stagnated as firms have been compelled to adopt labor-displacing production techniques.

While the combination of trade liberalization and increased access to the U.S. market under NAFTA should have provided some relief for SME producers on the export side, the latter report to be hampered by capacity limitations, the lack of affordable credit, poor marketing skills, and weak external demand for their products. Tellingly, less than 10 percent of small producers have taken advantage of the two government-sponsored export-promotion initiatives offered during the Salinas years, whereas nearly 40 percent of the large enterprises have benefited from the remaining forms of state support for exporters. Since the implementation of the March 1995 adjustment package, the SME sector, with its

---

24. This information is paraphrased from Enrique Vilatela Riba, general director of the Foreign Commerce National Bank, as reported in "Export Earnings up from Last Year," *El Financiero Internacional*, July 8–14, 1996, and confirmed by the authors' confidential interviews in Mexico's Ministry of Economics (Hacienda), October 1996.

25. See Jonathan Heath's chapter in this volume.

weak access to cheaper foreign financing and international export markets, has been particularly hard hit.[26]

The inability to expand urban employment significantly and the lack of any form of unemployment insurance have led to a rapid increase in economic activity within the country's informal sector.[27] It is now estimated that between 25 and 40 percent of the country's economically active population of 24.1 million has sought refuge in the informal economy. In the urban areas, the typical informal venture is a micro-level business operating in sectors where the entry barriers and infrastructure needs are low, such as commerce and services; not surprisingly, income and output are often as low as the barriers, and the informal sector has quickly become Mexico's workplace for the poor. As a result, over 50 percent of the country's most impoverished are now employed in the informal sector.

Government-Policy Responses

Mexican neoliberal reform did succeed in fostering a somewhat more regionally decentralized export-led model, which has thus far registered some impressive productivity gains within the tradables sector. But the social costs were mounting even before the December 1994 financial crisis, as manufacturing employment fell, informal activity rose, and assets became more concentrated. We have argued that these distributional stresses amount to more than just a longer-than-expected lag in the adjustment process; rather, they are directly related to the mix of policies that Mexico has embraced. Although the operative assumption of PRI technocrats since the mid-1980s has been that microeconomic innovation would follow naturally from macroeconomic reform, in hindsight the lack of consistency and coherence within the macroeconomic reform program and between the chosen macro- and microeconomic policies has stifled the potential gains from a more open economy.

Since 1982, there have been three main phases of government policy

---

26. Those smaller firms which are part of "commodity chains"—that is, linked to larger producers—will do better, but hard data on these linkages are scarce.

27. This analysis is based on Centro de Estudios Económicos del Sector Privado (CEESP), *La economía subterránea en México* (Mexico: CEESP, 1987); Anna Luiza Ozorio, Scott Graham, and Leandro Alves, "Poverty, Deregulation, and Informal Employment in Mexico" (World Bank, Washington, D.C., July 1994, mimeo); and the authors' interviews conducted in June 1995 with top policy makers at the Ministry of Social Development in Mexico City.

vis-à-vis the industrial sector. De la Madrid took the first step in dismantling the bulk of the country's old-fashioned sector-specific industrial
programs in the mid-1980s;[28] by the early 1990s, Mexico's industrial
policy had been drastically pared down to just two export-incentive
schemes and three sectoral programs in those industries dominated by
large transnational firms (autos, computers, and pharmaceuticals).[29] In
mid-1996, the Zedillo administration announced a new course involving
an eight-point plan to promote industrial competitiveness.[30] Of special
interest are the government's acknowledgment that more must be done
to facilitate the process of microeconomic adjustment, and its stated intention to pursue a more flexible and active approach to industrial development: "[C]ompetitiveness . . . cannot depend exclusively on the
availability of low-cost production factors, the isolated efforts of firms
and industries, or market forces alone. These and other factors must be
coordinated and complemented through active government participation, in the form of highly effective public policies that promote industrial growth."[31]

Will this be a case of too little, too late? In the SME sector, despite
strong evidence from the East Asian experience that effective competition requires a mix of large and small firms,[32] the general approach of
the Salinas technocrats was quietly to condone the collapse of small firms
as an example of a "survival-of-the-fittest" commitment to market discipline. As distributional stress mounted in the early 1990s, the government did attempt to help the SME sector via export-promotion measures
and indirect support programs for weaker industries, such as textiles.
The former approach has consisted in duty-free entry of imports that

28. A second phase of horizontal industrial promotion, based on policy tools that benefited the
manufacturing sector as a whole and did not add to the central government's fiscal burden, was
initiated by Salinas in 1989.

29. This section draws on Nora Lustig, *Mexico: The Remaking of an Economy* (Washington, D.C.:
Brookings Institution, 1992), 120–25; Peters, "From Export-Oriented to Import-Oriented Industrialization," 64–72; Jaime Ros et al., "Prospects for Growth and the Environment in Mexico in the
1990s," *World Development* 24, no. 2 (1996): 315; and Fernando Clavijo and S. Valdivieso, "La
política industrial de México, 1988–1994," in *La industria mexicana en el mercado mundial: Elementos para una política industrial,* ed. Fernando Clavijo and J. Casar (Mexico City: Lecturas de El
Trimestre Económico, FCE, 1994), 1:27–92.

30. Secretaría de Comercio y Fomento Industrial (SECOFI), "Mexico: Program of Industrial Policy
and International Trade" (Mexico City, May 1996, mimeo).

31. Ibid., 2.

32. Albert Fishlow et al., eds., *Miracle or Design? Lessons from the East Asian Experience* (Washington, D.C.: Overseas Development Council, 1994).

are crucial for expanding export production; the latter has attempted to encourage "internationalization" of weaker industries through the dissemination of technology and information concerning new market opportunities. The government has also encouraged large-scale firms to enter into subcontracting and procurement agreements with their smaller counterparts and to form joint ventures with small firms in securing finance and technology. This program, however, seems to have had little impact or publicity: in a 1992 survey of Mexican producers, less than one-third of the SME respondents were aware that a comprehensive industrial support program had been established for them in 1991,[33] suggesting a failure to reach the target population.

As one symptom of the adjustment difficulties, by the early 1990s SME borrowers reported severe problems in obtaining credit, even when they were paying interest rates that were double the prevailing deposit rates in the Mexican banking system. In 1991, the government responded by directing the state development bank (NAFIN) to set up a credit-card system to enable SME firms to finance their working-capital and fixed-asset needs. Unfortunately, this program quickly became a magnet for complaints over long delays and insufficient loan sizes, and could not begin to meet the needs of SME producers requesting support in coping with past-due loans and the exorbitant costs of financial intermediation that prevailed in the aftermath of the peso crisis.

As for government-policy responses to the severe decline in wages and jobs, labor-market reform in the context of Mexico's neoliberal model has been slow and erratic. For more than a decade, the underlying structure has been one in which wages are largely determined by the market but entry barriers and job mobility are still highly distorted.[34] This combination has fostered an increasing trend toward wage dispersion and a widening duality between the formal and informal sectors of the economy. Meaningful labor-market reform has been stunted by the PRI's reliance on nondemocratic official unions to guarantee an abundant supply of cheap labor power;[35] without a serious commitment to remove these structural distortions, the government's policy response to labor-market stress has basically been to chip at the margins. For example,

---

33. The general lack of awareness of government programs to assist smaller firms is indicated in our interviews with this sector between 1991 and 1994.

34. Sebastian Edwards, *Crisis and Reform in Latin America: From Despair to Hope* (New York: Oxford University Press, 1995), 277–86.

35. Peters, "From Export-Oriented to Import-Oriented Industrialization," 64.

some assistance has been provided through two separate adult-education programs, and through the Industrial Labor Force Training Program (CIMO) some 128,000 workers have upgraded their job skills to work in SME firms that are undergoing a process of modernization.[36] In the throes of the March 1995 stabilization program, the Mexican government finally stepped forward with a temporary emergency employment program (PEE) slated to provide 840,000 jobs through 1996 in the area of infrastructure projects to support private enterprise.[37]

To rationalize and legalize the informal economy, government strategies to date have centered on the streamlining of procedures for obtaining legal status and the strengthening of informal microenterprises through financial support. In this regard, the government did open a "one-stop window" in 1991, designed to enable microenterprise owners to legalize their businesses in a single transaction. However, the program is limited to microfirms in the manufacturing sector, and there is only one such "window" in all of Mexico City.[38] Not surprisingly, less than 1 percent of these manufacturing microentrepreneurs have taken advantage of this innovative regulatory reform. As for financial support, despite the opening of at least three special credit lines for microentrepreneurs at NAFIN, most of NAFIN's limited resources have been absorbed by small and medium-sized firms operating in the formal sector. Similarly, although Salinas's National Solidarity Program (PRONASOL) offered a very small percentage of its budget for microenterprise development, the urban portion of that program was canceled due to an inability to maintain ongoing contact with entrepreneurs operating at the micro level within the informal economy.[39] And since the 1994 devaluation, and the rapid multiplication of those who have literally been ejected from formal labor markets, even the informal economy is now becoming saturated as the country's workplace for the poor.[40]

In what ways might the Zedillo administration's launching of a new Program of Industrial Policy and International Trade help to alleviate

36. United Nations Economic Commission for Latin America and the Caribbean (ECLAC), *Strengthening Development: The Interplay of Macro- and Microeconomics* (Santiago: ECLAC, 1996), 80.

37. Authors' interview with Alberto Montoya, director of the Special Employment Program at the Ministry of Social Development, June 1995, Mexico City.

38. Ozorio, Graham, and Alves, "Poverty, Deregulation, and Informal Employment in Mexico," 36.

39. Authors' interview with Guillermo Bernal, general director of the Empresas de Solidaridad program, Mexico City, June 1995.

40. See Jonathan Heath's chapter in this volume.

the microeconomic stresses reviewed here? As noted earlier in this section, the government is now getting back into the business of promoting industrial development—but in a markedly different manner.[41] With regard to the SME sector, the government, apart from reiterating its commitment to broaden smaller firms' access to financing schemes, will promote regional and sectoral business "clusters" that focus on strengthening SME enterprises. This is to be done, for example, through tax incentives, technology training, "efficient import substitution," and more aggressive export promotion. The idea here is to restore the role of the SMEs in national production and to support them from the beginning to the end of the export chain. On the human-resource side, the new industrial policy offers to strengthen basic training and specialized education and to build closer ties between the educational system and industry. These are hopeful directions, but they are being undertaken within the context of acute adjustment fatigue and continued resource shortages; moreover, it remains to be seen whether this change represents a long overdue shift in the country's development strategy or yet another instance of the PRI's repackaging of itself in order to weather the current political storm.

The Rural Sector: Early Results of a Market-Based Agricultural Policy

When the Salinas team turned its attention to reform of the agricultural sector in 1990, the Mexican countryside had been struggling economically for at least three decades.[42] The stagnation of agriculture was a consequence of a long-standing policy bias that favored industry in the ISI era, and was compounded by a highly distorted set of ongoing gov-

41. SECOFI, "Program of Industrial Policy and International Trade," 1–26.

42. This section is based on the following background sources: Michael Foley, "Privatizing the Countryside: The Mexican Peasant Movement and Neoliberal Reform," *Latin American Perspectives* 22, no. 1 (1995): 59–76; Jonathan Fox, "Political Change in Mexico's New Peasant Economy," in *The Politics of Economic Restructuring: State-Society Relations and Regime Change in Mexico,* ed. Maria Lorena Cook, Kevin J. Middlebrook, and Juan Molinar Horcasitas (La Jolla: Center for U.S.-Mexican Studies, University of California at San Diego, 1994); Jonathan R. Heath, "Evaluating the Impact of Mexico's Land Reform on Agricultural Productivity," *World Development* 20, no. 5 (1992): 695–711; Cynthia Hewitt de Alcántara, ed., *Economic Restructuring and Rural Subsistence in Mexico: Corn and the Crisis of the 1980s* (La Jolla: Center for U.S.-Mexican Studies, University of California at San Diego, 1994); and Gary D. Thompson and Paul N. Wilson, "Ejido Reforms in Mexico: Conceptual Issues and Potential Outcomes," *Land Economics* 70, no. 4 (1994): 448–65, as well as confidential interviews with Mexican policy makers in June 1995.

ernment interventions. The 1980s saw a chaotic retrenchment of state participation in agriculture, exemplified by a 76 percent decline in public investment from 1982 to 1989.[43] By the early 1990s, agriculture's share of GDP had dropped below 5 percent, down from 20 percent in 1950, and the balance of trade in agricultural products was negative. However, some 26 percent of Mexico's economically active population remains in the rural sector, as opposed to 13.7 percent in Argentina or 14.1 percent in Chile—countries with more successful track records in agricultural development.

The goals of neoliberal reformers centered on the promotion of productivity and profitability in the agricultural sector, mainly through recapitalization and the encouragement of private initiative. However, a larger challenge loomed for Salinas as he sought the country's entry into NAFTA and membership in the OECD bloc of industrialized countries: although Mexico had registered some impressive gains in launching an export-led industrial model in the early 1990s, economic history offers few examples of countries that have successfully joined the ranks of the developed world without modernizing their agricultural sector;[44] in other words, a market overhaul of the rural economy, and a policy approach that cultivated more coherent linkages between agriculture and industry, were essential both for sustaining an export-led strategy and for lending credibility to the NAFTA and OECD membership applications still pending for Mexico.

Beginning in 1990, the Salinas administration swept away a complicated web of price supports that had evolved since land reform was first initiated by constitutional decree in 1917. Tariffs on most agricultural products were abruptly lowered, as were subsidies on production; the guarantee price was eliminated for all crops but corn and beans. At the same time, the government canceled its crop-insurance program, and the rural development bank (Banrural) announced that it would now target loans only to peasant growers whose operations were deemed profitable, and only at market rates. Under NAFTA, the agricultural sector's exposure to competition has been accelerated. Tariffs on 57 percent of the value of U.S.-Mexican agricultural trade were immediately eliminated in 1994, with 94 percent to be eliminated over the next ten years. Tariffs

---

43. Alain de Janvry et al., "NAFTA and Mexico's Maize Producers," *World Development* 23, no. 8 (1995): 1350.

44. See Kurt Shwedel, "La competitividad del sector agroindustrial," in *La industria mexicana en el mercado mundial,* ed. Clavijo and Casar, 2:7–13.

on the remaining 6 percent of "highly sensitive" products, like corn and sugar, will be done away with in a fifteen-year time frame.[45]

A second, bolder aspect of agricultural liberalization has involved the reconfiguration of asset ownership. The 1917 land reform produced a dualistic rural structure, characterized, on the one hand, by a patchwork of small communal landholdings (*ejidos*) that suffer from poor infrastructure and irrigation and, on the other hand, by privately held large farms estimated to be 30–50 percent more productive than their *ejido* counterparts.[46] Comprehensive reform geared toward privatizing the nearly 50 percent of arable land that constitutes the *ejido* sector was undertaken by constitutional amendment in early 1992. The most radical aspect of the reform—in the sense that the new law reverses the PRI's postrevolutionary commitment to communally held land—allows for the rental or sale of parcels of communal lands, including the sale of land to both domestic and foreign corporations.[47] Moreover, the individual or group holders can offer their land as collateral for loans from certified lenders, as opposed to the past practice of depending solely on Banrural or informal markets for credit.

Policy makers contend that this privatization of the *ejidos,* combined with low labor costs and a growing urban consumer market, will serve as a magnet for international investment in agriculture.[48] Thus, in the scenario envisioned by the designers of the reform package agribusiness will be encouraged by the new opportunity to secure land tenure through joint ventures, leasing, or direct purchase. The tough competition from the liberalization of agricultural trade is expected to be offset by productivity gains and increasing economies of scale, which, in turn, should help to reverse Mexico's status as a net importer of food. Critics are less sanguine.[49] The average size of small *ejido* holdings, only two-

45. Hufbauer and Schott, *NAFTA: An Assessment,* 126.

46. The estimate is cited in Thompson and Wilson, "Ejido Reforms in Mexico," 448; others, such as Heath ("Evaluating the Impact of Mexico's Land Reform on Agricultural Productivity") argue that there is little difference between productivity rates on *ejidos* and those on small private farms.

47. The new law did leave intact legal restrictions on the size of individual and group holdings. No one company can hold more land than the legal limit for individuals multiplied by the number of the company's members; the total landholding for any single corporation cannot exceed twenty-five times the individual limit. For more detail, see Foley, "Privatizing the Countryside," 64–67.

48. Confidential authors' interviews conducted with top PRI officials in Mexico City during August 1991.

49. This viewpoint is summarized in Lois Stanford, "The 'Organization' of Mexican Agriculture: Conflicts and Compromises," *Latin American Research Review* 28, no. 1 (1993): 188–201.

thirds of which have electricity, is just 9.5 hectares. The bulk of these lands are rain fed, and less than half have potable water or ready access to a paved road. While the exposure of this much weaker element of the rural sector to the new liberal-policy regime offers, in principle, new opportunities to shift crops and/or form more productive alliances with other growers, the lack of infrastructure, affordable credit, crop insurance, and price supports has been a strong deterrent.

The scarcity of reliable micro-level data on the rural sector makes it difficult to specify the impact of 1980s austerity and the 1990 neoliberal reform measures on the Mexican countryside. The two main areas of distributional stress that stand out in recent studies suggest (1) that greater asset concentration seems as real a possibility in agriculture as it has been in the industrial sector, and (2) that equally likely is a rise in migration from the rural sector. Certainly some of the increased social protest in the region—such as the Zapatista uprising in Chiapas in January 1994 and the Barzón debtors' movement in early 1995 to protest the astronomical interest rates and bank repossessions of land and farming equipment in the wake of the peso crisis—is related to the dramatic adjustment process now under way.[50]

The most solid evidence on asset reallocation in Mexico's rural sector stems from a 1990 countrywide survey of 1,582 households encompassing 276 *ejidos,* which was then compared against a 1994 survey of 1,523 households from the same sample.[51] Although the privatization of land tenure is still just getting under way, the early results suggest the gradual consolidation of a small-landholder class (2–10 hectares of farmland) in Mexico's rural economy, which increased its percentage share of land held from 46.9 percent in 1990 to 54.7 percent in 1994; over the same time span the *minifundios* (0–2 hectares) decreased from 27.4 percent to 19.4 percent, while larger ventures (10 hectares or more) held steady at approximately 25 percent. Underlying this reallocation of assets during the transition to a market economy is a highly differentiated pattern of adjustment, both by region and by farm size.

50. This was the tone of a talk given by Jose Maria Imaz, coordinator of foreign relations for the El Barzón movement, Latin American Studies Program, Johns Hopkins University, School of Advanced International Studies, Washington, D.C., April 18, 1996. For more on the Barzón movement, see Heather Williams, *Planting Trouble: The Barzón Debtors' Movement in Mexico* (La Jolla: Center for U.S.-Mexican Studies, University of California at San Diego, 1996).

51. This paragraph and the two following it are based on the survey findings cited in Alain de Janvry et al., "Ejido Sector Reforms: From Land Reform to Rural Development," in *Reforming Mexico's Agrarian Reform,* ed. Laura Randall (New York: Sharpe, 1996), 71–106.

Within the North, Pacific North, and Center regions, where this emergence of a smallholder class has been most pronounced, there are some incipient signs of the modernization of production practices and the diversification to higher-yield crops. In the Gulf and Pacific South regions, the persistence of impoverished *minifundio* holdings, many with strong indigenous ties, has been more pronounced. In the former, the smallholder class has grown at the expense of the larger farms; but in the latter, the redistribution of land ownership toward larger holdings has outpaced the emergence of a potentially productive smallholder contingent. It comes as no surprise that Chiapas and Oaxaca, two of the most socially volatile states in the 1990s, are both located in the Pacific South region.[52]

This pattern, whereby a smallholder sector appears to be gradually overtaking the traditionally impoverished *minifundios,* holds some promise for the eventual modernization of Mexican agriculture. However, small producers have been faced with an overvalued peso, the further contraction of public support, and falling commodity prices—all of which have worked against the widespread adaptation of commercial farming practices and diversification to higher-yield crops. Indeed, with 78 percent of Mexican farmers involved in corn production at the outset of the reforms, and given NAFTA's fifteen-year timeline on the liberalization of corn, the survival instincts of smaller producers has actually been to expand corn production for domestic and home consumption since 1990. In stark contrast, the larger farms, with ready access to credit, technology, and irrigation, are now leading Mexico's export boom in high-yield agricultural tradables (e.g., coffee, fruit, beverages, vegetables, sugar, livestock, and cut flowers) since the 1994 devaluation.[53]

A slow and painful adjustment in the rural sector has, indeed, provoked some out-migration, although recent research contradicts earlier predictions, which focused on the economically devastated *minifundio* population as the most likely group to depart the countryside in the 1990s.[54] Rather, it is the smallholder class, from farms of five to ten hectares in size, that is now the most likely to migrate. Survey data show,

52. Because of data-collection problems, Chiapas was not included in the de Janvry et al. survey.

53. See "Agriculture Leading NAFTA Trade Growth in 1996," *NAFTA Works* (SECOFI-NAFTA Office of the Mexican Embassy in Washington, D.C.), no. 6 (June 1996): 2.

54. Sherman Robinson et al., "Agricultural Policies and Migration in a United States–Mexico Free Trade Area" (Working Paper 617, Department of Agricultural and Resource Economics, University of California at Berkeley, 1991).

for example, that nearly 22 percent of adult family members have migrated from this smallholder sector, that these migrants have at least a medium-level education, and that around 64 percent of them head to the United States. For this group, many of whom are still trying to survive as farmers, remittances from the United States composed up to 13 percent of household income.[55] In contrast, of the approximately 20 percent of the rural population still active in the *minifundio* sector, only 16 percent of family members have migrated, and of these, just 35 percent have gone to the United States.

One explanation for today's comparatively lower levels of migration among this poorest income group is that the ongoing adjustment crisis of the 1980s had already provoked a large exodus of *minifundio* dwellers into the country's urban informal economy.[56] For those remaining on rural plots smaller than two hectares in the 1990s, the recently acquired right to rent out *ejido* land has provided the option to engage more actively in off-farm work.[57] Still, there is a sizable segment within this sector that has neither the resources to migrate to the United States nor the ability to defend its economic interests within local labor markets, be they rural or urban, formal or informal. Again, we argue that the alleviation of distributional stress for this particular group is hampered by more than just a longer-than-expected adjustment lag; particularly in the wake of the March 1995 austerity program, the proliferation of extreme poverty in such *minifundio* strongholds as Oaxaca and Chiapas suggests that a more targeted set of public policies will be necessary to support the adjustment of these struggling households to a market economy.

Government-Policy Responses

To ameliorate the distributional pressures in agriculture and discourage the outflow of migrants from the rural sector, the government has offered rural producers support through two main programs, PRONASOL and PROCAMPO. While PRONASOL offers many services that cut across the rural and urban sectors, such as infrastructure support for schools, electricity, and potable water, economically vulnerable segments of the rural sector have also received special attention. For example, PRONASOL

---

55. De Janvry et al., "Ejido Sector Reforms," 85–89.
56. De Janvry et al., "NAFTA and Mexico's Maize Producers," 1350–51.
57. De Janvry et al., "Ejido Sector Reforms," 76.

has provided social services to Mexico's estimated 3.6 million impoverished agricultural day laborers, support for small coffee growers, and assistance in the creation of diversified microindustrial enterprises in the countryside.[58] Since defaults in the small-farming sector can now result in loss of access to land, PRONASOL has also intervened in the restructuring or cancellation of Banrural's overdue loan portfolio for low-income producers.

The PROCAMPO program was launched in October 1993 as a fifteen-year direct income subsidy for producers of corn and other basic crops (beans, rice, sorghum, soybeans, wheat, cotton, and rye) who are likely to suffer losses due to trade-related competition.[59] In its first full year of operation, the government allocated U.S.$3.5 billion in income subsidies to some 3.3 million farmers through PROCAMPO—a significant welfare payment for low-productivity farmers. In theory, the program is meant to support farm income during the transition to a market-based rural economy, thus enabling those producers subsisting on peasant staple production to modernize and diversify into more commercial lines of agricultural production.

Not surprisingly, in view of the continued adjustment stress in the rural sector, both of these programs have been the object of at least three kinds of criticism. First, and perhaps most important, is that the resources that have been made available fall far short of what would be needed to enable a potentially productive farmer to make the improvements necessary for successful operation at the internationally competitive price level for these basic crops.[60] Second has been the misallocation of funds. In the case of PROCAMPO, for example, there is some evidence that these income payments ended up in the hands of larger producers, while smaller staple farmers with less than ten hectares received as little as U.S.$0.50 per day.[61] Similarly, although PRONASOL credits were disbursed evenly across farm sizes, they amounted to less than 10 percent

---

58. For a full description of PRONASOL activities, see Secretaría de Desarrollo Social (SEDESOL), *Solidarity in National Development: New Relations Between Society and Government* (Mexico City: SEDESOL, 1993).

59. As an income subsidy rather than a price prop, PROCAMPO is compatible with the dictates of the GATT and NAFTA. See Banco de México, *The Mexican Economy, 1994* (Mexico City: Banco de México, 1995).

60. Kirsten Appendini, "Transforming Food Policy over a Decade," in *Economic Restructuring and Rural Subsistence in Mexico*, ed. Hewitt de Alcántara, 155–56.

61. Marilyn Gates, "The Debt Crisis and Economic Restructuring: Prospects for Mexican Agriculture," in *Neoliberalism Revisited*, ed. Otero, 54.

of the loans available through Banrural or the commercial banks, and just 10 percent of the loans used by large farms.[62] While PRONASOL has distributed resources to a larger number of households (representing 61 percent of the credit available to small farms), the total amount of credit available to the *ejido* sector has fallen by 19 percent. It is this broad but shallow spending pattern that has fueled the opposition's claim that PRONASOL has been primarily geared toward winning PRI votes and quelling political protest.

Finally, in the sense that these programs do not begin to address long-term structural problems in the Mexican agricultural sector, they do not add up to a coherent strategy of rural integrated development. A main underlying problem is that trade liberalization has reduced the value of rain-fed land, since the goods produced on this land are mainly NAFTA's "losers"; conversely, the value of irrigated land, where more competitive agricultural goods such as fruits, vegetables, and flowers are grown, is increasing. Income subsidies only temporarily mask this shift in asset values and, hence, do little to prevent the likely concentration of more valuable land into fewer hands; what is needed is the implementation of a vigorous public-infrastructure program geared toward major land improvements (e.g., irrigation, drainage) and technical assistance that would help smaller farmers reorient production to higher-value crops.[63] If the government does not more strategically target state resources in this direction, the *ejido* reform will fail to attract the projected new investment, and the current trends of asset concentration and regressive distribution will continue.

The Social Sector: Market Restructuring and New Demands for Human Capital

In the social sector, Mexico's market-based development model faces a serious disjuncture between the increasing demand for highly productive human capital that would render the country more competitive internationally and the actual ability of the working population to rise to this occasion. The potential role of social policy for bridging this gap has not been well articulated in Mexico, or in the rest of the region, for that

---

62. De Janvry et al., "Ejido Sector Reforms," 81–84.

63. Santiago Levy and Sweder van Wijnbergen, "Transition Problems in Economic Reform: Agriculture in the Mexico-U.S. Free Trade Agreement" (Policy Research Working Papers, World Bank, August 1992), 17–19.

matter. There have, of course, been some efforts to raise education levels, improve housing, and enhance health care during the 1980s and 1990s, including President Salinas's ambitious poverty-reduction program, which targeted resources toward economically vulnerable segments of the population.

However, as Table 1.7 shows, although social spending rose as a percentage of government expenditure during the late 1980s, it fell as a percentage of GDP. While this rise in relative social spending reflects well on the government's priorities, it also suggests an increasing gap between social expenditures and the country's basic human needs. Because little progress has been made in raising the government's commitment to social spending as a percentage of GDP during the 1990s, policy makers are hard-pressed to ensure that social spending is better targeted to the truly needy, particularly since the steep recession of 1995.[64] Below, we review the two tracks on which Mexican social policy has moved since the mid-1980s, with an eye toward the ways in which social spending could better strengthen human capital and enhance income distribution.

Table 1.7. Social spending in Mexico, 1980–1990

	Education (% of GDP)	Health (% of GDP)	Housing, Social Security, Welfare (% of GDP)	Total (% of GDP)
1980	3.02	0.40	2.68	6.10
1985	2.87	0.34	2.41	5.62
1990	2.41	0.33	2.15	4.89

	Education (% of govt. spending)	Health (% of govt. spending)	Housing, Social Security, Welfare (% of govt. spending)	Total (% of govt. spending)
1980	18.0	2.4	16.0	36.4
1985	11.5	1.4	9.7	22.6
1990	13.9	1.9	12.4	28.2

SOURCE: World Bank, *World Tables, 1995* (CD-ROM).

64. Systematic and comparable World Bank data of the sort used in Table 1.7 are not available after 1990; analysis of social expenditure trends under the Salinas *sexenio* is further complicated by the considerable overlap between long-standing social spending categories and newer commitments under PRONASOL. Because of this, we base our assessment of the continued plateau in social spending as a share of GDP in the 1990s on the authors' interviews at the Ministry of Social Development, Mexico City, June 1995.

We begin with the traditional kinds of public goods that the state has always provided—education, housing, and health; we then evaluate the pros and cons of PRONASOL as a post-debt-crisis attempt to redefine the state's role in the provision of public goods under a market-based economic model that still faces tight resource constraints.

Education

Investment in primary education has long been touted by Mexican policy makers for its contribution to overall worker productivity and, subsequently, to restored economic growth under Salinas. However, Mexico's investment in primary education still lags behind other countries in the region. Whereas the average education of Latin American workers was 5.2 years in 1995, economists estimate that the region's level of development warrants a minimum of 7 years; because of its higher level of development, Mexico's educational gap is more than three years per worker.[65] This sector continues to be plagued by the following problems:[66]

- *Low educational achievement.* Mexican students consistently have performed below the average on standardized tests in Spanish, math, and science. The primary school repetition rate (the number of students who must repeat a grade as a percentage of the total) is 9.1 percent nationwide and has reached levels as high as 50 percent in some rural areas. Each year, 4.6 percent of enrolled students (some 700,000 students) drop out before they complete the third grade. At least half the attrition rate is due to poor nutrition, family economic hardship, and migration.
- *Poor teaching quality and teacher absenteeism.* These problems can be attributed to low salaries in the education field and to a backward incentive structure that encourages teachers to settle in teacher-rich urban areas and not in teacher-poor rural areas. Overall, teacher salaries fell 33 percent in real terms between 1983 and 1990; while teacher earnings have risen by 18 percent in real terms since 1990, they are still lower than pre-debt-crisis levels. The fact that rural

65. Juan Luis Londoño, *Poverty, Inequality, and Human Capital Development in Latin America, 1958–2025*, Latin American and Caribbean Studies, Viewpoints Series (Washington, D.C.: World Bank, 1996), 25.

66. See World Bank, "Mexico: Second Primary Education Project" (Staff Appraisal Report, World Bank, Washington, D.C., 1994).

teachers receive even lower wages than their urban counterparts ensures that the rural areas remain short of teachers.
* *Shortages of teaching materials, outdated curriculum, and poor physical
  facilities.* Many school buildings in Mexico are in dire need of repair,
  and almost all schools lack adequate library books and audiovisual
  aids—resource deficits that are considered a main cause of the country's low achievement-test scores in Spanish and the sciences.

While educational spending has rebounded somewhat, rising to 4.1
percent of GDP in 1993, the Mexican government still has done little to
rectify the problems above. This situation has been exacerbated by the
decentralization of primary and middle school management since mid-
1992. Such decentralization, while perhaps a necessary step toward fiscal
reform, has greatly increased the burden on state governments, which,
in turn, still sorely lack the required administrative and revenue-raising
capacities. Meanwhile, although recent research has shown a strong relationship between increased investment in primary education and higher
levels of employment and worker productivity,[67] the Mexican government continues to direct 41 percent of education expenditures toward
university subsidies, while primary education subsidies amount to just
12 percent of public expenditure on education. Although a university
education is also crucial to the pursuit of an economic model that demands high skills, it is not nearly as important as training an entire
workforce to read, write, and do simple math.

Housing

The availability of adequate housing, like the provision of a higher-
quality education, has the potential for creating large socioeconomic
benefits. Mexico is now experiencing a housing shortfall of at least three
million units. The reasons include a growing urban population, inefficient housing regulation, poor infrastructure to support housing construction, and a general decrease in government spending on housing
since the 1982 debt crisis. Moreover, the housing stock that is available
to lower-income groups often lacks proper sanitation and sewage facilities and tends to be far from where jobs are located, making it geographically difficult for the poor to exploit available work opportunities. Thus,
the connection between housing and productivity can be quite direct.

67. George Psacharopoulos, "Time Trends of the Returns to Education: Cross National Evidence," *Economics of Education Review* 8, no. 3 (1989): 225–31.

Both the federal and state governments have initiated serious changes in all facets of housing policy.[68] The regulation of housing construction, which in the past has added as much as 25 percent to the cost of a home, has been streamlined. The central government has also acted to increase the security of property rights by legalizing the ownership of 1.2 million properties that had been informally occupied, mostly by families in the very lowest income deciles. In November 1992 a uniform set of building standards and codes was established, and Mexico has increased spending on infrastructure that will provide sanitary water and sewage treatment to more areas.

Other reforms include the professionalization of FOVI, a special housing subsidy fund within the central bank for families with a monthly income below $600, which has now moved from an application process riddled with patronage to a more neutral auction system. Finally, in order to reduce mortgage costs and increase competition in the housing-finance industry, the central bank, the stock exchange commission, and several commercial banks are currently working to establish a secondary mortgage market. To its credit, the Zedillo administration, in the wake of the peso crisis, convinced the local private banks to collaborate with the government in rolling over the multitude of mortgages that had fallen into arrears. The distributional effects of this move are somewhat questionable—the bigger benefits go to middle-class homeowners—but the support of housing is welcome.

Health

In 1983, the Mexican Constitution was amended to include a guaranteed right to health care for every citizen. Despite this commendable goal, the imperatives of economic adjustment rendered the provision of universal health care impossible. By 1988, government spending on health care had increased by just 1.25 percent over the 1981 levels. Given this plateau in real public expenditure, policy makers were still able to deliver some important gains in the health arena: life expectancy increased from 67.1 years in 1982 to 70.3 years in 1991; infant mortality fell from 49 per 1,000 births in 1982 to 35 per 1,000 in 1991; and by 1987, 91 percent of the population had health insurance, compared with only 81.2 percent in 1982.[69]

---

68. See Thomas Zearley, "Creating an Enabling Environment for Housing: Recent Reforms in Mexico," *Housing Policy Debate* 4, no. 2 (1993): 239–49.

69. All trends cited here were drawn from the World Bank's "World Data" CD-ROM, 1994.

Apart from these advances, Mexico's health-care system has yet to undergo some fundamental reforms. One obstacle to better service lies in the allocation of health funding, which is still heavily skewed toward administrative (13–32 percent) and curative activities (59–75 percent), with few resources left over for the crucial areas of training and research. Recent studies have also found serious inequities: even though policy makers have succeeded in improving some key social indicators since 1982, austerity budgets and the decentralization of health-care services to the states have exacerbated the disparities in the quality of care received by rich and poor, urban sector and rural.[70] For example, an analysis of health-care delivery in two of the country's poorest states, Oaxaca and Guerrero, found that decentralization had resulted in an overall decrease in the number of people receiving health-care services (Oaxaca), and in reduced services to the poor (Guerrero), while the wealthier population in these states saw an increase in services.[71] It appears that attempts to improve and decentralize health care in order to make it more responsive to the needs of the local citizenry must be combined with increased efforts by the federal government to ensure equity in funding across states and across classes and sectors within states.

PRONASOL as a "New" Approach to Social Policy in Mexico
Faced with increasing distributional conflict and with some encouragement from the multilateral lenders, countries such as Bolivia, Chile, and Mexico launched compensatory social programs in the 1980s. To varying degrees, all of these social programs have relied on a combination of traditional social welfare compensation and on new "demand-based" criteria requiring that communities generate specific proposals for assistance. In all of these programs, the funds have primarily been spent on infrastructure; other kinds of social assistance (education and school materials, vocational training, and vaccinations) and production support (credit access, technology training, and employment creation) have lagged far behind.[72]

Mexico's version of a social compensation program was PRONASOL,

70. Carlos Cruz Rivero et al., "The Impact of Economic Crisis and Adjustment on Health Care in Mexico" (Innocenti Occasional Papers 13, Italy, February 1991).

71. Rene Gonzalez-Block et al., "Health Services Decentralization in Mexico," *Health Policy and Planning* 4, no. 4 (1989): 301–14.

72. See Carol Graham, *Safety Nets, Politics, and the Poor: Transitions to Market Economies* (Washington, D.C.: Brookings Institution, 1994).

launched by President Salinas in 1988 and now reincarnated as the Alliance for National Welfare under the Zedillo administration. While all of these safety-net programs are variations on a theme, PRONASOL was also very much a Mexican phenomenon in that it involved fairly heavy-handed government participation at every level. For example, during his tenure, President Salinas himself assessed local needs in weekly visits to the countryside, after which community groups and government officials designed government-funded projects. As a result, critics suggest that the real purpose of PRONASOL was to strengthen the PRI's control over local leaders and undermine the political opposition by handing out side payments to the loudest voices of potential protest. In this view, PRONASOL was little more than a "social tranquilizer" or an instrument of state patronage that the governing party used to mitigate the harsher effects of its economic policies.[73]

In fact, PRONASOL has been *both* a patronage slush fund for the PRI *and* a creative social compensation scheme staffed with a cadre of highly competent policy makers.[74] As the latter, it has faced a problem typical of many compensation programs: the mere introduction of a social safety net has inflated popular expectations and led some to mistake it as a successful answer to the long-term structural inequalities in Mexico's rural and urban sectors. However, PRONASOL's resources were never sufficient to accomplish such a daunting task. Although the program received an impressive-sounding $14 billion between 1988 and 1994, its annual budget never amounted to more than 1 percent of Mexico's GDP. As for triggering structural change in the long term, just 3 percent of the total PRONASOL budget went toward Empresas de Solidaridad—the main PRONASOL program that had been assigned the task of increasing productive opportunities for those on the economic margin.[75] In short,

73. See Denise Dresser, *Neopopulist Solutions to Neoliberal Problems: Mexico's National Solidarity Program* (La Jolla: Center for U.S.-Mexican Studies, University of California at San Diego, 1991), 1. The structure of PRONASOL made it very open to characterization as a social tranquilizer: Since recipient communities were required to organize to articulate their demands, the most organized of the poor—that is, those most likely to protest—were also the most likely to receive funds. At the same time, the demand-based nature of PRONASOL and the Latin American counterpart programs could be viewed as a positive in that it requires grassroots mobilization to trigger funding.

74. PRONASOL's mixed results and structure are discussed in the collection of essays on the program edited by Wayne A. Cornelius, Ann L. Craig, and Jonathan Fox, *Transforming State-Society Relations in Mexico: The National Solidarity Strategy* (La Jolla: Center for U.S.-Mexican Studies, University of California at San Diego, 1994).

75. Authors' interview with Guillermo Bernal, general director of the Empresas de Solidaridad program, Mexico City, June 1995.

PRONASOL was similar to other compensation programs: while effective in securing political breathing space in the wake of harsh adjustment measures, the limited resources and demand-based nature of such programs means that they cannot be expected to do much more than that.[76]

Conclusions: The Need for a "Second Phase" of Reform

Despite neoliberal claims that causally link economic opening with higher levels of growth and productivity, as well as broader access to a bigger economic pie, the Mexican case suggests that the path toward achieving these goals may be more complex than originally envisioned. In Mexico there has been an erratic pattern of growth, lackluster productivity gains, and an increasing concentration of income in the wealthiest groups over the past decade.[77] One reason for this poor performance is that Mexican policy makers focused on macroeconomic adjustment while leaving microeconomic restructuring to the market; unfortunately, the collapse of the macroeconomy in late 1994 and the explosion of violence and social upheaval—as well as the eventual political consequences for the PRI in 1997—have now made evident the costs of ignoring these micro-level issues of distribution and sectoral performance.

Since the debacle of 1994–95, macroeconomic stability has gradually been restored (see Pastor's chapter in this volume), with exports seeming to lead the way. Given the steep devaluations in Asian currency markets during 1997–98, and an associated loss of Mexican export competitiveness, policy makers are still not entirely out of the macroeconomic woods; nevertheless, the aggregate economic fundamentals underpinning this comeback, including the shift to a flexible exchange rate in 1995, are decidedly stronger than in the pre-1994 period.

Despite this impressive recovery, the underlying weaknesses and distributional stresses of the Mexican economy remain. In particular, the structural heterogeneity that we described in our analysis of the urban-

76. For an elaboration on this point, see Kathleen M. Bruhn, "Social Spending and Political Support: The 'Lessons' of the National Solidarity Program in Mexico," *Comparative Politics* 28, no. 2 (1996): 151–77.

77. Mexico, whose economy is the sixteenth largest in the world, now has the fifth largest collection of billionaires, outranking much larger economies such as those of Canada, Britain, France, and Italy on this indicator. See Rick Willis, "Savings Incentives Become a Priority," *El Financiero Internacional*, July 8–14, 1996.

industrial and the rural-agricultural sectors has become even more apparent in the post-1994 period, as the top tier of tradables producers within each sector has rapidly recovered but the ever-widening bottom tier continues to stagnate. For this latter group, operating within the nontradable service, agriculture, and manufacturing sectors, the neoliberal goal of achieving greater efficiency in the allocation of productive factors, and hence a more solid base for income gains, remains elusive.

Apart from long-term structural weaknesses related to low savings, investment, and productivity rates, this more vulnerable segment of the domestic market has also had less insulation from the tight fiscal and monetary contraction that formed the cornerstone of the 1995 austerity plan. The post-1994 data point to a further shrinking of real wages and an absolute worsening of income shares for the country's poorest groups.[78] Meanwhile, the explosion of such social protest movements as the Zapatistas, El Barzón, and the more violent People's Revolutionary Army, and the historic opposition victories in the 1997 midterm elections, suggest that an adjustment-weary populace is much less inclined to tolerate the PRI's cynical corruption scandals and its hollow promises of future prosperity.[79]

What kinds of strategies could help broaden productivity gains and economic prosperity? In the urban-industrial sector, the fallout from the peso crisis appears to have shifted the policy debate in favor of those within the president's technocratic ranks who have long argued for a more active, integrated approach to industrial policy.[80] The Zedillo administration now seems to recognize that such problems as asset concentration, the overall fragility of small and medium-sized firms, plummeting real wages, and the explosion of the informal economy are both endogenous to Mexican-style neoliberal reform and serious barriers to future productivity growth.

In this light, the government has renewed a number of commitments

78. Based on the authors' confidential interviews within Mexico's Ministry of Economics (Hacienda), October 1996.

79. See Alma Guillermoprieto, "Mexico: Murder Without Justice," *New York Review of Books,* October 3, 1996, 31–36. With the launching of its Alliance for the Recovery of Economic Growth in October 1995, the Zedillo administration has made modest efforts to alleviate adjustment stress, including a plan to cap credit-card rates and to purchase a share of troubled bank-loan portfolios through the government's Deposit Insurance Fund.

80. This view is expressed, for example, in the collection of essays edited by Clavijo and Casar, *La industria mexicana en el mercado mundial.*

concerning economic deregulation, the upgrading of technology and human resources, the strengthening of the SME sector, and stricter enforcement of antimonopoly legislation. More important, Mexican industrial policy has taken a potentially innovative turn with its stated intention to promote productivity through regional business clusters.[81] Such industrial clusters tend to encompass both large firms capable of effectively competing in world markets and smaller companion firms that provide supply flexibility and innovative backup. The government's decision to play a more active role in promoting horizontal and vertical ties between firms operating within this mode can create important multiplier effects, such as increased labor-market mobility and new kinds of technological adaptation. When combined with crucial investments in education, job training, and the creation of business associations related to these regional clusters, the very logic of production can shift quickly from today's low-wage, low-skill, slow-growth dynamic to one in which growth and income gains are driven by productivity and innovation.

In the rural-agricultural sector, Mexico City technocrats have settled for programs like PROCAMPO, which maintain an increasingly miserable status quo in the countryside. A more dynamic approach to incorporating the emergent class of small-landholding farmers into Mexico's rural economy would include the following: the creation of rural institutions to provide more equal access to credit and to promote modernization of farming techniques and diversification into high-yield crops; the implementation of a vigorous public infrastructure program geared toward expanding irrigation and transportation; and a more aggressive budgetary commitment to basic and technical education in the countryside.[82] The recent realignment of the peso has revealed Mexico's dynamic potential as an agricultural exporter under NAFTA; and the buoyant recovery of agricultural exports suggests that there is both room and reason for more aggressively targeting programs like PROCAMPO toward those

81. Recent industrial analysis suggests that businesses have increasingly grouped together into multisectoral clusters that share similar sorts of skilled labor and technology. For a view of this process in the United States, see Peter Doeringer and David Terka, "Business Strategy and Cross-Industry Clusters," *Economic Development Quarterly* 9, no. 3 (1995): 225–37.

82. For an elaboration of these policies, see Levy and van Wijnbergen, "Transition Problems in Economic Reform"; de Janvry et al., "NAFTA and Mexico's Maize Producers"; and de Janvry et al., "Ejido Sector Reforms."

who most need it, as opposed to those who are already thriving in the rural economy.

As for social policy, the period since 1988 has seen some creative innovations, albeit in an era of tighter budgets. However, the political baggage surrounding the PRONASOL safety-net program, a haphazard decentralization of fiscal responsibilities, and the inadequacy of social strategies in promoting long-term structural change have clearly been problems. Social policy, productivity, and potential income gains can be linked; in education, for example, a major reorientation of resources toward basic and technical education could foster large human-capital gains.[83] Yet, despite widespread social discontent concerning the difficulties of securing stable formal employment within Mexico's radically restructured economy, policy makers have still not mustered the political will to shift social priorities in a manner that would more aggressively harness human resources to a neoliberal development model.

Policy makers, in short, have thus far delivered on just half of what the neoliberal equation has to offer: markets are more open, certain economic units are more efficient, and Mexico has adjusted to the "shock" of the peso crisis without resorting to populist strategies. Unfortunately, what's missing—wage and employment gains, improvements in income distribution, and sustainable growth—may never follow "naturally" from the new market model. The gravity of the gap between relative macroeconomic stability and absolute microeconomic stress demands an explicit set of public policies to boost the adjustment process along. Although political-economy research since the debt crisis has identified an arsenal of policies that could readily jump-start the process of microeconomic adjustment in Mexico, PRI technocrats have opted to delay the adoption of such policies, apparently counting on the country's passive and downtrodden populace to remain as such.

In opting for more of the same, the PRI has gambled incorrectly on two counts. First, "voice" (Zapatistas, El Barzón) and "exit" (migration to the United States, defection to opposition parties at the polls) have more aptly characterized civic behavior in the 1990s, and this will ultimately diminish, not enhance, the stature of the PRI. Second, there is increasing evidence that sustainable growth may actually be induced, rather than hindered, by attention to improving distribution of income.[84]

83. Londoño, *Poverty, Inequality, and Human Capital Development in Latin America,* 10–16.

84. Alberto Alesina and Dani Rodrik, "Distributive Policies and Economic Growth," *Quarterly Journal of Economics* 109, no. 436 (1994): 465–90.

By overlooking these new dynamics, the Zedillo team could be condemning itself indefinitely to mediocre returns at the level of the real economy—not to mention a draining of scarce public resources into an expanding state-security network—as the social costs of neoliberalism in Mexico continue to accumulate.

2   Assessing the NAFTA Negotiations

U.S.-Mexican Debate and Compromise on Tariff and Nontariff Issues

Sylvia Maxfield and Adam Shapiro

This chapter steps back from the normative approach to NAFTA that has often dominated the debate over the agreement's economic impact. Our focus is on the outcome of sectoral negotiations, particularly between Mexico and the United States. The conventional wisdom is that Mexico had little leverage because it had lowered many tariffs unilaterally prior to the opening of the NAFTA negotiations and, hence, Mexican policy makers "had given away the store." Mexican tariff levels before NAFTA were still higher than those of the United States, and a strict focus on tariff-level changes does indicate that Mexico ceded more than the United States. However, our evaluation suggests that the NAFTA negotiations involved more than just tariff reductions. In fact, many have argued that Mexico's primary concern was to garner much higher levels of investment. Indeed, foreign capital flooded into Mexico upon announcement of the NAFTA negotiations, based partly on the implicit assumption that the U.S. government would become the de facto guarantor of Mexican government debt.

This chapter revisits the NAFTA negotiations with the benefit of hindsight and analyzes the outcomes on a sector-by-sector basis. Disaggregating NAFTA into its various sectoral negotiations adds nuance to the analysis of the bilateral balance of power between the United States and Mexico. It is also a necessary first step in any effort to evaluate how closely NAFTA conforms to different conceptions of the politics of international economic relations at the sectoral level. One such model focuses mainly on tariffs, arguing that industries with large actual or potential scale economies will favor, and by assumption obtain, the steepest regional tariff reductions.[1] More political variants of this argument suggest that trade policy in general will reflect the interests of the best-organized industries.[2] Crudely speaking, the research strategies used thus far in evaluating the outcome of intergovernmental trade bargaining hinge largely on the choice of the "independent" and "dependent" variables.

We recognize these debates, but at the same time argue that these approaches cannot answer the question of who "won" the NAFTA negotiations, mainly because the analysis of relative and absolute changes in tariff levels badly misconstrues the scope and content of the U.S.-Mexican trade relationship. For example, while Mexico, in its initial conception of the negotiations, focused on tariff reductions and increased market access, the United States clearly cared about such legal principles as intellectual-property rights and government procurement. As Table 2.1 details, the United States won on many, but not all, issues of legal principles, while Mexico held sway in crucial sectors like agriculture and energy. In view of this, our main point is that the respective winner within different sectors has as much to do with the preconceived goals of each country as it does with the actual outcome of the negotiations.

---

1. See Helen Milner, "Industries, Governments, and the Creation of Regional Trade Blocs," in *The Political Economy of Regionalism,* ed. Edward Mansfield and Helen Milner (New York: Columbia University Press, 1997), and Michael J. Gilligan, "Lobbying as a Private Good with Intra-Industry Trade" (New York University, n.d., mimeo).

2. See E. E. Schattschneider, *Politics, Pressures, and the Tariff* (Englewood Cliffs, N.J.: Prentice Hall, 1935); Raymond Bauer, Ithiel de Sola Pool, and Lewis Dexter, *American Business and Public Policy* (Chicago: Aldine, 1972); and Timothy McKeown, "Firms and Tariff Regime Change: Exploring the Demand for Protection," *World Politics* 36, no. 1 (1984): 215–33.

Table 2.1. NAFTA negotiation issues and outcomes by chapter

Chapter	Issues	Who Won Overall?
Market access	Protection for import-sensitive products Duty drawbacks/deferrals	United States
Automotive	Export-import ratios Domestic content Emissions standards for Mexican-produced U.S. cars Tariff phase-out	Mexico
Textiles/apparel	Exemptions to "yarn forward" Tariff phase-out	United States
Rules of origin	Special rule for auto parts	United States
Energy	Should it be discussed? Foreign participation Market access for U.S. electricity and natural gas sales Preferential energy prices for Mexican companies Energy crisis commitments	Mexico
Agriculture	Mexican orange juice sales in United States Sanitary standards Export subsidies	Mexico
Government procurement	Set-aside thresholds Over threshold contracts in energy State government procurement	United States
Investment	Mexican performance requirements for U.S. FDI Mexican government screening Definition of "NAFTA investor"	United States
Trade in services	Ground transport	(Draw)
Financial services	Market access National treatment	United States
Intellectual property	Enforcement commitments Expansion of copyrights and patents honored Compulsory licensing	United States
Review and dispute settlement	Should there by any? Arbitration procedures	Mexico

Because a full examination of all nineteen sectors is beyond the scope of this analysis, we focus here on twelve of the sectors negotiated under NAFTA.[3]

Overview of the Negotiations

Canadian Foreign Trade Minister Michael H. Wilson, Mexican Minister of Commerce and Industry Jaime Serra Puche, and U.S. Trade Representative Carla Hills oversaw the NAFTA negotiations. They, in turn, appointed chief and deputy chief negotiators. Under these negotiators, nineteen working groups were created, each with a lead negotiator. The first phase of the negotiations was exploratory and lasted from August through November 1991. In the second phase, beginning in late fall 1991, the working groups submitted text for most of the nineteen chapters. (Either the United States or Mexico failed to produce text for agriculture, energy, textiles, automobiles, and trade-dispute remedies.) A January 1992 meeting was the first with all working groups simultaneously present. This meeting yielded a first-draft "agreement" with points of discord printed in brackets. This gave way to the third phase of the negotiations, called the "bracket-reduction" phase, which lasted until July 1992. A marathon session at the Watergate Hotel in Washington, which began on July 29 and lasted several weeks, yielded the final agreement that was sent to the U.S. Congress for approval. Below we review the outcomes of the negotiations within those chapters that are most illustrative of the different goals and expectations that each country brought to the table—factors that complicate the simple assessment of gains and losses based strictly on the resulting tariff levels.

National Treatment and Market Access for Goods (Chapter 3)

The working group on market access was charged with resolving two contentious trade issues that prompted considerable lobbying in the United States. First was the question of how and how much to protect sectors that were deemed extremely import-sensitive; second was the

---

3. Unless noted otherwise, this discussion is based on the NAFTA text.

issue of whether to ban or perpetuate duty-drawback and duty-referral programs. Both of these issues affected many different segments of each country's economy and were areas of natural U.S.-Mexican conflict. Thus, the two together constituted difficult sticking points in the completion of NAFTA's third chapter.

Several import-sensitive sectors in the United States, such as glassware, rubber and plastic footwear, ceramic tiles, luggage, leather goods, orange juice, and sugar, pushed for permanent exemptions from free-trade exposure under NAFTA.[4] However, this request was opposed vehemently by the Mexican negotiating team, not to mention the General Agreement on Tariffs and Trade (GATT). Sensing lukewarm support from the U.S. negotiating team vis-à-vis permanent exemptions, most of the aforementioned sectors turned their attention fairly early toward achieving the longest possible phaseout periods on tariffs and quotas. (Not all sectors gave up so easily, as the discussion of sugar and orange juice in the agricultural negotiations reveals.)

Since import-sensitive sectors in the United States advocated phaseouts of twenty-five years or more, GATT provided the necessary "reality check" with its provision that free-trade agreements eliminate all restrictions within a "reasonable" time. Despite the vague wording, this generally has been interpreted to mean within fifteen years. This provision abetted the Mexican negotiating team, which sought the shortest possible phaseout of products placed in the "C+" (longest phaseout) category.[5] The United States, despite intense sectoral lobbying, made no visible effort to secure phaseouts of longer than fifteen years; however, it did succeed in placing more products on the C+ list than Mexico, perhaps as compensation for U.S. agreement on the fifteen-year cap. The United States achieved C+ status for three manufactured items (rubber footwear, ceramic tile, and household glassware) and for eleven agricultural products (sugar, orange juice, peanuts, broccoli, cucumbers, asparagus, dried onion powder, dried whole onions, dried garlic, and cantaloupes and other melons). Although negotiators technically considered Mexico's forest products (for example, paper products and furniture) as manufactured goods, which are highly sensitive to imports from the United States and Canada, Mexico placed no manufactured products

4. "Glassmakers Urge Administration for Exemption from NAFTA Duty Cuts," *Inside U.S. Trade,* August 30, 1991, 7.

5. "Final Deal on NAFTA Tariffs Restricts 15-Year Phaseout to Few Items," *Inside U.S. Trade,* August 14, 1992, 6–7.

in the C+ category. It placed only three agricultural products on that list: corn, dried beans, and nonfat dried milk.[6]

The second major issue confronted as part of the Chapter 3 negotiations was the future of duty-drawback and duty-deferral programs, which exist in various manifestations in both the United States and Mexico. Duty drawback and duty deferral are policies in which tariffs on imported components are waived or refunded if the components are later exported as part of a modified intermediate or final product.[7] One example of such a policy is Mexico's *maquiladora* program, in which components may enter the country duty-free as long as they are modified and exported to the United States. In exporting the end product under the *maquila* program, taxes are paid only on the value added in Mexico. The *maquiladora* program has led to the rapid industrialization of the Mexican border zone, boosting exports but also raising serious environmental and labor-market concerns.

As NAFTA was negotiated, many sectors in the United States feared that continued duty-drawback activity, combined with free trade, would transform Mexico into an export platform to the United States. Some argued that Mexico simply would become a countrywide *maquiladora* zone, with components from all over the world entering the United States duty-free under the guise of intermediate and finished products from Mexico.[8] Moreover, investment would be skewed toward Mexico, and the demand for U.S. components would drop. As a result of these fears, the U.S. negotiating team faced a steady call, spearheaded by the iron and steel industries, for the prohibition of duty-drawback programs as part of NAFTA. Unlike Mexico, vested interests in duty-drawback programs were fairly weak in the United States, as evidenced by the provision in the Canadian-U.S. Free Trade Agreement (CUSFTA) that eliminated such programs by 1994. For Mexico, on the other hand, the prohibition of duty drawback signaled the day of reckoning for the *maquiladora* program. Either Mexico would have to cease importing components

---

6. NAFTA also contains protections for import-sensitive sectors in the form of "snapback" and "freeze" provisions that can be implemented in case of import surges. These provisions were not negotiated as part of Chapter 3, however. Each such provision was designed as part of the chapter that corresponds to the sector to which it applies. For instance, snapback provisions pertaining to sugar and orange juice can be found in Chapter 7 ("Agriculture and Sanitary and Phytosanitary Measures"). Some of these negotiations are discussed below.

7. For simplicity, we use the term "duty drawback" to designate all such policies.

8. "North American AISI Members Push for Duty-Drawback Elimination in NAFTA," *Inside U.S. Trade*, July 10, 1992, 5.

duty-free, or it would have to end discrimination in duty-free importation and risk the possibility that products constructed from duty-free components would be sold domestically.

Despite its vested interests, the Mexican side seemed resigned to losing its duty-drawback programs. It did voice concerns, however, that the immediate elimination of such programs would create a "double tax" on those export sectors in which U.S.-Mexican tariffs were to be phased out over time. That is, where duty deferments were already prohibited but tariffs had not yet been eliminated, tariffs would be paid on the value of components when they were imported into Mexico but also later when they were exported to the United States as part of an intermediate or final product.

The resulting NAFTA rule addresses Mexico's concern while primarily reflecting the U.S. preference to eliminate duty-drawback/deferral policies. By the seventh year after NAFTA's initiation (two years later than the United States had advocated), the size of drawbacks must be limited to the lesser of the following two values: (1) the amount of duties paid to import the good into the intermediary country (NAFTA member); (2) the amount of duties paid to import the good into the target country (also a NAFTA member). By this rule, no duty drawback will be permitted in sectors where U.S.-Mexican tariffs are already zero. Moreover, double taxation will be averted where tariffs between the United States and Mexico still exist.

In this working group negotiators faced two particularly difficult issues: protection for import-sensitive sectors and duty-drawback/deferral programs. In both cases Mexico ceded more ground than the United States. Mexico wanted a very short phaseout period for the protection of import-sensitive sectors. However, faced with intense lobbying by such sectors, the U.S. negotiators pushed for and won a maximum fifteen-year phaseout period and placed many more products than Mexico in this maximum phaseout category. On the duty-drawback issue the Mexican negotiators yielded to more rapid and substantial duty-drawback/deferral rules than they originally had proposed.

Trade and Investment in the Automotive Sector (Annex 300-A)

The automotive sector inspired a relatively large number of disputes during the NAFTA negotiations.[9] The U.S. and Mexican positions were

---

9. NAFTA's Chapter 4 ("Rules of Origin") includes regional content rules for autos.

unusually polarized due to the fact that economic liberalization in Mexico had yet to fully permeate the automotive sector. Thus, the Mexican auto sector was still highly protected, while its U.S. counterpart was basically open. The corresponding number of disputes also reflected the complexity of the industry and its size and importance in the North American market.

In glaring opposition to free trade stood the export-to-import ratio requirements mandated by the five Mexican "Auto Decrees" for participants in the Mexican automotive industry. As a result of the decrees, which were issued over the 1962–89 period, the importation of automotive products into Mexico could only be performed by auto companies that also manufactured there.[10] Moreover, the monetary value of exports by each company had to be at least 2.5 times greater than the monetary value of its imports. These rules fostered some strange anomalies, such as Volkswagen's entering the honey export business. As NAFTA was being negotiated in 1991, the importation of auto parts all but filled the import allowances of the five automakers that were in operation there (three of which were American). As a result, no significant number of finished automobiles were being imported into Mexico.[11]

Although inconvenienced by the Auto Decrees, General Motors, Ford, and Chrysler did not advocate their immediate revocation. Instead, the "Big Three" argued that adaptation to these rules had been a "cost of entry" that they already had paid, and that new participants in the Mexican market ought to pay these entry fees as well. Against this backdrop, U.S. automakers lobbied for an extended phase out of export-to-import ratio requirements, while also claiming that automakers previously established in Mexico should enjoy a preferential (that is, more rapid) phaseout of such rules. The industry's main union, the United Auto Workers (UAW), was less patient on this issue, demanding the immediate elimination of export-to-import ratio requirements.[12]

On the home front, U.S. trade negotiators were determined that NAFTA provide for the complete elimination of Mexican export-to-import ratio requirements. The Mexican team, though resigned to losing

10. B. J. Zangari, ed., NAFTA: Issues, Industry Sector Profiles, and Bibliography (Commack, N.Y.: Nova Science Publishers, 1994), 51.

11. "Mexico Offers to Phase Out Auto Restrictions over 12 Years as Part of NAFTA," Inside U.S. Trade, May 8, 1992, 5–6.

12. Jorge Perez-Lopez, "The Automotive Sector in the NAFTA: Negotiating Issues from a U.S. Perspective," in Sectoral Labor Effects of North American Free Trade, ed. Rafael Fernandez de Castro, Monica Verea Campos, and Sidney Weintraub (Austin: University of Texas Press, 1993), 153.

the ratio requirements eventually, due to the realities of free trade and in light of the precedents set by GATT and other international trade agreements, still hoped to maintain them for as long as possible.[13] Ironically, the Big Three's position may have helped bring the U.S. and Mexican sides together. Though the automakers' demand for a preferential phaseout appears to have received little support from U.S. negotiators, the U.S. bargaining position did reflect the Big Three's preference for an extended phaseout of export requirements. The United States officially submitted a proposal in which the required export-to-import ratio would be cut immediately from 2.5:1 to 0.5:1, the balance of which would be phased out evenly over ten years. The Mexican side countered by offering an immediate reduction from 2.5:1 to 1:1, which would remain constant for twelve years, at which point the requirement would be eliminated. The two sides ultimately compromised on the following NAFTA rule: the export-to-import ratio requirement was to drop immediately from 2.5:1 to 0.8:1; equal annual reductions over ten years would phase the requirement down to 0.55:1; finally, the requirement would be eliminated after the tenth year of the agreement. After that, anyone, not just manufacturers, might import automotive products. The U.S. auto industry, which yielded a minor concession to established manufacturers in a rule that allows them to apply old surpluses on auto-parts trade to future balances, called the overall compromise "the single most significant accomplishment of the NAFTA automotive negotiations."[14]

Mexico's five Auto Decrees created a second major obstacle to U.S. participation in the Mexican automotive industry in the form of strict and complicated domestic-content requirements. For each supplier to the Mexican auto market, the total value of domestic (Mexican) components used by the manufacturer had to equal at least 36 percent of the value of its domestically sold fleets. These rules caused a number of problems for automobile manufacturers in Mexico, such as dependence on unreliable component suppliers, which led to a notable discrepancy in the quality of Mexican-made cars for export and Mexican-made cars for the domestic market.[15]

The Big Three's position on domestic-content requirements mirrored

---

13. "Canada May Accept 60 Percent Content in NAFTA Autos, but Seeks Phase-In," *Inside U.S. Trade*, July 3, 1992, 3.

14. Gary C. Hufbauer and Jeffrey J. Schott, *NAFTA: An Assessment*, rev. ed. (Washington, D.C.: Institute for International Economics, 1993), 39.

15. Zangari, *NAFTA*, 53.

their position on export-to-import ratio requirements. Again, the auto-makers argued that adaptation to these rules had been a steep "cost of entry" that new participants in the Mexican market ought to pay as well. They also repeated their demand for a relatively slow phaseout of requirements (fifteen years), as well as a preferential phaseout for compa-nies already established in Mexico (for companies already established, an immediate drop to 25 percent, then phaseout; for companies not es-tablished, a continued 36 percent requirement for five years, then phase-out).[16] The U.S. auto-parts industry, as represented by the Motor and Equipment Manufacturers Association (MEMA), advocated a faster and nonpreferential phaseout of all local-content requirements over five years.

The U.S. bargaining position largely followed the Big Three's pro-posal, although the degree to which the U.S. side pushed for a preferen-tial phaseout of requirements is unclear. The Mexican team, meanwhile, opposed any immediate drop in local-content requirements, as well as any preferential phaseout. Furthermore, the Mexicans wanted a back-ended phaseout of requirements over a ten-year period.[17]

The final result favors the Mexican side in its phaseout schedule. NAFTA provides for only a slight immediate drop in requirements from 36 percent to 34 percent local content. The requirement may stay at 34 percent for five years, after which it will be slowly phased down to 29 percent over the next five years. After the tenth year, all local-content requirements will be eliminated. However, the U.S. side did achieve a couple of preferential measures for manufacturers already established in Mexico. First, manufacturers that supplied the Mexican market during model year 1992 may produce fleets indefinitely with the same percent-age of domestic content as was achieved in 1992. That percentage was lower than 34 percent for most manufacturers.[18] Second, previously es-tablished manufacturers may calculate their domestic content as a per-centage of their domestically sold fleets' Mexican value added; new manufacturers must use a base figure that is closer to their domestically sold fleets' total value. Gary Hufbauer and Jeffrey Schott estimate that

16. "Special Report: U.S. Automakers Press for Preferences During 15-Year NAFTA Transition," *Inside U.S. Trade,* September 23, 1991, 1–7.

17. "NAFTA Negotiators Grapple with New Auto Proposals Before Ministerial," *Inside U.S. Trade,* July 24, 1992, 1, 14.

18. Zangari, *NAFTA,* 53.

these preferential rules result in a quick drop in domestic-content requirements to 20 percent for previously established manufacturers.[19]

A third point of contention in the automotive negotiations arose from
a Mexican request regarding the American corporate average fuel efficiency (CAFE) standards. Mexico proposed that U.S. automakers count
their Mexican production as part of their domestic fleets in calculating
average fuel efficiency. Mexico reasoned that such a stipulation would
attract greater U.S. investment in the Mexican production of small,
highly fuel-efficient cars.[20]

This new rule might have been attractive to the Big Three as an
optional provision by which they could choose whether to count Mexican production as part of their domestic fleets. However, the automakers
opposed an obligatory change in the calculation method. They also shied
away from this issue in deference to the UAW, which adamantly opposed
the rule change. However, Mexico succeeded on this issue in the face of
dispersed U.S. opposition.[21] As a result, for the first ten years of NAFTA,
U.S. automakers can choose whether to count Mexican-made cars as part
of their domestic fleets; after ten years, Mexican-made cars must be
counted as domestic for CAFE-standards purposes.

Finally, the U.S. and Mexican sides had to agree on a tariff-phaseout
schedule for automotive products. Despite the significance of this issue,
the negotiations surrounding it were fairly quiet, with few official positions made public. Mexican tariffs, which stood at 20 percent for U.S.-
built cars and 10–13 percent for auto parts, were significantly higher
than U.S. tariffs. However, the United States did maintain an unusually
high tariff of 25 percent on light trucks. The Big Three denounced the
relatively high Mexican tariffs and lobbied for their rapid phaseout.[22]
As usual, they also advocated a preferential phaseout for automakers
already established in Mexico. The U.S. bargaining team concurred that
tariffs should be eliminated as rapidly as possible, but apparently did
not push for a preferential phaseout. On the Mexican side, negotiators
simply tried to prolong tariffs for as long as possible.

The negotiation results included an immediate cut in Mexican tariffs

19. Hufbauer and Schott, NAFTA: An Assessment, 39.

20. "House Majority Leader Seeks ITC Study on Rules of Origin for Cars in NAFTA," Inside U.S.
Trade, August 16, 1991, 17.

21. "U.S., Mexico Strike Deal on Tariff Phaseout for Trucks, Fuel Economy Standards," Inside
U.S. Trade, August 7, 1992, 4–5.

22. "Special Report: U.S. Automakers Press for Preferences During 15-Year NAFTA Transition."

on finished autos from 20 percent to 10 percent, the remainder of which will be phased out over ten years. Furthermore, about 75 percent of Mexican tariffs on U.S. auto parts will be eliminated within five years, as will all Mexican tariffs on American-made light trucks. Mexican tariffs on medium and heavy trucks and buses from the United States will be phased out over ten years. On the U.S. side, tariffs on Mexican-made cars and auto parts were eliminated immediately. The 20 percent light-truck tariff was immediately cut to 10 percent, and will be phased out altogether in five years.

Four major trends stand out with regard to NAFTA's trade and investment rules in the auto sector. First, when all is said and done, Mexico compromised less than the United States. On export-to-import ratios the United States wanted an immediate reduction from 2.5:1 to 0.5:1 and the balance phased out over ten years, while Mexico wanted an immediate reduction to 1:1, with no change for twelve years, after which the ratio would go to zero. The compromise fell marginally closer to the Mexican position: immediate reduction to 0.8:1, with a ten-year phasedown to 0.55:1 and elimination in the eleventh year. Second, Mexico clearly won on the domestic-content issue: the United States wanted an immediate reduction from 36 percent to 25 percent and won only 34 percent. Third, Mexico also won on emissions standards. Whereas Mexican negotiators wanted U.S. car manufacturers to apply U.S. standards to cars sold in Mexico, the United States was reluctant because the UAW feared this would increase incentives for manufacturers to move from the United States to Mexico. In the end, the agreement stipulated a ten-year grace period during which U.S. manufacturers could apply U.S. standards to their Mexican-sold cars at their own discretion. Finally, on tariff phaseouts the result was a compromise. The United States sought the reduction of Mexican tariffs as quickly as possible, while Mexico desired the slowest possible phaseout. The outcome was an immediate reduction from 20 percent to 10 percent, and from 10 percent to zero over ten years.

Textile and Apparel Goods (Annex 300-B)

The negotiations surrounding Annex 300-B were relatively quiet in light of the sensitivity associated with the textile and apparel sectors. The first of two major issues to dominate the negotiations was a debate over how much regional content various textiles and apparel items had to contain in order to qualify for free trade.[23] As with all rule-of-origin deliberations, the objective was to establish criteria that would be strict enough to keep third parties from taking advantage of the free-trade agreement but flexible enough so as not to hinder free trade. The similarity of U.S. and Mexican preferences on this issue facilitated a relatively quick agreement.

The basic textile and apparel rule of origin emerged primarily from the earlier U.S.-Canadian negotiations over CUSFTA. Mexico sided with the United States in advocating the "yarn forward" rule of origin, which eventually won out. Since the United States and Mexico were not at odds over the basic rule of origin, the intricacies of "yarn forward" are not relevant to this discussion. Suffice it to say that this is a relatively strict rule of origin that was supported by nearly all textile and apparel manufacturers but opposed by most apparel retailers.[24]

More relevant to this discussion is the fight over what products would be exempted from "yarn forward," which was a point of U.S.-Mexican disagreement. American retailers and apparel manufacturers, arguing that a looser origin rule should be applied to various short-supply products, pushed for a long list of exemptions that included silk, linen, corduroy, lycra, spandex, rayon/nylon blends, cotton/polyester blends, and others.[25] The U.S. negotiating team heeded the retailers' and apparel manufacturers' argument, but adopted a shorter list of fabrics "in short supply" as a compromise with textile producers that opposed exemptions (a compromise that still failed to satisfy many producers). The United States requested that given quantities of silk, linen, Harris tweed, certain men's shirt fabrics, and certain corduroy fabrics enter the country under a "single transformation" rule of origin, as opposed to the "triple transformation" rule that was established by "yarn forward."[26]

---

23. Textiles, like automotive products, were made subject to specially designed rules of origin. However, unlike the automotive rules of origin, which appear with NAFTA's basic rules of origin in Chapter 4, the textile rules of origin are outlined in the annex dedicated generally to trade in textiles and apparel, Annex 300-B.

24. "U.S. Expected to Present Strict Textile Content Proposal in NAFTA Talks," *Inside U.S. Trade,* January 24, 1992, 1–2.

25. "Apparel Group Seeks Removal of Tariff and Quota Barriers for Imports in NAFTA," *Inside U.S. Trade,* October 18, 1991, 7–8, and "Textile and Apparel Producers Push Strict NAFTA Rules of Origin," *Inside U.S. Trade,* October 25, 1991, 9.

26. "Canada May Pull out of NAFTA Textile Agreement as U.S., Mexico Near Deal," *Inside U.S. Trade,* May 28, 1992, 1–2, 21.

Although opposed, Mexico expended almost no energy on this issue, and the U.S. proposal was adopted.[27]

The second major issue facing textile and apparel negotiators was the construction of a tariff-phaseout schedule. As with the rule-of-origin deliberations, the United States and Mexico brought similar preferences to the bargaining table. A three-tiered schedule that earmarked various textile and apparel goods for either immediate ("A" list), medium-term ("B6" list), or long-term ("C" list) tariff elimination was quickly agreed upon. However, the details relating to how this schedule would be implemented became a sticking point between the United States and Mexico. The B6 category, which contained the greatest number of textile and apparel products, became the focal point of this dispute.

The disagreement revolved around a Mexican demand that the United States phase out its tariffs more quickly than Mexico on B6 products. Specifically, Mexico wanted the United States to cut tariffs immediately by 50 percent and then phase out the balance in equal annual reductions over five years. Under this proposal, Mexico simply would phase out its tariffs in 20 percent annual reductions over five years. This type of phaseout, known as "relative reciprocity," was unacceptable to U.S. negotiators due to its potential for inviting a future political backlash. For example, such a concession by the United States would have been a liability during the Uruguay Round of the GATT negotiations because other developing countries would have demanded similar treatment. Moreover, relative reciprocity could have hindered NAFTA's ratification by serving as further ammunition for the agreement's numerous opponents. The U.S. side, after initially submitting a symmetrical five-year phaseout proposal, eventually offered a compromise in which both sides would make initial tariff cuts equal, in percentage terms, to the rates of the tariffs, and then eliminate the remaining tariffs in equal installments over five years.[28] This proposal, which resulted in larger initial tariff reductions for the United States than for Mexico, was accepted by Mexico as the NAFTA rule.

To summarize, the two controversial issues facing negotiators in this working group were the exemption from "yarn forward" rules (NAFTA

27. "U.S., Mexico Resolve Remaining Hurdles on NAFTA Textile Deal, Anger Retailers," *Inside U.S. Trade,* May 29, 1992, 1, 16–18.

28. "Canada Likely to Accept Textile Deal but U.S., Mexico Grapple on Tariff Phaseout," *Inside U.S. Trade,* May 22, 1992, 7–8, and "U.S., Mexico Resolve Remaining Hurdles on NAFTA Textile Deal, Anger Retailers."

adopted the U.S. proposal on this issue) and the relative reciprocity in tariff phaseouts (where the U.S. position also prevailed). On the latter, Mexico did not want to follow relative reciprocity, but ultimately conceded. Considering these two U.S. victories in a wider context, it is not surprising that the United States was able to impose its preferences on the details of the textile agreements, given that its general stipulations represent a historic break from a protectionist U.S. past. As Hufbauer and Schott note, "NAFTA represents the first attempt by the United States or Canada to subject its heavily protected textile and apparel sector to significant trade liberalization with a large developing country."[29] Mexico, grateful to be the large developing country selected, was not in a position to haggle over relatively minor issues.

Rule of Origin (Chapter 4)

U.S. and Mexican negotiators had little trouble arriving at a basic rule of origin under NAFTA. However, the effort to create a special rule of origin for automotive products engendered significant controversy. "Sound bite" coverage of this debate focused solely on what percentage of North American content an automotive product had to contain in order to qualify for free trade. But, as numbers like 50 percent and 60 percent regional content were boldly debated, two other criteria that would determine exactly what constituted 50 percent or 60 percent regional content were being discussed more quietly. The first criterion was whether the regional-content rule would permit "roll-up," which is the practice of counting components as 100 percent regional if at least 51 percent of their subcomponents originated regionally. Obviously, the prohibition of roll-up would make for a stricter rule of origin. The second criterion was whether regional-content requirements would have to be met on a plant-by-plant, model-by-model, or company-wide basis. (Company-wide averaging is the least strict valuation method.)

The CUSFTA's automotive rule of origin set some loose precedents for NAFTA. Under this agreement, automotive products had to contain at least 50 percent U.S.-Canadian combined content to qualify for free trade. Furthermore, the CUSFTA used a regional-content formula in which

29. Hufbauer and Schott, *NAFTA: An Assessment*, 45.

roll-up was permitted and the average production of each plant had to satisfy the 50 percent requirement. Both Mexico and Canada wanted an almost identical rule of origin written into NAFTA. Despite these precedents, however, the U.S. automotive industry considered the CUSFTA rule of origin far too permissive. Nearly every faction of the U.S. industry supported a stricter provision for NAFTA, at least with regard to U.S.-Mexican trade.

The UAW, which advocated an 85 percent North American–content rule, held the most extreme position. The Big Three automakers were split, with Ford and Chrysler seeking a 70 percent rule and General Motors preferring 60 percent. The Big Three uniformly advocated a formula that eliminated roll-up and calculated regional content on a company-wide basis. The U.S. automotive parts industry backed a 60 percent rule of origin. Finally, the U.S. International Trade Commission, after studying the subject at the request of the House Committee on Ways and Means, suggested a nonnumerical rule of origin in which certain "critical processes" had to take place in North America.

The U.S. negotiating team eventually adopted a position that most closely reflected the Big Three's average preferences. The U.S. side officially submitted a 65 percent rule of origin in which roll-up would be eliminated and regional content would be calculated on a company-wide basis. Mexico countered with a 50 percent rule of origin proposal in which roll-up would continue and regional content would be calculated on a plant-by-plant basis. The United States essentially won this exchange; in NAFTA, a 62.5 percent rule of origin covers cars, light trucks, transmissions, and engines, and a 60 percent rule of origin covers other vehicles and parts, although this requirement will be phased in over eight years. Roll-up was eliminated, as per the U.S. proposal, and regional content is calculated on a model-by-model basis, which represents a U.S.-Mexican compromise.[30]

---

30. Information for the discussion of rule of origin was compiled from the following articles: "Special Report: U.S. Automakers Press for Preferences During 15-Year NAFTA Transition"; "ITC Study Notes 'Utility' of EC-Like Auto Origin Rule for NAFTA," *Inside U.S. Trade,* December 13, 1991, 1, 12–17; "U.S., Canada Auto Negotiators Seek to Clarify Mexican Offer on Auto Decree," *Inside U.S. Trade,* April 17, 1992, 3–4; "Lawmakers Urge That NAFTA Deal on Autos Be Seen as Single Package," *Inside U.S. Trade,* April 24, 1992; "Mexico Offers to Phase Out Auto Restrictions over 12 Years as Part of NAFTA"; "UAW Challenges Administration over Auto Rule of Origin in NAFTA," *Inside U.S. Trade,* June 5, 1992, 8–9; and "Auto Deal Gives Special Treatment to Canadian Joint-Venture Plant," *Inside U.S. Trade,* August 14, 1992, 1–2.

Energy and Basic Petrochemicals (Chapter 6)

NAFTA's hardest-fought and most enigmatic negotiations were those surrounding the energy chapter.[31] Mexico adamantly defended its traditional protection of the energy and basic petrochemicals industries to the point of initially refusing to discuss liberalization of these sectors as part of NAFTA. Not surprisingly, the United States refused to accept an unqualified exemption of energy and basic petrochemicals from the discussions. With support from the GATT's provision that free-trade agreements liberalize all trade to the fullest extent possible, the United States managed to establish a working group on energy and basic petrochemicals that would deal with several hotly contested issues.

Easily the most sensitive and difficult issue that had to be resolved as part of the Chapter 6 negotiations was foreign investment and participation in the Mexican hydrocarbon and basic (or "primary") petrochemical industries. Mexico's policy banning foreign investment in those industries was long-standing and partially based in its constitution. Former president Carlos Salinas de Gortari (1988–94) had in 1989 liberalized the petrochemicals industry to some degree by permitting majority foreign ownership in the production of more than seven hundred "final" petrochemical products and up to 40 percent foreign ownership in the production of sixty-six "secondary" petrochemical lines, but most hydrocarbon operations were still largely closed to foreign participation. Foreign ownership of oil reserves was strictly banned, as was foreign ownership of firms engaged in the exploration, exploitation, and refining of petroleum and natural gas and in the production of nineteen primary petrochemicals (those made directly from petroleum rather than from petroleum derivatives).

Mexico maintained a protectionist stance vis-à-vis these sectors despite mixed incentives. On the one hand, foreign participation in the Mexican hydrocarbon and basic petrochemical industries would have contradicted decades of political rhetoric on the part of the ruling Revolutionary Institutional Party (PRI), as well as threatening the monopolistic status of PEMEX, the state-owned oil company and a major source of public revenue. Foreign participation might also have led to a more rapid depletion of domestic oil reserves. On the other hand, liberalizing these sectors was the only way Mexico could hope to reverse drastic underin-

---

31. NAFTA's Chapter 10 also includes special government-contract rules for the energy sector.

vestment and poor capacity use in these industries. PEMEX, for instance, was hoping to raise $30 billion in capital to modernize its antiquated facilities.[32] Some observers have gone so far as to claim that Mexico would benefit more than the United States from liberalization of investment in Mexico's petroleum industry.[33]

As part of its initial bargaining position, Mexico would not concede to foreign ownership of its oil reserves, to foreign production of any primary petrochemical products, or to foreign involvement in the exploration, exploitation, and refining of oil and natural gas. Its only initial concession was that it would consider raising the 40 percent ceiling on foreign ownership in the production of secondary petrochemicals, but only if the change could be phased in over time. The United States, meanwhile, pushed for as much liberalization as possible in primary and secondary petrochemical production and in the exploration, drilling, and refining of oil and natural gas. The United States, furthermore, wanted immediate, rather than phased-in, concessions.[34]

Overall, Mexico succeeded in keeping its hydrocarbon industries closed to foreign participation. NAFTA specifically reserves to the Mexican state the right to control all activities and investment in the exploration, exploitation, refining, transportation, storage, and distribution of crude oil and natural gas, as well as the production, transportation, storage, and distribution of artificial gas, primary petrochemicals, and all other goods obtained from the refining of crude oil and natural gas. Mexico did make some limited concessions, however. For one thing, NAFTA redefined "primary" (prohibited) petrochemicals in such a way that fourteen petrochemicals were taken off the list, while three petrochemicals were newly put on. Thus, eight primary petrochemicals remain closed to foreign participation. Furthermore, all nonprimary petrochemicals, including the sixty-six "secondary" petrochemicals, would be open to 100 percent foreign participation within three years.

32. "U.S. Chemical Firms Press for Eased Mexican Curbs on Petrochemicals in NAFTA," *Inside U.S. Trade,* July 5, 1991, 15–18, and "Special Report: U.S. and Canada Press for National Treatment of Utilities in NAFTA Energy Talks," *Inside U.S. Trade,* February 28, 1992, 1–2.

33. Hufbauer and Schott, *NAFTA: An Assessment,* 34.

34. "Mexico to Keep Direct Ownership of Petroleum out of FTA Talks, Official Hints," *Inside U.S. Trade,* September 14, 1990, 5; "U.S. Seen Acquiescing to Mexican Demands for Exclusion of Oil, Gas from NAFTA," *Inside U.S. Trade,* November 1, 1991, 1, 18; "Mexico Makes Offer to Open Up Petrochemicals Sector to Foreign Investors," *Inside U.S. Trade,* May 8, 1992, 5; and "Key Details in Energy Sector Remain Unresolved in NAFTA, Official Says," *Inside U.S. Trade,* August 14, 1992, 1, 18.

Mexico also made some loosely related concessions regarding foreign participation in the production of electricity. Despite these mitigating provisions, however, the agreement on investment in the Mexican energy sector has been noted as an important shortcoming in NAFTA, and thus as an important U.S. loss.[35]

Another issue that had to be resolved as part of the Chapter 6 negotiations was market access in energy, where Mexican barriers were again the focus. U.S. objectives on this issue included the right to sell natural gas directly to industrial end users in Mexico, guaranteed permission to make cross-border sales of electricity to northern areas of Mexico, and the elimination of Mexico's 10 percent tariff on coal.[36] Mexico's position on these issues is not entirely clear.

As a result of NAFTA, Mexico's tariff on coal was eliminated immediately. However, the results of efforts to achieve the other two major U.S. objectives are ambiguous. While NAFTA legalized the sale of natural gas by U.S. firms directly to industrial end users in Mexico, it did not guarantee access for U.S. firms to PEMEX's pipelines. Thus, PEMEX has de facto veto power over these sales. Nonetheless, the U.S. side considered this something of a victory because it believed that pressure by Mexican end users would keep PEMEX from abusing its veto power. Finally, although Mexico conceded certain investment opportunities in electricity generation as part of NAFTA, it in no way guaranteed permission to make cross-border sales of electricity. Such sales will likely continue, but at the government's discretion.

A third issue that entered these negotiations was a U.S. protest that the Mexican government was using its control of the oil and electricity monopolies to give domestic companies preferential energy prices over U.S. firms operating in Mexico.[37] This practice was in clear conflict with the "national-treatment" principle that appears in GATT and that was also adopted as a general NAFTA stipulation. These factors made it almost impossible for Mexico to resist a ban on preferential energy pricing, and such a ban was adopted as part of NAFTA.

Finally, the United States and Canada pushed adamantly for a Mexican commitment not to restrict energy exports to the other NAFTA countries during times of energy crisis. The United States and Canada, as

35. Hufbauer and Schott, *NAFTA: An Assessment,* 34.
36. "Mexico Makes Offer to Open Up Petrochemicals Sector to Foreign Investors."
37. "CEOs Recommend that U.S. Press for U.S. Investment in Mexican Energy Sector," *Inside U.S. Trade,* June 14, 1991, 14–15.

members of the International Energy Agency, had signed an agreement in 1974 that limited the amount by which energy exports to member countries could decrease during a crisis. In the CUSFTA, the United States and Canada reaffirmed this commitment to each other. Despite united U.S. and Canadian demands, however, the Mexican side steadfastly refused to accept such a provision as part of NAFTA.[38] The Mexican team eventually won out, and Mexico remains unbound by any such commitment.

The United States can be considered to have "won" in this sector simply by virtue of energy's inclusion in NAFTA. The United States also won with the elimination of preferential energy pricing for Mexican firms, in compliance with national-treatment standards. But on the question of foreign participation in primary products and exploration, drilling, and refining, Mexico held tight to its closed-door policy. Mexico also responded only minimally to U.S. pressure for the free sale of electricity and natural gas by foreigners to Mexicans. The United States also sought, and did not secure, Mexico's commitment not to restrict energy exports to NAFTA partners in times of shortage. On balance, Mexico came out ahead in this chapter of the NAFTA negotiations.

Agriculture and Sanitary and Phytosanitary Measures (Chapter 7)

The turbulent negotiations that dealt with agriculture and sanitary and phytosanitary measures involved a tremendous amount of politicking by various agricultural interests on both sides of the border. Of the sectors in the United States agriculture was one of the least united with regard to free trade, as growers of certain crops clamored for liberalization, while a smaller number opposed it forcefully. The resulting disagreement over the U.S. negotiating team's mission made for secretive negotiations and, in some instances, inconclusive outcomes.

A mostly Florida-based conglomeration of fruit and vegetable producers was the largest group to make a zealous push for exemption from free trade. This contingent, which was headed by orange growers and included tomato growers, argued that fifteen-year phaseouts of tariff and

---

38. "Special Report: NAFTA Energy Text Would Supersede U.S.-Canada Free Trade Pact," *Inside U.S. Trade*, July 31, 1992, 1–7.

quota protections would only "delay the pain" of free trade's ruinous effects. They said that they could not compete with Mexico, even fifteen years down the road, as long as Mexican growers had economic advantages such as free or subsidized land, child labor, loosely enforced minimum-wage laws, almost nonexistent worker compensation and occupational safety laws, and no stringent environmental controls. Although Mexico is currently very inefficient in producing crops like oranges, due to deficiencies in infrastructure, equipment, and experience, U.S. growers feared the effects of rapid agricultural modernization. A modernized farming sector in Mexico would compete directly with Florida growers because the two share similar crop capabilities and almost identical growing seasons.[39]

Despite lobbying by the state of Florida and various agriculture groups, no Florida crops received a permanent exemption from free trade. Their position was challenged by, among others, the National American Wholesale Grocers Association, which praised liberalization in these crops, saying it would lower prices and increase product diversity and availability, thus better serving the U.S. consumer.[40] Far more threatening to the Florida growers, however, was the extent to which Mexico coveted access to the U.S. market in these very products. Mexico saw fruits and vegetables as critical in its effort to transform "a stagnated and crisis ridden agricultural sector into an internationally competitive industry."[41] Orange juice (along with similar products) was thus a powerful card in the horse trading that occurred in the agriculture negotiations: the United States found that it could achieve significant new access to Mexican markets in corn and other products if it would concede access in orange juice. This is the compromise that was enacted.[42] The decision represents a virtual abandonment of corn in Mexico; it was made based on the fact that Mexico's inefficient corn producers have little chance of ever becoming internationally competitive.[43]

39. "De La Garza Predicts That NAFTA Negotiations Will Extend Past Mid-April," *Inside U.S. Trade,* March 6, 1992, 17–18, and "Florida State, Industry Demand Fruit and Vegetable Exemption in NAFTA," *Inside U.S. Trade,* May 29, 1992, 10–11.

40. "Florida Government, Industry Urge NAFTA Rejection over Fruits, Vegetables," *Inside U.S. Trade,* September 25, 1992, 6.

41. Kirstin Appendini, "Agriculture and Farmers Within NAFTA: A Mexican Perspective," in *Mexico and the North American Free Trade Agreement: Who Will Benefit?* ed. Victor Bulmer-Thomas, Nikki Craske, and Mónica Serrano (New York: St. Martin's Press, 1994), 59.

42. "U.S.-Mexico Agriculture Talks Lag Despite Mexican Concessions on Corn," *Inside U.S. Trade,* July 10, 1992, 9–10.

43. Appendini, "Agriculture and Farmers Within NAFTA," 68.

On orange juice, Mexico significantly increased its access to the U.S. market with a tariff-rate quota of forty million gallons, which will be lifted after fifteen years. Right away, the most-favored-nation (MFN) tariff of $.35 per gallon was to be cut 50 percent for Mexico for the first forty million gallons per year. After forty million gallons, Mexico would be subject to the full MFN tariff. Once the Uruguay Round was ratified, the rate on in-quota trade was to be cut another 15 percent. Then the tariff would be phased out over years ten to fifteen of the agreement. After fifteen years, there will be no quota or tariff.[44] In exchange, Mexico conceded to a fifteen-year phaseout of its corn tariff.

Another group that was active in lobbying during the NAFTA negotiations was the U.S. sugar industry, which sought to prolong the strict protections against foreign competition that it had long enjoyed. These protections were powerful enough to drive the U.S. price of raw sugar up to $.21 per pound, about $.12 above the average world price. Thus, the sugar industry had strong incentives to oppose liberalized sugar trade and presented the following arguments against it: free sugar trade with Mexico would discriminate against the Caribbean Basin Initiative countries that already hold quota privileges; the U.S. sugar industry was already facing competition due to the Uruguay Round negotiations; and liberalization of the sugar sector would create a potential arbitrage situation in which Mexico could buy foreign (perhaps even Cuban) sugar, substitute it for domestic sugar, and then sell domestic sugar in the high-priced U.S. market.[45]

The U.S. negotiating team was secretive in its treatment of sugar. Some claim that the administration wanted to "lose" on this issue in order to loosen the sugar industry's grip on American politics. Whatever the reason, the United States submitted a vague official proposal that involved a fairly small initial increase in Mexico's market access from 7,500 metric tons to 25,000 metric tons. Mexico, however, pushed for a dramatic increase in sugar access to 1.5 million metric tons. Facing a stiff

---

44. The tariff-rate quotas on orange juice serve as a volume-based safeguard against import surges during the fifteen-year phaseout period. A similar system was set up to protect six of the approximately sixteen import-sensitive Florida crops, including tomatoes, which are protected between November and July of each of the phaseout years. Although the remaining crops are not covered by a special safeguard mechanism, they are still eligible for NAFTA's general safeguard provisions under Chapter 8.

45. "Senators Challenge Administration Not to Open U.S. Sugar Market in NAFTA," *Inside U.S. Trade*, April 17, 1992, 16–17.

Mexican position, which some say was inspired by the financial interests of a key private-sector adviser to the Mexican negotiators, the U.S. team accepted a NAFTA rule that protects the sugar industry for six more years and provides for significant Mexican access after that.[46]

For each of the first six years of the agreement, Mexico's market access will be 25,000 metric tons of sugar. After that, the figure increases to 150,000 tons in the seventh year and 110 percent of the previous year's access for years eight through fourteen. However, in the unlikely event that Mexico becomes a net exporter of sugar for two years running at any point in the agreement, it is then eligible, after year six, to ship to the United States its entire surplus production. This alternative rule was designed to allow Mexico considerable access, while also controlling for the potential arbitrage effect mentioned above.

A third important agriculture issue concerned the demands of various producers that NAFTA bring some kind of harmonization, or at least transparency, to the process by which U.S. and Mexican sanitary and phytosanitary (SPS) standards are set. For cases in which SPS measures were in dispute, moreover, those interests called for a fast resolution mechanism that could provide rulings before perishable goods would have a chance to spoil. This issue became salient when, during the early stages of the NAFTA talks, Mexico abruptly instituted a sweeping ban of livestock and tree imports from the United States and justified the measures as health precautions. U.S. industry quickly protested that the measures were nontariff barriers to trade with purely economic, not scientific, incentives.

The idea of making firm SPS commitments, such as harmonization of standards, was problematic for negotiators from both sides. For both the United States and Mexico this issue raised sovereignty concerns, since a binding SPS policy would limit government discretion and hamper each government's ability to prevent harmful products from entering its territory. The particular concern of the United States was that harmonization would mean a lowering of its standards, thereby raising opposition from environmental interests and creating general health anxieties. For its part, the Mexican team feared that conforming to stricter SPS standards would be economically debilitating. Although both sides had reasons to

---

46. "U.S., Mexico Appear Far Apart over Sugar in NAFTA Agriculture Talks," *Inside U.S. Trade*, March 20, 1992, 1, 17–18, and "Sugar Industry Challenges Administration over Plans to Lower Tariffs in NAFTA," *Inside U.S. Trade*, May 15, 1992, 1, 10–11.

balk, the benefits of an SPS agreement were likely to be greater for the United States because of Mexico's history of using SPS measures to create trade-distorting effects.

The rules covering SPS measures in NAFTA are fairly imprecise, though not necessarily impotent. They stipulate, for instance, that NAFTA members may apply any SPS measure, even measures more stringent than the international standard, as long as the measure is "based on scientific principles" and doesn't create "a disguised restriction to trade between parties." Each NAFTA member is also obligated to use "relevant international standards, guidelines or recommendations with the objective, among others, of making its sanitary and phytosanitary measures equivalent or, where appropriate, identical to those of the other Parties." Due to this lack of specificity, the success and strength of these provisions will depend largely on future cooperation between the United States and Mexico and on the initiative taken by the relevant dispute-resolution committees, which, as per many requests by agricultural interests, must rule on disputes within fifteen days when perishable goods are involved.

Finally, the agriculture talks dealt similarly with the issue of export subsidies, which commanded attention because they help domestic growers undersell foreign growers in target markets. Because of this, export subsidies are considered to offer an unfair trade advantage for farmers operating within target markets. The American Farm Bureau, for one, supported the concept that "all trade-distorting government subsidies be subjected to progressive and substantial reductions."[47] Again, however, NAFTA's wording on this issue is imprecise. Provisions regarding export subsidies contain such statements as "Each Party shall take into account the interests of the other Parties in the use of any export subsidy on an agricultural good, recognizing that such subsidies may have prejudicial effects on the interests of the other Parties." As with SPS measures, the wording of the provisions is vague enough that their success and strength will depend heavily on future cooperation between the United States and Mexico and on the actions of the relevant dispute-resolution committees.

Mexican negotiators won the agricultural chapter, although not resoundingly. The centerpiece of a horse trade equally acceptable to both sides was Mexican access to the U.S. orange juice market. Vague lan-

---

47. "Farm Bureau Letter on NAFTA," *Inside U.S. Trade,* January 31, 1992, 15.

guage left the SPS and export-subsidy issues effectively unresolved. Nonetheless, the Mexicans won access to the U.S. sugar market. Finally, looking beyond individual crop issues, we find that Mexico achieved an overall victory in that it may delay liberalization for 60 percent of its agricultural products, while the United States achieved delayed liberalization for only 33 percent of its agricultural goods.[48]

Government Procurement (Chapter 10)

The U.S. negotiating team saw NAFTA as an opportunity to achieve greater access to Mexican government contracts, which were relatively closed to U.S. participation at the outset of the talks. Specifically, the United States sought to reduce or eliminate the number of contracts set aside for domestic bidders and increase the number of contracts that would be open to bidding, on a nondiscriminatory basis, by both U.S. and Mexican firms. The two sides agreed early on that contracts larger than a to-be-determined threshold would have to be open to foreign bidding, while contracts smaller than the threshold could be set aside for domestic bidders. What followed was some fairly simple haggling over threshold levels, with four categories of thresholds being debated: goods-and-services contracts procured by federal government entities, such as the U.S. Department of Agriculture or the Mexican Ministry of Finance and Public Credit; goods-and-services contracts procured by federal enterprises, such as the U.S. Tennessee Valley Authority or the Mexican National Company for Basic Commodities (CONASUPO); construction contracts procured by federal government entities; and construction contracts procured by federal enterprises.

The U.S. negotiating team proposed thresholds of $25,000 for goods-and-services contracts procured by federal government entities, $175,000 for goods-and-services contracts procured by federal enterprises, and $6 million for construction contracts procured by federal government entities. It released no specific proposal for construction contracts procured by federal enterprises. Mexico countered by proposing $200,000 for goods-and-services contracts procured by federal government entities and $400,000 for goods-and-services contracts procured by federal enterprises. Furthermore, Mexico sought to exclude all con-

---

48. Appendini, "Agriculture and Farmers Within NAFTA," 70.

struction contracts from guaranteed access by American firms.[49] The deal reached by the two sides fell closer to the U.S. numbers. NAFTA provisions state that firms from all member countries must be allowed to bid on all contracts larger than the following: $50,000 for goods-and-services contracts procured by federal government entities, $250,000 for goods-and-services contracts procured by federal enterprises, $6.5 million for construction contracts procured by federal government entities, and $8 million for construction contracts procured by federal enterprises.

However, Mexico achieved a mitigating provision that allows it to set aside for domestic firms a total of $1 billion in nonenergy government contracts, regardless of size, for each of the first nine years of the agreement, and $1.2 billion annually in nonenergy government contracts indefinitely afterward, subject to certain conditions.

Mexico also succeeded in setting up specialized talks to deal with government procurement in energy. Although the same thresholds were accepted for energy contracts as for nonenergy contracts, Mexico demanded that 80 percent of over-threshold energy contracts still be off-limits to foreign bidders. The United States said that it would accept phased-in access to over-threshold energy contracts but rejected Mexico's 80 percent rule. Instead, the United States proposed that foreign bidders have access to a list of major goods, services, and construction services. The list would grow over a ten-year phase-in period, after which foreign bidders would have access to all over-threshold energy contracts.[50] Ultimately, a percentage system was used in NAFTA under which Mexico is allowed to reserve for its own firms 50 percent of PEMEX and Comisión Federal de Electricidad (CFE) contracts in 1994. This percentage will be phased down to 30 percent by 2002 and then to zero in 2003. However, beginning in 2003, Mexico may set aside for domestic firms $300 million in contracts procured by PEMEX and CFE.

Finally, Mexico raised the issue of government procurement by state governments. The United States had little interest in this subject because federal spending dominates overall public spending in Mexico. Thus, contracts procured by Mexican states are fairly small and scarce. However, Mexico pushed hard for access to the considerable market for pro-

---

49. "NAFTA Government Procurement Talks Focus on U.S., Mexico Negotiations," *Inside U.S. Trade*, May 22, 1992, 1, 14–15, and "NAFTA Procurement Chapter Sets Out Schedule for Further Negotiations," *Inside U.S. Trade*, September 11, 1992, 20–21.

50. "NAFTA Energy Talks Hampered by Mexico's Interpretation of Constitution," *Inside U.S. Trade*, May 29, 1992, 14–15.

curement by U.S. state entities and enterprises. Specifically, Mexico proposed delaying implementation of the procurement chapter until such time as the majority of U.S. states had agreed to abide by its guidelines.[51] This push by Mexico was largely in vain, however, since the following vague principle was incorporated into NAFTA: "[T]he Parties shall endeavor to consult with their state and provincial governments with a view to obtaining commitments, on a voluntary and reciprocal basis, to include within this Chapter procurement by state and provincial government entities and enterprises." Thus, government-procurement negotiations were a victory for the United States, since the NAFTA text falls closer to the initial U.S. positions on general thresholds for set-aside projects, on over-threshold rules for the energy sector, and on procurement by state governments.

Investment (Chapter 11)

The working group on investment was charged with creating rules that would govern foreign participation in the majority of commercial sectors. These talks focused far more on Mexico's foreign-investment policies than on those of the United States, since Mexico's policies were far more restrictive. Mexico was able to exempt a number of sectors from these generalized rules, however, and to subject those sectors to specialized investment provisions. Specialized rules apply, for instance, to certain subsectors of energy, financial services, and basic telecommunications. Mexico also proposed special investment rules for the automotive-products sector, but the provisions that eventually were adopted conform with NAFTA's general investment rules.

As with the automotive talks, the most disputed and complex issue that had to be resolved by the working group on investment was the future of Mexico's strict performance requirements for U.S. firms operating in its territory. As was mentioned earlier, Mexico was basically resigned to losing its performance requirements as a result of free trade and the precedents set by GATT and other international trade agreements. Mexico's strategy was to maintain performance requirements for as long as possible and then institute an incentive program in which a

---

51. "NAFTA Procurement Text to Phase Out Tariff, Contract Limits over 10 Years," *Inside U.S. Trade*, August 14, 1992, 3.

company could voluntarily agree to meet certain performance criteria in exchange for an advantage such as a subsidy or tax concession. The U.S. side was amenable to an extended phaseout of performance requirements, but it sought ultimately to ban not only performance requirements but also performance "incentives."[52] The outcome is a compromise in which, after performance requirements are phased out over periods of up to ten years, Mexico may offer incentives in certain performance categories but not in others. Mexico may *not* offer incentive advantages contingent upon a U.S. firm's achieving a given level or percentage of domestic content, purchasing local goods, limiting imports to some given relation to exports or foreign-exchange inflows, or restricting local sales to some given relation to exports or foreign-exchange inflows. However, Mexico may offer incentive advantages to U.S. firms that locate production in a specific area, sell certain services, train or employ local workers, construct or expand particular facilities, or carry out research and development in its territory. This compromise seems to favor the United States slightly, since the more trade-distorting performance incentives are eliminated.

A second important investment issue was the question whether Mexico would continue to have veto power over foreign acquisitions of domestic companies. Before NAFTA, Mexico reserved the right to screen foreign takeovers based on such factors as national security, effects on employment and training, technological contribution, or general contribution to industrial productivity and competitiveness. This issue was fairly straightforward in terms of proposals. The United States wanted the elimination of all these so-called screening mechanisms, except when national security was an issue. Mexico wanted to retain the provisions, but offered to limit such screening to takeovers that involved firms over a certain purchase value.[53] This latter proposal was accepted, and NAFTA therefore permits Mexico to screen takeovers with a purchase price greater than $25 million for the first three years of the agreement, $50 million for the next three years, $75 million for the seventh through the ninth years of the agreement, and $150 million from the tenth year on. These figures are adjusted annually for inflation, and this rule applies only where foreign investors come to own over 40 percent of a Mexican

52. "NAFTA Working Group on Investment Still in Early Stages of Negotiations," *Inside U.S. Trade,* January 31, 1992, 1, 10–11.
53. "U.S., Mexico Agree on Investor-State Arbitration in Investment Text," *Inside U.S. Trade,* May 22, 1992, 11.

enterprise. Despite these conditions, this settlement represents a victory for the Mexican side.

A third important rule concerned the type of presence a company would need to have in the United States, Mexico, or Canada to qualify for NAFTA investment privileges. The United States pushed for a broad definition of "NAFTA investor," in which any firm doing real business in a NAFTA country, regardless of the nationality of its owners, would qualify to invest under Chapter 11 rules. Mexico wanted a far narrower definition that would exclude all companies that were not owned by nationals of a NAFTA country.[54] The United States, quite simply, won this debate. As a result, any firm that is "constituted or organized" in a NAFTA country and has "substantial business activities" in the territory of that country may take advantage of NAFTA's investment privileges. The only exception, which appeared to be fueled by U.S. preferences, is that privileges may be denied by a NAFTA member to companies owned by nationals of a country with which the NAFTA member does not have diplomatic relations.

Finally, the working group on investment had to determine how to arbitrate investment disputes between NAFTA members. The United States proposed arbitration procedures that would use existing institutions such as the World Bank or the International Chamber of Commerce. Under the U.S. proposal, the plaintiff in an investment dispute would be allowed to choose from several such arbitration forums. Mexico, in contrast, resisted subjugation to multilateral bodies such as the World Bank because it wanted to preserve its policy-making autonomy. Mexico offered no feasible counterproposal, however, and a version of the U.S. system was adopted. Under NAFTA, investors may submit disputes for arbitration to the International Center for the Settlement of Investment Disputes (ICSID), the Additional Facility Rules of the ICSID, or the United Nations Commission on International Trade Law (UNCITRAL).

On balance, U.S. negotiators can claim modest victory in the investment-chapter negotiations. The resolutions of three of the four issues dominating working-group efforts lie closest to the U.S. position. On performance requirements for U.S. companies in Mexico, Mexican negotiators wanted to maintain these as long as possible and stipulated permanent financial incentives to meet performance standards. The United States could tolerate a phaseout but not financial incentives. In the end,

---

54. "NAFTA Working Group on Investment Still in Early Stages of Negotiations."

the most trade-distorting financial incentives were eliminated in a marginal victory for the U.S. side. Mexico wanted a strict, nationality-based definition of the kind of investor eligible for NAFTA treatment, while the United States sought, and gained, a broader definition. The U.S. outline for arbitration procedures also was adopted. Mexico, however, retained the right for government screening of foreign investment, over U.S. protests.

Cross-Border Trade in Services—Ground Transport (Chapter 12)

Easily the most contentious services issue was liberalization of the ground-transport sectors in both Mexico and the United States. Before NAFTA, strict Mexican regulations essentially banned U.S. firms from servicing and investing in the Mexican ground-transport market. For instance, since U.S. tractors and drivers were not allowed to enter Mexico, freight originating from the United States had to be transloaded at the border. Mexico was not alone in protecting its ground-transport sector, however. The U.S. land-transport sector had its own restrictions, which were closely defended by domestic trucking and railroad interests. These two groups, though eager to exploit new access to the Mexican market, did not relish one-on-one competition in the United States with their Mexican counterparts.[55]

Nonetheless, the United States pushed for a symmetrical opening of land-transportation markets, including investment, to be phased in over six years. In response to industry anxieties, the United States also pursued requirements that Mexican drivers meet the same standards as U.S. drivers with regard to competency, insurance, vehicle safety, and regulatory oversight. Mexico consented to liberalizing international land transport, albeit over a longer phase-in period, but wanted to exempt all domestic cargo from liberalization.

Mexico succeeded in maintaining strict regulations banning U.S. firms from servicing and investing in domestic land transport in Mexico. International land transport, however, was opened almost exactly as the United States had hoped. Within six years, U.S. firms will be allowed

55. "Special Report: De La Garza Proposes Six Year Land Transportation Plan for NAFTA," *Inside U.S. Trade*, April 3, 1992, 2–3.

to deliver international cargo directly to Mexican destinations, while investment in Mexico's international land-transport market will be restriction-free within ten years. Furthermore, the United States secured some harmonization of technical and safety standards through NAFTA and non-NAFTA agreements.[56]

On the prime trade-in-services issue, ground transport, Mexican and U.S. negotiators met in the middle. Although the United States had sought to open both international and domestic land transport, the compromise centered on Mexico's conceding only in the area of international transport.

Financial Services (Chapter 14)

The negotiations dealing with financial services were some of the most polarized and difficult. Mexico was adamant about limiting competition in financial services because the Mexican banks had been privatized only recently and were still in the process of restructuring. Mexican negotiators feared that these formerly public enterprises, which had long enjoyed strict government-sponsored protection, would not be able to compete with their highly efficient U.S. counterparts. The Mexican side maintained a staunch position, moreover, despite the benefits of cheaper credit for Mexican firms that liberalization of the sector would likely bring about.[57] The U.S. side, meanwhile, saw tremendous opportunity in the Mexican financial-services market and pushed hard for its liberalization.

Whether U.S. firms could establish wholly owned subsidiaries or branches in Mexico was easily the most important market-access issue regarding financial services. With regard to all market-access issues, both Mexico and the United States treated four financial subsectors individually: banking, securities, insurance, and "limited-scope" financial services such as auto loans. Mexico's original proposal involved a complete prohibition of foreign affiliates in all four subsectors of its financial-services market through 1998. Then, in 1999, foreign affiliates would be allowed to occupy in each subsector a market share that would begin at

56. Hufbauer and Schott, NAFTA: An Assessment, 68.

57. For a more complete look at the pros and cons for Mexico, see Ignacio Trigueros, "The Mexican Financial System and NAFTA," in Mexico and the North American Free Trade Agreement, ed. Bulmer-Thomas, Craske, and Serrano, 43–57.

1 percent and increase by 1 percent per year until it reached 7 percent, at which point it would freeze permanently. Under this proposal, subsidiaries of each foreign firm would be limited permanently to a 0.5 percent market share in each subsector.[58]

The United States considered this proposal grossly inadequate and staunchly opposed any permanent caps on foreign market share in Mexico, although it expressed willingness to have permissible market share phased in. Early in the negotiations, Mexico upped its offer to 5 percent immediate market share, 12 percent ultimate market share, and a 1.5 percent single-firm limit. This second proposal was still far from acceptable to the U.S. side.

Based on the NAFTA results, the United States won this standoff. Although permissible market share is phased in slowly in line with the Mexican proposal, no permanent caps on market share are maintained. In banking, for instance, foreign affiliates can occupy 8 percent of the Mexican market in 1994, 15 percent in 2000, and an unlimited percentage beginning in 2001. As a safeguard, however, Mexico can institute a one-time, three-year market-share freeze if foreign participation reaches 25 percent before 2004. Furthermore, during the seven-year phaseout period, a 1.5 percent per-firm market share limit will apply; starting in 2001, per-firm market-share limits will be eliminated. NAFTA provisions regarding foreign affiliates in insurance, securities, and limited-scope financial services are nearly identical to those for banking. All four sets of provisions share identical time frames for the complete elimination of market-share caps; only the market-share limits during the seven-year phase-in period vary, and only slightly.

Mexico did achieve two mitigating provisions as part of this settlement. First, Mexico will maintain strict permanent caps of 25–30 percent on foreign ownership of commercial banks and investment houses based in Mexico. Second, NAFTA allows Mexico to prohibit cross-border solicitation of financial services. This option, however, is not considered particularly relevant, because restrictions on cross-border financial transactions "are in general absent or ineffective" given Mexico's geographical situation and the technologies used in financial transactions.[59] Furthermore, neither U.S. concession will provide much protection to

---

58. "U.S., Mexico Still Unable to Resolve NAFTA Financial Services Dispute," *Inside U.S. Trade,* May 22, 1992, 17–18, and "Mexican Market Access Major Obstacle in Financial Services Deal," *Inside U.S. Trade,* May 8, 1992, 22.

59. Trigueros, "The Mexican Financial System and NAFTA," 45.

Mexico's financial-services industry once foreign subsidiaries have established themselves firmly in Mexico.

Mexico did raise one issue—the treatment of foreign financial subsidiaries by subnational governments—that related primarily to its firms' operations in the United States, rather than vice versa. Mexico was quick to point out that state and local governments in the United States maintained many of their own laws with regard to financial markets, and that these laws often discriminated against foreign firms. Since they would not be subject automatically to trade commitments made at the federal level, Mexico wanted specific wording in NAFTA that would eliminate the potentially discriminatory aspects of these laws. Furthermore, Mexico tied this issue to that of national treatment, which is the guarantee that foreign firms enjoy the same competitive opportunity as local firms. Mexico argued that without specific commitments from its subnational governments, the United States would be unable to afford national treatment to Mexican firms, and therefore Mexico shouldn't have to reciprocate.[60]

The United States, by the same token, would not accept anything less than national treatment for its financial firms operating in Mexico. With regard to subnational governments, the United States proposed a "standstill" provision that would grandfather any existing discriminatory treatment at the state level but prohibit the enactment of any future discriminatory regulations.[61] The United States basically won this confrontation. With the enactment of NAFTA, state governments could pass no new law that would create less favorable business opportunities for a Mexican financial firm than for an American firm from a different state. However, states were allowed to submit a list of discriminatory rules already in place, which would continue to apply indefinitely after NAFTA was enacted. With regard to national treatment, moreover, the agreement states that federal laws must afford "equal competitive opportunities" to firms of all NAFTA members. Thus, although Mexico is not required to treat U.S. firms identically to its own firms, the principle of national treatment is incorporated into the Chapter 14 provisions.

Although the financial-services text fell short of the demands made by U.S. financial institutions, it was nonetheless a victory for U.S. nego-

60. "NAFTA Talks Stall in Financial Services Market Access Working Group," *Inside U.S. Trade,* June 5, 1992, 10–11.

61. "Negotiators Remain Far Apart in NAFTA Talks on Financial Services," *Inside U.S. Trade,* January 31, 1992, 1, 19.

tiators. Caps on market access for U.S. institutions were limited, and national treatment holds.

Intellectual Property (Chapter 17)

NAFTA's comprehensive chapter on intellectual property was basically dictated by a determined U.S. negotiating team. For example, U.S. preferences fueled extensive talks dealing with the enforcement of intellectual-property laws. Whereas the United States was fairly impressed with Mexican intellectual-property laws as they appeared on paper—thanks in part to an extensive industrial-property and copyright law enacted in 1991—poor enforcement of these laws was a major concern. U.S. pressure resulted in a number of Mexican commitments regarding improved enforcement. Besides basic guarantees covering punishment and compensation, Mexico agreed to begin policing the border for pirated goods, rather than check for them after shipments had cleared customs, as was its preference. Mexico also agreed to start prosecuting those engaged in the theft of satellite signals.[62]

At U.S. insistence, Mexico also agreed to expand the types of international copyrights and patents that it would honor. One notable example is computer software, which Mexico now will consider literature for copyright purposes. Another example is plant inventions, which Mexico has committed itself to protecting through one of two possible mechanisms.[63]

The United States did encounter Mexican resistance, however, in its effort to ban most uses of compulsory licensing. Compulsory licensing occurs when a government forces a patent holder in a foreign country to license production of his or her invention to a domestic producer at a discounted price or even for free. This practice occurs frequently in pharmaceuticals, since the licensing government can claim that national health is at stake. The United States wanted to restrict the use of compulsory licenses to "cases of declared national emergency, or cases where the license is used to remedy an adjudicated violation of competition laws." The U.S. proposal also required that the patent owner be "fully"

---

62. "Industry Group Calls for Strong Intellectual Property Agreement in NAFTA," *Inside U.S. Trade*, March 13, 1992, 17–19.

63. "Special Report: NAFTA Negotiators Far Apart on Intellectual Property, Financial Services," *Inside U.S. Trade*, March 24, 1992, 1–14.

compensated for the loss of revenue due to the issuing of the license. Mexico, however, wanted NAFTA to allow compulsory licensing in a wider range of circumstances. It proposed further that patent holders receive only "adequate" compensation.[64]

Mexico basically prevailed in this dispute. NAFTA permits compulsory licensing any time a domestic market is deemed underexploited for a particular invention and a potential licensee has tried and failed to obtain authorization under "reasonable commercial terms." Furthermore, NAFTA states that compensation to the license holder need only be "adequate in the circumstances of each case." The United States did achieve, however, a provision that compulsory licenses be used "predominantly for the supply of the Party's domestic market." This provision quelled some fears that firms producing under compulsory licenses would export inventions back into the country where they were originally patented.

U.S. negotiators prevailed in two of three issues disputed by the intellectual-property-rights working group. Mexico increased its enforcement commitment, as the United States demanded, and also expanded the types of copyrights and patents honored, in line with U.S. preferences. Mexican commitment to honor software copyright was an important U.S. victory. However, Mexican negotiators forced the U.S. team to accept compulsory licensing.

Review and Dispute Settlement in Antidumping and Countervailing-Duty Matters (Chapter 19)

The main disagreement between the United States and Mexico regarding antidumping measures and countervailing duties was whether NAFTA would provide for dispute settlement in these areas. Opposition to a new and specific way in which parties to NAFTA could challenge countervailing duties and antidumping measures adopted by other parties was strong in the United States. Critics argued that such a system would set a precedent whereby all future free-trade partners would have excessive power to alter U.S. trade law. Some also claimed that the avenues of appeal against countervailing-duty and antidumping determinations in

---

64. "Negotiators Close on NAFTA Intellectual Property, but Obstacles Remain," *Inside U.S. Trade*, May 8, 1992, 10–11.

the United States were already sufficiently impartial and transparent. However, many critics, including the U.S. steel industry, gave in fairly early to a dispute-settlement mechanism after accepting that such a system was inevitable.[65] Mexico, which had pushed for such a system, was the winner in these negotiations. Interestingly, once it was clear that NAFTA would cover dispute settlements in countervailing duties and antidumping measures, this became a quiet issue. The CUSFTA contained an adequate precedent, and the United States and Mexico hammered out the logistics uneventfully.

Conclusions

Although U.S. negotiators were victorious more often than Mexican negotiators, this analysis does not necessarily indicate that Mexico "gave away the store" in the NAFTA text itself. The pattern of victory/loss thus far, although wrought with methodological problems,[66] reflects that the United States "won" more often on issues of trade law, while Mexico's gains were registered more fully at the sectoral level. This suggests that the politics of trade negotiation may be more clearly sectoral in Mexico than in the United States.

It is in line with patterns of post–World War II American foreign policy for U.S. trade negotiators to be more intransigent about international trade principles than about defending particular economic sectors. As a leading world power, the United States had an interest in, and was able to bear the cost of, promoting liberal trade and monetary regimes. Vestiges of the liberal mind-set of those years kept U.S. policy on a liberal course even as U.S. hegemony declined in the 1970s and 1980s. However, beyond hegemony and its concomitant ideology of openness lie other possible explanations of the difference in U.S. and Mexican trade-policy priorities.

In negotiations over energy, agriculture, and automobiles, our analysis suggests that Mexico compromised less than the United States, while

---

65. "Mexican Proposal to Debate Reforms of Trade Laws Hits U.S. Brick Wall," *Inside U.S. Trade,* July 12, 1991, 1, 16–18.

66. These include delineating success or failure across chapters, without explicit weighting of the issues disputed within the chapter. Another problem is using the final chapter subjects as the denominator in measuring the overall percentage of chapters "won." The United States, for example, wanted a chapter on wage and price controls, an issue the Mexicans refused to put on the agenda.

the reverse held true in discussion of trade principles such as market access, rules of origin, investment, and intellectual property. Two explanations are plausible here: One is that the U.S. government is more insulated from particularistic pressures of sectoral business associations than is the Mexican government. Another is that U.S. businesses more often cut across sectoral lines or, for other reasons, have more at stake in the definition of trade principles than do Mexican businesses.

The existing literature does not include any serious evaluation of the relative insulation of the Mexican and U.S. governments in the making of trade policy. But one obvious point is that U.S. business is more international than Mexican business. Lobbyists for U.S. companies would thus naturally be more concerned than their Mexican counterparts with the global implications of bilateral agreements. For companies that operate globally, the cost-benefit calculation regarding NAFTA provisions extended far beyond the impact on tariff levels for specific sectors. Examination of this hypothesis, which links trade policy to the degree of internationalization of a nation's business sector, would build on the literature concerning industry characteristics and trade policy, while highlighting the need for studies associating industry characteristics with different aspects of trade policy beyond tariff levels.

3   Pesos, Policies, and Predictions

Why the Crisis, Why the Surprise, and Why the Recovery?

Manuel Pastor Jr.

Celebrated at the December 1994 Summit of the Americas as the pacesetter for regional trade reform, Mexico basked in both the approval of its senior partner in the North American Free Trade Agreement (NAFTA), the United States, and the admiration of its Latin American neighbors eager to secure their own free-trade pacts.[1] Returning from the accolades of the summit to the realities of a desperately shrinking base of international reserves, however, the Mexican government had no

A less technical version of this research, "Globalization, Sovereignty, and Policy Choice," focuses more on whether the Mexican overvaluation decision and subsequent crash reflected domestic policy choice or simply international pressure, and is forthcoming in *The State Still Matters*, ed. David Smith, Dorie Solinger, and Steve Topik.

1. For a review of the summit and its optimistic tone, see Howard J. Wiarda, "After Miami: The Summit, the Peso Crisis, and the Future of U.S.–Latin American Relations," *Journal of Interamerican Studies and World Affairs* 37, no. 1 (1995): 43–68.

choice but to devalue the peso just two weeks later. A step devaluation of 15 percent came on December 20, and a free float—or, better put, a free fall—ensued just two days thereafter.

With panic in the air, the peso continued its decline through the early months of 1995. Nervous investors reacted by pulling assets not only from Mexican financial markets but also from Argentina, Brazil, and other emerging markets in Latin America. As Woods outlines in this volume, the United States responded by coordinating with the International Monetary Fund (IMF) to produce a $53 billion loan package in late February 1995 (with $20 billion coming from the United States, $18 billion from the IMF, $10 billion from the Bank for International Settlements, and the rest from commercial banks and others). In March 1995, Mexico sought to calm financial markets further by announcing the outlines of a harsh new adjustment program, reminiscent of the sort of orthodox demand-restraint policies common throughout Latin America during the early years of the 1980s debt crisis. The economy proceeded to fall into a deep recession, but then staged a sharp and surprisingly rapid recovery by 1996.

The sequence of events in Mexico raises a series of important questions for economic theory and policy. First, why was a financial crisis of this magnitude not anticipated by rational agents, especially those international investors whom economic theory considers to be so well informed in their predictions concerning market behavior? Second, was there an alternative to both the policy that provoked the crisis and the policy response that followed—that is, could Mexico have avoided the debacle of December 1994, and were there any viable alternatives to the austerity plan that followed? Finally, what lessons does the Mexican peso crisis and recovery offer for the future of Mexico and for other Latin American countries striving to maintain macroeconomic stability in today's context of open markets and greater regional integration?

This chapter is organized as a series of responses to these questions, intended in part to complement the coverage by Woods on the reasons behind the international response to the Mexican crisis. My argument is as follows: While the timing of the crisis was clearly related to an unfortunate convergence of political pressures and economic mismanagement, the specific causal variable was an overvalued exchange rate that had long required correction. Failure to anticipate the crisis was partially rooted in the belief held by Mexican policy makers and multilateral officialdom that within a free market the exchange rate would "self-adjust"—and in the faith of international investors in the pronouncements of both groups.

One alternative to the crisis would have involved a slow and controlled devaluation when the exchange rate began to lose parity in 1992; unfortunately this was precluded by the perception of the Salinas administration (1988–94) that any tinkering with the exchange rate would alienate portfolio investors and perhaps jeopardize Mexico's chances at entering NAFTA. Once the crisis began, there was little immediate alternative to the tough adjustment program launched in March 1995, largely because government officials had lost the credibility necessary for a less painful disinflation.

The postcrisis Mexican experience offers both positive and negative lessons for other Latin American reformers. On the one hand, the surprisingly quick recuperation of the Mexican economy, mostly through a devaluation-induced boom in manufactured exports, suggests that years of restructuring has rendered the economy more flexible than many observers once believed possible. On the other hand, the recession-recovery cycle has done little to ameliorate the underlying distributional difficulties that have plagued Mexico (see Pastor and Wise in this volume). This has led to a political backlash that threatens to tie reformers' hands in the future. Moreover, it remains unclear whether there has been full appreciation of the exchange-rate warning raised by the December 1994 experience: overvaluation remains a problem in Mexico and many other countries, and the peso crisis will probably not be the last financial "surprise" in the region.

What Happened?

As with Mexico's 1982 debt crisis, the December 1994 financial shakeout was a long time in the making.[2] The crisis of the early 1980s had called into question the inward-looking strategy that had undergirded Mexi-

2. The longer-term history in this section draws from Nora Lustig, *Mexico: The Remaking of an Economy* (Washington, D.C.: Brookings Institution, 1992); David Barkin, *Distorted Development: Mexico in the World Economy* (Boulder, Colo.: Westview Press, 1990); and James D. Cockcroft, *Mexico: Class Formation, Capital Accumulation, and the State* (New York: Monthly Review Press, 1983). Analysis of the more recent period is taken from Manuel Pastor Jr. and Carol Wise, "The Origins and Sustainability of Mexico's Free Trade Policy," *International Organization* 48, no. 3 (1994): 459–89, and Rudiger Dornbusch and Alejandro Werner, "Mexico: Stabilization, Reform, and No Growth," *Brookings Papers on Economic Activity*, no. 1 (1994): 253–315.

co's economic development for several decades. That model, state-driven import-substitution industrialization (ISI), was rooted in both the nationalism of the Mexican Revolution and the subsequent *profundización* (deepening) of this ethos under President Lazaro Cárdenas (1934–40), a period that included the acquisition by the state of the assets of international oil producers in Mexico and the first substantial attempts at land reform.

ISI hit its economic and political stride in the 1960s and the "golden years" of the 1970s, when annual growth rates of nearly 6 percent suggested that this protectionist strategy had much to offer in terms of the government's modernization and industrialization goals. In retrospect, however, this vibrant GDP growth was often driven by increased government spending on both public infrastructure and the subsidization of key state-owned industries. As the 1970s gave way to the 1980s, expansionary public expenditure relied increasingly on borrowed money, and the government hoped rising oil revenues would allow for continued growth and endless access to foreign savings. When the debt crisis broke in 1982 and oil prices tumbled through the ensuing decade, it became clear that debt-backed, state-led growth simply could not be sustained. A new development model was needed.

In fits and starts, Mexico embarked on what is now viewed as a vigorous program of structural adjustment, including liberalization, privatization, and deregulation. Despite the seeming thematic continuity of this post-1982 "neoliberal" approach, Mexican economic policy actually underwent several important variations over the course of the 1980s. The initial stabilization package prescribed by the de la Madrid administration (1982–88), for example, was much more focused on macroeconomic stability than microeconomic reform and leaned heavily on the usual tools of currency devaluation and fiscal tightening. Unfortunately, the results were less than impressive: inflation remained stubbornly high and the sharp recession of 1983 was followed by an anemic recovery, then another sharp fall in 1986 as the decline in world oil prices reverberated through the economy. By 1987, inflation stood at 159 percent, an all-time high for modern Mexico, while GDP limped along at a 1.9 percent annual rate.[3]

---

3. The "shock therapy" adopted by de la Madrid failed partly because the government underestimated the extent of structural reform necessary to restore external and internal equilibrium. In light of the magnitude of the external shocks affecting Mexico, complete macroeconomic adjustment would have required an increase in access to outside credit and assistance in rescheduling loan

The revised neoliberal model adopted by President Salinas in 1988 shifted direction in both micro and macro policy. On the micro side, the Salinas administration was much more far-reaching in its efforts to privatize state enterprises, particularly the banks, and to liberalize both domestic prices and foreign trade and investment. Yet the real center-piece was a new anti-inflation strategy that sought to break inertial in-flation by applying wage and price controls, but against the backdrop of tight fiscal and monetary policy. (It was the last part of this strategy that distinguished Mexican incomes policy from the much less successful approach employed by "heterodox" reformers in Argentina, Brazil, and Peru.) Moreover, wage and price controls were not simply imposed by fiat; as budget secretary under de la Madrid, Salinas helped design and implement a social "pact" (or *pacto*) in 1987 that committed the govern-ment, business, and labor to price restraints.[4] Particularly important was the government's decision simultaneously to halt the peso's depreciation and to liberalize imports, a combination based on the rationale that im-port competition would serve as an additional brake on inflation.[5]

The mix of sound fiscal policy, increased trade liberalization, and a creative incomes policy helped restore some degree of stability to the Mexican macroeconomy. Economic growth during the Salinas years av-eraged 2.8 percent, while inflation fell from the aforementioned level of 159.2 percent in 1987 to 7.1 percent in 1994. Real interest rates also fell from 16 percent in 1988 to the 4–6 percent range in 1991–92, before rising above 8 percent in 1994. This temporary interest-rate decline, combined with an increase in the availability of consumer credit, fi-nanced an expansion in domestic aggregate demand that helped propel both overall growth and a general rise in the sense of consumer well-being.

Yet, while the Mexican government was successful at controlling in-

---

payments, neither of which was provided by foreign lenders. For a more complete review of this period, see Lustig, *Mexico: The Remaking of an Economy,* 34–38.

4. See Dornbusch and Werner, "Mexico: Stabilization, Reform, and No Growth," 287–89, for a detailed account of the various agreements concluded under the rubric of the *pacto* from 1987 to 1994.

5. Mexico had been on a more gradual schedule to liberalize imports in anticipation of its 1986 entry into the GATT, but it moved ahead of its GATT commitments in order to create a second level of price control via import competition; for example, the first *pacto* halved the tariff rate and eliminated import permits (see Dornbusch and Werner, "Mexico: Stabilization, Reform, and No Growth," 288). It should be noted that exchange-rate fixing was not fully incorporated into the various *pactos* until mid-1988, several months before the presidential elections.

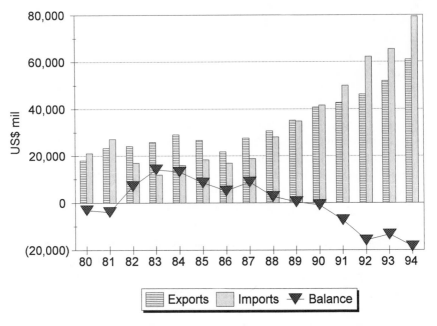

Fig. 3.1. Mexican trade figures, 1980–94

flation and facilitating short-term economic growth, the use of the ex-change rate as a price "anchor" within the context of the *pacto* led to an increasingly overvalued real peso. The first negative consequence of this strategy was reflected in the trade figures: between 1987 and 1993, exports grew by 88 percent (with *maquila* sales included), while imports rose 247 percent, reversing Mexico's 1987 trade surplus of $8.8 billion, to a trade deficit of nearly $13.5 billion by 1993; as can be seen in Figure 3.1, this pattern worsened significantly in 1994.[6] The trade-deficit problem was compounded by the government's decision to increase personal credit for domestic spending. Imports burgeoned as Mexican consumers used their new easily obtained credit cards to purchase a wide range of U.S. goods that had previously been unavailable.[7]

6. Trade figures include imports and exports related to the *maquila* (in-bond) industry, as taken from the IMF's *International Financial Statistics*. Previously, net earnings on *maquila* operations were included as services, and so earlier long-term historical analyses of Mexican trade may not quite match these figures (although the trends are generally the same).

7. As noted in Daniel Oks and Sweder van Wijnbergen, "Mexico After the Debt Crisis: Is Growth Sustainable?" *Journal of Development Economics* 47, no. 1 (1995): 167, real consumer credit jumped at an annualized rate exceeding 50 percent between March 1989 and April 1992, fueling imports as well as domestic demand.

To finance the trade imbalance, Mexico turned to foreign investment. Unfortunately, as can be seen in Figure 3.2, the bulk of incoming capital consisted of highly mobile portfolio investment (the figures for "other flows" include debt-related borrowing, which peaked in 1982; the brief resurgence in 1990 and 1991 reflects refinancing in the wake of the implementation of Mexico's Brady Plan for debt relief).[8] While flows of foreign direct investment (FDI) increased a healthy 57.6 percent from 1989 to 1993, portfolio investment rose more than 8,000 percent. By 1993, portfolio investment accounted for 86.8 percent of total foreign investment flows in Mexico, compared to just 11.3 percent in 1989.[9]

Thus, by 1994, yawning trade deficits and the increased influence of portfolio investors had left Mexico susceptible to rapid changes in investor expectations and confidence. As long as investor confidence remained high, the large level of portfolio investment was not particularly worrisome. However, as can be seen in Figure 3.2, the flow of external finance began to dry up in 1994, partly as a result of higher interest rates in the United States. Just as important, however, were the political uncertainties associated with the March 1994 assassination of Revolutionary Institutional Party (PRI) presidential candidate Luis Colosio and the national elections held in August of that year.

Investors soon began to demand higher interest rates to compensate for the perceived political risk as well as ongoing increases in U.S. rates. Eager to calm investors' nerves and concerned that an interest-rate hike in mid-1994 would provoke a mild recession as the nation headed into a presidential election, the government instead converted much of its short-term peso-denominated *Cetes* debt to dollar-denominated *Tesobonos* in mid-1994.[10] Whereas dollar-denominated *Tesobonos* constituted only 6 percent of the total foreign holding of government securities in December 1993, just a year later these new financial instruments accounted for 87 percent of the total.

The conversion to *Tesobonos* did not stem the tide, particularly as local investors became worried (appropriately) about the viability of the

---

8. See the detailed analysis of debt flows in ibid., 161.

9. All data on capital flows are based on the IMF's *International Financial Statistics*, CD-ROM, March 1996.

10. The reluctance to raise interest rates was also due to legitimate concern about the fragility of the banking system, a topic addressed below. See Jeffrey Sachs, Aaron Tornell, and Andrés Velasco, "The Collapse of the Mexican Peso: What Have We Learned?" (NBER Working Paper 5142, National Bureau of Economic Research, Cambridge, Mass., June 1995), 13.

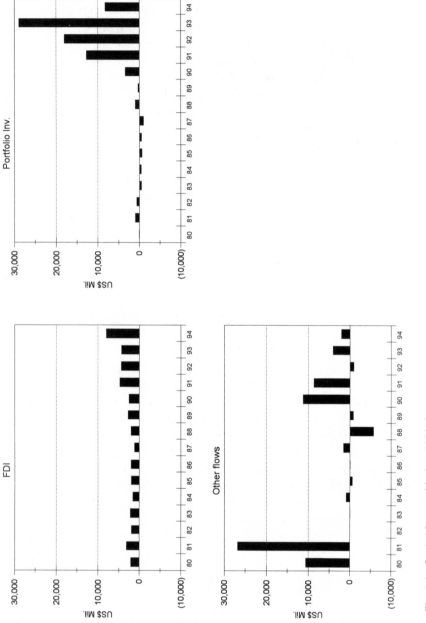

Fig. 3.2. Capital flows to Mexico, 1980–94

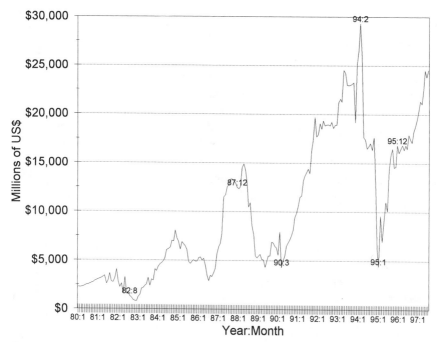

Fig. 3.3. Total reserves minus gold

exchange rate. With trade still far from balanced, foreign reserves (minus gold) plummeted from a high of $29.3 billion in February 1994 to just $6.3 billion in December 1994 (see Fig. 3.3), a particularly alarming turn when one realized (and some soon did) that nearly $30 billion worth of *Tesobonos* were due to mature in 1995.[11] The decision to announce a step devaluation finally came on December 20, 1994, when dollar reserves were nearly depleted. Two days later, the peso was set to float freely (that is, sink) as capital continued to hemorrhage outward.

Why Wasn't the Crisis Anticipated?

The Mexican case presents a striking anomaly for political economy. The December 20, 1994, devaluation and the forces that continued to drive

11. The reserve figures are drawn from the IMF's *International Financial Statistics*, CD-ROM, September 1997; *Tesobono* obligations are given in Paulo C. Leme, "Rebuilding Confidence in Mexico" (report of the Economic Research Division of Goldman Sachs, New York, February 1995).

the peso downward seemed to have caught international investors, academic economists, and even many high-ranking officials in the United States (with supposedly close ties to the upper ranks of the Mexican Finance Ministry) completely off guard.[12] Yet, much of economic theory is built on the assumption that rational actors should be able to anticipate such market movements and adjust accordingly.[13] Following this logic, the persistence of investors in Mexican markets—and their shock at the consequent loss in their asset values—is more of a surprise than the devaluation itself.

In the wake of the devaluation, a virtual cottage industry has cropped up to provide explanations, ranging from Mexico's unexpectedly unstable political environment to the shift from peso-financed government debt to dollar-financed government debt.[14] But while all these explanations may shed light on the timing of the crisis, they tell us little about why the crisis itself was not successfully anticipated. After all, the figures on *Tesobono* financing were widely known to investors active in these markets, and the political roller coaster of 1994 could hardly have been a surprise to knowledgeable analysts on Wall Street and policy makers in Washington and elsewhere.[15]

12. As reported in Sebastian Edwards, *Crisis and Reform in Latin America: From Despair to Hope* (New York: Oxford University Press, 1995), 297, a "number of international investment firms were still recommending Mexican securities to their clients" right up until December 20.

13. While such assumptions are particularly true of the "rational expectations" school of macroeconomics, they are part and parcel of most economists' analyses.

14. See, for example, IMF, *International Capital Markets: Developments, Prospects, and Policy Issues* (Washington, D.C.: IMF, 1995); Rudiger Dornbusch, Ilan Goldfajn, and Rodrigo O. Valdés, "Currency Crises and Collapses," *Brookings Papers on Economic Activity*, no. 2 (1995): 219–93; Sachs, Tornell, and Velasco, "The Collapse of the Mexican Peso"; and Gary L. Springer and Jorge L. Molina, "The Mexican Financial Crisis: Genesis, Impact, and Implications," *Journal of Interamerican Studies and World Affairs* 37, no. 2 (1995): 57–81. Jonathan E. Heath, "The Devaluation of the Mexican Peso in 1994: Economic Policy and Institutions" (Policy Papers on the Americas, Study 5, Center for Strategic and International Studies, Washington, D.C., June 1995), also offers an explanation that focuses on money managers choosing new mixes (or target stocks) of Mexican and non-Mexican assets. According to this view, ambitious market reforms prompted high capital inflows from 1988 to 1993, as money managers strove to meet their new asset targets; the 1994 slowdown in flows was natural, since this desired stock of assets had been obtained. Heath, however, offers no explanation why it would take four years (1989–93), rather than some other time frame, to reach this saturation point.

15. Some investors have claimed that they were not sufficiently informed of Mexico's reserve figures, and there is some truth to this claim. As pointed out in IMF, *International Capital Markets: Developments, Prospects, and Policy Issues*, 56, a decline of over 25 percent of Mexico's stock of international reserves during the month of November 1994 was not announced until *after* the

There were some pundits who worried out loud about a coming currency crisis.[16] As Rudiger Dornbusch notes, the government seemed to believe that the real exchange rate was an economic outcome and not a policy tool; from this standpoint, the massive capital inflows and the peso's appreciation over the 1988–93 period reflected increasing levels of confidence in the Mexican economy. On the other hand, the "disequilibrium" view developed by Dornbusch and others suggests that the real exchange rate is a "policy-influenced or even policy-dominated variable."[17] According to this view, the use of the nominal exchange rate as an anti-inflation tool tends to produce real appreciation because there are lags in reducing inflation; the challenge is to shift away from exchange-rate targeting at the appropriate point and to live with slightly higher inflation but stronger trade competitiveness.[18]

The Mexican case certainly seems to exhibit this disinflation-*cum*-overvaluation phenomenon. As can be seen in Figure 3.4, the Mexican peso gained value steadily over the 1987–94 disinflation process (following standard economic practice, the real exchange rate depicted in the figure is the inverse of the real currency value). By 1994, the peso was more valuable against the dollar than it had been before the debt "crack" of 1982. That this was likely to induce a new crisis could have been

---

December devaluation. However, this notion of an information gap fails to explain why money managers seemed to believe that Mexico's current-account deficits were sustainable over the longer term. Moreover, as made clear by Barry Eichengreen and Albert Fishlow (*Contending with Capital Flows: What Is Different About the 1990s?* [New York: Council on Foreign Relations, 1996], 40), "the virtual unanimity that more and better information is necessary enables portfolio fund managers to find an excuse for their poor predictions. Once there is fuller information, the next crisis will fail to be foreseen for other, and also initially profitable, reasons."

16. See, for example, Dornbusch and Werner, "Mexico: Stabilization, Reform, and No Growth"; Manuel Pastor Jr., "Mexican Trade Liberalization and NAFTA," *Latin American Research Review* 29, no. 3 (1994): 153–73; and Pastor and Wise, "The Origins and Sustainability of Mexico's Free Trade Policy." Rogelio Ramirez de la O, a respected business economist in Mexico, wrote little in traditional academic outlets, but was advising investors through late 1993 and 1994 that a devaluation was inevitable.

17. Dornbusch, Goldfajn, and Valdés, "Currency Crises and Collapses," 251.

18. In a slightly different take on the peso crisis, Andrew Atkeson and José-Víctor Ríos-Rull ("How Mexico Lost Its Foreign Exchange Reserves" [NBER Working Paper 5329, National Bureau of Economic Research, Cambridge, Mass., 1995]), offer a postmortem suggesting that Mexico's exchange rate (and fiscal and monetary) policy was "credible"; the problem arose when Mexican policy makers met constraints on further international borrowing and, hence, were forced to devalue. Yet, it is difficult to understand how an exchange-rate policy can be credible while a government is known to be bumping up against volume constraints in international credit markets.

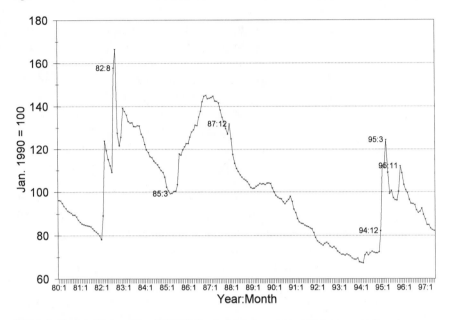

Fig. 3.4. Real exchange rate, 1980–97 (period average, using Mexican CPI, U.S. WPI)

anticipated if economists and investors had compared Mexican macroeconomic policy from 1988 to 1994 to the similar strategy employed by
Chile in 1978–81; in both cases, trade liberalization was combined with
a fixed exchange rate as a way to tame domestic inflationary pressures,
and in both cases, the exchange rate subsequently collapsed.[19]

To illustrate the parallels, I periodize the Chilean and Mexican cases
along the following lines: (1) pre-reform (including a precipitating crisis,
which for Chile was the socialist/populist regime of Salvador Allende,
and for Mexico the impending debt crisis during the last years of the
Lopez Portillo government from 1976 to 1982); (2) monetarist stabilization (for Chile, the initial response of the Pinochet dictatorship that took
over in 1973, and for Mexico, the de la Madrid administration's reliance
on the traditional macroeconomic tool of devaluation); (3) exchange-rate
targeting (coupled in both cases with trade liberalization to dampen inflationary pressures); and (4) the immediate aftermath (of two years in

19. Dornbusch, Goldfajn, and Valdés ("Currency Crises and Collapses") also draw a comparison
with Chile.

each case).[20] A close look at Table 3.1 and Figures 3.5 to 3.8 suggests just how reminiscent the evolution of Mexico's crisis is of Chile's a decade earlier; there is some divergence in the aftermath experience, explored in more detail below.

Why did savvy international investors miss what old-fashioned "exchange-rate fundamentals" could easily have predicted? The answer lies in three interrelated phenomena: a set of ideological priors that convinced key policy makers and private-sector analysts that a country playing so strongly by the market's rules could hardly wind up getting it wrong; a perception that the political costs of devaluation were so prohibitive that no rational Mexican official would even contemplate this option; and a "herd instinct" on the part of investors that caused the stampede away from Mexican assets to be more dramatic than may have been necessary.

On my first point, it is important to recall that Mexican policy makers underwent a sharp ideological shift during the de la Madrid and Salinas presidencies. The obvious failures of ISI led to a firm embrace of the so-called Washington consensus, a view that held that markets could do little wrong and governments could do little but. The macroeconomic counterpart to this pro-market orientation was the notion that if the government budget was balanced, then large trade imbalances simply reflected foreign optimism and willingness to finance excess investment opportunities.[21]

This was certainly the macroeconomic faith projected in numerous interviews conducted with high-level Mexican policy makers in 1993 and 1994: the budget was more or less balanced; foreign capital was

20. The periodization scheme for Chile is drawn from the analysis in Manuel Pastor Jr., *Inflation, Stabilization, and Debt: Macroeconomic Experiments in Peru and Bolivia* (Boulder, Colo.: Westview, 1992), and Joseph Ramos, *Neoconservative Economics in the Southern Cone of Latin America, 1973–1983* (Baltimore: Johns Hopkins University Press, 1986).

21. Some observers argue that, in fact, the Mexican trade balance was related to a budget deficit, albeit one that was nontraditional. The logic (see, for example, Heath, "The Devaluation of the Mexican Peso in 1994") runs as follows: while public-sector spending was largely covered by revenues, Mexican authorities allowed the rapid expansion of credit via the state's development banks (4 percent of GDP in 1994), a policy that was obscured by the government's 1993 decision to remove such financial intermediation from public-sector balance figures. Sachs, Tornell, and Velasco ("The Collapse of the Mexican Peso," 6) counter that "most or all of such activities do not belong in an economically meaningful definition of a budget deficit," primarily because total lending is only a cost (rather than an asset) in the event of a bad loan and because regulations on such development banks (in order to prevent losses) had also been tightened in 1993.

Table 3.1. Exchange-rate targeting in Chile and Mexico

Chile

		GDP Growth	Inflation Rate	Real Effective Exchange Rate (1976 = 100)	Wage Share of Manufacturing Value-added (1976 = 100)	Exports (FOB) (Millions of US$)	Imports (FOB) (Millions of US$)	Merchandise Trade Balance (Millions of US$)
Pre-reform	1971	9.2	26.7	105.5	156.0	1,000	927	73
	1972	−0.7	149.2	110.7	202.6	851	1,012	(161)
	1973	−4.8	558.6	123.1	111.9	1,316	1,329	(13)
Monetarist stabilization	1974	2.5	376.0	107.3	83.0	2,152	1,901	250
	1975	−11.6	340.7	115.0	84.0	1,590	1,520	70
Exchange-rate targeting	1976	3.5	174.3	100.0	100.0	2,116	1,473	643
	1977	8.6	63.4	96.9	119.7	2,186	2,151	35
	1978	7.5	30.3	112.2	122.9	2,460	2,886	(426)
	1979	8.7	38.9	100.3	124.5	3,835	4,190	(355)
	1980	8.2	31.2	86.2	125.9	4,705	5,469	(764)
	1981	4.8	9.5	77.4	157.3	3,836	6,513	(2,677)
Aftermath	1982	−10.4	20.7	90.6	139.3	3,706	3,643	63
	1983	−3.7	23.1	95.9	116.9	3,831	2,845	986

Mexico

		GDP Growth	Inflation Rate	Real Exchange Rate (1988 = 100)	Wage Share of Manufacturing Value-added (1988 = 100)	Exports (FOB) (Millions of US$)	Imports (FOB) (Millions of US$)	Merchandise Trade Balance (Millions of US$)
Pre-reform	1980	8.4	29.8	84.0	185	18,031	21,087	(3,056)
	1981	8.8	28.7	76.5	192	23,307	27,184	(3,877)
	1982	−0.7	98.9	113.0	191	24,056	17,009	7,047
Monetarist Stabilization	1983	−4.1	80.8	120.8	134	25,953	11,848	14,105
	1984	3.7	59.2	104.4	119	29,101	15,915	13,186
	1985	2.7	63.7	100.8	118	26,758	18,359	8,399
	1986	−3.9	105.7	125.2	113	21,803	16,784	5,019
	1987	1.9	159.2	124.8	99	27,599	18,813	8,786
Exchange-rate targeting	1988	1.3	51.7	100.0	100	30,692	28,081	2,611
	1989	3.5	19.7	94.7	106	35,171	34,766	405
	1990	4.3	29.9	88.5	113	40,711	41,592	(881)
	1991	3.9	18.8	77.6	122	42,687	49,966	(7,279)
	1992	2.8	11.9	69.3	NA	46,196	62,130	(15,934)
	1993	0.4	8.0	65.1	NA	51,885	65,366	(13,481)
	1994	3.8	7.1	66.8	NA	60,879	79,346	(18,467)
Aftermath	1995	−6.2	52.0	95.2	NA	79,543	72,454	7,089
	1996	5.0	27.7	85.8	NA	95,999	89,469	6,530

SOURCE: GDP growth, wage share, and Chilean trade from World Bank, *World Tables, 1995* (CD-ROM). December-to-December inflation from IMF, *International Financial Statistics*. Chilean real exchange rate from Ramos (1986); Mexican real exchange rate calculated using the period average exchange rate, domestic CPI, and U.S. WPI, with data from *World Tables, 1995* (CD-ROM) and IFS (CD-ROM, September 1997). Mexican trade data include *maquila* operations; 1996 Mexican trade (and GDP) is based on data from the New York Mexican Consulate Web page; 1996 inflation and real exchange rate based on IFS (CD-ROM, September 1997).

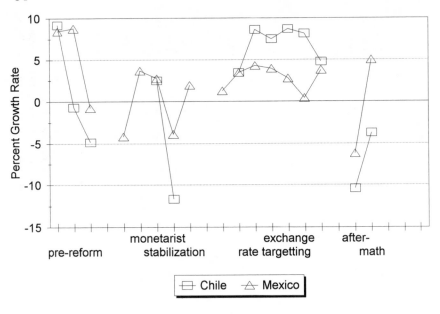

Fig. 3.5. GDP growth rates, Chile and Mexico

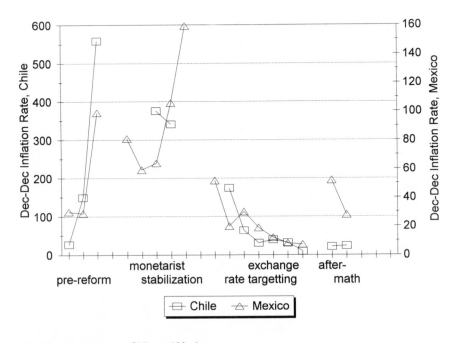

Fig. 3.6. Inflation rates, Chile and Mexico

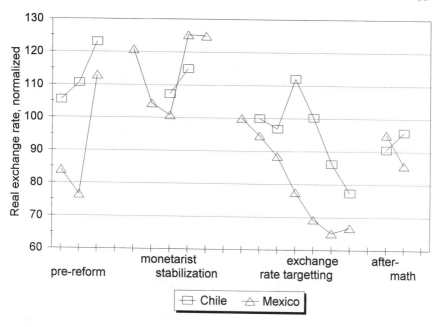

Fig. 3.7. Real exchange rates, Chile and Mexico

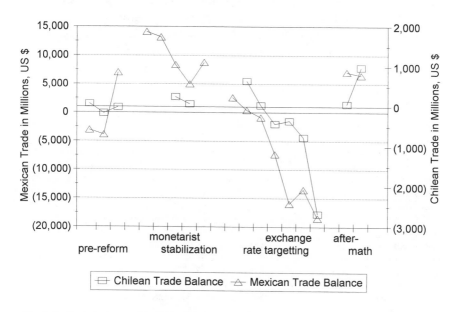

Fig. 3.8. Trade balance, Chile and Mexico

clearly interested in Mexico; and the resulting overvalued exchange rate was thought to reflect a "ratification" of the country's economic policy.[22] A closer analysis would have suggested that Mexico's imbalances were actually the result of low savings and not simply high investment possibilities; more wariness about the market would have sent some warning flags that the main form of foreign financing, portfolio investment, was exposing the country to some potentially destabilizing external shocks in the event of an adverse shift in investor sentiment. Instead, both domestic and foreign decision makers bought into the government's own confidence.

Such confidence in exchange-rate stability also reflected the view that the political costs of a devaluation were too high, not an unreasonable position in light of the actual aftermath of the December 1994 devaluation.[23] It was thought that any devaluation would have slowed (and eventually did slow) the flow of portfolio investment (see the discussion of speculative attacks below), thereby imposing a large macroeconomic adjustment burden. Moreover, the peso's overvaluation helped "mask" an underlying deterioration in income distribution that continued through the Salinas epoch. As noted by Pastor and Wise in this volume, the upper tenth decile of households gained during the 1980s, especially in the first period of "monetarist stabilization," while the bottom 70 percent saw flat or negative returns during the period of more intense market reform under Salinas.[24] Yet, the distributional costs associated with trade liberalization, privatization, and other aspects of the neoliberal package were muted, partly because overvaluation bolstered pur-

---

22. See the discussion in Heath, "The Devaluation of the Mexican Peso in 1994," as well as the argument along these lines in Pedro Aspe, *El camino mexicano de la transformación económica* (Mexico City: Fondo de Cultura Económica, 1993), 190–93. Edwards (*Crisis and Reform in Latin America*, 274) concurs that high-level Mexican policy makers thought that since the capital "inflows were largely private . . . this was an equilibrium phenomenon that did not call for policy action," and offers statements from the Bank of Mexico that reflect this view.

23. This period of Mexican policy making conforms neatly to models of political economy in which governments try to solve time, inconsistency, and credibility problems by committing to policies that would be extraordinarily costly to reverse and thereby convincing investors of the sustainability of such policies. See Dani Rodrik, "Promises, Promises: Credible Policy via Signalling," *Economic Journal* 99, no. 397 (1989): 756–72, and idem, "Understanding Economic Policy Reform," *Journal of Economic Literature* 34, no. 1 (1996): 9–41.

24. Preliminary analysis of the change between 1992 and 1994 suggests that distribution did not improve, that only the top two deciles enjoyed absolute gains. See Manuel Pastor Jr. and Carol Wise, "State Policy, Distribution, and Neoliberal Reform in Mexico," *Journal of Latin American Studies* 29, no. 2 (1997): 419–56.

chasing power. Mexicans felt richer, and there was understandably little incentive for policy makers to remind them that they were not.

However, once reserves fell to a critical level and the government had no choice but to accept the political costs of depreciation, any ideological blinders were quickly lifted, and capital wasted no time in fleeing. In the two-day period between the step devaluation and the decision to float the peso, Mexico's international reserves fell by $4 billion.[25] That this classic speculative attack played a role in exacerbating the peso crisis is true; the question, however, is whether it caused the crisis.

In its influential postmortem, the IMF has identified the Mexican case as one in which investors, increasingly aware of "deteriorating fundamentals," decide to abandon a particular currency and cash in their gains before the inevitable devaluation.[26] This stampede naturally intensifies the economic pressure associated with deteriorating fundamentals and contributes to the overshooting of the exchange rate when it is finally devalued.[27] Although this explanation enables us to understand better the severity of the peso's decline, it does *not* capture the element of complete surprise that seems to characterize this episode. After all, the difference in the rate of return between peso- and dollar-denominated government debt instruments was not very large through most of 1994, a fact that indicates that few investors were lying in wait for a devaluation.[28] Moreover, "catching on" to the economic fundamentals after the government's desperate measures on December 20 suggests little prescience by economic actors; abandoning the currency in a panic instead reflects the usual fragility of financial markets.[29]

25. IMF, *International Capital Markets: Developments, Prospects, and Policy Issues,* 57.

26. There is a certain inconsistency to this literature. Individuals who become aware that the exchange rate will be unsustainable on date *x* should wait until date *x-1* so as to maximize profits in the meantime. However, waiting until that date simply tempts others to abandon the currency on *x-2* in order to beat the crowd and realize extra profits. Continuing with this logic, any economic news that changes the perception of sustainability should result in an immediate adjustment today, making any exchange-rate shifts small and unlikely to be of the magnitude associated with speculative attacks and crises.

27. Such overshooting occurred with the steep depreciation of the real rate up until March 1995 (see Fig. 3.6), which was then followed by some recovery of the peso's value.

28. See IMF, *International Capital Markets: Developments, Prospects, and Policy Issues,* 75.

29. The analysis provided in Nora Lustig, "The Mexican Peso Crisis: The Foreseeable and the Surprise" (Brookings Discussion Paper 114, Brookings Institution, Washington, D.C., 1995) differs in its details, but Lustig's insistence that the financial crisis followed (and was due to) the devaluation essentially squares with my notion that any speculative attack came after the Mexican government's announcement and actions on December 20.

The failure to anticipate the crisis, then, was due largely to the belief held by both Mexican policy makers and their international counterparts that there was only one possible outcome for Mexico's market opening, that of success.[30] Compounding this was the perception in Mexico City that any attempt to depreciate the peso would impose prohibitively high political costs. Yet, once these ideological and political thresholds were crossed, the volatile dynamics of financial markets took over, propelling the peso downward. And while the anticipation of these events was entirely possible, this would have required a more realistic assessment of the Mexican strategy from the beginning, as well as a more sober comparison of this strategy with the earlier Chilean experience discussed above.

One factor preventing such an assessment was the highly exclusionary arrangements that have long characterized the Mexican political system. While the tight insulation of Mexican policy makers was central to their ability single-handedly to force through a sweeping program of liberalization and privatization, insulation and insistence on consensus among technocrats stifled any constructive dialogue within the government over the need for a shift in the exchange rate. Pastor and Wise argue that such removal from popular pressures can prevent policy makers from learning how to build a "winner's circle" for reform, and hence lead to political miscalculations.[31] In this sense, a more democratic and accountable style of management might have prevented the crisis and could be essential for sustained recovery.

Was There an Alternative Before the Crisis—or After?

If the crisis could have been anticipated, could it also have been avoided? In the wake of the crash, many authors have sketched out

---

30. To be fair, some U.S. Treasury officials were concerned about Mexico's potential overvaluation problem and relayed their concerns to Mexican authorities quietly; obviously, both sides found it easier to downplay this concern, for fear of "spooking" the markets into the sort of speculative attack that eventually occurred. See David Wessel, Paul B. Carroll, Thomas T. Vogel Jr., "How Mexico's Crisis Ambushed Top Minds in Officialdom, Finance," *Wall Street Journal*, July 6, 1995, A1.

31. Borrowing from Dani Rodrik, "The Rush to Free Trade in the Developing World: Why So Late? Why Now? Will It Last?" in *Voting for Reform: Democracy, Political Liberalization, and Economic Adjustment*, ed. Stephan Haggard and Steven B. Webb (New York: Oxford University Press, 1994), Pastor and Wise develop a model of policy determination in which decision makers balance

scenarios of possible "soft landings." For example, Heath suggests that the Mexican government was hoping that the award of an "investment-grade" rating would attract new pension-fund-based capital flows, even as exports and foreign direct investment were on the rise; this would have allowed both the exchange rate and growth to be sustained.[32] Others argue that Mexican monetary policy should have been tightened, forcing a peso-protecting recession that would have resulted in a temporary but small adjustment and eventually resuscitated the "Mexican miracle."[33]

These scenarios are unrealistic. Portfolio investment and reserves were on the decline through 1994; expecting an investment-rating upgrade in this context was as unrealistic as expecting typically risk-averse pension-fund investors to come streaming into Mexico in the quantities needed. Tightening monetary policy to defend the peso would also have been problematic, not simply because of electoral concerns but also because banks were carrying a large portfolio of nonperforming loans, a trend that made policy makers fear the prospect of interest-rate hikes. Both the electoral and financial worries help to explain why authorities opted to convert peso-denominated government securities to dollar-denominated ones, hoping thereby to avoid the domestic interest-rate hikes necessary to cover the risk of depreciation.

The real issue, as I have suggested above, is whether the government could have engineered a devaluation without triggering a financial panic—particularly since a more neatly executed devaluation could have promoted the surge in exports and foreign direct investment Mexico was counting on in its own "soft-landing" scenario. There were at least two opportune moments for such a policy. The first was immediately after the March 1994 assassination of PRI presidential candidate Luis Colosio.

---

distributional costs against aggregate efficiency gains to calculate a politically optimal degree of liberalization; if they have a high demand for reform (for ideological or other reasons), they can "artificially" lower the perceived costs via asymmetric information and institutional exclusion (to misinform "losers" and limit their influence). This, however, does not change the optimum point of reform, and a "snapback" can occur, as it did in Mexico's crisis of 1994–95. See Pastor and Wise, "The Origins and Sustainability of Mexico's Free Trade Policy."

32. See Heath, "The Devaluation of the Mexican Peso in 1994."

33. The IMF suggests this possibility in its discussion of the inappropriate sterilization of reserve losses in the second half of 1994; see IMF, *International Capital Markets: Developments, Prospects, and Policy Issues*. See also the discussion of options in Council on Foreign Relations, *Lessons of the Mexican Peso Crisis: Report of an Independent Task Force* (New York: Council on Foreign Relations, 1996).

While this political event did raise the anxiety level in both domestic and international circles, as reflected in a round of capital flight, such a political shock also created an opportunity to shift policy and cast the blame elsewhere without a major loss of credibility;[34] moreover, the United States and Canada immediately stepped forward after Colosio's death with a $7 billion swap facility to help cushion any adjustment. The Mexican government did take advantage of this moment to force through a 10 percent decline in the peso's value, but this gesture was too little, especially so late in the game.[35]

The second opportunity to devalue came after the August 1994 elections, when Salinas could have forced a change in the currency sometime in the fall, allowing the newly elected President Zedillo to take office with a more sustainable peso and little of the blame for the depreciation. That he did not is noteworthy, especially since de la Madrid granted Salinas this very same favor by devaluing significantly in 1987 to provide the leeway that allowed Mexico more or less to freeze the exchange rate and employ it as an anti-inflation anchor. Some have attributed Salinas's refusal to devalue to his desire to end his administration on a successful note and thus clinch his candidacy for the directorship of the new World Trade Organization. While such personal motives are plausible, perhaps more significant was the lack of coordination between the outgoing and incoming economic teams and the institutional exclusion that had, on the one hand, allowed Salinas and his technocrats to finesse a major economic restructuring while, on the other hand, allowing them to ignore the entreaties of Zedillo and especially Guillermo Ortiz, who eventually became Zedillo's treasury minister.[36]

34. Sachs, Tornell, and Velasco ("The Collapse of the Mexican Peso," 20–21) concur that "it is plausible that the investor community would have understood that the devaluation [at the time of the assassination] was prompted by a political disaster which was painfully observable to all." Dornbusch and Werner ("Mexico: Stabilization, Reform, and No Growth," 285) also suggest that there were "several days following the assassination of candidate Colosio during which the nation rallied behind the official party and that could have provided the cover for a realignment." The Zedillo team may have had such a political "cover" in mind when, in December, it devalued in the wake of an upsurge in fighting in Chiapas, hoping, it seems, that investors would blame Subcomandante Marcos and not Finance Minister Jaime Serra Puche for the depreciation. However, by this late in 1994, reserves were much lower, and exchange-rate declines were far more likely to provoke a speculative attack. Moreover, the resurgence of conflict in Chiapas was not an entirely unexpected event and did not provide the same sort of political cover for the shift in policy as the assassination would have.

35. The actual mechanism for the devaluation was to let the peso float up to the top of the exchange-rate band that had been established and widened systematically over the previous year.

36. See Rosario Avilés and José Luis Gaona, "The Errors of December, 1994," El Financiero (International Edition), December 25, 1995–January 7, 1996, 7.

In short, there was an alternative to the crisis, although it would have required some degree of political courage and the willingness of Salinas to "fall on his sword" in order to smooth the way for his successor. However, once the crisis began, there may have been little alternative to the harsh policies initially undertaken by the Zedillo administration. Significantly, the original adjustment program unveiled in January did little to calm markets or stem inflation. Obviously, no program would have been credible until there was strong evidence that multilateral support would be forthcoming, something not clarified until late January and formally agreed to in mid-February by the United States, the IMF, and other Paris Club leaders. With the mammoth $53 billion loan package in place, the March program was able to halt the slide in the peso, restore some degree of voluntary capital inflows, and calm jittery nerves.

The program achieved this success by applying the same sort of orthodox medicine that had been common during the de la Madrid era, including a tightening of fiscal policy, with reductions in real spending and increases in the value-added tax; tight limits on monetary growth; and a floating exchange rate designed to allow for further depreciation.[37] This return to the past raises a significant question: why couldn't the Mexican government simply have revived the incomes policies of 1988–94, albeit on the basis of a realigned real exchange rate (and therefore an output mix more tilted to the tradable-goods sectors)?

The answer hinges on credibility. An incomes policy essentially involves an agreement by which business, labor, and government make promises—and keep them. Having lost the public's confidence, the government was unable to secure a credible level of sectoral cooperation on a new pact. Thus, it was fighting inflation the old-fashioned way—with sharp increases in unemployment and a compression in real wages to signal to foreign investors that Zedillo's team was serious about stabilizing the economy.[38] That there were few options to this costly form of inflation fighting did not make it any easier to administer yet another

37. See Council on Foreign Relations, *Lessons of the Mexican Peso Crisis.* In keeping with Mexico's recent emphasis on social "safety nets," the program included a shift of expenditures toward social and rural programs and the development of a modest public-employment scheme for building new infrastructure.

38. See Rodrik, "Promises, Promises: Credible Policy via Signalling," on how governments sometimes need to "overdo" adjustment in order to restore credibility. It should be noted that a new *pacto* was signed in late October 1995, but it eschewed exchange-rate fixing in favor of a commitment to an anti-inflationary monetary policy. Unfortunately, inflation continued upward in the months after the *pacto* was signed.

round of austerity to a population already reeling from deepening distributional cleavages and frustrated by the unrealistically high expectations that Mexican policy makers had built around NAFTA's implementation. In this light, it is not surprising that the government party continued to face a decline in popularity, culminating with the loss of its congressional majority in the 1997 elections.

Why the Recovery—and Can It Be Sustained?

The initial economic scenario in postcrash Mexico was not encouraging. In 1995, Mexican GDP plunged by over 6 percent, and unemployment rose sharply. After surges in March and April, inflation tapered down but then shot back up to a 3 percent monthly rate at the end of 1995. Real wages in manufacturing fell by 15–20 percent, due to the combination of depreciation, rising joblessness, and increasing informality. Political discontent was clearly on the rise, as middle-class debtors, battered by the crisis-induced increase in interest rates on their mortgages and credit cards, formed the so-called Barzón movement to seek debt relief.[39]

Yet bubbling up in the background was a startling improvement in the trade picture. Figure 3.9 uses monthly data to chart the dramatic shift in the Mexican trade picture after the crisis broke.[40] As can be seen, the turnaround in the trade balance was extraordinarily rapid, occurring only two months after the devaluation, and was obtained not only via the usual recession-induced reduction in import demand but also via a striking rebound in exports. A revitalized *maquila* sector helped drive the export boom, and by mid-1995, manufacturing employment had actually begun to increase, reversing a long slide that had begun in 1990 and then accelerated in the first months of the crisis (Mexico's overall unemployment remained high because of the collapse of services and domestic demand).

39. The Barzón movement was originally focused on rural debtors seeking to prevent bank foreclosure on their farms but quickly spread to urban areas. The Zedillo administration took the Barzón's demands seriously, partly because it is usually the middle class that prompts major political realignments. Thus, the government agreed to a Debtor's Aid Program in September 1995 that included measures to postpone foreclosures and cap the interest rates affecting most credit-card holders for at least one year. While this helped stabilize politics, it raised the costs of the bank bailout by forcing the government to absorb interest losses and requiring that the banks continue to hold potentially bad loans.

40. The trade data come from the web pages of Mexico's National Institute of Statistics (INEGI) and include *maquila* sales.

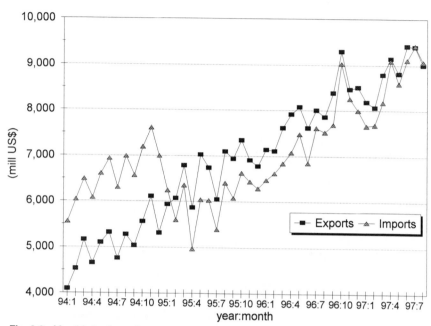

Fig. 3.9. Monthly trade performance, 1994–97

By 1996, Mexican aggregate GDP was on the upswing, with the pre-crisis level of output reattained by early 1997. In comparison to the Chilean experience, the recovery was far more rapid in both trade and GDP (see Figs. 3.5 and 3.7). While NAFTA helped by providing privileged access to the U.S. market, the ability of the manufacturing sector to respond to the new price incentives created by the devaluation speaks volumes about the decade-long, and frequently painful, transformation of the Mexican economy. As can be seen in Figure 3.10, Mexico has fundamentally altered its earlier reliance on oil exports; price-sensitive manufactures are now around 85 percent of total exports, implying that devaluation can spur significant increases in volume and sales revenues.[41] Moreover, interviews with the business sector suggest that local investors are far more responsive to price signals and external markets, partly because the traditional avenue of protecting profits through gov-

41. As can be seen in the figure, some of the stated increase in manufactured exports is due to a shift between 1990 and 1991 in the way *maquila* exports were counted. However, it is also true that *maquila* sales were a much less significant part of the economy in 1980 and grew significantly through the following decade, implying that the compositional shift between 1982 and 1990 is understated.

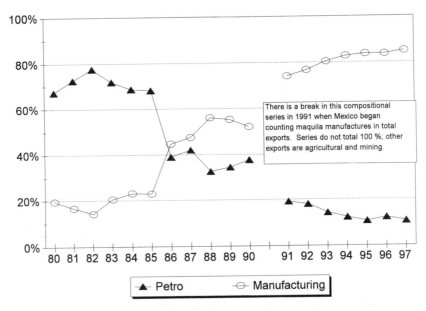

There is a break in this compositional series in 1991 when Mexico began counting maquila manufactures in total exports. Series do not total 100 %; other exports are agricultural and mining.

Fig. 3.10. Petroleum and manufacturing as percent of Mexican exports, 1980–96

ernment restrictions has been limited by neoliberal reforms. Mexico, in short, is in a new era.

At the same time, Mexico's future prospects—that is, the medium-term sustainability of its recovery—are dampened by old problems, such as an underdeveloped financial structure, distributional inequities, and a lumbering political system. On the financial side, the peso crisis reverberated sharply through an already shaky banking system. The percentage of bad loans rapidly doubled between December 1994 and October 1995 (up to 17.7 percent), and the government responded by taking over failing banks and buying up nonperforming loans from larger banks in order to assure their survival.[42] It is estimated that the bank bailout will cost at least $11 billion, just about equal to the proceeds the Salinas administration earned by selling the previously state-owned banks back to the private sector in 1992–93.[43]

The crisis in the financial sector has had negative effects on distribu-

42. See Chris Kraul, "Mexico's Banks Are Again in Crisis," *Los Angeles Times*, December 4, 1995.

43. See Mark Stevenson, "Mexico's Bad Year for Banks," *El Financiero* (International Edition), December 25, 1995–January 7, 1996, 9, and idem, "Still Much to Do in Modernizing Banks," *El Financiero* (International Edition), October 13–19, 1997, 5.

tion as well. Income equity is usually thought of in terms of factoral, or class, distribution, and most observers acknowledge that Mexico has suffered in this regard since 1994, particularly in light of a steady fall in real wages that seemed to bottom out finally in mid-1997. Yet another feature of Mexico's political economy is the concentration of business opportunities and finance in the hands of a select group of large companies. This concentration has actually been made worse by the new reliance on exports, since this is an arena in which larger firms benefit from economies of scale and the ability to maintain quality standards. Small and medium-sized enterprises can cluster with their larger brethren in externally oriented production chains, but the strained and oligopolistic financial system limits the ability of smaller firms to secure the credit necessary to modernize operations.[44] Helping the poor, elevating wages, and propping up small business will require some measure of state intervention, yet the government's longer-term strategy, as reflected in the "National Development Plan" President Zedillo unveiled in mid-1995, essentially favors a continued reliance on market mechanisms.

On the political side, the administration has lost significant ground even as the economy has done much better than anyone thought possible. In 1997, the government party lost its majority in Congress, and the Left's perennial candidate for the presidency, Cuauhtémoc Cárdenas, won the first popular election for mayor of Mexico City. Certainly one of the factors in the loss was the public's sense of previous economic mismanagement; despite the export boom and GDP upswing, the lingering memories of the peso crisis and the ongoing distributional difficulties led voters to be less fearful about handing over at least part of the policy reins to opposition forces. And as with the peso crash, PRI technocrats seemed to be surprised at the electoral rejection, once again reflecting the unique combination of political insulation and ideological blinders that has characterized neoliberalism in Mexico.

What is the future for Mexico? The country does have important long-term advantages: a developed, and now seemingly nimble, industrial base; a relatively skilled and hardworking populace; and continued access via NAFTA to both external consumer demand and capital investment. Yet the air of self-congratulation that marked the December 1994

---

44. See Manuel Pastor Jr. and Carol Wise, "State Policy, Distribution, and Neoliberal Reform in Mexico."

Summit of the Americas—immediately before the crash—is still influencing policy makers as they now revel in their newfound ability to export. In particular, the very success of the recovery, like the success of the anti-inflation strategy of 1988–94, has obscured fundamental problems with regard to the exchange rate and income distribution.

On the first issue, it is useful to recall that, in the wake of its own crisis, Chile wisely abandoned its attachment to fixed exchange rates and learned to live with slightly higher inflation but a more competitive exchange rate. Mexico has followed the same strategy in form but not in result; slowly but surely, the peso has reappreciated (recall Fig. 3.4). This reduced Mexico's trade balance through 1996, and monthly trade figures fell into deficit in July 1997. Worried about the same phenomenon of currency revaluation, Chile through the 1980s departed from a purely "hands-off" market orientation and instituted measures to tame financial surges, including taxes on capital movements and requirements that incoming capital commit itself to a minimum stay before exiting the country. Mexico has eschewed such measures, and the peso remains vulnerable.

As for distribution, Chilean policy makers worked toward improving equity by combining a social safety-net scheme with stable macroeconomic management, particularly after the Pinochet regime gave way to a democratically elected government.[45] This last aspect of the Chilean reform process remains to be seriously tackled in Mexico. Because of the government's lack of leadership on distribution, policy consensus is elusive, and the opposition is tempted to adopt populist positions, such as reducing the value-added tax (a levy that is regressive but is also arguably necessary for maintaining budget balance), for political gain. If the government wishes to avoid either irresponsible measures or policy paralysis, it will have to launch a serious, credible effort to empower the poor and spur development opportunities at the lower end of the income and business structure.

Given the current political strains, some may suggest that the key element in the Chilean turnaround was not exchange-rate policy or other measures but rather the authoritarian ability to force through, and stick to, reform in general. Such a view is misleading. After all, the Pinochet

---

45. For various perspectives on the Chilean reform during the 1980s, see Barry Bosworth, Rudiger Dornbusch, and Raúl Labán, eds., *The Chilean Economy: Policy Lessons and Challenges* (Washington, D.C.: Brookings Institution, 1994).

regime was also responsible for the economic disaster of the early 1980s, and the authoritarian insulation of Mexican policy makers proved to be no antidote to bad economic policy. As a result, many Mexicans, including those enamored of the government's neoliberal approach to economics, have welcomed the new debate on the shape of economic policy that is being forced by a significant oppositional presence in the domestic political system.

Indeed, the peso crash of 1994—particularly the failure of policy makers and markets fully to anticipate the problem—highlights the weakness of policy frameworks that are excessively ideological and decision-making institutions that are overly exclusionary. Mexico now faces a choice between ideology or pragmatism, traditional politics or further democratization. Perhaps the biggest lesson from 1994 is that if we are to avoid another "surprise" in Mexico or in any other Latin American country—and achieve a longer-term path to sustainable growth—what will be needed is greater modesty about the benefits of market liberalization, a stronger commitment to equitable distribution, and a renewed emphasis on openness, transparency, and flexibility in the policy-making process.

4 · International Financial
· Institutions and
· the Mexican Crisis

· *Ngaire Woods*

· More than three years after the announcement that the
· United States, Canada, and Mexico would pursue a
· North American Free Trade Agreement (NAFTA), the bill
· was finally passed by the U.S. House of Representatives
· on November 17, 1993. From the Mexican perspective,
· the agreement reflected wide and sweeping changes. In
· principle, NAFTA signaled exchange-rate stability and
· the prospect of fresh capital flows from investors now
· reassured about the future direction of Mexican eco-
· nomic policy. Indeed, although NAFTA was technically a
· free-trade agreement, one prominent Mexican economist

· I am especially grateful for the helpful comments of Valpie Fitzgerald, Peter
· Garber, Sylvia Maxfield, Frances Stewart, and Carol Wise on an earlier ver-
· sion of this chapter.

stated at the time that "[i]ncreased capital mobility is, of course, what both the public and the trade negotiators have in mind."[1] NAFTA also promised an improved set of economic arrangements between Mexico and the United States based on new possibilities for economic growth and diversified investment. In this context, we might well have expected the role of the international financial institutions (IFIS) in Mexico— especially the International Monetary Fund (IMF) and the World Bank— gradually to be replaced by regional institutions.

By early 1995, NAFTA's hoped-for returns had become ephemeral. In December 1994, after a period of mounting economic instability, the Mexican government widened the exchange rate band by 15 percent. What followed was a virtual financial nightmare.[2] Investors quickly fled, and within weeks Mexico was on the verge of default. The new regional free-trade area was experiencing its first crisis. Yet the management of this crisis quickly became international, as opposed to being handled on a bilateral or trilateral basis within NAFTA.

Mexico's difficulties were immediately perceived as a broader threat to international financial stability, partly because of what was called the tequila effect, whereby the flight of portfolio capital spread rapidly across the entire region. But I argue that the United States also had a direct interest in defining aspects of the Mexican crisis as international. Just as in the 1980s, when Mexico's debt crises were cast partly as threats to international financial stability and thus dealt with jointly by both public and private international institutions, so too in this case was the United States able to remit the crisis to international forums— especially the IFIS—and again spread the burden of assisting Mexico. Having effectively put an international spin on the peso crisis, subsequent discussions focused on two core issues: how to manage the crisis, and how to prevent such crises in the future. These two issues are addressed in this chapter.

---

1. Jaime Ros, "Mexico and NAFTA: Economic Effects and the Bargaining Process," in *Mexico and NAFTA: Who Will Benefit?* ed. Victor Bulmer-Thomas, Nikki Craske, and Mónica Serrano (London: Macmillan & Institute for Latin American Studies, 1994), 11–28.

2. For different interpretations of Mexico's peso devaluation, see Nora Lustig, "The Mexican Peso Crisis: The Foreseeable and the Surprise" (Brookings Discussion Papers 114, Brookings Institution, Washington, D.C., 1995); Jeffrey Sachs, Aaron Tornell, and Andrés Velasco, "The Collapse of the Mexican Peso: What Have We Learned?" (NBER Working Paper 5142, National Bureau of Economic Research, Cambridge, Mass., June 1995); and Manuel Pastor's chapter in this volume.

Crisis Management, NAFTA, and the International Financial Institutions

Mexico's financial crisis of 1994–95 was one of the first major challenges to confront the NAFTA bloc, and one response was to ask why NAFTA's institutions had not been designed to deal with such a situation.[3] Since they had not, management of the crisis, as with earlier crises involving Mexico, was internationalized by the U.S. Treasury, with the IMF and the Bank for International Settlements (BIS) being drawn immediately into the rescue and the World Bank becoming involved later on in providing assistance to soften the impact of increased austerity.[4]

The response to Mexico highlighted a dilemma for U.S. policy makers. On the one hand, by internationalizing the crisis, the United States reduced the political and economic costs of the assistance package. It did so not only by sharing costs with other states but also by diluting U.S. domestic opposition to "bailing out" Mexico, as well as Mexican resentment over conditions for assistance imposed by the United States. On the other hand, there were costs to the internationalization strategy—namely, the danger of setting a precedent for assistance, even if in subsequent cases (such as those not involving Mexico) that precedent was greatly watered down. We saw this dynamic at work throughout the debt crisis of the 1980s.[5]

The United States had several reasons for intervening in Mexico's financial crisis.[6] For one, the launching of NAFTA represented a hard-won victory for the Clinton administration, whose reputation in the foreign-economic-policy arena was riding on the success of the agreement. Furthermore, significant financial losses would have occurred if U.S.-based mutual and pension funds heavily invested in Mexico had been allowed

3. Part of the answer lies in the fact that it had been impossible for U.S. negotiators to provide for financial stability within NAFTA without an overt sacrifice of Mexican monetary sovereignty, as in the proposal, for example, that Mexico be made a member of the U.S. Federal Reserve Board.

4. Although international agencies helped to manage the crisis, the existence of NAFTA ensured the immediate and large-scale U.S. lead in the response. See Nora Lustig, "Mexico in Crisis, the U.S. to the Rescue: The Financial Assistance Packages of 1982 and 1995" (Brookings Discussion Papers, Brookings Institution, Washington, D.C., July 1996).

5. Stephany Griffith-Jones, *Managing World Debt* (London: Harvester Wheatsheaf, 1988), and Ngaire Woods, "Ethics and Interests in the International Political Economy: The Management of Mexican Debt, 1982–1989" (Ph.D. thesis, Oxford University, 1992).

6. Bradford De Long, Christopher De Long, and Sherman Robinson, "The Case for Mexico's Rescue: The Peso Package Looks Even Better Now," *Foreign Affairs* 75, no. 3 (1996): 8–14.

to collapse. Yet, although the political logic favoring a rescue package was compelling for Clinton-administration officials, the U.S. Congress was of another mind. The initial proposal put to Congress for a rescue package (essentially a $40 billion loan-guarantee program) was soon withdrawn when the political reaction on Capitol Hill became overtly hostile.

In the U.S. Congress, the "antirescue" lobby represented a number of different interests and groups, including budget balancers who saw the assistance package as jeopardizing efforts to reduce the U.S. budget deficit; tax cutters who more generally resented this use of taxpayers' money; those concerned about the fall of the U.S. dollar through 1994 and its further weakening in response to a bailout; free-marketeers who believed in avoiding moral hazard, preferring to leave the solution to the market; labor groups who opposed NAFTA and any measure that might strengthen it, thereby jeopardizing U.S. jobs; and, finally, a small contingent concerned about the impact of the so-called rescue on the poor in Mexico, given the explicit conditions that the Mexican government launch a massive austerity program in exchange for financial assistance of the magnitude being discussed. These antirescue sentiments were summed up most vociferously by Senator Alfonse d'Amato, chairman of the Senate Banking Committee; at its most extreme, this debate included a CATO Institute critique that called on the United States to withdraw from both the IMF and the World Bank.[7]

The emotional tone of the antiassistance forces reflected the extent to which earlier opponents of NAFTA were still alive and kicking. In opposing assistance, Ralph Nader, for example, used the same arguments he had during the NAFTA debate: that Mexico is "a political dictatorship that has long run rife with the corruption of its super-oligarchs . . . implicated in crimes, judicial cover-ups and the exploitation of public offices to amass enormous fortunes."[8] Representative Dana Rohrabacher, from the conservative Orange County district of southern California, argued, "I am extremely upset, along with other members of Congress, . . . [since] it appears that congressional authority has been circumvented in order to send tens of billions of dollars basically to a corrupt Mexican

7. W. Lee Hoskins and James W. Coons, "Mexico: Policy Failure, Moral Hazard, and Market Solutions" (Policy Analysis 243, CATO Institute, Washington D.C., 1995).

8. Ralph Nader, cited in *Report on the Mexican Economic Crisis*, presented to the Senate Committee on Banking, Housing, and Urban Affairs by Chairman Senator Alfonse d'Amato, June 29, 1995, 12.

elite and to Wall Street speculators."[9] A more moderate argument about the intrinsic flaws of the U.S.-Mexican relationship was expressed in the following terms: "There is no way to integrate two societies as disparate in economic and social and political development as are Mexico and the United States."[10]

The arguments in Congress against a rescue package for Mexico offered powerful domestic incentives for the Clinton team to move as quickly as possible in spreading the costs and responsibility of managing the crisis to international actors. Politicians who had supported NAFTA needed to prove that the close interdependence this new arrangement implied was not disastrous. Moreover, if assistance was framed too heavily as a U.S. obligation under NAFTA, it would further weaken popular support for the free-trade agreement.

In the end, the arguments in support of the assistance package were the traditional ones familiar to any student of the 1980s debt crisis. Direct financial intervention was said to be the least costly way to quell the panic in international markets and keep U.S.-Mexican relations on track. The Department of State wheeled out its standard arguments that the difficult issues called up by the peso crisis—trade, financial stability, the control of drugs, and immigration—were of immediate concern to U.S. national interests.[11]

In 1995, various special interests were also keen to support an assistance package. These included fund managers anxious to prevent a Mexican rescheduling or reissuing of government bonds, and commercial banks hoping to avert any collapse that might jeopardize their own assets and increase pressure for heavier regulation. As an aside, it is

9. House International Relations Committee, *Hearings on Economic Support for Mexico*, March 7, 1995.

10. Representative Tom Lantos, in ibid. See also Riordan Roett, "The Mexican Devaluation and the U.S. Response: Potomac Politics, 1995-Style," in *The Mexican Peso Crisis: International Perspectives*, ed. Riordan Roett (Boulder, Colo.: Lynne Rienner, 1996).

11. Undersecretary of State for Political Affairs Peter Tarnoff argued that because Mexico is the third largest U.S. trading partner, its economic stability affects U.S. exports, jobs, and investments. Because of the exposure of U.S. banks and investors, financial instability in Mexico puts international financial security at risk. Furthermore, Mexico's population of some 90 million shares a two-thousand-mile border with the United States, and therefore political and economic uncertainty in Mexico cannot but exacerbate problems of illegal migration, law enforcement, and narcotics interdiction. In contrast, political and economic cooperation facilitate the orderly management of these problems. Finally, Tarnoff argued that the United States must preserve its leadership in the Western Hemisphere. See House International Relations Committee, *Hearings on Economic Support for Mexico*.

worth noting that those who argued for intervention by the Group of Seven, or the G-7, governments and multilateral assistance in January 1995 are not necessarily still doing so in the aftermath. Fund managers, for example, reportedly having pressured the Mexican government to maintain an overvalued peso right up until the December 1994 crash,[12] were relieved to be bailed out in 1995. However, these same investors now fear that any future bailouts that involve the IFIs may subject them to some kind of involuntary "freeze" of repayments. Hence, having had their way in 1995, some now support a limited role of the IFIs in managing the crisis and a greater reliance on market discipline.

The rescue package drew heavily on the resources of the IMF and the Bank for International Settlements, as well as on Mexican compliance with a tight austerity policy and strict reporting requirements. More specifically, the final package (which constituted an alternative to that which the Clinton administration withdrew from Congress) included an IMF loan of up to $17.8 billion, amounting to nearly 700 percent of Mexico's quota in the Fund and constituting the largest loan in Fund history; a pledge of short-term bridging loans of approximately $10 billion arranged by the BIS; and assistance of up to $20 billion from the U.S. Exchange Stabilization Fund (ESF)—a fund situated in the U.S. Treasury Department that has been drawn on some six times since 1982 to provide financing to Mexico on a strictly short-term basis and one that requires no congressional approval.[13] Once the package was prepared on February 21, 1995, the U.S. secretary of the treasury entered into four agreements with the Mexican secretary of finance and public credit:

1. *The U.S.-Mexico Framework Agreement for Mexican Stabilization* defined the terms on which U.S. assistance of up to $20 billion was contingent. These included rigorous monetary, fiscal, and structural policies, including obligations to pursue negative real money growth and a budget surplus of half a percent of GDP. (Mexico had agreed to some of these terms in its January 1995 agreement with the IMF.)

12. Reports suggested that representatives of fund managers met with Mexican central bank officials and the undersecretary of finance to urge them to maintain the exchange rate in return for continued investment from the United States. See, for example, Douglas Payne, "Wall Street Blues," *New Republic*, March 13, 1995, 20. The pressures on fund managers are highlighted by Roger Taylor, "After Mexico: The Backlash," *Financial Times*, January 7, 1995, and Stephen Fidler, "The Lessons of Mexico," *Financial Times*, January 27, 1995.

13. The Mexican Debt Disclosure Act of 1995 now assures that Congress will be informed of such arrangements through a monthly report submitted by the secretary of the U.S. Treasury.

Furthermore, the Mexican authorities agreed to strict and more transparent financial reporting requirements, including monthly data on government securities and banking operations and quarterly reporting on a host of monetary aggregates such as fiscal revenues, public-sector borrowing operations, development-bank operations, and trade and balance-of-payments statistics. The interest rates on this financial package began at 2.25 percent above treasury-bill rates, which Undersecretary of Treasury Lawrence Summers referred to as "a price that recognizes and indeed substantially exceeds any possible risks." The intention was to "encourage Mexico to return as rapidly as possible to private market sources for capital."[14]

2. *The Medium-Term Exchange Stabilization Agreement* authorized Mexico and the United States to purchase and repurchase Mexican pesos and U.S. dollars using ESF resources. Maturities for the medium-term swaps were provided for up to five years. Some $1.5 billion was also disbursed from the Federal Reserve for short-term swaps.

3. *The Guarantee Agreement* authorized the U.S. Treasury (through the ESF) to guarantee the payment of the principal and interest on Mexican debt securities of up to ten years' maturity.

4. *The Oil Proceed Facility Agreement* required PEMEX, the Mexican state-run oil company, to give irrevocable instructions to its foreign customers to direct payments owed to Mexico for oil purchases to the United States, in the event that Mexico failed to repay the United States under any of the financing agreements.

Despite the ultimate definition of the Mexican peso crisis as international, these agreements reveal the dominance of U.S. preferences in the overall rescue plan. The stringency of the terms pressed upon Mexico, particularly with respect to the Oil Proceed Facility, was more expressly bilateral and tougher than any of the agreements negotiated during the 1980s. Yet, as in the 1980s, the United States could still rely on the IMF to monitor these policies. Herein lay an important reason for internationalizing the crisis. If these conditions had been imposed explicitly within a NAFTA framework, the United States would have borne the financial brunt of the bailout, and there certainly would have been a larger reac-

---

14. See the testimony of Undersecretary of State Peter Tarnoff and Undersecretary of the Treasury Lawrence Summers in House International Relations Committee, *Hearings on Economic Support for Mexico.*

tion against the United States within Mexico. Yet, the involvement of the IMF lessened the economic burden for the United States while also reinforcing the strict program of economic reform that had to be undertaken in order for Mexico to receive multilateral assistance. This obviated the need for deeper NAFTA institutions within which Mexico might or would have had a stronger voice. It also demonstrated that further conditions would have to be imposed on Mexico if integration were to continue smoothly. In other words, integration would not follow automatically from those measures which Mexico had already undertaken (an assumption about which I say more below).

An International Mechanism for Crisis Management

The internationalization of Mexico's crisis had one less felicitous implication for the United States: it gave impetus to the idea of creating an international mechanism for managing future crises. Such a mechanism had been proposed by the IMF's managing director, Michel Camdessus, to the IMF Executive Board in September 1994. Camdessus wanted to create a new "Short-Term Financing Facility" that would permit countries access of up to 300 percent of their quota for up to three months in order to send a signal of confidence to the markets—with the proviso that only countries with a sound policy record and no fundamental balance-of-payments problem would be able to draw on the facility. Naturally, as the managing director was quick to point out, the Fund would need more resources to set up such a mechanism. After the Mexican rescue, the idea reemerged at the Halifax Summit of the seven leading industrialized countries in June 1995 under the heading of an Emergency Financing Facility, along with a proposal to double the Fund's resources to more than $50 billion. And indeed the G-7 soon endorsed a plan to create a new emergency financing mechanism along these lines.

The Fund, of course, had its own interests in bailing out Mexico, but I would argue that the proposal for an Emergency Financing Facility also highlights the Fund's interest in backing U.S.-determined priorities. Similar to the evolution of the debt strategy throughout the 1980s, Mexico's 1995 crisis gave the Fund a chance to carve out a more prominent role for itself and claim additional financial resources. But beneath the bureaucratic facade of the IMF's role in the Mexican bailout lay political tensions and compromises that suggest there will be strong limitations on the repeat of any such "rescue" in the future.

In the first place, there was considerable disagreement among the industrialized countries that make up the board of the IMF with regard to the Mexican rescue. In the vote to authorize the Fund's $17.8 billion contribution to the Mexican assistance package, for example, both Germany and Britain abstained. The implication is that even if an adequate fund existed within the IMF, there is a real question whether the core group of industrialized countries would agree on where and when to use it. The case of Mexico illustrates only that when U.S. interests are at stake, the Fund can be cajoled into action, since the United States is quite willing to "push and shove" on the board until it gets its way.[15] The next time around, particularly if U.S. interests are not directly involved, it simply is not clear whether a consensus will be reached on the use of the planned Emergency Financing Facility. The more recent Asian financial crisis is a case in point.

In the second place, there is a real limitation on the potential effectiveness of the proposed emergency-assistance fund, and that is its size. The Fund's proposal recognizes that its largest contributor, the United States, is reluctant to increase its contributions to the organization. And so a compromise figure has been arrived at that would almost certainly be inadequate. As one economist notes, in June 1995 the United States, Germany, and Japan spent $20 billion in a single day to defend the dollar, and during the European exchange-rate crisis of 1992, the German Bundesbank mobilized some $130 billion in defense of six European currencies whose combined IMF quotas came to $23 billion. Under the proposed 300 percent rule, these countries could have drawn only $70 billion from the Fund under its emergency financing mechanism.[16] The limited funds available for the IMF to use in a crisis highlight yet again the tension in U.S. policy between using the IFIs to promote foreign-policy goals and having to accept that this use requires a much greater allocation of financial resources for these institutions.

The rescue package and subsequent emergency financing mechanism were just one part of the international response to Mexico's financial crisis. The other response concerned foreseeing and preventing such crises in the future. In this second part of the response, there was an im-

15. This phrasing is cited from a confidential interview with an IMF board member.

16. E.V.K. Fitzgerald, *Intervention Versus Regulation: The Role of the IMF in Crisis Prevention and Management* (Oxford: Queen Elizabeth House, 1995).

plicit attribution of blame for Mexico's crisis, and in this too, the IFIS were brought to center stage.

The Role of the IMF in Preventing Future Crises

At the Halifax Summit in June 1995, President Clinton stressed the need to identify crises and to strengthen the international capacity to respond to them. He and the other leaders present called not just for an emergency financing mechanism but also for more "rigorous surveillance" of potentially high-risk countries, including requirements that they disclose critical monetary and financial information.[17]

These proposals reflect a particular interpretation of the Mexican crisis, and one that deflected attention from (1) the need to establish NAFTA institutions, (2) the need to regulate investors, and (3) the possible fallibility of the economic reforms undertaken by Mexico in the late 1980s and early 1990s. The official interpretation of the crisis implicitly blamed inadequate information and crisis management within the Mexican government;[18] from this flowed proposals for better monitoring and the development of an early-warning system to detect signs of crisis. The first candidate seized upon for (and that seized upon) this role was the IMF. Yet, despite signs throughout 1994 that the Mexican economy was running into significant difficulties, neither the IMF nor the World Bank seemed to recognize this—or, if they did, their doubts were not acknowledged publicly.[19] What, then, constrained these institutions, and could they play a different and more active role in identifying and preventing future crises? The Mexican crisis highlights several aspects of the workings of these institutions that severely inhibit their capacity to serve as part of an "early-warning system" for financial crises in their member countries. My analysis thus suggests that the IFIS cannot be expected to play such a role.

17. Chairman's Statement, Halifax Summit, June 17, 1995; Press Briefings, Office of the Press Secretary, White House, June 16, 1995; and Economic Communiqué, Halifax Summit, June 1995.

18. For alternative interpretations, see Francisco Gil-Díaz and Agustin Carstens, "One Year of Solitude: Some Pilgrim Tales About Mexico's 1994–1995 Crisis," *American Economic Review* 86, no. 2 (1996):164–69, and Guillermo A. Calvo and Enrique G. Mendoza, "Petty Crime and Cruel Punishment: Lessons from the Mexican Debacle," *American Economic Review* 86, no. 2 (1996): 170–75.

19. The IMF has since conducted its own inquiry into the Mexican crisis, and both the Bank and Fund have published "official" accounts in their annual publications. See IMF, *International Capital Markets: Developments, Prospects, and Policy Issues* (Washington D.C.: IMF, 1995).

IFIs and Their Members

A first important constraint on the capacity of the IFIS to act as crisis monitors emerges simply from their structure and rules.[20] In all their endeavors, the IMF and the World Bank rely upon the cooperation and openness of their member countries. Although both organizations have various instruments of leverage, they have no automatic right of entry into the financial affairs of member countries. Rather, they must persuade governments to give them access to confidential statistics and sensitive policy documents. Once granted access, the IFIS must use this information very carefully in order to ensure that good relations continue. An example of this delicate balancing act occurred on the eve of the debt crisis in 1981, when the World Bank was about to publish a report expressing some reservations about Mexican economic policy; the Mexican government, having gotten wind of the report, dispatched Carlos Salinas de Gortari (then a junior finance official) to Washington to stress that any negative comments on the Bank's part would surely catalyze the pending crisis. The final report reflected a more positive interpretation of the state of the Mexican economy, even if there was little real cause for optimism.

In short, it is difficult to see how the Fund and the Bank might publish more statistics or give clearer warnings to the international financial community without breaching the confidentiality required by governments in return for access to their ministries of finance and planning and their central banks. In subsequent negotiations, governments would simply close off access to the necessary information—something that happened frequently during the 1980s in countries such as Brazil and Peru, thus preventing the IFIS from performing their most basic functions. If such an early-warning system were required within the NAFTA economy, a differently structured institution would need to undertake this role—an institution in which the question of access would not be so sensitive.

Reputation and Credibility

After the 1994 peso crisis in Mexico, many accused the Fund (and to a lesser extent the Bank) of not having given an early (or, for that matter, even a late) warning of the impending crisis. These critics argued that

---

20. A good account of decision-making strengths and weaknesses is given in Ian Clark, "Should the IMF Become More Adaptive?" (IMF Working Paper, Washington, D.C., 1996).

the Fund has a responsibility to monitor and inform the international financial community about events in the world economy, especially incipient trends that could threaten international financial stability. Moreover, since both the Fund and the Bank are in the business of providing a "stamp of approval" for their member economies, these institutions ostensibly bear the responsibility for informing the financial community of events or changes that might negate this approval rating.

Such arguments are sometimes made disingenuously, evading the fact that, if either institution did publicize a warning along the lines mentioned above, this would no doubt trigger a crisis whether or not one was in the making. But there is yet another problem with charging the international institutions with this duty. The IFIs are under constant pressure to justify their deployment of resources and to protect their reputation. And here Mexico provides an excellent example. Both the Bank and the Fund had committed significant resources to Mexico in the early 1990s, placing their credibility directly on the line. Tables 4.1 and 4.2 illustrate the level of IFI resources committed to Mexico, which were higher than for any other country.

The reforms undertaken by Mexico during the late 1980s and early 1990s had been perceived by many within the international financial community, including the World Bank and IMF, as "spectacular, lasting, and the envy of any reform economy."[21] Mexico's efforts to project itself

Table 4.1. Mexico's total IMF credit and loans outstanding

	1992	1993	1994	1995
Total in SDRs (millions)	4,683.6	4,231.1	3,327.1	7,765.7
% of Mexico's quota	401.8	241.3	189.8	442.9

SOURCE: IMF, *International Financial Statistics,* 1992–95.

Table 4.2. Mexico's total loans from the IBRD

	1990	1991	1992	1993	1994
Total loans					
(thousands of US$)	13,548,537	14,389,480	15,830,000	16,108,000	17,287,000
% of Total IBRD					
loans outstanding	11.39	11.61	11.91	11.86	11.93

SOURCE: World Bank, *Annual Reports,* 1990–94.

21. Rudiger Dornbusch and Alejandro Werner, "Mexico: Stabilization, Reform, and No Growth," *Brookings Papers on Economic Activity,* no. 1 (1994): 266.

as a role model for other developing countries is reflected in *Economic Transformation: The Mexican Way,* the account by former Mexican finance minister Pedro Aspe of Mexico's "recipe for success."[22] The involvement of the IFIs in (and the commitment of their resources to) Mexico was a sign of their confidence that the country had hit its economic stride and would continue to implement liberalizing reforms to good effect.

The figures in Tables 4.1 and 4.2 reveal the extent of the IFIs' stake in Mexico's ongoing success. Not only would a warning or pessimistic note from the Bank or the Fund risk triggering a crisis in international financial markets; even worse, it would signal a failure of the IFIs' long-running policy of persuading countries to liberalize and deregulate their economies. Indeed, in the wake of Mexico's crisis, other countries, such as Brazil, India, and South Korea, have argued for more gradual and flexible approaches to reform, pointing to the failure of IFI prescriptions in Mexico.[23] During the crisis of 1994, the IFIs had their reputations on the line, and this, I would argue, influenced their judgment.[24] Furthermore, the IFIs' interpretation of and stake in Mexico's success reflected a more broadly held belief that neoliberal economic reforms were sufficient to set in train a smooth process of integration within NAFTA. This was the assumption that the crisis of 1994 proved untrue. The constraint on the IFIs' judgment, however, goes much deeper, as elaborated below.

Orthodoxy Within the IFIs

A third and final constraint on the IFIs contributed to reinforce the view that Mexico's policy reforms were enough to further a spontaneous process of integration. The IMF had long persisted in the orthodoxy upon which this assumption was founded, despite its very mixed returns. Since their founding in the 1940s, both the Fund and the Bank have

22. In *Economic Transformation: The Mexican Way* (Cambridge, Mass.: MIT Press, Lionel Robbins Lectures, 1993), Pedro Aspe describes the "profound transformation of the economy" that rendered it in 1993 "much better prepared to face the uncertainties of a rapidly changing and challenging world and to respond more effectively to the social needs of our population" (xiii).

23. Brazil is making this argument before many institutions in Washington. On India and South Korea, see David Hale, "Lessons from the Mexican Crisis of 1995 for the Post–Cold War International Order" (draft chapter for *The World Bank Report on Mexico,* February 1996), 2 and 21.

24. For a public-choice analysis of the incentives and pressures faced by actors within the IMF, see Roland Vaubel, "The Political Economy of the International Monetary Fund," in *The Political Economy of International Organizations,* ed. Roland Vaubel and Thomas Willett (Boulder, Colo.: Westview Press, 1991).

been bound institutionally by a particular way of thinking that has permeated the internal structure and operation of these organizations. The institutionalization of orthodoxy has made it extremely difficult for staff to challenge the mainstream view or to offer alternatives—another telling comment on the weaknesses of the IFIs when it comes to monitoring economic crises. With regard to the Mexican crisis, for example, we might recall that throughout 1994 some highly respected economists were insisting on the need for a major macroeconomic adjustment.[25] Again, most warnings focused on the overvaluation of the peso, the lack of growth, and increased fragility in monetary and exchange-rate policy. After the crisis, Sebastian Edwards—a senior World Bank official at the time of Mexico's crisis—argued, "What is to some extent intriguing . . . is not that the Mexican economy faced a major currency crisis, but that so many observers were shocked by this turn of events." In his view, the "prophetically similar crisis" suffered by Chile in the 1970s should have alerted officials.[26]

Yet, while questions about the sustainability of Mexico's reforms were being debated by prominent economists, there was an overwhelming tendency in the international financial community to "go" with the success story. Along with credit-rating agencies and many private financial institutions, the IFIs held fast to the view that the appreciation of the Mexican currency was a natural companion to capital inflows and foreign investment, reflecting simply a high rate of absorption in the Mexican economy.[27] According to this view, the burgeoning current-account deficit and mounting dollar-denominated debts were not a problem so long as they were being financed by the private sector.

Overall, the optimism of the IFIs rested on the belief that Mexico's successful program of stabilization, privatization, and deregulation, now formally institutionalized within NAFTA, gave Mexico the credibility and

25. See Dornbusch and Werner, "Mexico: Stabilization, Reform, and No Growth," and the comments by Guillermo Calvo, which follow this article in the same issue, 298–303. While Dornbusch and Werner advocated an immediate currency devaluation, Calvo called for a stabilization arrangement with the U.S. Treasury.

26. Sebastian Edwards, "Exchange-Rate Anchors, Credibility, and Inertia: A Tale of Two Crises, Chile and Mexico," *American Economic Review* 86, no. 2 (1996): 176–80.

27. See the private-investors' forecasts cited in Hale, "Lessons from the Mexican Crisis of 1995 for the Post–Cold War International Order." World Bank and IMF views are recounted in Sebastian Edwards, *Crisis and Reform in Latin America: From Despair to Hope* (New York: Oxford University Press, 1995), and the IMF Country Report following Article IV consultations with Mexico, January 1994.

strength necessary for weathering temporary difficulties. The maintenance of this view, despite some very convincing evidence to the contrary, can be ascribed to two factors. First, the belief of the IFIS and of
the wider international financial community in Mexico's success constituted a self-defeating form of "groupthink." Second, although we might
expect the IFIS as public entities to be less susceptible to this tendency,
in fact their rigid organizational structure militates against bucking the
prevalent orthodox view. I elaborate on these factors below.

Groupthink Within the International Financial Community and the IFIS

Many outsiders see the Fund and the Bank as institutions with large,
professional staffs of economists whose role it is to present independent
and objective analyses. Unlike private-sector investors, whose technical
expertise is devoted to analyzing returns on investment, the IFIS are
also charged with independent monitoring and reporting on micro- and
macroeconomic-policy trends in their member countries. One might thus
expect the IFIS to be a step removed from the dynamics of groupthink
that are exhibited in the marketplace by private investors. Yet, the IFIS
seem as vulnerable to this phenomenon as other members of the international financial community.

Research into the dynamics of groups involved in decision making
reveals that dissent becomes particularly difficult because groups with
shared beliefs form "illusions of invulnerability" and "illusions of unanimity."[28] The former causes the policy-making group to become overly
optimistic and more willing to take greater risks than any one individual
of the group would be. The latter causes the group to rationalize and
justify decisions—no matter what they might be—and to screen out
warnings and counterinformation that might lead to a reconsideration
of decisions. Any individual prone to counterargument is likely to be
pressured into self-censorship.

Group illusions, it has been argued, capture an important dynamic
within the Fund and the Bank, as well as within the wider international

---

28. Early research on these trends is found in *Group Dynamics: Research and Theory*, ed. Dorwin
Cartwright and Alvin Zander (Evanston, Ill.: Row, Peterson, 1953). The specifics referred to here
derive from the work of Irving Janis, who investigated major foreign-policy decisions such as the
Bay of Pigs invasion in 1961, the setting up of the Marshall Plan, and the decision to escalate the
war in Vietnam. See Irving Janis, *Groupthink* (Boston: Houghton Mifflin, 1982).

financial community.[29] Indeed, this group dynamic extends to the small number of finance officials in countries where the international financial community is deeply involved, such as Mexico. The result is a circle of officials who are jointly committed to a particular set of beliefs and reforms. During the 1980s an elite cadre of technocrats in Mexico had come to believe that the country had gotten the economic fundamentals "right" and that therefore nothing serious could go wrong if the overall policy direction was maintained. In such an atmosphere it was all too easy for standards of evidence within the group to slide.[30] Within this context, the insights of groupthink point to an interface of psychology and group process that explains why it was so difficult for any member to conceive of, let alone voice, doubts about Mexico's policy and prospects—even when faced with solid evidence of fragility and risk.

This analysis is borne out by the way in which the IFIs responded to trends that challenged the optimistic scenario for Mexico. For example, the Fund's Country Report on Mexico of January 1994 recognized some danger signs: that the Mexican exchange rate was appreciating and that net capital inflows to the public sector were increasing. Yet, the report concluded that such a small appreciation "would not affect export competitiveness significantly because of the positive effects of the structural reforms." Later in this same report, Fund staff observed that "[d]uring 1993 the peso continued to appreciate in real effective terms as customarily measured and eroded further the margin obtained in the 1980s. However, the strong expansion in manufacturing exports would indicate that the structural reforms in recent years and wage restraint have compensated so far."[31] Here, as well as in a raft of other Fund and Bank publications, we find the belief in Mexico's reform process buttressing optimistic accounts of Mexico's prospects and obscuring warnings or evidence to the contrary.

29. See the convergence in various forecasts made by major financial and investment institutions in the latter half of 1994, such as Robert S. Gay, "Looking Beyond the Haze into 1995," *Perspectives on Emerging Markets* (Bankers Trust Research), November 7, 1994, and David Malpass, "Latin America Outlook 1995," *Bear Stearns Global Development*, November 16, 1994. These are analyzed in David Hale, "Lessons from the Mexican Crisis of 1995 for the Post–Cold War International Order."

30. Indeed, officials on all sides whom I have interviewed spoke of a growing "trust and confidence" among the IFI staff and Mexican policy makers. This meant, to cite one official, that "the *i*'s no longer had to be dotted and the *t*'s no longer had to be crossed." For a deeper elaboration of the 1994 process of decision making and its flaws, see Ngaire Woods, "Getting It Wrong: Groupthink, the IMF, the World Bank, and Mexico's 1994 Crisis" (Oxford University, 1997).

31. IMF Country Report, January 1994, 7 and 12.

Although the IFIs have a large staff of highly trained and intelligent economists, there is a group dynamic at work that prevents alternative views from being expressed. Furthermore, the process by which views are mediated within these organizations serves to prevent dissenting opinions from surfacing.

Organization and Hierarchy Within the IFIs

The intellectual and professional climate of the IFIs has been described as "closed" and "hierarchical," as indicative of "a class structure in which people rise and self-promote." In the words of one World Bank official, "The ethos of the Bank is that no one challenges his supervisor, there is no room for boat rocking."[32] This comment is borne out by the findings of contributors to the World Bank History Project, who argue that the hierarchical way in which both the Bank and the Fund are run ensures that particular ideas are perpetuated and that change is top-down.[33] This view is reinforced by Pedro-Pablo Kuczynski, a banker and analyst who works closely with the IMF. He writes of the Fund as having a deliberate policy of keeping its staff small, with low turnover; although this has been a source of sound research, it also has meant that the staff are slow to "experiment and innovate."[34] This undervaluation of critical or alternative thinking is illustrated by an episode that occurred before Mexico's 1982 debt crisis: a young Chilean economist working on the World Bank's Mexico team dared to take an alternative (very pessimistic, and in retrospect correct) line on Mexico, only to find himself swiftly moved off the team and into another area of the Bank.[35]

Conformity in thinking within the IMF and the World Bank has both political and organizational underpinnings. At a practical level, the fact

32. Cited by Donald R. Sherk, "Emerging Markets and the Multilateral Development Banks," *Columbia Journal of World Business* 29, no. 2 (1994): 52 n. 19.

33. Furthermore, the authors highlight the homogeneity of staff appointed, reporting that some 80 percent of high-level staff in the Policy, Research, and External Affairs Department of the Bank in 1991 had trained in economics and finance at institutions in the United States and the United Kingdom. See Nicholas Stern (with Francisco Ferreira), "The World Bank as 'Intellectual Actor'" (Development Economics Research Programme Discussion Paper, DEP/50, STICERD, London School of Economics, 1993). So too in the IMF: some 90 percent of staff with Ph.D.'s received them from universities in the United States and Canada. See Clark, "Should the IMF Become More Adaptive?"

34. Pedro-Pablo Kuczynski, *Latin American Debt* (Baltimore: John Hopkins University Press, 1988), 124.

35. This episode was related to me by three Bank officials who were involved with Mexico at the time or shortly thereafter.

that these organizations assign junior officials to field offices in countries all over the world necessitates a clear, standardized framework for analyzing economic performance and for prescribing the most appropriate adjustment policies. The content of this framework, however, is politically determined. At the head of each organization sits an executive board, and within this board—more often than not—the preferences of the U.S. government have prevailed. This is not to say that all decisions of the IFIs are influenced by the United States. Rather, where decisions touch upon U.S. interests, the preferences of the United States frequently will determine the outcome. This is illustrated both in major shifts in philosophy within the IFIs as well as in lesser policy changes.[36]

For example, in the 1980s, the Reagan administration stamped on the mandates of both organizations an emphasis on the private sector and a tougher neoliberal reform agenda. So, too, neither the Fund nor the Bank moved on debt reduction until U.S. Secretary of Treasury Nicholas Brady gave the go-ahead in 1989.

The argument here is not a theory of conspiracy. Indeed, that type of argument would link the IFIs' underplaying of Mexico's problems in 1994 with the U.S. Treasury's suppression of negative reports about Mexico, suggesting that all were acting on behalf of powerful U.S. economic interests. (The U.S. Treasury, it has been alleged, was trying to bolster the strong peso in order to maintain high levels of U.S. exports to Mexico and prevent an increase in imports, which would inflame the anti-NAFTA lobby.)[37] Rather, the IFIs were caught up in a groupthink process that held neoliberal orthodoxy as the unquestionably "correct" policy course; this orthodoxy has gone unchallenged because of its close integration into the IFIs' hierarchical organizational structures and daily professional practices. The orthodoxy is important to our understanding of NAFTA because it assured all parties that integration could proceed on the basis of policy changes that had already been undertaken.

As mentioned at the outset of this chapter, Mexico's December 1994 crisis was attributed partly to poor information and monitoring of the Mexican economy. From this diagnosis followed proposals that the IFIS

---

36. Miles Kahler, "The United States and the International Monetary Fund: Declining Influence or Declining Interest?" in *The United States and Multilateral Institutions,* ed. Margaret Karns and Karen Mingst (Boston: Unwin Hyman, 1990). For a more historical view of U.S. power in the IMF, see Frank Southard, "The Evolution of the International Monetary Fund" (Essays in International Finance 135, Department of Economics, Princeton University, 1979).

37. See Senator d'Amato, *Report on the Mexican Economic Crisis.*

should play a greater role in the transmission of information to the international financial community. Yet, even if we accept this interpretation of Mexico's crisis, several factors impede both the Fund and the Bank from effectively monitoring the economies on which they work. In the first place, the IFIS' modus operandi, coupled with concern for their reputation and the credibility of their economic prescriptions, impedes objective analysis of emerging market economies. In the second place, the IFIS are not immune to the groupthink that influences other members of the international financial community. Indeed the very structure and hierarchy of these institutions has been framed around the tenets of neoliberal orthodoxy, which groupthink processes have reinforced. These factors provide strong reasons why financial crises such as that of Mexico in 1994–95 will not be prevented by additional monitoring and reporting undertaken or facilitated by the international financial institutions. If institutions for monitoring and crisis management are necessary within the NAFTA economy (and the experience of 1994–95 suggests they are), then the parties to the agreement need to develop these institutions themselves.

Conclusion

Mexico's financial crisis of 1994–95 has been interpreted in a variety of ways, many of them self-serving. Some other developing countries have taken it as an indictment of neoliberal adjustment and reform. The Mexican government continues to blame the external sector and the volatility of capital flows. Investment institutions, anxious to avoid any further regulation, insist that the crisis stemmed from inadequate information and secretive Mexican economic policy. The U.S. government, rather than admit to any institutional or policy flaws intrinsic to NAFTA, immediately cast the crisis in international as opposed to regional terms and sought a solution that directly involved the IFIS. Called to active duty, the IMF seized the opportunity to expand its role and increase its resources by pushing for a new emergency financing mechanism.

The prevailing interpretation in Washington has focused on the need for more information and realistic assessments of economies at risk and on the need to coordinate assistance when a crisis poses a threat to international financial stability. Yet I have argued that the proposed solutions fall far short and place demands on the IFIS that they were not designed to meet. In fact, the politics and structure of both the IMF and the World Bank contributed to their failure to foresee the Mexican crisis. Their subsequent participation in providing exceptional assistance to Mexico, far from paving the way for an international emergency financing mechanism, simply mirrored their largest shareholder's political priorities. More profoundly, the 1994 crisis demonstrated the shallowness of the assumption that NAFTA could proceed without deeper integration or institutions.

Part II Assessing the Impact:
Jobs, Immigration, Drugs,
and Politics

5 The Impact of Mexico's Trade Liberalization

Jobs, Productivity, and Structural Change

Jonathan E. Heath

Mexico has undergone dramatic changes during the past decade. Profound economic and political reforms are taking place that will transform the country permanently. This reorganization of Mexican society is comparable in magnitude to other key moments in Mexico's history, such as the independence from Spain, the battle for reform led by Benito Juarez, or the revolution of 1910. The economy is shifting from an inward-looking, highly protected, import-substitution development model, to one that is outward-looking and market-oriented. The political system is slowly evolving from an authoritarian regime with little regard for the rule of law to a more democratic society. This transition is taking place within a society plagued by an extremely skewed distribution of income, as evidenced by the existence of huge belts of poverty throughout the country.

Change has been so rapid that it is hard to use the

word "evolution"; "revolution" seems more appropriate. At the core of this revolution are several simultaneous transformations. On a worldwide level, technological innovation has been advancing at a rapid pace, causing fundamental improvements in productivity as countries adapt more automated technologies. The downside has been a systematic increase in unemployment rates in many countries. On a regional level, developing countries (especially in Latin America) are struggling to reduce government intervention and to foster a development model based on higher growth and greater equity. This change has been induced by the general failure of past policies on these fronts and by the fall of the Berlin Wall, which further delegitimated state-led policies. On a national level, Mexico is undergoing the transition from a closed to an open economy, with immense implications for employment, efficiency, and resource allocation. Politically, the country is trying to introduce the rule of law, true federalism, and a balanced structure of power, following sixty-five years of absolute control by the ruling Revolutionary Institutional Party (PRI). All this coincides with a severe recession in which the economy is at the trough of a pronounced business cycle.

The transformation of the Mexican economy has tremendous implications. At the macroeconomic level, the reduction of large fiscal deficits implies an end to cross-subsidies and price distortions and introduces a new set of priorities in public expenditures. At the sectoral level, the privatization process and broad deregulation efforts have shifted the standing of each sector vis-à-vis the others. Industrial conversion, or the adaptation of new technologies under a more open economy, has become a necessity. Most large firms, which have better access to capital, already have advanced substantially in this area, while medium and small firms have remained stagnant and dependent on outdated technologies. In a much more competitive environment, the death rate of these firms has increased considerably, as the survival-of-the-fittest rule separates the efficient from the inefficient. Although this process is viewed not only as natural but also as necessary for Mexico's future economic strength, the complicated political environment has slowed the pace of adjustment.

The move from a closed to an open economy is not simply a matter of eliminating quantitative restrictions, reducing trade tariffs, and doing away with nontariff barriers. Rather, it is an extremely complex transformation of technologies, administrative processes, values, and ways of thinking. The Mexican entrepreneurial spirit, along with labor relations and the role of the government in society, must undergo major changes. This process takes time, and Mexico has, at best, now reached the midpoint of this transformation. Michael Bruno warned of this struggle almost ten years ago, when he wrote, "[T]he transition strategy from a pre-reform regime to a post-reform open economy is more important than the choice of the end product."[1] Bruno was referring in particular to the sizable unemployment costs that would be incurred during the transition period if policy makers did not tread carefully—a warning that, as this analysis shows, was not heeded by Mexican policy makers.

Where Mexico stands within the transformation now under way must be understood in order to evaluate the current state of the economy and to appreciate the country's long-term possibilities. High unemployment, low growth, a banking crisis, business fragility, and many other current issues cannot be examined adequately outside of this transitional context. While criticisms of the so-called neoliberal policies that Mexico has been applying are increasing sharply on the domestic front, it is still too early to judge the move to an open economy, especially since Mexico's *apertura* (opening) has yet to be completed. Given the lack of any viable alternatives, a more valid line of criticism would question the specifics of the adjustment process and not its necessity. Should the opening of the economy have been so sudden? Should the government have taken a more active role in helping firms adjust to the new competitive environment? Was a more explicit industrial policy necessary? Did the government anticipate and adequately address the true costs of adjustment? Was the exchange-rate policy appropriate under the circumstances? Was more aggressive political reform warranted at an earlier stage?

The purpose of this chapter is to probe these questions from a microeconomic standpoint, with a focus on the multiple changes that have occurred at the sectoral and firm level. My main hypothesis is that Mexico's trade liberalization has had a fundamental impact on the majority of firms, causing major changes in their way of doing business. The short-term impact, on balance, has been negative, given the sharp increase in unemployment and the high level of mortality among firms. Moreover, most firms are struggling to understand the new rules of the game as the

---

1. Michael Bruno, "Opening Up: Liberalization with Stabilization," in *The Open Economy: Tools for Policymakers in Developing Countries,* ed. Rudiger Dornbusch and Leslie Helmers, EDI Series in Economic Development (Washington, D.C.: Oxford University Press for the World Bank, 1988), 224.

old protectionist scheme is slowly dismantled. Unfortunately, these initial costs have been an unavoidable part of Mexico's transformation into a more efficient, competitive economy, and a necessary condition for net job creation once the transition to a market model is completed. The long-term impact, however, must be positive as inefficiency gives way to a more competitive industrial base.

My analysis is presented in five parts: first, the original expectations of trade liberalization are explored as a reference point for examining the outcomes thus far; second, the effects on employment and productivity are examined, given their central importance to this transition; third, different regulatory reforms and their impact on the economy are discussed; fourth, structural changes within different economic sectors are examined; finally, conclusions are drawn concerning the significance of these developments for the individual firm.

Mexican Trade Liberalization: Policy Makers' Initial Expectations

Toward the end of the 1960s, Mexico began questioning the validity of its development model. While impressive for having generated three decades of high growth, this model also had fostered a pattern of deteriorating income distribution. It had become clear that economic prosperity was benefiting only a small portion of the population, while the majority of Mexicans were seeing little increase in their standard of living. Since the early 1940s, the development strategy that created these income disparities has been based on the expansion of an incipient industrial sector in a country that was predominantly rural and agricultural.

The classic infant-industry argument was used to justify a highly protectionist scheme with multiple state subsidies. The industrial growth that followed brought with it rapid urbanization and a quick displacement of agricultural employment in favor of both industry and services. In spite of strong industrial growth, the combination of very high population growth and sprawling urbanization made it difficult for the industrial sector to create enough jobs. Thus the service sector emerged as a residual absorber of excess labor, although with very low paying and unproductive activities.

When President Luis Echeverria took office in December 1970, it was felt that the government should take an even more active role in the economy and that the improvement of income distribution and the reduction of poverty should be its primary goal. However, under this aggressive interventionist approach, public expenditures increased without a concomitant increase in revenues, provoking inflation and external imbalance through a growing current-account deficit. These imbalances were exacerbated by the protectionist nature of the import-substitution model, which created high rates of return on domestic investment and production, but low rates of return on exports, since Mexican products could not compete effectively in international markets. As a result, exports as a percentage of GDP decreased steadily between 1940 and 1982.[2] The decline in export revenue forced Mexico to borrow abroad in order to finance its growing current-account deficit, which led to an increasing debt-service burden.

As the government's presence in the economy grew, the number of public enterprises expanded dramatically. In order to reduce unemployment, the state took on the obligation of buying any firm or business that was going bankrupt, while at the same time creating new firms. Public tariffs and utility fees were kept artificially low in order to alleviate financial hardship on the bulk of the population. Finally, the wages and salaries of public employees were raised as a means of improving income distribution. Because no revenue adjustments were made to offset expenditure outlays, the public deficit increased ever more rapidly. At the same time, the financing of the current-account deficit became more difficult, and foreign-exchange reserves began to dwindle. Not surprisingly, Mexico had no other choice but to devalue the currency in 1976, after twenty-two years of a fixed exchange rate.

As early as 1976, it was obvious that Mexico needed to implement major changes in its economic strategy. Although the previous strategy had sufficed for over three decades, it was no longer viable. What was needed was an approach that could generate foreign exchange in order to finance a growing demand for imports and complement a low domestic savings rate. However, instead of opening up the economy and encouraging export-led growth, Mexico relied on large new oil reserves in the context of increasing world oil prices. While oil revenues helped Mexico

---

2. This trend applies mainly to non-oil exports, since oil exports started to grow substantially in 1977.

grow for five more years and created extraordinary leverage for foreign borrowing, in hindsight it is clear that this only postponed the necessary structural changes.[3]

When oil prices fell in 1982, at a time of record-high world interest rates, the Mexican economy found itself in a much worse situation than it had faced in 1976. Both inflation and the public deficit had grown substantially, and the current-account deficit and debt-service burden were far above previous levels. The number of public enterprises had risen, along with the number of unproductive state employees. Unfortunately, the government responded to the financial crash of August 1982 with measures that only complicated Mexico's recovery and the possibilities for structural change, while strongly undermining faith in the authorities' ability to weather the crisis successfully. Dollar-denominated bank accounts were frozen and converted forcibly into pesos at a below-market exchange rate. Foreign-debt-service payments were suspended temporarily, while a renegotiation of the terms of the debt was forced upon the international banking community. Exchange controls were introduced and private banks expropriated. Public confidence was exhausted, as huge levels of capital flight made clear.

In 1983, beginning with the administration of Miguel de la Madrid, Mexico finally faced the enormous challenge of undertaking a major structural transformation of its economy. The initial difficulty was to reduce both the fiscal and the external deficits, while finding a viable source of foreign exchange that would not only permit Mexico to continue servicing its debt, but also enable a return to sustained economic growth. The logical choice was to liberalize the economy, which involved the elimination of price distortions, export barriers, and government intervention.[4] However, the shift to a more market-oriented economy was much more complex than originally thought. Most government officials were convinced of the necessity of change, but no immediate consensus appeared regarding its direction or pace. Should Mexico open all markets through a type of shock treatment, or should the country's exposure to greater competition be more gradual? If liberalization was to be gradual, which markets should be liberalized first? How much liberalization was necessary?

---

3. Miguel de la Madrid, "Doce años de cambios en México," *Este País,* no. 53 (August 1995).

4. This approach later became known as the "Washington consensus"—a phrase coined by John Williamson in 1990.

These questions emerged within a society that had been under heavy state sponsorship for decades. The political system had fed on government controls and regulations as a means for power sharing among the elite. This meant that any type of deregulation or liberalization would diminish the government's hold on power, while generating enormous opposition from the existing political structure. Thus Mexico initiated its first phase of structural change timidly and with great reserve.

When examining the results of structural adjustment between 1983 and 1987, little improvement is evident. Although inflation averaged 102 percent in 1983, by the end of 1987 it had risen to 159 percent. The public deficit represented 16.9 percent of GDP in 1983 and 16.0 percent in 1987. Growth for the period averaged a negative 0.3 percent per year. Foreign debt was restructured three times. The financial crisis deprived Mexico of all voluntary international lending, forcing the economy to maintain a current-account surplus in order to finance its capital account. The resulting exchange-rate policy of sustaining an undervalued currency exacerbated inflation. This meant that Mexico maintained a steady capital transfer abroad, limiting domestic investment possibilities. One of the main implications was that it took the industrial sector 105 months (almost nine years) to be able to reach a higher level of production than that achieved toward the end of 1981.

Although certain structural changes were initiated in 1983, both the pace and scope were limited. The privatization process began slowly and was limited to marginal firms. Deregulation was unconvincing and fiscal retrenchment unsuccessful. Uncertainty about the direction and commitment of reform during this period only delayed policy action and the reestablishment of confidence. Moreover, the perceived lack of results hindered further advances. Finally, after the worldwide stock-market crash in October 1987, the government reconsidered its strategy and initiated a "heterodox" stabilization program, which later adopted a much more aggressive approach to structural change. Upon examining the process of economic opening, Michael Bruno pointed out that "a very rapid trade liberalization process in the product market may be preferable to a gradual process for reasons of credibility and long-term efficiency."[5]

During this period, Mexico closely observed the heterodox stabilization efforts undertaken in Brazil, Argentina, Bolivia, and Israel. Ortho-

5. Bruno, "Opening Up: Liberalization with Stabilization," 224.

dox stabilization by itself seemed to have failed in all countries because the driving force behind inflation was no longer just a chronic fiscal deficit. Inflation had reached a stage in which it entered a vicious circle, causing what is known as "inertial" inflation. For example, high inflation called for high salary increases, which in turn caused further inflation. Expectations had become the driving force behind inflation.

Heterodox stabilization programs used strict wage and price controls, usually backed by a "social pact," or agreement, to cut inflation quickly. If everyone agreed at the same time not to raise prices, the inertial component of inflation would be eliminated. Both Brazil and Argentina brought triple-digit inflation rates down to nearly zero very quickly. But after some time, inflation returned, as demand pressures broke down price controls and policy makers lost sight of their commitment to fiscal discipline. Israel, however, combined orthodox and heterodox elements to eliminate inflation altogether and bring about a successful stabilization effort. The heterodox component brought inflation down quickly, while the orthodox component helped reduce the fiscal deficit, which had caused inflation in the first place.

The October 1987 stock-market collapse created an extremely vulnerable situation for an economy like Mexico's, especially since renewed capital flight was likely. Yet, high foreign-exchange reserves and an undervalued currency allowed Mexican policy makers to borrow from the Israeli experience and implement a combined heterodox and orthodox shock stabilization program. The effect was immediate. By the end of 1988, annual inflation had dropped to one-third its previous rate. The government followed up with restrictive fiscal and monetary policies, which began to bring down the public-sector deficit. These results were all that Mexican policy makers needed to convince themselves that the gradual approach to stabilization and structural change was all wrong, while shock treatment could be highly effective.

Thus, in December 1988, when Carlos Salinas de Gortari took office, the government initiated a much more aggressive structural-change strategy. Confidence and renewed credibility were apparent at once. For the first time since the financial crash of 1982, Mexico began to attract capital inflows, and the promise of a development strategy that could be financed began to emerge. It seemed that Mexico had finally found its course: a consistent macroeconomic strategy combined with market liberalization, which became a magnet for portfolio and direct investment after the long dry spell of the 1980s.

Mexico's first attempt to open up its economy came in 1986, when the government applied for membership in the General Agreement on Tariffs and Trade (GATT). This signaled the beginning of the end for the highly protectionist policies of the past. By 1987, the government decided to pursue a unilateral tariff reduction and the all-out elimination of import permits, exposing Mexican industry to international competition for the first time. As a result, the government expected an increase in export revenue—a strong incentive for capital inflows from abroad—and an overall improvement in efficiency and resource allocation. This meant renewed possibilities for growth and employment creation.

The failure of the earlier gradual approach to reform and the apparent success of the subsequent shock-treatment strategy convinced Mexican authorities that the complete dismantling of all restrictions was the road to follow. However, many of the costs of large-scale reforms were overlooked. Policy makers ignored the fact that sweeping reforms would require many inefficient industries to shut down, leading to higher unemployment, and that a significant time lag would be required before new and more efficient industries began to appear.[6] Moreover, these new industries would have considerably different skill requirements than those that had collapsed. Protracted unemployment was certain to surface, with high political costs.

As an open border increases the pressure on firms to become more efficient and competitive, they struggle immediately to reduce costs and increase productivity. For firms established under a highly protectionist economy, the easiest cost to reduce is labor. Firms will try to produce the same or higher levels of output with fewer workers. Thus, during the transition period between a closed and an open economy, the job-generation capacity of the economy is reduced markedly. As a result, most of Mexico's growth between 1989 and 1994 seems to be explained by productivity increases rather than by job generation.

An interesting example of this serious oversight by the Mexican government surfaced during the NAFTA negotiations. At the core of the NAFTA debates in the United States was the jobs issue.[7] Those who argued against NAFTA held that the job loss created by factory reallocations would entail high costs in terms of retraining displaced workers.

6. Raghbendra Jha, *Macroeconomics for Developing Countries* (London: Routledge, 1994), 265–81.

7. Gary C. Hufbauer and Jeffrey J. Schott, *NAFTA: An Assessment,* rev. ed. (Washington, D.C.: Institute for International Economics, 1993), 11–32.

Thus, they claimed that special assistance bonds or unemployment compensation should be introduced, given that the transition period in which all displaced workers were reallocated could last up to ten years. At the same time, even in the case of a net job gain, the political costs from job losses would outweigh the benefit from job creation. Multiple studies were carried out analyzing the effects on real wages and net job gains or losses. Articles appeared voicing strong opinions. Conclusive findings were cited, like those of Alan Deardorff, Drusilla Brown, and Robert Stern of the University of Michigan, which showed that the job displacement and ensuing reallocation costs would be much higher in Mexico than in the United States.[8] In spite of all the importance this issue was given in the United States, it was hardly discussed in Mexico, even though it was widely acknowledged on both sides of the border that the employment effect of NAFTA on Mexico would be immensely greater than in the United States.

Still, the initial expectations of Mexico's trade liberalization and other structural changes were that a much more efficient economy would appear. Mexico would develop the ability to generate enough foreign exchange to avoid future balance-of-payments crises. Low inflation rates and overall stability would help economic growth. Sustained growth rates would enhance the ability to generate more and better jobs. Soon, the country would be closer to First World status.

The Impact of Trade Liberalization on Employment

When examining employment patterns in Mexico, it is essential to establish some definitions. Although the definition applied by the National Institute of Statistics (INEGI) in the calculation of the open-unemployment rate corresponds to that of the International Labor Organization (ILO), it is now commonly believed that this figure understates significantly the unemployment picture in Mexico. The ILO and INEGI define a person as unemployed if he or she has not worked at least one hour in a

---

8. The University of Michigan findings are summarized in Drusilla K. Brown, "The Impact of a North American Free Trade Area: Applied General Equilibrium Models," in *North American Free Trade: Assessing the Impact*, ed. Nora Lustig et al. (Washington D.C.: Brookings Institution, 1992), 26–68; see also Jonathan E. Heath, "NAFTA: El debate" (El indicador especial 4, Dirección de Análisis Económico y Bursátil, Grupo Financiero Serfín, October 1993).

given week, is actively looking for a job, and is able to accept it once found. This definition has been criticized for being too narrow, since a person is not considered unemployed if he or she worked at least one hour in a given week.

In a country like Mexico, with no safety net (that is, no unemployment insurance, welfare benefits, or accumulated family wealth), it is much more common for a person who is actively looking for a job to work part-time in any endeavor in order to make ends meet. This might involve selling light consumer goods on a street corner, helping out a relative, or accepting a lower-paid job until a better one is found. It also is typical for someone looking for a job, for example, to work from fifteen to thirty-five hours a week in some sort of menial capacity. The all-or-nothing alternative, more customary in developed countries, is much less an option in Mexico. Given this situation, INEGI began publishing complementary indicators in 1991 that provide a better picture of the country's labor market (see this chapter's Appendix for details).

Although these additional definitions compensate for the narrowness of the open-unemployment rate, most of these statistics have been available only on a quarterly basis since 1987, making historical comparisons difficult. However, INEGI has begun to release more of these rates on a monthly basis and has promised to release all of them soon. Another problem is that INEGI has adopted, not one, but seventeen alternative definitions. Because of this, different analysts may be using different definitions, making forecast comparisons impossible. Nevertheless, regardless of what definition one uses, it can be assumed that the different indicators tend to move together. So, instead of observing the actual level of the unemployment rate, we could concentrate on changes from one month to the next. INEGI has pointed this out, saying that the actual definition used is not that important, as long as it captures relative increases or decreases in unemployment. This is the case for most of the indicators, but not for all of them (see the Appendix).

To some degree, we should expect a negative correlation between unemployment indicators and GDP growth, given that an increase in economic activity should fuel job creation and thus reduce unemployment. However, if we bracket this expectation within the context of Mexico's recent trade liberalization, then we also would expect an initial deterioration in the job-generation capabilities of the economy. The data indicate that the latter expectation appears to be dominant, although at a low level of correlation.[9] Although trade liberalization has been one factor in the country's slow rate of job generation, other variables also have influenced the demand for labor, such as capacity use, wage rates, and productivity.[10] In trying to understand Mexican unemployment, one must consider the changing role of productivity in the transition from a closed to an open economy. As the Mexican economy has become more open, it has been subject to much more competition and pressures to increase efficiency.

In the initial period of trade reform, competitiveness is usually increased through productivity gains as firms struggle to decrease costs, especially by reducing labor overhead. This translates into lower levels of job generation. Analysis of the open-unemployment rate between 1987 and 1994 shows a slow downward trend in unemployment through 1992, which at first glance seems to contradict the expectation of deterioration in employment generation from trade liberalization. Unemployment did increase slightly in 1993, but this can be explained by a period of stagnant growth in the economy from the second quarter of 1993 through the first quarter of 1994.

Nevertheless, the open-unemployment rate does not capture sufficiently the phenomenon of disguised unemployment in Mexico, which has grown strongly during the 1990s. In other words, given that a very high percentage of the workforce is either unskilled or semiskilled and receiving very low levels of remuneration, people who are laid off are likely to accept any type of employment, even if it does not meet their expectations. People will accept jobs below their established wage category, will be willing to work longer hours with no extra pay (in order to keep their current job), and will accept jobs with fewer working hours per week. These situations generally do not appear in the labor statistics.

However, Social Security statistics show the number of registered workers, which is a good approximation of employment in the formal sector. Whereas data up through 1991 show increasing employment, as of 1992 formal employment stagnates and shows no growth at all for the next three years. Given that the open-unemployment rate did not in-

9. Correlations with lagged values of unemployment were also calculated with no visible improvements.

10. We could also expect a lag between the drop in economic activity and an increase in the unemployment rate. Interestingly, no visible relationship was found, with the exception of the insufficient-income and unemployment rate (TIID), which responds, albeit with a low correlation, up to four quarters behind changes in GDP.

crease by much, it can be assumed that the informal sector of the economy started absorbing a larger share of the labor force. Nevertheless, it becomes quite clear that the formal sector lost its capacity to generate enough jobs.

The unemployment figures examined so far are for the economy as a whole. The impact of trade liberalization should become more apparent when analyzing sectoral changes in employment creation. For example, we would expect strong shifts from the manufacturing and industrial sectors to the services sector under a more open-trade regime. Given that the service sector cannot absorb all of this labor, we should expect a systematic increase in the informal economy and in disguised unemployment. On this question, the data strongly reflect a contraction in manufacturing jobs. As Figure 5.1 shows, there was a systematic drop in the number of jobs held in the manufacturing sector over the five years from 1988 through 1993. In fact, there is an uninterrupted downward trend that lasts for seventy consecutive months, from mid-1990 through April

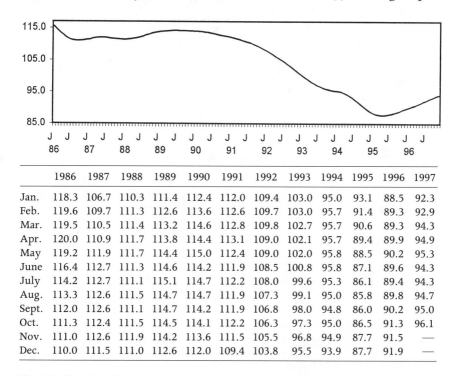

	1986	1987	1988	1989	1990	1991	1992	1993	1994	1995	1996	1997
Jan.	118.3	106.7	110.3	111.4	112.4	112.0	109.4	103.0	95.0	93.1	88.5	92.3
Feb.	119.6	109.7	111.3	112.6	113.6	112.6	109.7	103.0	95.7	91.4	89.3	92.9
Mar.	119.5	110.5	111.4	113.2	114.6	112.8	109.8	102.7	95.7	90.6	89.3	94.3
Apr.	120.0	110.9	111.7	113.8	114.4	113.1	109.0	102.1	95.7	89.4	89.9	94.9
May	119.2	111.9	111.7	114.4	115.0	112.4	109.0	102.0	95.8	88.5	90.2	95.3
June	116.4	112.7	111.3	114.6	114.2	111.9	108.5	100.8	95.8	87.1	89.6	94.3
July	114.2	112.7	111.1	115.1	114.7	112.2	108.0	99.6	95.3	86.1	89.4	94.3
Aug.	113.3	112.6	111.5	114.7	114.7	111.9	107.3	99.1	95.0	85.8	89.8	94.7
Sept.	112.0	112.6	111.1	114.7	114.2	111.9	106.8	98.0	94.8	86.0	90.2	95.0
Oct.	111.3	112.4	111.5	114.5	114.1	112.2	106.3	97.3	95.0	86.5	91.3	96.1
Nov.	111.0	112.6	111.9	114.2	113.6	111.5	105.5	96.8	94.9	87.7	91.5	—
Dec.	110.0	111.5	111.0	112.6	112.0	109.4	103.8	95.5	93.9	87.7	91.9	—

Fig. 5.1. Manufacturing employment (moving average 1993 = 100)

1996, in which each month shows fewer people employed in the manufacturing sector compared to the same month of the previous year.

The downward trend in jobs held in the manufacturing sector can also be observed in Figure 5.2, which measures annual growth rates. The open-unemployment rate did not really increase until 1995, meaning that the jobs lost in the manufacturing sector must have been absorbed by other sectors. As mentioned above, the most likely candidate would be the services sector. Upon examination of the number of jobs in commercial establishments, we find supporting evidence for such a trend, as viewed in Figure 5.3.[11] The interesting finding is that, while there is a definite increase in jobs in retail services until the beginning of 1995,

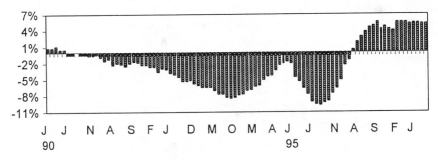

	1990	1991	1992	1993	1994	1995	1996	1997
Jan.	0.9%	−0.4%	−2.3%	−5.9%	−7.7%	−2.0%	−4.9%	4.3%
Feb.	0.9	−0.9	−2.6	−6.1	−7.1	−4.5	−2.3	4.0
Mar.	1.2	−1.6	−2.7	−6.4	−6.9	−5.3	−1.4	5.6
Apr.	0.5	−1.1	−3.6	−6.4	−6.3	−6.6	0.6	5.56
May	0.5	−2.3	−3.0	−6.5	−6.0	−7.6	1.9	5.65
June	−0.3	−2.0	−3.0	−7.1	−5.0	−9.1	2.9	5.25
July	−0.3	−2.2	−3.8	−7.7	−4.4	−9.6	3.8	5.48
Aug.	0.0	−2.4	−4.1	−7.6	−4.1	−9.7	4.7	5.46
Sept.	−0.4	−2.0	−4.5	−8.3	−3.3	−9.3	4.9	5.32
Oct.	−0.3	−1.7	−5.2	−8.4	−2.4	−9.0	5.5	5.26
Nov.	−0.5	−1.8	−5.3	−8.3	−2.0	−7.6	4.3	—
Dec.	−0.5	−2.3	−5.2	−7.9	−1.7	−6.6	4.8	—

Fig. 5.2. Manufacturing employment growth

11. INEGI increased the coverage of commercial establishments from three cities to thirty-three as of January 1994. The new series suggests that the loss in the number of jobs is much more pronounced than that presented in the old series. However, the old series is used in the figures in order to show the trend before 1994.

	1994		1995		1996		1997	
	Wholesale	Retail	Wholesale	Retail	Wholesale	Retail	Wholesale	Retail
Jan.	−4.60%	4.51%	−0.80%	−0.20%	−4.15%	−3.59%	−0.53%	−5.38%
Feb.	−5.04	5.66	−2.71	−1.50	−2.99	−4.37	0.21	−2.98
Mar.	−4.04	3.97	−4.40	−1.82	−1.26	−3.20	0.21	−3.20
Apr.	−2.64	4.11	−5.89	−4.33	0.53	−1.37	−0.21	−2.77
May	−3.29	5.93	−6.70	−5.14	1.71	−1.28	−0.11	−0.97
June	−3.02	6.41	−10.31	−5.84	6.36	−3.21	0.00	1.66
July	−3.39	3.69	−8.00	−5.97	3.15	−1.61	1.16	1.42
Aug.	−1.88	3.50	−8.69	−5.91	3.61	−2.55	2.32	1.64
Sept.	−3.93	0.54	−8.98	−5.73	3.51	−3.52	2.33	3.32
Oct.	−1.78	−0.50	−8.87	−5.91	3.72	−3.09	3.16	2.64
Nov.	−1.99	−0.18	−8.03	−4.23	3.93	−5.34	—	—
Dec.	−0.42	−0.02	−8.94	−3.68	4.14	−5.13	—	—

Fig. 5.3. Growth in employment in commercial establishments

the number of jobs in wholesale services shows the same systematic drop as manufacturing jobs, indicating an increase in efficiency in this sector.

This difference between wholesale and retail can be explained intuitively. Wholesale commercial establishments are dominated by larger firms, which have pursued increases in efficiency and labor productivity in the same fashion as the manufacturing sector. By contrast, the retail business is made up of many smaller, often family-owned establishments that have yet to modernize. Small retail stores are easier to set up because of their low start-up costs. They have become the mainstay of the low-productivity–low-wage job market in Mexico, absorbing workers expelled from the more modern sectors. As of 1995, with the recession aggravating consumer sales, these jobs were no longer being created, which explains the increase in the open-unemployment rate displayed in Figure 5.3.

Further examination of available data shows a systematic drop in job creation during the 1990s in all modern sectors that produce tradable goods and services. The more traditional sectors and those dominated by smaller firms had been able to maintain their employment levels or even register small increases through the end of 1994. This suggests strongly that trade liberalization has increased efficiency and labor productivity in the tradable-goods sector, creating a sizable net job loss. Until the currency devaluation of 1994, the nontradable-goods sector and the informal economy absorbed a large number of these workers. Nevertheless, the jobs created were lower paid and less productive, meaning a net loss for those workers moving into this sector.

Starting in mid-1996, the evidence points toward an end of the net-job-loss phase as the drop in manufacturing employment reached its trough. The number of people registered with a job in the Social Security system started increasing, and the open-unemployment rate showed an important fall. If this evidence is correct, then we can estimate the net-job-loss period to have lasted approximately six years.

What about the impact of the December 1994 currency crisis and subsequent recession on the domestic labor market? In light of the above trends, it comes as no surprise that the unemployment figures observed in 1995 are far higher than those that emerged in the wake of the 1982–83 recession. Unemployment tends to respond quickly to an abrupt drop in economic activity, but reacts very slowly once the economy starts to pick up. The data bear out this pattern: the high point of unemployment in 1983 was 6.1 percent, compared to an estimate of 7.6 percent reached in August 1995.[12]

Finally, an obvious question from an economist's point of view is whether this recomposition of Mexican labor is Pareto efficient. Such a shift would be Pareto desirable (or efficient) for labor if the wage increase for those who were able to retain their jobs in the modern sector compensated the wage decrease of those who lost their jobs, as well as those who accepted a wage cut in transferring from the modern sector to either the services or the informal sector. Intuitively, the short- to medium-term effect is definitely not a Pareto improvement, since employment

---

12. These numbers are not strictly comparable, since the Monthly Employment Survey has changed methodology and increased coverage substantially.

suffered severe losses and real wages only increased marginally. Moreover, both real wages and employment suffered large losses during the 1995 recession. This would mean that the change induced so far by trade liberalization on the labor sector has not been viewed by society as a whole as desirable.

If trade liberalization does not provide a Pareto improvement, then why would the government favor an open economy? In order to answer this, the above argument must be rephrased to examine outcomes over time. Once the transition phase has been completed, there should be net job creation as firms achieve efficiency and further increases in output are met through greater employment expansion. Recent evidence seems to point toward net job creation, suggesting that eventually trade liberalization will provide an overall improvement. Thus, policy makers must believe that future gains and wage increases will outweigh these losses, creating a Pareto improvement over time.

Unfortunately, it is clear that, thus far, Mexico has suffered a tremendous loss in labor welfare. The recent gains in employment have not been felt in all sectors and regions of the country. As can be expected, initial recovery is very heterogeneous. Nevertheless, evidence in the labor market as of mid-1997 points toward an incipient real-wage recovery, while employment registered through Social Security shows annual growth rates of 9 percent.

Productivity Gains Under an Open-Trade Regime

One of the main arguments in favor of trade liberalization is that it brings about a much more efficient allocation of resources. An open economy increases competition, pushing firms to a more efficient use of all production factors in order to minimize costs. Thus, trade liberalization should result in increased productivity, which measures efficiency in terms of physical production divided by the amount of labor used, or output per labor unit employed. This measure does not identify which part of output is explained by labor productivity and which by capital productivity. Thus output per unit of labor may increase due to a better use of capital (a different technology) and/or a more efficient use of labor, but we cannot know which is at work. However, an increase in efficiency, induced by further competition, does not have to be gained through a specific factor.

In an open economy, competitiveness plays a much more important role. An economy can increase its competitiveness through several means. Interest rates, which reflect the cost of capital, and wages, which are the cost of labor, are two basic elements in the determination of competitiveness. It is assumed that Mexico has a competitive advantage in wages and a disadvantage in interest rates, given an abundant supply of labor and a scarcity of capital. In order for the economy to be competitive, the labor advantage must outweigh the capital disadvantage. Both wages and interest rates are determined by the market and therefore will adjust according to supply and demand. Thus it is hard for firms to influence these prices directly. Still, productivity is a result of firms' striving to become more efficient and, as a result, more competitive.

INEGI publishes manufacturing-productivity indices for both Mexico and the United States, based on the same methodology. If we take the ratio of these two measures, we can arrive at a relative measure of the degree to which Mexico has been able to close the productivity gap between the two countries. We would expect to find a sharper increase in Mexico's productivity under trade liberalization, with a relative increase vis-à-vis the United States. As can be seen in Figure 5.4, Mexico's productivity hardly increased at all between 1980 and 1987, before trade was liberalized. Taking 1980 as the base year, the accumulated increase until 1987 was 7.1 percent, an unimpressive increase of 0.98 percent per year, compared to the U.S. average of 3.8 percent per year. Productivity in the United States increased 21.5 percent above Mexican productivity during the same period, underlining Mexico's need to increase its competitiveness.

As of 1989, a little more than one year after Mexico opened its borders by reducing tariffs unilaterally, productivity began to increase quickly, averaging 6.6 percent per year between 1988 and 1993.[13] As Figure 5.5 shows, the gap between Mexico and the United States widened until 1988, after which trade liberalization began forcing the Mexican manufacturing sector to increase its productivity at a higher rate than the United States, closing this gap significantly.

In sum, the data strongly suggest an all-out improvement in Mexican manufacturing productivity as a direct result of trade liberalization.

---

13. Unfortunately, INEGI has been slow to update these data beyond 1993. However, other evidence seems to suggest that the recent trend persists.

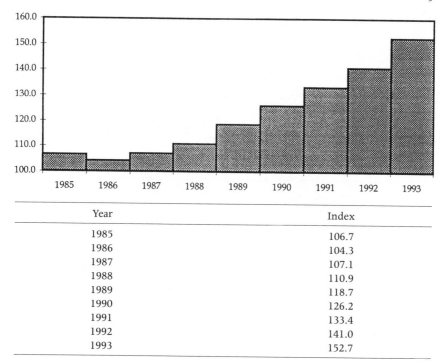

Year	Index
1985	106.7
1986	104.3
1987	107.1
1988	110.9
1989	118.7
1990	126.2
1991	133.4
1992	141.0
1993	152.7

Fig. 5.4. Manufacturing productivity (1980 = 100)

When this observation is combined with the employment figures discussed above, it seems safe to conclude that most of the growth achieved by Mexico during this period was through gains in efficiency and not through a more intensive use of labor. Support for this conclusion is found in the latest Mexican Economic Census, showing a decrease in the average number of people employed per firm in the manufacturing sector from 18.8 in 1988 to 12.0 in 1993.[14]

As productivity continues to increase and the net-job-loss phase comes to an end, it can be assumed that real wages should soon start to show a positive growth rate. This is important in order to provide an overall improvement in the labor sector through time and to gain support for trade liberalization and other complementary policies in the future.

14. INEGI, *Censos económicos 1994: Resultados oportunos* (Aguascalientes: INEGI, 1994).

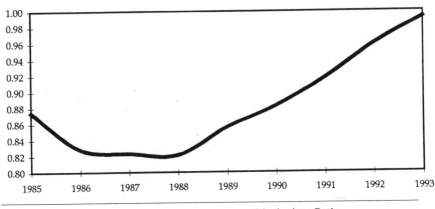

Year	Mexico/USA Ratio
1985	87%
1986	83
1987	82
1988	82
1989	86
1990	88
1991	92
1992	96
1993	99

Fig. 5.5. Mexico/U.S. productivity ratio (1980 = 100)

Regulatory Changes

Mexico has tried to approach its economic transformation as an integrated process, seeking both increased overall efficiency and a better allocation of resources. Trade liberalization is but one of several measures implemented in pursuit of this goal. The privatization and deregulation policies enacted over the past ten years are also part of this process. Because of high preexisting levels of government intervention, Mexican policy makers have undertaken an aggressive deregulation strategy, particularly during the Salinas years. The result has been numerous changes in laws and regulations, some even at the constitutional level.

The driving idea behind this process has been to establish a more transparent and market-based environment in virtually all sectors of the economy. According to the government, the aim is to lower barriers to entry and participation in economic activities, foster free competition, eliminate obsolete regulations, and establish clear rules that will make market conditions more certain.[15] By the end of 1993, more than seventeen laws had been reformed and more than forty regulations altered.[16]

Some of the main actions have been the elimination of regulations that limited economic activity by firms and individuals; the redefinition of the government's role in society so as to open access to various activities where private-sector participation was formerly restricted; the redefinition of regulations whose ambiguity had reduced investment flows; the granting of legal guarantees required for planning long-term investments in undeveloped fields; the streamlining of the decision-making process by reducing the discretionary powers of certain authorities and decentralizing decisions; and the removal of unnecessary or unjustified rules.[17]

This process is still going on as the government continues to deregulate. For example, in May 1995, Article 27 of the Mexican Constitution was amended in order to permit private-sector investment in the transportation, storage, and distribution of natural gas. Foreign companies, which may own up to 100 percent of a Mexican firm, are now permitted to build, operate, and own pipelines, plants, and equipment.[18]

Nevertheless, this is the one area that most businessmen complain about in terms of what still needs to be done. For example, a major reform in tax laws is long overdue and continually postponed in spite of constant complaints. Many surveys carried out by the central bank and other institutions underline the failure to deregulate as one of the main factors that limit competitiveness of the private sector.

Structural Changes at the Sectoral Level

Another way of assessing the impact of trade liberalization on the Mexican economy is to compare the evolution of the main sectors between 1988 and 1993 (the most recent date for which sectoral data are available through the Economic Census carried out by INEGI every five years).

15. Bank of Mexico, *The Mexican Economy, 1993* (Mexico City: Bank of Mexico, 1993), 68.
16. Reforms have been carried out in all of the major economic sectors—including electricity, mining, health, ports, petrochemicals, tourism, financial services, agriculture, transportation, telecommunications, sugar, coffee, water, and fishing—as well as in intellectual-property rights, consumer and environmental protection, immigration, customs agencies, and foreign investment.
17. Bank of Mexico, *The Mexican Economy, 1995* (Mexico City: Bank of Mexico, 1995), 68.
18. Ibid., 191.

Since Mexico joined the GATT in 1986 and began reducing tariffs a year later, 1988 is the most appropriate starting point for analyzing the changes that have occurred. The data for 1993 should provide some indication of the initial effects of trade liberalization. The next Economic Census will be carried out by INEGI in 1998, with results due to be disclosed by late 1999.

Interestingly, in broad sectoral terms, there is no visible major change in the composition of the economy during this five-year period. In 1988 manufacturing employed 29 percent of all labor, and in 1993 it employed 27 percent, implying a certain net expulsion of labor during the time frame. The only major sector showing a change of more than two percentage points over this period is private services, which increased its labor share from 19 percent to 22 percent. This is consistent with observations made previously about employment shifts in Mexico.

However, when these percentages are broken down into numbers of workers per firm, a sharp reduction in the average number of persons employed per firm emerges in every sector. These workforce reductions, shown in the Table 5.1, reflect the increased efficiency gains that have been registered since 1988. This downward employment pattern remains evident upon further breakdown of the above sectors. In the manufacturing sector, for example, the only exception is in basic-metals industries, which increased the number of persons employed from 116 to 143. At the same time, the manufacturing sector registered 871 firms in 1988 and only 401 in 1993, while employing a total of 100,694 persons in 1988 and only 57,396 five years later. This suggests a large restructuring that resulted in a 43 percent drop in the number of people employed, during a period in which the industry itself grew briskly.

Closer scrutiny of the manufacturing sector reveals that real wages

Table 5.1. Average number of people employed per firm

Sector	1988	1993
Total	6.6	5.2
Mining and oil	94.0	34.4
Manufacturing	18.8	12.0
Commerce	2.8	2.5
Government services	29.4	26.7
Private services	4.1	3.8
Communication services	56.6	23.8

SOURCE: INEGI.

increased in all subsectors during the 1988–93 period, although in a heterogeneous fashion. While there is a direct relationship between real-wage increases and the change in the number of people employed in each subsector of manufacturing, Table 5.2, which tracks the average annual growth rate in real wages within the manufacturing sector, also shows that the smaller wage increases tend to be within those sectors that are more labor-intensive (including *maquila*, or in-bond, industries). At the same time, the capital-intensive industries have registered larger wage increases. This is most likely a result of higher productivity gains within these capital-intensive industries.

Another change that we should expect as a result of trade liberalization is a reduction in profitability. Past protectionism had resulted in monopolistic profits, as firms enjoyed reduced competition under regulatory barriers that impeded market entry. The increased competition resulting from an open border should force down profit margins. The data strongly support this expectation, since gross profit margins in all subsectors of manufacturing dropped from an average of 35.6 percent in 1988 to 30.2 percent in 1993, although with wide variance. Only after a detailed breakdown do some exceptions come to light, such as in petrochemicals and other chemical products. This is very likely a result of deregulation and the elimination of price controls. Other exceptions are found in meat production, beverages, shoes, cellulose, glass, and cement.[19]

Table 5.2. Real wage growth in the manufacturing sector, 1988–1993 (average per annum)

Printing and editorials	9.1%
Beverages	7.8
Plastic products	6.2
Chemical products	5.6
Metallic products	5.2
Automotive industry	3.6
Clothing	2.8
Machinery and electrical equipment	2.5
Electronic equipment	2.3
Textiles	1.1
Others	2.6

SOURCE: INEGI.

19. According to the estimates of Grupo Financiero Serfín, the increase in profitability in cellulose can be explained by the huge variation observed in world prices over the same period.

The largest drop in profit margins emerged in sectors that were highly protected before the reforms. For example, machinery and equipment in general decreased in profitability from 40.3 percent to 27.5 percent, while the office-equipment subsector dropped from 40.5 percent to 12.2 percent. The same trend can be observed in both wholesale and retail trade, which decreased from 19.4 percent to 15.6 percent on average. Consistent with these expectations, the services sector shows a much smaller drop, from a profit margin of 49.5 percent to one of 47.5 percent, given that services are usually nontradable. Again, most of the exceptions are explained easily by the impact of deregulation or privatization. For example, the profitability of financial institutions increased sharply as a result of privatization.

Another trend that can be observed in INEGI's Economic Census is changes in the average number of employees per firm in the manufacturing sector. Between 1988 and 1993 there was a sharp increase in the number of smaller firms vis-à-vis the number of larger ones, as can be observed in Table 5.3. The number of firms with fifteen employees or fewer represented 92 percent of all firms in 1993, compared to 87 percent five years earlier. Accordingly, these smaller firms employed 21 percent of the workforce in 1993, compared to only 14 percent in 1988. At the other extreme, only 1 percent of all firms employed more than 250 people. But these large firms accounted for 44 percent of the workforce in 1993, compared to 50 percent before in 1988. Upon examination of the commerce and services sectors, this same trend holds, although the shift is smaller in services than in manufacturing. Again, we can assume that this is because the effects of trade liberalization have been felt more in the tradable than nontradable sectors.

Table 5.3. Characteristics of manufacturing firms

Number of Employees	Number of Firms (%)		People Employed (%)		Income (%)	
	1988	1993	1988	1993	1988	1993
0–15	87	92	14	21	4	9
16–100	10	6	20	20	13	14
101–250	2	1	16	15	14	14
251 +	1	1	50	44	69	63
Total	100	100	100	100	100	100

SOURCE: INEGI.

The figures above suggest that larger firms have increased efficiency by reducing their labor overhead, while smaller firms have absorbed most of the layoffs. This would also confirm the earlier hypothesis that the more productive jobs are in the larger firms, while smaller businesses generally offer less productive and lower-paid jobs. If this is the case, then the fragility of smaller firms can be at least partially explained as a consequence of inefficiency and a failure to adapt to the modernization process brought about by trade liberalization.

The results of a survey carried out by the Bank of Mexico in mid-1995 suggest that a large number of firms still face problems associated with the transition from a closed to an open economy.[20] For example, 24 percent of the firms surveyed complained about too much competition, while an additional 8 percent mentioned excessive regulation and bureaucratic red tape. Lack of adequate infrastructure, insufficient transportation, and lack of knowledge concerning export markets also were mentioned.

More to the point, one of the main complaints put forth by firms is that of high financing costs and lack of access to credit. Over half the firms surveyed mentioned this as one of their main disadvantages. While manufacturing firms are struggling to adapt modern technologies, they are reducing their labor overhead and investing in new capital equipment. This is the case despite the cheaper cost of labor and higher capital costs. As a result, Mexico now tends to export more in capital-intensive goods than in labor-intensive goods.

These survey responses and accompanying trends again drive home Mexico's problem of low job generation. In general, labor-intensive goods are less profitable than capital-intensive goods, in spite of the factor-price differences. In the same business survey, a significant number of firms admitted that they are still considering further layoffs in order to increase efficiency, and most are now in the process of incorporating new technologies.

Conclusions

From this analysis, it is clear that Mexico had little choice but to shift policy tracks by the mid-1980s. The most immediate challenge was to

20. Bank of Mexico, *The Mexican Economy, 1995.*

devise a strategy that would reduce both the fiscal and the current-account deficits; provide a viable source of foreign exchange, which would enable the country to service its external debt; and lay the groundwork for economic recovery and sustained growth.

Policy makers first attempted a gradual approach to economic liberalization and structural change but met with disappointing results. The decision to accelerate the market-reform process in the late 1980s was unavoidable. While reforms are moving basically in the right direction, it is clear that the costs of large-scale reform were greatly underestimated; Mexico's shift to a market-oriented economy was a much more complex undertaking than originally perceived, particularly in the crucial areas of employment and productivity.

On the employment front, a brief examination of Mexico's postliberalization labor-market structure highlights some nagging problems. The initial expectation was that an open economy would substantially increase the country's capacity to create jobs, given that one of Mexico's main comparative advantages lies in lower wages. However, the data indicate a systematic drop in job creation between 1990 and 1995 in all modern sectors that produce tradable goods, while the more traditional service sectors and those dominated by smaller firms have shown a small increase in jobs. This pattern, which could continue for some time, is not unique to Mexico: global competition is inducing firms to adapt more efficient technologies, which so far have resulted in large productivity gains but a less intensive use of labor. This suggests that labor-intensive technologies are still less efficient than capital-intensive technologies, in spite of large factor-price differences.

A big part of Mexico's employment problem seems to be related to inefficiencies in the use of labor, resulting in a loss of competitiveness. For example, although smaller firms are traditionally the source of employment creation, these companies are less profitable and more inefficient than the larger firms even after paying out lower wages. This suggests that the marginal productivity in labor employed by the larger firms more than offsets the higher wages. At the same time, multinational firms can finance their operations through global capital markets, offsetting the higher domestic cost of capital. By applying the same global technology, they can achieve a higher profit margin through a lower labor cost, compared to other countries. However, there is little incentive to use a more labor-intensive technology to minimize capital requirements. This would seem to explain why larger firms have been able to adapt more efficient technologies, reduce labor costs, and achieve higher profit margins vis-à-vis smaller firms.

Another problematic aspect of the Mexican labor market is the use of a definition for open employment that understates the true employment picture. Moreover, the open-unemployment rate does not reflect job layoffs from trade liberalization. Keeping these methodological limitations in mind, and given the economy's reduced capacity to generate jobs, the increase in unemployment since the 1994 peso crisis is probably higher than the layoffs that accompanied the 1982–83 recession. Until the recent devaluation, the nontradable-goods sector and the informal economy absorbed a large number of these laid-off workers, although at much lower wages. One of today's main worries concerns the fate of these disenfranchised workers, who no longer have access to the "safety net" provided by the informal sector during highly recessionary times.

The flip side of this difficult employment scenario is Mexico's impressive gains in productivity. Indeed, the data show that trade liberalization has increased efficiency and labor productivity in the tradable goods sector, thereby contributing to a net job loss. Although profit margins have been reduced in virtually all sectors, especially in tradable goods, real wages have still increased in capital-intensive industries—again suggesting large productivity gains. Large firms have advanced substantially in adapting new technologies, while medium and small firms have remained stagnant. The mortality rate of smaller firms is explained by continuing inefficiency under a more competitive environment and failure to adapt to the modernization process.

Even though the impact on unemployment seems to be larger in the 1995 recession than in the 1982–83 recession, the benefits of a more efficient economy are today quite apparent. Whereas industrial production in the 1980s took 105 months to return to its precrisis levels of 1981, it only took 22 months following the 1995 recession for industrial production to exceed 1994 levels. The difference is that the industrial base in Mexico during the 1980s was quite inefficient under the inward-looking import-substitution model, whereas efficiency and competitiveness were greatly enhanced during the 90s. As a result, industry was able to find and sustain export markets once the domestic economy collapsed in 1995. Sustained export performance has since helped the Mexican economy jump back from a serious blow and is slowly but surely filtering into the rest of the economy.

In sum, Mexico's transition from a large inefficient economy to one that is globally competitive has been more painful and prolonged than originally envisioned. The combination of productivity increases with the rise in unemployment strongly suggests that growth during 1989–94 was a result of gains in efficiency and not a more intensive use of labor. Capital investments carried out during this period were used mainly for updating technology and modernizing industrial plants, rather than for expanding productive capacity.[21] This does not necessarily cast doubt on the benefits of a more efficient economic structure achieved through trade liberalization, but rather reflects the failure of policy makers to anticipate the magnitude of the costs of this transition. In short, Mexican policy makers are learning the hard way that "the transition strategy from a pre-reform regime to a post-reform open economy is more important than the choice of the end product."[22]

Appendix

Additional INEGI unemployment indicators (initials in parentheses are those used by INEGI in Spanish):

Alternative Open-Unemployment Rate (TDAA) includes open unemployment, those who have actively given up job searching, and those who currently do not hold a job but have stated that they will begin working within a month.

Effective Economic-Pressure Rate (TPEE) represents the percentage of the economically active population that is openly unemployed, plus those who have a job but are actively looking for an additional one.

Effective Preferential-Pressure Rate (TPEP) refers to the percentage of the workforce that is unemployed, in addition to those who have a job but are actively looking for an alternative job with the intention of voluntarily changing jobs.

General Pressure Rate (TPRG) combines the TPEE and TPEP definitions— that is, it includes open unemployment, plus those who have a job but

21. However, as of 1996, private-sector investment has started to show large growth rates. Most of this is explained by investments in export-oriented sectors aimed at capitalizing on installed capacity. As a result, these firms are now creating jobs.
22. Bruno, "Opening Up: Liberalization with Stabilization," 224.

are actively looking for another one, either in order to change jobs or to hold on to multiple jobs. In other words, this reflects the pressure on the labor market for new jobs.

Partial-Employment-for-Market-Reasons and Unemployment Rate (TOPRMD) consists of open unemployment, plus those who, due to market conditions, work less than thirty-five hours a week (that is, involuntary underemployment).

Partial-Employment (of less than fifteen hours a week) Rate (TOPD1) adds both open unemployment and those who work for less than fifteen hours a week (for whatever reason).

Partial-Employment (of less than thirty-five hours a week) Rate (TOPD2) adds both open unemployment and those who work for less than thirty-five hours a week. The difference between this rate and TOPRMD is that this includes those who work less than thirty-five hours a week for whatever reason, rather than solely for market reasons.

Insufficient-Income and Unemployment Rate (TIID) mixes open unemployment and those who have a job but earn less than one minimum wage.

Critical-Employment-Conditions Rate (TCCO) combines those who work less than thirty-five hours a week (due to market conditions), those who work more than forty-eight hours a week while earning less than twice the minimum wage, and those who work more than thirty-five hours a week while earning less than the minimum wage.

In terms of the correlation between the various indicators, the partial-employment rate (TOPD2), the insufficient-income and unemployment rate, and the critical-employment-conditions rate do not move together with the open-unemployment rate (TDA), but rather display a distinct pattern. All the other indicators tend to correlate strongly. This means that the open-unemployment rate reflects the same pattern of six other indicators, while only the TOPD2 and the TIID represent a different trend in the domestic labor market.

The different behavior in the insufficient-income and unemployment rate can be explained by the deterioration in the real minimum wage over the past six years. During the Salinas administration, the minimum wage increased steadily but remained below the rate of inflation, resulting in a steep drop in the real wage over time. The intention was to eliminate the wage indexing that had played a role in fueling high inflation during the 1980s, and at the same time reduce the significance of the minimum wage as a barrier to entering the labor market. Thus the percentage of those who claimed to hold a job, but earned less than one minimum wage, dropped from over 30 percent in 1987 to near 7 percent by 1994. However, most of the adjustment took place in 1988, when this figure dropped abruptly to about 15 percent.

As for the variance in the partial-employment rate (TOPD2), this shows a very strong seasonal pattern, with a notable improvement every third quarter (July, August, September). Recall that this category includes those who work for less than thirty-five hours a week regardless of the reason. The decrease shown during these months means that more people are working thirty-five hours or less, which might be explained by an increase in students finding part-time jobs during the summer. Still, this phenomenon, which is quite common in the United States, is not that common in Mexico.

6 The Paradox of Integration

Liberalizing and Criminalizing Flows Across the U.S.-Mexican Border

Peter Andreas

Even as state controls over the flow of goods, services, information, and capital loosen under the North American Free Trade Agreement (NAFTA), state prohibitions against two of Mexico's leading exports, drugs and migrant labor, tighten. Jagdish Bhagwati has noted that immigration controls are "the most compelling excep-

Part of this chapter is adapted from "U.S.-Mexico: Open Markets, Closed Border," *Foreign Policy*, no. 103 (summer 1996). The research was supported by a fellowship from the Foreign Policy Studies Program at the Brookings Institution, and the Social Science Research Council's SSRC-MacArthur Foundation Fellowship on Peace and Security in a Changing World. I also wish to acknowledge the support of the Cornell Peace Studies Program and the Institute for the Study of World Politics. Philip Cerny, Kate Doyle, Martha Finnemore, Jonathan Kirshner, James Kurth, Nicholas Onuf, Cathy Schneider, Kenneth Sharpe, Janice Thomson, Carol Wise, and Carolyn Wong provided helpful comments on an earlier draft. A previous version of this chapter was presented at the annual meeting of the American Political Science Association, Chicago, Ill., August 31–September 3, 1995, and at the Latin American Studies Association meeting, Washington, D.C., September 28–30, 1995.

tion to liberalism in the operation of the world economy."[1] Drug controls are an equally striking exception. In both cases, the advice of otherwise influential free-market proponents has fallen on deaf ears,[2] and the political expedience of prohibition has eclipsed the economic logic of liberalization.

On the one hand, the practice and ideology of market liberalization signal a retreat of the state in the form of deregulation, privatization, the opening up of national economies, and the erosion of boundaries. The fundamentals of market prohibition, on the other hand, are about the reassertion of the state and economic regulation through criminalization and the sharpening of boundaries. The status of state intervention in the market under today's NAFTA-style arrangement is therefore ambiguous: widespread support for market deregulation is matched by rising support for increased regulation of prohibited markets. The difference, however, is that the form of regulation in the latter case is through the state's policing apparatus. The police function of the state thus appears to be expanding as a punitive form of economic regulation.

The retreat and reassertion of state regulation, while seemingly separate processes, are in some ways intimately related. The unleashing of market forces—the loosening of government controls over the flow of goods, services, information, and capital—has unintentionally encouraged and facilitated not only legal economic activity but illegal economic activity as well. As all forms of cross-border activity have become more extensive and intensive, so too have state efforts to "weed out" the illicit from the licit. This task has fallen primarily on the state's law-enforcement apparatus. Thus, even as some state regulatory functions and capacities contract through market liberalization and integration, other regulatory functions and capacities (the enforcement of market prohibitions) expand. Consequently, the state, far from simply retreating in the face of economic integration and market liberalization (as some orthodox liberal theorists claim), is actually being reinvigorated and redeployed.

In this chapter I offer a preliminary analysis of how market liberalization and economic integration unintentionally facilitate and encourage illegal-drug and migrant-labor flows, and how this, in turn, is being matched by a reassertion and expansion of the state's policing authority

---

1. Jagdish N. Bhagwati, "Incentives and Disincentives: International Migration," *Weltwirtschaftliches Archiv* 120, no. 4 (1984): 680.

2. For example, Milton Friedman and the *Economist* promote drug legalization, and the *Wall Street Journal* advocates open borders for labor flows.

and law-enforcement apparatus. I highlight how these dynamics of state retreat and reassertion are transforming the 1,951-mile U.S.-Mexican boundary, where the United States is moving simultaneously to open the border (to the legal flow of goods) and to close the border (to the illegal flow of drugs and labor).

Lawrence Herzog has argued that "[t]he internationalization of the world economy—the evolution of transnational markets, production-sharing strategies, labor migration, and banking systems—has led to an inevitable reshaping of boundary functions. The most obvious change has been the shift from boundaries that are heavily protected and militarized to those that are more porous, permitting cross-border social and economic interaction."[3] While there is much truth in this view, the trends along the U.S.-Mexican boundary suggest a more complex and contradictory dynamic: the intensification of cross-border economic activity due to economic liberalization and integration is paralleled by an intensification of border law enforcement to deter a perceived invasion of "undesirables." In short, as old barriers between the United States and Mexico are being torn down under NAFTA and the two nations drawn closer together, new barriers are rapidly being built up to keep them apart.

Market Reforms and Prohibitions

The simultaneous opening and closing of the U.S.-Mexican border is part of a broader transformation of inter-American relations in the post–Cold War era. Much of U.S. policy toward Latin America in recent years has been driven by two sharply contrasting agendas: the promotion of liberal market reforms and the enforcement of market prohibitions. The United States has encouraged the free flow of virtually everything except migrant labor and drugs. As the export of illegal drugs (primarily cocaine, heroin, and marijuana) and migrant labor (especially Mexican, but from the rest of the region as well) to the United States has grown, so have U.S. efforts to suppress them. Strategies have focused primarily on curbing the supply and secondarily on targeting the source of demand (consumers of drugs and employers of migrant labor).

3. Lawrence A. Herzog, "Changing Boundaries in the Americas: An Overview," in *Changing Boundaries in the Americas*, ed. Lawrence A. Herzog, U.S.-Mexican Contemporary Perspective Series 3 (La Jolla: Center for U.S.-Mexican Studies, University of California at San Diego, 1992), 5–6.

In the case of drug control, this has involved intense law-enforcement efforts to cut the supply at the point of production abroad, at the point of entry at the border, and at the point of distribution and sales domestically. Federal drug-control spending has increased from less than $1 billion in 1981 to a budget request of over $15 billion in 1997, with about 70 percent of the budget devoted to law enforcement. While the primary focus of immigration control is on domestic and border enforcement, operations are also expanding beyond U.S. boundaries. According to Robert Bach, now a senior official at the Immigration and Naturalization Service (INS), this is part of a broader process of reconceptualizing and internationalizing immigration control. As Bach observes, "In order to control events in countries which export migrants, receiving states are increasingly connecting their migration regulatory efforts with new methods of international law enforcement and changes in post–Cold War military doctrine."[4]

The continued influx of illegal migrant labor and the failure of U.S. supply-side approaches to halt the incoming flow of drugs is propelling a fusion between U.S. national-security and domestic law-enforcement agencies. For example, the Defense Department has taken on important policing tasks (such as drug interdiction), the National Security Council now oversees efforts to deter the smuggling of aliens, law enforcement has become more sophisticated and internationalized,[5] and the intelligence community and State Department have placed such issues as transnational organized crime more centrally on their agendas.[6] Of course, this is driven partly by the scramble for new agency missions in the post–Cold War security environment. Between the early 1980s and the early 1990s, for example, the Pentagon underwent a metamorphosis, transforming itself from a reluctant ally on the sidelines of the U.S. anti-drug campaign to a frontline advocate. Similarly, the CIA has begun to overcome its traditional reluctance to engage in drug-related intelligence work.

But these institutional changes are not merely the result of bureau-

---

4. Robert Bach, "Processes of Migration," in *The Challenge of Integration: Europe and the Americas,* ed. Peter Smith (New Brunswick, N.J.: Transaction Publishers, 1993), 217–18.

5. See Ethan Nadelmann, *Cops Across Borders: The Internationalization of U.S. Law Enforcement* (University Park: Pennsylvania State University Press, 1993).

6. The popular press is beginning to recognize these changes. In the case of the United States, for example, see David Johnston, "Strength Is Seen in a U.S. Export: Law Enforcement," *New York Times,* April 17, 1995.

cratic opportunism. They also reflect domestic political pressure to "do something" about drugs and illegal immigration. Foreign-policy priorities clearly have shifted in the public's mind. In a Gallup poll commissioned by the Chicago Council on Foreign Relations in late 1994, respondents were asked to rank sixteen foreign-policy goals by their order of importance. Curbing the flow of illegal drugs into the United States was their first priority (89 percent), followed by protecting the jobs of U.S. workers (83 percent), preventing the spread of nuclear weapons (82 percent), and curbing illegal immigration (72 percent).[7] Policing, it should be noted, is a central tool in government responses to three of these problems.

While drug trafficking and migration have long been U.S. policy concerns, it is only in recent years that they have become the defining source of tension in U.S.–Latin American relations. In the Cold War era, controlling the spread of Communist insurgents was the key preoccupation of U.S. leaders. Today, however, the degree of hemispheric conflict or harmony depends to a large extent on how the influx of migrants and drugs are managed politically. Just as politicians of an earlier era did not want to appear "soft on Communism," in the current political climate they do not want to appear "soft on drugs" or "soft on illegals." Consequently, relations between the United States and a number of Latin American countries are "narcotized," as development assistance and diplomatic favor increasingly are tied to compliance with U.S. drug-control objectives.[8] Similarly, fears of uncontrollable waves of migration play an increasingly pivotal role in U.S. foreign policy toward its southern neighbors.

This situation has been exacerbated by the fact that both illegal migrant labor and drugs are crucial exports from the region. During a period in which the value of traditional exports has fluctuated, the boom in these illegal goods (or "bads," depending on your perspective) has been a vital source of revenue for many debt-burdened Latin economies. For example, remittances generated by migrant workers in the United States (many of them illegal) is a major source of foreign exchange for

7. Cited in Jim Lobe, "United States: New Poll Fuels Growing Foreign Policy Debate," *Interpress Service*, March 6, 1995.

8. See Peter Andreas, Eva Bertram, Morris Blachman, and Kenneth Sharpe, "Dead End Drug Wars," *Foreign Policy*, no. 85 (winter 1991–92): 106–28. For an overview of U.S. drug policy and the Latin American drug trade, see Bruce M. Bagley and William O. Walker III, eds., *Drug Trafficking in the Americas* (New Brunswick, N.J.: Transaction Publishers, 1994).

countries such as Mexico, El Salvador, Haiti, and the Dominican Republic.[9] Illegal drugs easily have been Latin America's most successful export industry in the past decade, serving as a leading generator of
foreign exchange for countries such as Peru, Bolivia, Colombia, and
Mexico.[10] From Chile to the Cayman Islands, most Latin American countries have tapped into the region's thriving drug trade in roles ranging
from crop producers and processors to shippers and money launderers.
Moreover, illegal migration and the drug trade help cushion the bleak
employment prospects in some countries, since hundreds of thousands
of the unemployed find work through these clandestine activities.

For those countries enmeshed in the region's drug trade, the distinc-
tion between legal and illegal economic activity is increasingly blurred.
In some cases, the drug-export sector is not isolated from, but integrated
into, the national economy.[11] Thus, even as the United States seeks to
expand the role of market forces and the private sector throughout the
region, the awkward reality in a number of countries is that the drug-
export industry is a leading market force and an integral component of
the private sector. Indeed, the drug trade is in many ways the quintes-
sential expression of the kind of high-risk, aggressive entrepreneurialism
advocated by U.S. free-market proponents.

An unintended side effect of the market-reform process in Latin
America has been to facilitate and encourage the export of illegal drugs
and migrant labor. This can be explained in part by simple economic
logic: the pressures from increased competition under a market model
make it more difficult for those who are economically displaced to resist
the temptation of economic gains related to drug production and illegal
migration; moreover, the opening of the economy through liberal market
reforms reduces the ability of the state to withstand external market

9. More broadly, a 1993 United Nations report estimated that total annual remittances from
international migrants amount to about $66 billion—second only to oil in value and greater than
all international development assistance from governments. Report cited in Ian Mather, "Fortress
Europe Has Porous Walls," *Calgary Herald*, July 18, 1993, B3.

10. It is, of course, impossible to provide more than rough estimates of the size of the illegal-
drug trade. Commonly cited figures for the size of the U.S. drug market range from $40 billion to
$100 billion annually. For a useful analysis of estimates of the size of the drug-export sector in
Colombia, Bolivia, and Peru, see Humberto Campodónico, "La política del avestruz," in *Coca, cocaína y narcotráfico*, ed. Diego García Sayan (Lima: Comisión Andina De Juristas, 1989).

11. See, for example, Vito Tanzi, *The Underground Economy in the United States and Abroad* (New
York: Lexington Books, 1982), and Alejandro Portes, Manuel Castells, and Lauren Benton, eds., *The
Informal Economy: Studies in Advanced and Less Advanced Countries* (Baltimore: Johns Hopkins
University Press, 1989), especially the chapter by Jose Blanes Jimenez.

pressures—particularly as U.S. demand for illegal drugs and migrant labor remains buoyant. Overall, this process represents what Robert Cox has called the "internationalization of the state," whereby national policies bend more easily to the exigencies of the international economy.[12] Ironically, these trends are perfectly in line with the dictates of neoclassical economic theory, which encourages countries to specialize in those exports that enjoy a comparative advantage. The clandestine side of the international economy, I argue, is part and parcel of this process. For a country like Mexico, two important "market niches" lie in the export of migrant labor and drugs.[13]

The Clandestine Side of U.S.-Mexican Integration

Raul Hinojosa-Ojeda and Sherman Robinson have observed that the United States and Mexico "share by far the most extensive and complex network of linkages of any two countries on opposite sides of the North-South divide. Mexican-U.S. interdependence includes the largest trade relation and the largest debtor-creditor relation between any two developed and developing countries, the largest foreign investment flows, the largest in-bond coproduction relations (maquiladoras), and the longest contiguous border with the highest levels of border crossings and border commerce, both legal and illegal."[14] Whether acknowledged or not by the United States and Mexico, the illegal flow of drugs and migrant labor may be as significant a part of their deepening economic relationship as legal economic flows. As noted earlier, these clandestine flows have been influenced powerfully by the liberalization of markets and the deepening process of economic integration. I do not mean to suggest that market liberalization and economic integration are somehow the underlying

12. Robert Cox, *Production, Power, and World Order* (New York: Columbia University Press, 1987).

13. Trade theory accepts Adam Smith's conclusion that "man is of all sorts of luggage the most difficult to be transported," and therefore assumes that labor does not cross borders. Yet this assumption has been undermined by recent advances in transportation and communications technology and broader transformations in the global economy that have made labor much more mobile. The Adam Smith quotation is from Philip Martin, *Trade and Migration: NAFTA and Agriculture* (Washington D.C.: Institute for International Economics, 1993), 27.

14. Raul Hinojosa-Ojeda and Sherman Robinson, "Labor Issues in a North American Free Trade Area," in *North American Free Trade: Assessing the Impact*, ed. Nora Lustig et al. (Washington D.C.: Brookings Institution, 1992), 70.

cause of drug and migration flows. I am arguing, however, that these economic processes in some ways unintentionally facilitate and encourage such clandestine forms of exchange. Unfortunately, the policy implications of this complicated dynamic have not been addressed sufficiently by officials on either side of the U.S.-Mexican border.

The illegal flow of drugs. The State Department estimates that the percentage of cocaine entering the U.S. market through Mexico was negligible in the mid-1980s, but increased to as much as 70 percent by the mid-1990s. Mexico also supplies about 20–30 percent of the heroin and up to 80 percent of the marijuana consumed in the United States. The U.S. Drug Enforcement Administration (DEA) estimates that Mexico earns more than $7 billion a year from the illicit-drug trade.[15] Some estimates from Mexico's prosecutor general's office place the figure much higher.

While Mexico has a long history of involvement in the drug trade, the nature and scope of this involvement has undergone a transformation in the past decade. Most significant has been the country's emergence as the primary shipping point for Colombian cocaine into the United States. A strategic alliance has developed between Colombian and Mexican trafficking groups,[16] greatly increasing the power and wealth of Mexico's drug traffickers, while expanding already high levels of political corruption. Colombian traffickers turned to Mexico as a major entry point to the U.S. market in the early 1980s after the United States began to crack down on cocaine shipping through the Caribbean. In addition to Mexico's geographical advantages, increasing economic ties between Mexico and Colombia and between Mexico and the United States made the country an ideal transshipment point. Mexican imports of legal goods from Colombia increased from $17 million in 1980 to $121 million in 1985 (at the same time, Mexican imports from the rest of Latin America decreased from $768 million to $630 million).[17]

Richard Friman suggests that expanding trade between Mexico and Colombia helped establish broad economic linkages within which illegal

15. Cited in Tim Golden, "Mexican Connection Grows as Cocaine Supplier to U.S.," *New York Times,* July 30, 1995, A1.

16. For an analysis of strategic alliances among drug-trafficking organizations, see Phil Williams, "Transnational Criminal Organizations: Strategic Alliances," *Washington Quarterly,* winter 1995, 57–72.

17. IMF, *Direction of Trade Statistics, Yearbook 1981* (Washington D.C.: IMF, 1981), 265–66, and IMF, *Direction of Trade Statistics, Yearbook 1992* (Washington, D.C.: IMF, 1992), 280, both cited in Richard Friman, "Just Passing Through: Transit States and the Dynamics of Illicit Transshipment," *Transnational Organized Crime* 1, no. 1 (1995): 75.

economic flows could be hidden.[18] The U.S. cocaine market, in turn, became even more penetrable as economic ties between the United States and Mexico deepened and spread. Legal exports from Mexico to the United States doubled between 1986 and 1993. Hiding drug shipments within the growing volume of U.S.-Mexican trade has become an increasingly favored method for smuggling drugs. As one observer notes, "Contrary to popular belief, most drugs do not cross American borders on low flying Cessnas or aboard fast-moving 'cigarette' boats. Most reach their markets by way of commercial conveyances."[19]

These trends are accelerating under NAFTA. A 1993 report written by an intelligence officer at the U.S. embassy in Mexico City claims that cocaine traffickers are establishing factories, warehouses, and trucking companies as fronts in Mexico to take advantage of the boom in cross-border commerce now occurring under NAFTA. The report was obtained through the Freedom of Information Act by the National Security Archive, a private research group in Washington that seeks to declassify government documents. Assistant U.S. Attorney Glenn MacTaggart has acknowledged that "[i]f NAFTA provides opportunity for legitimate businesses, it may clearly provide opportunities for illegitimate businessmen."[20]

The trucking industry offers the most concrete illustration. In May 1993 it was reported that 1,700 trucks crossed over to the United States from Juarez, Mexico, each day. One U.S. customs official conceded that "most trucks that go through customs go through almost unimpeded." According to another senior customs official, to inspect every truck coming across the border would create a traffic jam all the way to Mexico City. Under the NAFTA agreement, trucking into the United States from Mexico is growing exponentially. In 1994, 2.8 million trucks crossed the border from Mexico, up from 1.9 million in 1993. In addition, U.S. customs officials counted 82.3 million cars crossing into the United States from Mexico in 1994.[21]

Transportation links between Mexico and the United States will continue to expand significantly in coming years to accommodate the rise in

---

18. See, for example, Friman, "Just Passing Through."

19. Stephen E. Flynn, "Worldwide Drug Scourge," *Brookings Review*, winter 1993, 9.

20. Quoted in Tim Weiner (with Tim Golden), "Free Trade Treaty May Widen Traffic in Drugs, U.S. Says," *New York Times*, May 24, 1993.

21. Peter Slevin, "Agents Face Impossible Task Along the Border," *Austin American-Statesman*, July 2, 1995, D8.

cross-border commerce. To encourage this trend, the U.S. Southwest Border Capital Improvement Program will provide infrastructure to support more than double today's traffic levels, or as many as 8.4 million trucks annually.[22] Mexican truckers will soon be allowed to operate freely throughout the border states of California, Arizona, New Mexico, and Texas.[23] And they will eventually be able to travel anywhere in the United States and Canada. Trucks, of course, can carry illegal goods as easily as legal goods. For example, one truck that was stopped near San Diego carried eight tons of cocaine stuffed into cans of jalapeño peppers. Law-enforcement officials believe that the cocaine belonged to a businessman who owns one of the biggest trucking companies in Mexico.[24]

As part of their effort to hide drug shipments within legal shipments, some Mexican traffickers reportedly have hired trade consultants to determine which products move most quickly through border inspection under NAFTA guidelines. "They have very specific issues," notes Craig Chretien of the DEA. "Does a perishable get through quicker than a load of steel? What kind of cargoes go through faster than others?"[25]

Drug-control concerns were not discussed during the NAFTA negotiations. As Gary Hufbauer of the Institute for International Economics observes, "This was in the 'too hot to handle' category."[26] According to a former U.S. customs commissioner, NAFTA is openly called the North American Drug Trade Agreement by U.S. Customs and drug-enforcement personnel.[27] In short, as one press report puts it, Mexican drug traffickers "seem to have embraced a vision of North American integration not unlike that with which NAFTA . . . was sold to skeptics in Washington."[28]

At the same time that trade liberalization and economic integration have helped Mexico's traffickers penetrate the U.S. market, the deregu-

---

22. See Stephen E. Flynn, "The Erosion of Sovereignty and the Emerging Global Drug Trade" (paper presented to the annual conference of the International Studies Association, Chicago, Ill., February 22, 1995), 9, citing *Assessment of Border Crossing and Transportation Corridors for North American Free Trade: Report to Congress* (Washington D.C.: U.S. Department of Transportation, Federal Highway Administration, 1993).

23. Howard LaFranchi, "The Dawn of Borderless Trucking," *Christian Science Monitor*, December 11, 1995, 1.

24. Weiner, "Free Trade Treaty May Widen Traffic in Drugs, U.S. Says."

25. Quoted in Golden, "Mexican Connection Grows as Cocaine Supplier to U.S."

26. Quoted in Weiner, "Free Trade Treaty May Widen Traffic in Drugs, U.S. Says."

27. William von Raab and F. Andy Messing Jr., "Will NAFTA Free the Drug Trade? Cocaine Businessmen Too Will Exploit Open Borders," *Washington Post*, August 15, 1993, C2.

28. Golden, "Mexican Connection Grows as Cocaine Supplier to U.S."

lation of the Mexican banking system and the privatization of state-owned enterprises has facilitated the laundering of their drug profits. The *Economist Intelligence Unit* reports that "[l]iberalisation of the Mexican financial services sector and capital markets in recent years has provided opportunities for money-laundering and the investment of the illicit gains from the drugs trade."[29] U.S. officials acknowledge that drug traffickers are taking full advantage of the privatization process. For example, according to the Federal Bureau of Investigation, many of the state-owned companies privatized under the Salinas administration were bought up by drug traffickers.[30]

Not only does the buying-up of state-owned enterprises facilitate the laundering of drug profits, but this in turn provides a large and immediate influx of desperately needed foreign exchange for the Mexican financial system. Given Mexico's critical balance-of-payments problems and heavy debt-servicing obligations, there is an incentive to tolerate funds from any source (this is especially true after the collapse of the Mexican peso in December 1994).

Finally, it should be noted that the liberalization of agriculture and the cutting of state subsidies in rural areas increases the incentives for peasant farmers to produce illegal crops such as marijuana. As one group of researchers reports, "[S]ocial disruption and economic pressure from free-market reforms have intensified in rural areas, fueling the tendency to grow illicit crops as a household survival strategy."[31] Drug production has expanded in Mexico's more remote rural regions. The State Department reports that "[a]dverse agricultural and economic conditions have forced farmers in nontraditional areas to turn to cultivating illicit crops."[32]

The illegal flow of migrants. The INS estimates that there are some five million illegal immigrants living permanently in the United States, of which 54 percent are believed to be from Mexico. While migration flows from Mexico are the product of a complex mix of "push" and "pull"

29. "Political Outlook: Party Stability," *Economist Intelligence Unit Country Forecast*, May 30, 1995.

30. Cited in Golden, "Mexican Connection Grows as Cocaine Supplier to U.S."

31. T. Barry, H. Browne, and B. Sims, *Crossing the Line: Immigrants, Economic Integration, and Drug Enforcement on the U.S. Mexican Border* (Albuquerque, N.Mex.: Resource Center Press, 1994), 59.

32. Department of State, Bureau of International Narcotics Matters, *International Narcotics Control Strategy Report* (Washington D.C.: U.S. Government Printing Office, March 1991), 162.

factors that have deep historical roots,[33] market liberalization and growing economic integration between the United States and Mexico help
explain the recent influx. The focus here is on the most important sup-
ply-push factors that encourage cross-border labor migration: the
growth of the export-assembly industry along the U.S.-Mexican border,
the liberalization of agriculture in Mexico, and pressures from NAFTA
itself.

   Although U.S. officials have long argued that market liberalization
and economic integration with Mexico will help deter illegal migration,
some of these policies actually have had the opposite effect.[34] For example, the border industrialization program initiated in the 1960s, which
U.S. officials argued would curb illegal migration by providing employment in Mexico, led to a proliferation of export-assembly plants in
northern Mexico. A number of scholars suggest that the program, rather
than deterring migration, has encouraged migration from the interior of
Mexico to the border, leading in turn to increased migration to the
United States.[35] Many illegal migrants who enter the United States from
Mexico are, in effect, unintended imports from this export-processing
zone. This area has experienced particularly rapid growth in recent
years. For example, the number of *maquiladoras* along the Californian-
Mexican border has quadrupled in the past decade. The assembly plants
are largely foreign-owned and export almost exclusively to the U.S. market. The end result, according to Saskia Sassen, is that "the maquila
program has consolidated a transnational border economy, within which
trade, investment, and people move rather freely."[36]

   The liberalization of Mexican agriculture is another factor contributing to increased migration. A computable-general-equilibrium model developed by Raul Hinojosa-Ojeda and Sherman Robinson predicts that
NAFTA could lead to the uprooting of about 1.4 million Mexicans from
the countryside. Between 30–50 percent of all days worked in Mexican
agriculture are devoted to corn and bean cultivation. Since the United

---

33. Current Mexican migration patterns resulted in large part from the U.S. demand for labor by
Southwest agricultural interests earlier in the century. This was formalized in the Bracero Program,
which brought 4.6 million Mexican farmworkers into the United States from the early 1940s to the
mid-1960s.

34. For an analysis of how economic linkages shape migration patterns, see Saskia Sassen, "America's Immigration Problem," *World Policy Journal,* fall 1989.

35. Ibid. See also Saskia Sassen, "Why Migration?" *NACLA Report on the Americas,* July 1992.

36. Saskia Sassen, "Free Trade and Immigration," *Hemisphere,* winter/spring 1991.

States produces both crops far more cheaply, the gradual liberalization of agriculture under NAFTA will lead to an influx of U.S. imports. The Hinojosa-Ojeda and Robinson study estimates that 800,000 of those peasant farmers expected to be displaced would remain in Mexico, while 600,000 would migrate illegally to the United States over a five- to ten-year period.[37]

As discussed in more detail in Chapter 2 of this volume, the impact of market opening has been exacerbated by state retrenchment in the countryside. For example, since the late 1980s, the Mexican government has been reducing electricity, fertilizer, water, and credit subsidies to peasant farmers. Price supports for crops, which have traditionally helped to inhibit rural emigration, also have been cut. Moreover, restrictions on the sale of communal farmlands (about 70 percent of Mexico's cropland and one-half of its irrigated land) have been lifted. Although the government in late 1993 initiated a fifteen-year direct income-subsidy program (called PROCAMPO) for producers of corn and other basic crops, this has served primarily as a limited form of welfare payment rather than provide the kind of public investment (affordable credit, crop insurance, infrastructure improvements such as irrigation and drainage) needed to modernize Mexican agriculture and make small-scale farmers more productive and competitive.[38]

These sweeping changes in the Mexican countryside tend to uproot peasants from traditional modes of existence and stimulate a mass exodus from the land. Luis Tellez, the former undersecretary for planning in Mexico's Ministry of Agriculture and Hydraulic Resources, estimates that one million peasants are likely to leave the land every year, and that as many as fifteen million peasants will leave agriculture in the next decade or two.[39] Mexico's already bloated cities can hardly accommodate the influx. While it is impossible to know exactly how many of these peasants will end up in the United States, crossing the northern border understandably will be a logical option for some. As Philip Martin observes, "With projections that 20 percent to 50 percent of Mexico's farmers could leave the land over the next decade, the stage is set for a repeat

---

37. Cited in Philip Martin, "Mexican-U.S. Migration: Policies and Economic Impacts," *Challenge*, March 1995.

38. See Santiago Levy and Sweder van Wijnbergen, "Transition Problems in Economic Reform: Agriculture in the Mexico-U.S. Free Trade Agreement" (Policy Research Working Papers, World Bank, Washington, D.C., August 1992).

39. Cited in Martin, "Mexican-U.S. Migration: Policies and Economic Impacts."

of a great migration similar to what the United States experienced in the 1950s and 1960s, when structural changes in U.S. agriculture and cotton harvest mechanization brought sharecroppers from Mississippi to Chicago. Mexico is on the verge of a similar agricultural revolution, but potential destination cities for ex-farmers include Los Angeles and Houston."[40]

The main impact of NAFTA will be to reinforce and institutionalize these migratory waves from Mexico's interior to the U.S.-Mexican border. In an effort to promote the trade agreement domestically, Clinton-administration officials argued that NAFTA would help advance U.S. immigration objectives by laying the groundwork for a more buoyant job market in Mexico. Attorney General Janet Reno, for example, warned that if NAFTA were not passed, "effective immigration control [would] become impossible."[41] Without NAFTA, she said, illegal immigration "is only going to get worse. I don't have the numbers, but every bit of logic . . . would confirm it."[42] Yet even those migration specialists who argue that the trade pact will help curb illegal migration in the long term due to NAFTA-induced economic development in Mexico point out that through at least the end of this decade the combination of NAFTA and Mexico's own domestic economic reforms will add as many as several hundred thousand to the number of Mexicans who migrate to the United States annually.[43] This will deepen the already extensive cross-border migration networks that have proved so crucial as a social base and bridge for later migration flows. Thus, the long-term reduction of migration hoped for under NAFTA is questionable.

Finally, economic liberalization not only helps fuel the population flow across the border, but also provides a crucial cushion for the Mexican state as it carries out its market-reform program. Mexico, by exporting part of its unemployment problem, reduces social and political tensions, as well as population pressures on urban areas. Some estimate that a third of the new entrants in the labor force in Mexico's western region end up in the United States. According to a July 1995 OECD report, remittances from Mexican migrants total $3 billion annually, mak-

---

40. Martin, *Trade and Migration*, 6.

41. Quoted in Wayne Cornelius and Philip Martin, "Perspective on NAFTA: Take the Long View on Immigration," *Los Angeles Times*, November 2, 1993.

42. Quoted in Lyndsay Griffiths, "NAFTA Best Hope to Stem Immigration: Reno," *Reuters Business Report*, November 1, 1993.

43. These studies are reviewed in Martin, *Trade and Migration*.

ing this one of the country's leading sources of revenue. Mexican politicians routinely travel to lobby their constituents in the United States to keep the money flowing back to their hometowns. One-fifth of the total Mexican workforce is employed in the United States. The migration "safety valve" is so important to Mexico that Jorge Domínguez has suggested that "the only realistic response to the problem posed by Mexico's difficult internal situation is for the president of the United States to quietly subvert" U.S. immigration laws.[44]

Policing the Border

As economic integration between the United States and Mexico—both legal and illegal—has deepened and expanded in recent years, so too have U.S. border-policing efforts. These efforts are propelled primarily by concerns over drug and immigration control, which have become intertwined operationally along the U.S.-Mexican border. Thus, even while the United States promotes some aspects of integration and erosion of economic sovereignty, it rejects others in the name of sovereignty. The emphasis on policing is reflected in funding for border enforcement. For example, the number of Border Patrol agents jumped 65 percent between 1990 and 1996, and the number is expected to increase even more rapidly through the end of the decade. This is part of a broader increase in funding for the INS, the Border Patrol's parent agency: the budget of the INS has more than doubled since 1993, with most of the increase devoted to southwest-border enforcement. The number of INS inspectors at official ports of entry along the U.S.-Mexican border increased by 50 percent in 1996 alone—the largest port-of-entry staffing increase in history. The U.S. Customs Service is also expanding its border presence. In February 1995, Customs announced as much as a 20 percent increase in resources devoted to inspecting cross-border traffic, as part of an initiative along the U.S.-Mexican border called Operation Hard Line. According to George Weise, the U.S. commissioner of customs, "We intend to blitz this border with Operation Hard Line. This is a war."[45]

44. Jorge I. Domínguez, "Immigration as Foreign Policy in U.S.–Latin American Relations," in *Immigration and United States Foreign Policy*, ed. Robert W. Tucker, Charles B. Keely, and Linda Wrigley (Boulder, Colo.: Westview Press, 1990), 164.

45. Cited in B. Drummond Ayres Jr., "Drug Crackdown Planned Along the Mexican Border," *New York Times*, February 24, 1995; see also idem, "Border War Against Drugs Is Stepped Up," *New York Times*, February 26, 1995.

To help filter out illegal flows from legal flows, the United States is creating an elaborate net of state-of-the-art electronic surveillance technology. Alan D. Bersin, the U.S. attorney for the Southern District of California explains it this way: "Our border is intended to accomplish twin purposes; on the one hand, it is intended to facilitate trade in order to bring our nation the significant benefits of international commerce and industry. At the same time, it is geared to constrain and regulate the free movement of people and goods in order to block the entry of illegal migrants and unlawful merchandise. The key to resolving these apparently contradictory purposes lies in the strategic application of modern technology. We can and must have a border that is both secure and business-friendly."[46]

Surveillance technology is a major component of a multiyear $540 million border-enforcement strategic plan announced in February 1994. According to INS commissioner Doris Meissner, "[W]e will install 17 long-range infrared nightscopes during FY 1995. . . . By the end of 1996, we intend to deploy low-level light television systems, acquire and install hundreds of ground sensors, install miles of fences, complete encrypted two-way radio systems in seven localities, deploy a new positive identification system which tracks recidivism. . . . We have already maximized agent effectiveness through these improvements."[47]

Border enforcement relies increasingly on technologies and equipment designed initially for military purposes. For example, magnetic footfall detectors and infrared body sensors, originally used in Southeast Asia, are scattered along the more remote stretches of the border. The Border Patrol is testing a photo-identification system developed by Hughes Aircraft Co. According to Robert Bach of the INS, "The technology came out of the CIA and the Department of Defense. They used it, and it was made available to the INS." The system, he said, "is a clear example of this administration's initiatives to convert military and intelligence technology to domestic applications."[48] Along the border south

---

46. Prepared statement of Alan D. Bersin, U.S. attorney, Southern District of California, before the House Appropriations Subcommittee of the Department of Commerce, Justice, and State, the Judiciary and Related Agencies, March 29, 1995.

47. Testimony of Doris Meissner, commissioner of the Immigration and Naturalization Service, before the Committee on the Judiciary Subcommittee on Immigration Concerning the Programs and Operations of the Immigration and Naturalization Service, May 11, 1995.

48. Cited by Sandra Dibble, "Star Wars Arrives at the Border: High Tech Developed by the Military, CIA May Aid Enforcement," *San Diego Union-Tribune*, March 18, 1995.

of San Diego, army reservists have constructed a ten-foot-high steel wall made up of 180,000 metal sheets originally designed to create temporary landing fields for military operations. Mexicans call it the "iron curtain." Graffiti on the steel barricade reads: "Welcome to the new Berlin Wall."[49]

Other devices include an electric current that disables a fleeing car, a camera that can see into trunks for hidden passengers, an ion scanner designed to detect drugs hidden in vehicles, and a computer that identifies commuters by voiceprint. A Border Research and Technology Center opened in March 1995 to test these devices. The purpose of the Center, which is managed by the Department of Justice, the Office of National Drug Control Policy, and the Treasury Department, is to adapt military and intelligence technology to the problems of border control.[50]

While border law enforcement has suffered from predictable turf battles between government agencies (especially between the INS and Customs), some progress has been made toward institutionalizing interagency cooperation. Operation Alliance, established in 1986 "to foster interagency cooperation and to interdict the flow of drugs, weapons, aliens, currency, and other contraband across the Southwest border,"[51] coordinates the enforcement activities of fifteen federal and four state and local agencies.

Interagency cooperation increasingly involves links between the military and law-enforcement.[52] This is explained in part by the end of the Cold War, which has made the military more enthusiastic about its border-control mission. As one former army officer has suggested, with the military looking for a new job, a "more easily accomplished mission for existing forces would be patrolling the borders. It is, of course, absurd that the most powerful nation on earth cannot prevent a swarming land invasion by unarmed Mexican peasants. The U.S. Army is entirely capable of plugging the holes permanently, and border duty would be excellent military training."[53]

Strict rules against the use of the military for law-enforcement functions have been loosened gradually since the early 1980s. By amending

49. *Wall Street Journal,* January 6, 1995, A2.
50. Dibble, "Star Wars Arrives at the Border."
51. Barry, Browne, and Sims, *Crossing the Line,* 78.
52. Timothy Dunn has described it in the following way: "It's when cops act like the military and the military act like cops." Quoted in ibid., 77.
53. Christopher Bassford, "What Wars Can We Find for the Military Now?" *Newsday,* September 17, 1991.

the Posse Comitatus Act in 1981, Congress paved the way for the military to assist in the detection and monitoring of border-crossing activities in cooperation with law enforcement. The role of the military in border interdiction was expanded by the Omnibus Drug Control Act of 1986, and the 1989 Defense Authorization Act designated the Department of Defense as the lead agency for border drug interdiction.

Although not authorized to make arrests, military personnel engage in a variety of support activities, such as surveillance and intelligence, cargo inspection, road and fence maintenance, and training. Military equipment, including helicopters and interceptor and radar planes, is also provided.[54] Even the North American Aerospace Defense Command (NORAD), originally created to track incoming Soviet bombers and missiles, has redirected some of its activities toward targeting drug smugglers.

In response to this buildup of border policing, many illegal border crossers are adapting rather than being deterred. For example, as border controls are tightened, illegal migrants rely increasingly on "coyotes" (professional smugglers), who take them across the border for a fee. Forcing illegal migrants to depend on smugglers has created a more profitable and sophisticated binational underground business in human trafficking. Each border-enforcement tactic, such as higher and stronger fences and more sophisticated surveillance technology, has been countered with new tactics by the smugglers, such as the use of more remote entry points, payoffs to corrupt officials, and a significant increase in the use of fraudulent border-crossing documents. This, in turn, reinforces the U.S. resolve to devise new methods and devote more resources to controlling the migration flow.

For example, in September 1993 the Border Patrol in El Paso, Texas, initiated Operation Blockade (later renamed Operation Hold-the-Line) in which some 450 agents working overtime covered a twenty-mile area of the border. Illegal border crossings plummeted. The limits of such a Maginot Line–type strategy, however, became clear as new crossing points for illegal migrants emerged quickly on both sides of the twenty-mile El Paso "blockade." The Border Patrol's El Paso operation has been adapted and modified for border-control efforts in neighboring states. In

---

54. For a fuller account, see Timothy J. Dunn, *The Militarization of the U.S.-Mexico Border, 1978–1992: Low Intensity Conflict Doctrine Comes Home* (Austin, Tex.: Center for Mexican-American Studies, 1996).

1994, Operation Gatekeeper was initiated in the San Diego area. This enforcement effort sparked a dramatic but predictable rise in illegal crossings in the more remote portions of eastern San Diego County and along the Arizona border. In response, the Border Patrol began Operation Safeguard in Arizona and has extended Operation Gatekeeper to cover the sixty-six westernmost miles of the border. More recently, Operation Rio Grande was initiated in August of 1997 along the border in eastern Texas, which includes plans to line thirty-one miles of the Rio Grande with floodlights. And so the game of cat and mouse generates its own logic of escalation.

Despite its apparent limits, the escalation of border enforcement has a powerful political logic. Policing campaigns have enormous symbolic appeal and help appease domestic political pressure to "do something." At the same time, policing helps sustain government agencies struggling to preserve their funding in a period of austerity and slashed budgets. Law-enforcement agencies—especially those charged with the missions of immigration and drug control—have largely been insulated from the current movement to shrink the state and cut spending. Indeed, despite the otherwise tarnished image of state regulation, there is a great deal of public support for a highly interventionist state when it comes to drug and immigration control.

Conclusion

In contrast to conventional wisdom, which holds that the liberalization of markets and intensification of cross-border economic activity signals the retreat of the regulatory state, I have argued that these same economic processes are helping stimulate the expansion of the state's policing powers and law-enforcement apparatus. The basic dilemma facing many states is that their embrace of market liberalization and integration can encourage and facilitate not only legal but also illegal economic activity, such as clandestine drug and migrant-labor flows. Nowhere is this dynamic more evident than in the deepening economic integration between the United States and Mexico. The United States has turned increasingly to its criminal laws and policing apparatus in an effort to resolve this dilemma.

The perceived threat posed by many illegal cross-border activities is generating a domestic backlash, and it is the state that is expected to enforce "law and order" and maintain at least the appearance of controlling the border. Thus, even as state intervention is being rolled back in the name of market liberalization and economic integration, it is also being extended in the name of market criminalization and territorial sovereignty. Nowhere is this more strikingly apparent than along the U.S.-Mexican border—a line that is being blurred and sharpened at the same time.

7   Post-NAFTA Politics in Mexico

Uneasy, Uncertain, Unpredictable

Denise Dresser

Mexican poet Octavio Paz wrote in *The Labyrinth of Soli-*
tude that "Mexico's character, like that of any other people, is an illusion, a mask; at the same time it is a real
face. It is never the same and it is always the same. It is
a perpetual contradiction; each time we affirm part of us
we deny another." Paz captured the essence of a profoundly contradictory country. The First World Mexico
of skyscrapers and cellular phones exists side by side
with the Third World Mexico of shoe shiners and flame-
throwers. World-class technocratic teams have ruled in
tandem with dinosaur-like members of the country's
longtime political class. Many Mexicans figure prominently on the *Forbes* international billionaire list, yet
over 40 percent of the population lives in extreme poverty. Former president Carlos Salinas was considered a
thoroughly modern leader when in office, while today
he is an international pariah.

Mexico's dichotomies and contradictions have surfaced with a ven-
geance since the enactment of NAFTA. An indigenous uprising, political
assassinations, kidnappings, and former president Salinas's dramatic political demise transformed the icon of predictable politics in Latin
America into an emblem of uncertainty. Along with unprecedented political turbulence, Mexico was racked by severe economic crisis, fueled
by the December 1994 devaluation of the peso. This combination of
events contributed to the rapid unraveling of one-party rule, loosening
the grip on government held by the Revolutionary Institutional Party
(PRI) since its inception in 1929 and opening new avenues of political
change. Mexico undoubtedly has embarked on a transition from authoritarian rule, but the final outcome of this process—despite the optimism
fueled by highly competitive midterm elections in 1997—remains unclear. Mexican leaders seem committed to economic liberalization, but
the deepening of market-oriented reform and the persistence of problems
in U.S.-Mexican relations have created difficult problems of political
management.

As Mexico inches toward recalcitrant economic recovery and more
pluralistic politics, several questions loom large: Will Mexico's ruling
technocracy stay the course of the neoliberal reforms enacted since 1982,
or will economic policy succumb to volatile political pressures and electoral cycles? Has an adjustment-weary civil society finally reached its
limits with eternal promises of future prosperity? Will increasingly democratic politics be enough to contain social dissatisfaction? Will internal
strife prevent the ruling PRI from once again regrouping, or will the
party display its traditional resilience? What impact will these heightened domestic uncertainties have on U.S.-Mexican relations, particularly
given the propensity of NAFTA to intensify them? In addressing these
questions, I focus on four main trends that are currently shaping Mexican politics:

- a decline of presidential authority and the increasing decentralization
  of power to other regions, political entities, and actors, including
  Congress;
- the growing importance of parties and elections as a determining
  force in the country's political life;
- the continuing emergence of extra-institutional players (such as the
  Zapatista army and other guerrilla organizations, the El Barzón debtors' movement, narco-politicians, and disaffected politicians within

the ruling party) and the likelihood of greater turbulence in Mexico's political future; and

* a closer alignment of Mexican foreign and domestic policies with U.S. interests in the 1990s, notwithstanding recurrent episodes of confrontation between the two countries.

From the Imperial to the Invisible Presidency

Among the most significant political developments in the era of post-NAFTA politics is the decline of presidential authority in Mexico. Since the creation of the ruling party in 1929, the president traditionally has exercised a broad range of discretionary powers.[1] As head of a disciplined, loyal, and united PRI, and at the helm of a system devoid of checks and balances, the president ruled supreme.[2] However, the political and economic turmoil that has plagued the country since 1994 has reduced many of the sources and instruments of presidential power, including the unchallenged hegemony of the dominant party.[3] As a result, the Mexican presidency has become much less omnipotent. The decline of *presidencialismo* (presidentialism) is based partly in today's economic and political turbulence, but is also the product of a deliberate decision by the current president, Ernesto Zedillo, who has inaugurated a new presidential style.

Less than two weeks after Zedillo's arrival in office on December 1, 1994, the country was plunged into its worst economic debacle since the debt crisis of 1982. Zedillo's immediate response to the political challenges created by the devaluation was to announce what he called the

1. The Mexican president's extraordinary range of powers has included the capacity to reform the constitution by proposing amendments unchallenged by Congress; designate his own successor; nominate most of the congressional candidates of his party; remove mayors, governors, and members of Congress from their posts; designate members of his cabinet and remove them at will; and fill the judicial branch with his appointees. See Jeffrey Weldon, "The Political Sources of Presidentialism in Mexico," in *Presidentialism and Democracy in Latin America,* ed. Scott Mainwaring and Matthew Schugart (New York: Cambridge University Press, 1996).

2. Enrique Krauze, "La presidencia imperial," in *Tiempo contado* (Mexico City: Editorial Océano, 1996), 157–60.

3. According to Weldon, there are four necessary conditions that explain presidentialism in Mexico: a presidentialist system based in the constitution; unified government, where the ruling party controls the presidency and at least both houses of Congress; discipline within the ruling party; and acknowledgment that the president is the leader of the ruling party. See Weldon, "The Political Sources of Presidentialism in Mexico."

"modernization" of the Mexican presidency. Zedillo's personal preference was to transform a historically activist and interventionist presidency into a neutral arbiter and enforcer of the rule of law. He promised
to reduce discretionary policy making, promote a new federalist pact,
decentralize power, and bring an end to the symbiotic relationship between the presidency and the ruling party. Zedillo argued that a presidential retreat would allow other institutions, such as the judiciary and
Congress, to flourish.

Zedillo's detached form of leadership stemmed largely from the pecu-
liarities of his arrival in office. After the assassination of PRI presidential
candidate Luis Donaldo Colosio in March 1994, Zedillo was handpicked
by outgoing president Salinas as a last-minute replacement. Trained as
an economist, the accidental candidate had technical expertise but little
political experience to offer. As an outsider to the PRI, Zedillo did not
feel beholden to the clientelist networks within the party, and he and
his close-knit team of advisers were not previously tied to the beneficiaries of state largesse. Zedillo's overriding policy goal was to achieve macroeconomic stability; as a result, he tended to discount the political and
economic demands of the ruling party. Zedillo also believed that the
legitimacy provided by his relatively clean election gave him a mandate
to deepen economic reform, and that subsequent efforts to build popular
consensus were less important.

Although Zedillo was distinctly different from his predecessors, his
insulated governing style reflected the age-old vices of the Mexican political system. Since the birth of the ruling party, Mexico's presidents
and their *camarillas* (cliques) have governed in a relatively uncon-
strained fashion. The arrival of highly trained economists to political
office in the 1980s made policy making more efficient, but not more
accountable.[4] The havoc unleashed by the 1994 devaluation was the unfortunate economic manifestation of a political crisis, rooted in insulated
techno-bureaucratic rule. Since the 1982 debt crisis, the imperatives of
managing the economy had created incentives for government elites to
insulate economic policy making from societal pressure and centralize
decision making in the economic cabinet.[5] However, this pattern of insu-

    4. See Stephanie R. Golub, "'Making Possible What Is Necessary': Pedro Aspe, the Salinas Team,
and the Next Mexican 'Miracle,'" in *Technopols: Freeing Politics and Markets in Latin America in the
1990s*, ed. Jorge Domínguez (University Park: Pennsylvania State University Press, 1997), 95–143.
    5. See Miguel Centeno, *Democracy Within Reason: Technobureaucratic Revolution in Mexico* (Uni-
versity Park: Pennsylvania State University Press, 1994).

lation and centralization perpetuated Mexico's widespread lack of accountability—hence the institutional backdrop that enabled Salinas to postpone indefinitely a much-needed currency devaluation.

Salinas's reasons for not devaluing the peso before leaving office were both political and personal; he was intent on guaranteeing a PRI victory in the August 1994 presidential election, assuring his place in history as Mexico's great modernizer, and becoming the head of the World Trade Organization. No other institution within the Mexican government—not even the central bank—had the power or autonomy to question the soundness of the president's judgment. Salinas placed economic policy at the service of his own political interests, regardless of the potentially deleterious economic implications of such a decision. Yet, even under the reign of the modernizing technocrats, epitomized by Salinas, the traditional ways of doing politics prevailed. Mexico's political and economic stability was jeopardized routinely by the lack of rules to govern by and the absence of institutions to govern with.

The initial lesson the Zedillo government learned from the postdevaluation crisis was that bureaucratic insulation should be increased rather than decreased; that is, economic adjustment should be implemented without catering to social groups, electoral imperatives, or the ebb and flow of politics. Whereas Salinas overpoliticized economic reform, Zedillo sought to depoliticize it. Zedillo and his top economic advisers stressed routinely that economic policy would not be modified despite social pressures and criticisms voiced by members of the business class and the rank and file of the ruling party. The Zedillo team sought to establish strong ties with business groups that benefited from the devaluation (namely, exporters), while simultaneously ignoring the remainder of the population, which comprised the losers. These top policy makers viewed economic decisions as largely technical in nature and believed that these decisions should not be subject to bargaining and politicking. The technocratic and exclusionary approach adopted by the economic cabinet rendered futile much of the lobbying effort of disaffected business and political groups. For the Zedillo team, microeconomic instability and popular disaffection was the price to be paid for macroeconomic stability.[6]

6. Denise Dresser, "Conflicting Imperatives: The Political Economy of the Crisis," in *Mexico 1994: Anatomy of an Emerging Market Crash*, ed. Sebastian Edwards and Moisés Naím (Washington D.C.: Carnegie Endowment for International Peace, 1998).

The retrenchment of presidential authority under Zedillo had significant political implications. On the one hand, a leaner presidency strengthened other political actors, including legislators and opposition-party leaders, thus contributing to the creation of a more pluralistic and accountable political system. A decline in presidential activism also led toward establishment of a system of checks and balances, which had been so sorely lacking in Mexico. On the other hand, Zedillo's seclusion was criticized by many pundits and politicians as an abdication of responsibility that created problems instead of solving them.[7] Members of traditional factions in the PRI took advantage of perceived presidential weakness to strengthen their personal fiefdoms, while hard-liners at the helm of several PRI-controlled governorships continuously opposed the president, questioned his decisions, and jeopardized governability.

The regionalization of politics has created important challenges for economic-policy coordination at the national level.[8] In some geographic regions and economic activities, Mexico is still characterized by powerful *cacicazgos* (political fiefdoms), which rallied behind Zedillo because they perceived him as a weak candidate and knew that their own survival as members of a weakened PRI was at stake. However, in the face of the modernizing directives announced by Zedillo once in office, many traditional governors and local *caciques* (power brokers) closed ranks and opposed the central government's plans. Mexico seems to be witnessing the growing "feudalization" of the PRI, whereby hard-line power brokers govern their states in the way they see fit, often resorting to violence, fraud, and repression. In order to win the election, Zedillo allied himself with several of the PRI's traditional factions. As a result, he was constrained by political commitments and seemed reluctant to pursue a significant political modernization agenda that challenges these authoritarian fiefdoms.

Political developments in the states of Tabasco, Guerrero, and Puebla during the mid-1990s illustrated the dilemmas and negative consequences of diminished presidential authority. In Tabasco, the Party of the Democratic Revolution (PRD) charged the PRI governor, Roberto Madrazo, with electoral fraud and took the case to the attorney general's office, which in turn returned the case to state authorities. The PRD pro-

---

7. Lorenzo Meyer, *Liberalismo autoritario* (Mexico City: Editorial Océano, 1995).

8. Robert R. Kaufman and Guillermo Trejo, "Regionalism, Regime Transformation, and PRONA-SOL: The Politics of the National Solidarity Program in Four Mexican States" (Columbia University, October 1995, unpublished paper).

duced thirteen boxes of documents proving that Madrazo spent seventy times the legal limit during his gubernatorial bid. In response to public outrage, local members of the PRI organized mass demonstrations in support of the governor and threatened to instigate a nationwide PRI revolt if the governor were forced to resign. Despite the overwhelming evidence against him, Madrazo was exonerated and even publicly supported by Zedillo during a presidential tour of the state in 1996. In Guerrero, the Supreme Court found evidence linking another PRI state governor, Rubén Figueroa, to the massacre of seventeen peasants who belonged to an organization that repeatedly challenged the governor's corrupt and repressive practices. Although the governor was forced out of office after a video of the massacre was broadcast on national television, state authorities subsequently declared him innocent of all charges. In Puebla, PRI governor Manuel Bartlett boldly announced that he would not wait for the presidential "dedazo" (whereby the incumbent president handpicks his successor) and publicly declared his intention to run as a candidate for the ruling party in the presidential election in the year 2000. In the three cases, strong regional leaders were able to thwart presidential directives, challenge Zedillo, and proceed with politics as usual.

Zedillo's perceived lack of consistent leadership sabotaged many of his reform efforts and heightened conflicts within Mexico's already divided political class. Many members of the PRI felt that they were paying at the polls for the economic cabinet's incompetence, and their loyalty to the president became tenuous at best. Neither the "hawks" nor the "doves" in the political elite trusted Zedillo. Traditional factions of the PRI resented Zedillo for breaking the unwritten rules that had governed the country since the PRI's creation, while modernizing groups resented him for not dismantling the old guard quickly or thoroughly enough. Zedillo's reluctance to build coalitions of support for economic or political reform led to a recurrent pattern of erratic policy maneuvers wherein the president announced a specific policy, was confronted with opposition from affected interests, and subsequently abandoned the initiative. For example, Zedillo pledged to promote clean elections throughout his term, but then proceeded to support a fraudulently elected PRI governor in the state of Tabasco. Zedillo vowed to establish the "rule of law," and forced the resignation of the governor of Guerrero for his involvement in the June 1995 massacre of seventeen peasants, only to exonerate him later. Zedillo launched an attack against the Salinas family, only to postpone indefinitely investigations into the Salinases' alleged involvement in corruption and assassination scandals. A combination of bad counsel from key advisers, presidential stubbornness, and Zedillo's failure to address key political problems generated a vicious cycle of political mishaps.

The dilemmas created by the weakening of dominant-party rule transformed the presidency into a key factor shaping the prospects and limits of the Mexican transition. In the past, Mexico has been unable to achieve full democratic rule due to the unlimited power of the presidency; in the future, presidential strength will be required for the critical task of institution building and asserting political control over antireform groups. Zedillo and whoever succeeds him will need to use the presidency to strengthen representative institutions that can order the country's political life and eventually act as counterweights to the presidency and to the PRI. As a result of divisions within the PRI and the growing representation of opposition parties, the Mexican Congress has begun to shed its reputation as a pliant and submissive political entity.[9] Moreover, a gradual decentralization of economic resources has started taking place between the federal and state governments, especially in the key area of social spending. Both developments could eventually lead to the creation of more responsible and effective government, without presidential intervention.[10]

However, greater legislative independence will be insufficient to bring about real change within the Mexican Congress unless the current one-term limit for Congress is revised and reelection is allowed. In addition, unsupervised decentralization may not be an unmitigated blessing. Without real political reform that injects greater accountability and transparency into the way public money is spent at the state level, decentralization could merely strengthen the clout of local *caciques*. Thus, the real challenge for the Mexican presidency will be to inaugurate a "modern" form of presidential rule. The president will need to decentralize power, but retain enough leadership to sanction and control mem-

---

9. Alonso Lujambio, *Federalismo y congreso en el cambio político de México* (Mexico City: Universidad Nacional Autónoma de México, 1995).

10. For an analysis of the implications of Zedillo's proposals for a "new federalism," see Alberto Díaz Cayeros, "Federalismo Mexicano," *Enfoque*, June 23, 1996, 12–14; "Nuevo federalismo," *El Nacional*, May 7, 1995; and Victoria E. Rodríguez, *Decentralization in Mexico: From Reforma Municipal to Solidaridad to Nuevo Federalismo* (Boulder, Colo.: Westview Press, 1997).

bers of the old guard who want to defend PRI dominance as a way of life.[11]

The Rise of the Ballot Box

In the past, PRI electoral victories were the norm, and opposition parties occupied a symbolic and secondary role; today, exactly the reverse is the case. Competitive elections at the state and municipal level are changing the very nature of the political system. In 1995 alone, the center-right National Action Party (PAN) became an electoral force to be reckoned with, especially in urban areas. The PRD won the first-ever election for the mayor of Mexico City in 1997 and aspires to win the presidency in the year 2000. The PRI is no longer an unchallenged hegemonic party; in almost every area of the country it faces stiff electoral competition, and in all likelihood this trend will prevail in the future.

Among the most interesting political developments between 1989 and 1995 was the increasing competitiveness of local elections and the growing electoral clout of the PAN in areas traditionally controlled by the PRI.[12] In Chiapas, the southern state that is home to the left-wing Zapatista National Liberation Army (EZLN), the conservative PAN won the municipal presidency of the state's capital in local elections in 1995. This victory was largely the result of dissatisfaction among local elites (landowners and cattle growers) with the PRI's ability to contain the indigenous uprising or assure social peace in the state. Since the EZLN uprising in January 1994, different groups within the PRI, including the state's governor, have been pitted against each other, creating the perception of a power vacuum. The PAN took advantage of this void, nominated a well-known and respected businessman, courted disaffected *priístas* (PRI supporters), and managed to win the election. The Chiapas victory fit well with the PAN's overall strategy—to make inroads at the

---

11. See José Antonio Crespo, "El rol de la presidencia en el cambio político," in *Jaque al Rey: Hacia un nuevo presidencialismo en México* (Mexico City: Joaquín Mortiz, 1995), 159–81.

12. For an account of the PAN's electoral inroads during the Salinas period and an analysis of its local strategies, see Victoria E. Rodríguez and Peter Ward, *Political Change in Baja California: Democracy in the Making* (La Jolla: Center for U.S.-Mexican Studies, University of California at San Diego, 1994).

municipal and state level in order eventually to win a majority in Congress.[13]

Through the early 1990s the PAN was able to extend its support gradually beyond the confines of the urban middle class and garner a growing number of votes in the countryside. The PAN's strong electoral performance in rural areas in the 1994 election in Michoacán proved that the Center-Right has the capacity to weaken the PRI's grip over rural voters. However, despite its growing rural clout, the party was still encumbered by the widespread perception that the PAN remained an elitist and cadre-based party.

On the left of the political spectrum, the PRD also faced significant dilemmas in the post-Salinas era.[14] During the 1994 presidential race the PRD was caught in debilitating struggles between factions and personalities.[15] Since then the party has oscillated between radicalism and moderation, losing potential bases of support in the process. The PRD spent years attempting to determine whether it should hold to the purist, combative, and delegitimizing behavior of the Salinas period or should reposition itself as the flexible, modern, institutionalized Center-Left, willing to participate in "normal" politics, provide representativeness to the party system, demand greater micro-level government intervention, and exert useful pressure for deepening the process of political reform.

Table 7.1. Growth of the PAN

	1989	1995
States governed	1	4
Population governed	3.5[a]	24.7[a]
Mayors	29	218
Local congressmen	115	240
Federal congressmen	101	119
Senators	1	25

SOURCE: *Reforma* database.

[a]Millions of people.

13. For a review of the PAN's political performance in 1995, see Mario Alejandro Carrillo and Rigoberto Ramírez, "El Partido Acción Nacional en el primer año de gobierno de Ernesto Zedillo," *El Cotidiano* 75 (March–April 1996): 12–18.

14. See Kathleen M. Bruhn, *Taking on Goliath: The Emergence of a New Left Party and the Struggle for Democracy in Mexico* (University Park: Pennsylvania State University Press, 1997).

15. For an account of power struggles in the PRD, see Adolfo Aquilar Zínser, *Vamos a ganar: La pugna de Cuauhtémoc Cárdenas por el poder* (Mexico City: Editorial Océano, 1995).

The PRD won 17 percent of the national vote in the 1994 presidential election; however, until 1997 the party had been steadily losing ground to the PAN in states that had been traditional strongholds of the Left, such as Chiapas, Oaxaca, and Michoacán. The severity of the economic crisis did not translate into increased support for the PRD, in large part due to the party's incapacity to devise a viable alternative to the government's economic policy. In addition the party displayed a schizophrenic attitude toward electoral reform. The more moderate and conciliatory faction led by Porfirio Muñoz Ledo supported negotiations with the Zedillo government and advocated active participation in the design of a new electoral law. However, the more purist antigovernment groups—spearheaded by Cuauhtémoc Cárdenas—were reluctant to endorse electoral reform.

Although Cuauhtémoc Cárdenas remained an important moral force within the party during the 1994–97 period, his political protégé and party president, Andrés Manuel López Obrador, emerged as a prominent and popular national leader in 1996. López Obrador had gained recognition as a result of his unsuccessful gubernatorial bid in Tabasco in 1994 and his subsequent crusade to dislodge his fraudulently elected PRI rival from power. López Obrador headed a political current within the PRD that supported *partido-movimiento* (party movement)—a hybrid incarnation for the party—which sought to combine organizational and institutional development with mass mobilizations and marches to protest electoral irregularities and government policies.[16] Through popular demonstrations that pressured the government into negotiating on key issues—such as forcing the government oil monopoly, PEMEX, into investing in development projects in Tabasco—López Obrador inaugurated a tough but compromising strategy that gradually became the PRD's trademark during the Zedillo term.

Under López Obrador's guidance, the PRD demonstrated an increasing willingness to negotiate with the government in the process of elaborating what opposition leaders called a "definitive" electoral reform. Although the 1994 presidential election was generally perceived as the cleanest in Mexico's history, the consensus among opposition parties was that many of the structural imbalances of the electoral system prevailed. Among the main sources of contention stemming from that elec-

16. See Andrés Manuel López Obrador, *Entre la historia y la esperanza* (Mexico City: Editorial Grijalbo, 1995).

tion were issues of campaign financing, unequal access to the media, the role of the Federal Electoral Institute, and the many sources of government support for the ruling PRI. The reforms were designed to create more equal access among parties and address numerous areas where unfair competition still prevailed.[17] After months of difficult negotiations, the PRI, PRD, PAN, and the Worker's Party (PT) finally arrived at an accord that established the following fundamentals:[18]

- the autonomy of the Federal Electoral Institute (the entity that supervises Mexico's electoral processes) and its independence from the federal government;
- for the first time, the direct election of the governor of Mexico City (that is, the mayor) in 1997;
- the integration of the Federal Electoral Tribunal (which resolves electoral disputes) into the judiciary—in other words, independent judges will have the final word on postelectoral differences among the parties;
- the creation of rules related to party financing and media access.

Although these reforms constitute a significant improvement over current electoral legislation, several major flaws remain. No agreement was reached on the constitutional rule established by the PRI majority that grants any party that wins 35 percent of the vote an automatic majority in Congress. Designed to assure the PRI's predominance, the provision constitutes one of the greatest existing obstacles to fair political representation. The proportion of public financing for parties (90 percent, with only 10 percent private) hurt parties, such as the PAN, that rely heavily on private contributions. In other areas the PRI was willing to make concessions because it needed opposition parties to recognize its legitimate victories at the local level and could not afford for every election to become a battleground. Electoral reforms combined with the political backlash created by the 1994 economic crisis thus strengthened the prospects for a highly contested midterm congressional race in 1997.

17. Pedro Aguirre, Ricardo Becerra, Lorenzo Córdova, and José Woldenberg, *Una reforma electoral para la democracia* (Mexico City: Instituto de Estudios para la Transición Democrática, 1995).

18. Poder Legislativo Federal, "Decreto de Reformas y Adiciones a la Constitución Política de los Estados Unidos Mexicanos," Doc. 148/LVI/96; Ricardo Becerra, Pedro Salazar, and José Woldenberg, *La reforma electoral de 1996: Una descripción general* (Mexico City: Fondo de Cultura Económica, 1997).

On the night of July 6, 1997, left-wing candidate Cuauhtémoc Cárdenas swept triumphantly into the Zócalo, the main square in Mexico City, and as he waved to an exuberant crowd, Mexican politics changed, probably forever.[19] After sixty-eight years of dominance by the ruling Revolutionary Institutional Party (PRI), the terms "coexistence," "cohabitation," and "divided government" were incorporated into the country's vocabulary. Congress was transformed from a rubber-stamping, subordinate entity into a testing ground for democratic politics. The PRI lost its majority in Congress, and the Mexican stock market did not crash.

Indeed, Mexicans voted peacefully, abundantly, for change and against the ruling party. The government did not tell the electorate what the future augured; instead, citizens themselves interpreted through the ballot box. The country's destiny was not decided by the president or imposed by PRI officials; the population chose its own path at the polls.

However, despite the euphoric mood, the election proved that news about the PRI's death had been greatly exaggerated. The PRI emerged very much alive from the race: the ruling party won 40 percent of the national vote, four out of six governorships, and managed, thanks to the lifeboat provided by its traditional voters, to retain several of its usual bastions. Once again, the PRI sought refuge (and found it) in the rural areas: the southern states of Oaxaca, Chiapas, and Guerrero remained in the PRI's grip. A mixture of intimidation and inertia, clientelism and conviction, presidential stumping and fear of change guaranteed the party another lease on life, another uncertain remission.

However, the PRI did face important defeats. The party lost 112 congressional seats, the majority in local congresses in seven states, and the governorships in two states—Nuevo León and Querétaro—that are economic powerhouses. The jewel in the crown, the federal district, was placed squarely on the head of an opposition that was perceived as the ruling party's worst enemy, the PRD. President Zedillo had proclaimed that economic recovery had set in; the results of the July 6 election proved that most Mexicans did not believe him. The party was punished for a multiplicity of sins. Although the worst of the financial debacle of 1994 was over and the population had learned new survival tactics, the campaigns rubbed salt over a wound that had not fully healed. People

19. This section, on the 1997 midterm election, draws from Denise Dresser, "Mexico After the July 6 Election: Neither Heaven nor Hell, *Current History*, February 1998.

relived their grievances and voted against the party that had produced them. Although geographically removed from the eye of the storm, former president Carlos Salinas de Gortari was omnipresent, and Mexicans lashed out against him and his legacy at the ballot box.

In the 1997 midterm election, the PRI seemed downtrodden, bewildered, out of sync with the times. Eight out of ten Mexicans between the ages of eighteen and twenty-five—Mexico's "Generation X"—voted against the ruling party. Although there were several exceptions, PRI campaigns were low risk, without surprises, without new proposals, without luster. PRI candidates kissed babies, distributed bottles of what later proved to be contaminated water, organized mass meetings, and relied on the carcass of the party's corporatist machine. The electoral demise of Alfredo del Mazo, the PRI's candidate for mayor of Mexico City, proved that even a well-known *priísta* supported by one of the strongest political clans in the PRI—the Atlacomulco group, named after a town in México state—can lose. Burdened by the blunders of its president, Roque Villanueva, the party suffered the absence of a coherent national strategy. Trapped in an identity crisis, the PRI continued to win but by less and less, on fewer occasions, and by smaller margins. The party became more and more fragmented, less national, and more regional: a strong PRI in Tamaulipas and Coahuila coexisted with a weak PRI in Mexico City and Querétaro. The PRI unraveled in the state of Veracruz, but reinforced its grip in Tabasco.

In a paradoxical twist, president Zedillo was the winner, but also the loser, of this election. His political capital rose as a result of clean, peaceful, and well-run elections. Also, his statesmanship in the face of Cárdenas's victory was commended; instead of lambasting the arrival of an opposition mayor, he applauded it. But in the aftermath of the election, the president was faced with a resentful and undisciplined party that felt it was paying at the polls for the president's economic policy. The PRI was left with few incentives to toe the presidential line on legislative issues, and its loyalty to neoliberal economic reform remained tenuous at best. In reaction to the PRI's perceived electoral demise, a splinter group of *priístas* in the Mexican Senate formed a political coalition—the Grupo Galileo—that questioned the top-down directives and discipline that characterized the PRI in the past. In addition, several hard-line governors from the Southeast declared their intentions to question Zedillo's technocratic leadership, seize control over the PRI, and resurrect the party's standard operating procedures.

The 1997 race also underscored that, contrary to the prevailing wisdom before the election, Cuauhtémoc Cárdenas was not a political has-been. In the aftermath of Cárdenas's second failed bid for the presidency in 1994, many pundits and politicians had signed Cárdenas's death certificate: Cárdenas was over, done, forgotten, spent. The greatest surprise of the electoral season was his electoral renaissance: his metamorphosis from a wooden, sullen, superior, Mexican messiah to a smiling, successful, serene candidate. Not only did Cárdenas reinvent himself, he was also helped by a peculiar coincidence that surfaced during the campaign. In several ways, the 1997 elections were a replay of the 1988 elections. Now, as then, Mexico lived in a *clima oposicionista:* an opposition climate. Now, as then, many Mexicans felt that their economic situation was worse, not better. Now, as then, many Mexicans felt the need to punish the PRI. In 1997, over 70 percent of those polled supported the need for change.

In an unexpected turn of events, the PRD was better suited to capitalize on this simmering discontent than the PAN. To begin with, Cárdenas changed his political style, and his party ran a better campaign than three years previously: both read the polls better, modified their strategy, and redesigned their platform accordingly. The PRD discarded the plaintive, whining tone of past campaigns and developed a forward-looking optimistic message. Cárdenas replaced his purist positions of the past with a new pragmatism, and took advantage of opportunities that his rivals squandered. In a country where decency had become a scarce commodity, Cárdenas was perceived as the only decent candidate. Among an electorate who considered collaboration with Salinas as tantamount to treason, Cárdenas was viewed as a victim of the former president and not as his lackey.

Cárdenas also benefited from the dismal campaign that National Action Party candidate Carlos Castillo Peraza ran in the city, and from the capital's traditional, antigovernment attitude. In addition, the Zapatista National Liberation Army's silence and virtual disappearance from the national political scene exorcised fears that a Cárdenas victory would fuel instability and violence. In 1997, aided by a "teflon" effect, whereby all accusations from his opponents simply slid off, Cárdenas came into his own.

Cárdenas's performance as mayor of Mexico City will help determine the future of the Mexican Left. Almost overnight, the Left experienced a political renewal. Since its creation in 1989 the PRD had lagged behind its adversaries by a wide margin and seemed condemned to winning no more than 17 percent of the national vote. Trapped in an apparently never-ending struggle between personalities and factions, the PRD had become the beleaguered third wheel of Mexico's party system. In 1994, the PRD trailed behind as the third electoral force in Mexico City with just 20 percent of the vote. And yet in 1997, the PRD garnered over 45 percent of the vote, twenty-nine out of thirty federal deputies, and thirty-eight out of forty seats in the Asamblea de Representantes (the city council).

The July elections placed a feather in the cap of party president Andrés Manuel López Obrador. His *brigadas del sol* (brigades of the sun) infused the PRD's campaign with a vitality it hadn't witnessed since 1988, and his dynamic and pragmatic style accounted to a large extent for the party's electoral inroads. Thanks to the party's stunning performance, some of its heavy hitters have gained representation in the Mexican Congress.

The PRD's stance on concrete policy issues has become difficult to predict given the party's ideological ambiguity. The PRD's leadership has said that it will govern without losing its principles. The problem is that few in the party seem to know exactly what principles they are unwilling to lose. Party leaders seem to believe that all of the country's ills can be solved by a strong dose of democracy combined with political goodwill. Caught by surprise by the magnitude of its congressional victory, the PRD began to develop a legislative agenda in late 1997. Included in its list of potential political battles are establishment of committees to investigate past corrupt practices by PRI officials, creation of new laws that would regulate public office, and promotion of an electoral reform that would make funding fairer. Whether the PRD succeeds in passing these laws will depend on its ability to establish voting coalitions with the PAN, with members of some of the smaller parties, or even with disaffected *priístas*.

Along with the resurrection of the Mexican Left, among the most interesting developments throughout the 1997 electoral season was the new role of the media. More vigilant journalists and more critical coverage guaranteed a degree of unprecedented competitiveness and accountability. For the first time in the country's history, the media behaved like an incipient "fourth estate," and young, aggressive journalists seemed more intent on breaking the news than on supporting the PRI. The written press spearheaded a dual process of professionalization and modernization, embodied by the Mexico City daily *Reforma* and its sister publication in the northern city of Monterrey, *El Norte*. In recent years these iconoclastic newspapers have published polls showing the PRI's demise, written stories about the symbiosis between drug traffickers and politicians, and placed pictures of former untouchables like Raúl Salinas de Gortari—mistress on lap, á la Gary Hart—on the front page.

The country's political transition also forced television to march to the beat of a more democratic drummer. In the past, the private television monopoly Televisa effectively functioned as a public-relations firm for the Mexican government, and its owner, Emilio Azcárraga, constantly declared that he was "a soldier of the PRI." As a result, during the 1988 presidential race, opposition candidates were invisible men. Televisa and tightly controlled government networks only allotted 5 percent of their time to Cárdenas, although he probably won the election. However, in 1997, more competitive and privatized television stations were obligated—both by ratings and the demands of the autonomous Federal Electoral Institute—to provide more inclusive and fair-minded coverage.

Television (despite persistent biases) placed the three contenders of the federal district on equal footing. Instead of standing passively by, the population participated, observed, and judged what it saw on the television screen. The government-Televisa cufflink didn't mistranslate Cárdenas to the population; he translated himself via his access to the screen. Under the harsh and unforgiving glare of the television cameras, PAN candidate Carlos Castillo Peraza proved to be the only politician capable of losing a debate with himself. Scrutinized by probing journalists, the PRI's del Mazo was exposed as a stereotypical member of the old guard. Media access magnified the virtues of good candidates and the vices of bad ones. Via television, radio, and the press, political competition reached people's homes and psyches, and thus undermined the PRI's arguments that opposition politicians were Antichrists. In what amounted to a turning point in Mexican political history, Cárdenas, minutes after learning he had won, appeared on a Televisa talk show and engaged in a lively conversation with Lorenzo Meyer, a prominent historian and commentator who in the past had been banned by the pro-government television conglomerate.

For the first time in Mexican history, candidates and campaigns mattered. Perhaps no other party learned this lesson as bitterly as the PAN. Despite its announcement in January 1997 of a victory foretold in Mexico City, this party was the clear loser in the nation's capital. Acción Nacional thought that it was enough to have a good brand—the PAN—

and that the party's prestige and growing electoral clout would be enough to assure individual victories. But the party's selection of a bad product—Carlos Castillo Peraza—cost the PAN a probable triumph in the city and numerous votes in the provinces.[20] With 40 percent support in the polls at the beginning of the race, this was Castillo's election to lose, and he lost it. Both Castillo and the PAN have had to come to terms with the disastrous results, and recognize that Castillo Peraza was the Bob Dole of Mexican politics, a good party leader but an unfortunate candidate.

Millions of *capitalinos* voted against him for reasons that were more visceral than rational. Castillo was crucified not because of his proposals but because of his arrogance. In the final count, the intelligence of his message and the weight of the PAN were buried by the personal deficiencies of the candidate. The PRI also learned this lesson the hard way, after a bad campaign by front-runner Fernando Ortiz Arana cost the ruling party the crucial governorship of Querétaro. The quality (or lack thereof) of campaigns and candidates altered predictions and produced surprises. A volatile, unpredictable, and increasingly sophisticated electorate rewarded those who ran good races and punished those who didn't. The predictable voter had become a thing of the past.

After the election , the PAN engaged in an unprecedented amount of soul-searching, which led to a gradual alteration of the power balance within the party. The more traditional, purist faction in the PAN— epitomized by Castillo Peraza—began to give way to the neo-*panístas,* the pragmatists, the wing of the party that cares more about winning power than about protecting principles. Castillo's demise strengthened the political hand of politicians with electoral and governmental experience, including Ernesto Ruffo, Francisco Barrio, Carlos Medina, and Vicente Fox. As a result, the PRI no longer found an easy or unconditional ally in the National Action Party, as it had in the past. Under the leadership of the *bárbaros del Norte* (the barbarians from the North)—and with the presidency in mind—the PAN tried to undermine the PRI at every turn. The PAN's recalcitrance in Congress during the last months of 1997, including its willingness to establish strategic, short-term alliances with the left-wing PRD, was testimony to this shift.

20. Armand B. Peschard-Sverdrup, "The 1997 Mexican Midterm Elections Report" (Western Hemisphere Election Study Series, Center for Strategic and International Studies, Washington, D.C., August 30, 1997).

As a result of the midterm election, the process whereby economic policy making was made in Mexico changed, irrevocably and for the better. In a complete break with its docile past, the Mexican Congress turned into a battlefield, complete with frontal attacks, strategic retreats, endless negotiations, and potential stalemates. For the first time during a budget negotiation—in November and December of 1997—government technocrats were forced to explain why their proposals were best, why budget deficits were dangerous, and why taxes should not be cut. Congress thus became, as historian Enrique Krauze predicted, a "laboratory of democracy."

Not everyone in Mexico welcomed or understood these changes. President Zedillo, for example, declared after the election that "economic policy will not change." And a prominent economist from the Instituto Tecnológico Autónomo de México (ITAM)—the breeding ground for Mexico's ruling technocracy—stated during the 1997 budget debate that opposition congressmen were "crazy" for even discussing a new economic route. The president, however, no longer had the prerogative to make such a sweeping claim. And even the most narrow-minded Mexican economists and businessmen were eventually forced to recognize that a democratic Congress was not, by definition, an irresponsible Congress.

Emboldened by their electoral success in the midterm election, Mexico's opposition parties initially banded together to form an "opposition bloc" to confront the PRI in Congress. Led by prominent leaders from the major parties—Porfirio Muñoz Ledo, Santiago Creel, Carlos Medina Plascencia—the bloc wrestled several of the most important congressional committees away from the PRI, including the Governance and Budget Committees. Both parties had a major incentive to maintain a united front and defeat the PRI. The PRD wanted to be recognized as a responsible political force, and therefore needed to avoid radical stances; the PAN, on the other hand, felt forced to banish the perception of coziness with and proximity to the government (a perception rooted in the party's collaborative relationship with Carlos Salinas de Gortari). Thus, the parties began to hammer out a unified legislative agenda, only to be confronted in November 1997 with the first real challenge to the survival of the bloc: the battle over the budget.

Negotiations over the budget proved to be the new Congress's trial by fire, as major differences surfaced among government and opposition parties over taxes and the size of the deficit. The Zedillo team wanted to stay the current neoliberal course, while the opposition "bloc" called for lower taxes and higher government spending. Ultimately, however, ideological and strategic differences between the PAN and the PRD led the former to abandon the bloc, vote with the PRI, and pass the budget.

After heated negotiations, the end result was an Aristotelian middle ground: a budget with no tax cuts, an expanded deficit, and major modifications—introduced by the opposition—to budget disbursement: in short, more social spending, less political slush for the PRI. This outcome actually constituted a "win-win" situation for both the government and the opposition. The Zedillo team claimed a political victory by refusing to budge on the tax issue, while the PAN argued that its newfound political muscle was strong enough to reorient government spending for the coming year. And the PRD once again was able to declare that the PRI-PAN alliance had sabotaged democracy, thus demonstrating that the Left was the only force capable of defending popular interests.

The budget wars augured a new era in Mexican politics, an era defined by congressional and party politics. Bills went back and forth, congressmen defected from their party's voting blocs, and lobbying became an integral part of the country's political landscape. In other words, Mexico began to experience the vagaries of a true legislative life. And as a result, the central axis of Mexican politics changed. In the past, in order to decipher Mexico, analysts focused on the presidency and the PRI. After the 1997 election, the spotlight shifted to Congress.

Actors Outside of Established Institutions

Economic adjustment during the 1980s and 1990s has created a Mexican electorate that is much more volatile and less loyal to the PRI, and has opened windows of opportunity for opposition parties on both the left and right of the political spectrum. However, these parties were not able completely to bridge the chasm of distrust that separated them from an increasingly disaffected populace. Among some sectors economic decline also led to disillusionment with the existing political options offered by parties and to the strengthening of opposition movements working outside of party channels.

Although the party system matured over the last decade, parties and elections did not entirely represent the demands of several social groups. As a result, parties recently have often been eclipsed by other protago-

nists in civil society, such as the EZLN and its sympathizers, nongovernmental organizations (NGOs), business leaders, the media, and groups of
disaffected intellectuals and politicians. Although electoral politics became more institutionalized and more actors were willing to play by the
rules of the game, several key groups and individuals continued to operate at the margins of established politics.

One clear example of the insufficiencies of the party system was the
Chiapas conflict.[21] Peace talks to resolve the Zapatista revolt took place
between 1994 and 1996 in Chiapas, with no conclusive results. The government's strategy to contain Chiapas, place the conflict on the back
burner, negotiate *ad nauseam,* and bore the Mexican populace with a
strategy of "negotiation overkill" functioned effectively during those
three years. The power balance tilted in the government's favor for a
variety of reasons: First, the EZLN was spatially contained and no longer
controlled the municipalities that it took over during its 1994 military
initiative. Second, by wresting a significant portion of territory during
its own military onslaught in January 1995, the government diminished
the ability of the EZLN's charismatic leader, Subcomandante Marcos, to
influence civilians in the local towns. Third, before the government's
military crackdown in 1995, the EZLN demanded the total retreat of the
army. Afterward, it insisted only that the army proceed no further and
that dialogue replace confrontation. Fourth, by unmasking Marcos and
exposing him as Sebastian Vicente Guillén, a university professor and
"urban terrorist," the government successfully reduced Marcos's popularity among certain sectors of the population, including members of the
middle class, business groups, the intelligentsia, and the media. Finally,
the slow pace of the peace talks weakened support for the EZLN among
previously loyal groups, who began to view the Zapatistas as intransigent and uncompromising.

The January 1998 massacre in the town of Chenalhó—in which a
paramilitary group linked to the ruling PRI killed forty-five villagers—
proved that Chiapas remained a political time bomb. The killings constituted a dramatic indicator of the political turbulence prevalent in the
state, and sad testimony to the Zedillo government's lack of efficacy. The
Zedillo team's strategy (ignore the conflict and postpone the search for

---

21. For an analysis of the Chiapas uprising, see Neil Harvey, "Rural Reforms and the Zapatista
Rebellion: Chiapas, 1988–1995," in *Neoliberalism Revisited: Economic Restructuring and Mexico's
Political Future,* ed. Gerardo Otero (Boulder, Colo.: Westview Press, 1996), 187–208.

any real solution) reached its limits in Chenalhó. The Zedillo team's response in the months before Chenalhó was a combination of stall tactics and outright militarization. The Mexican army spent most of its time combing the Chiapas hillside in an effort to detect and deactivate pro-Zapatistas and their sympathizers. But by granting so much power and presence to the military and simultaneously ignoring the existence of paramilitary groups such as Paz y Justicia (the group involved in the Chenalhó massacre), the government followed a dangerous path. Allegations of human-rights abuses continued to rise; according to human-rights organizations in the state, an average of fifteen people die daily in Chiapas as a result of unbridled political violence.[22]

Although several people—including the mayor of Chenalhó—were arrested for their alleged involvement in the killings, the turmoil did not abate. At the heart of the crisis was a bitter ongoing debate over the possibility of granting "autonomy" to the indigenous communities of the state. In February 1996, the government signed the Accords of San Andrés Larráinzar with the EZLN. Since the signing, however, the government has attempted to backtrack on its commitment, for fear of the full implications of indigenous autonomy.

After Chenalhó the situation reached another impasse, a stalemate marked by increased tension and escalating violence. It seemed that the only possible solution would be for the EZLN to accept a renegotiation of San Andrés, a process that would take the issue of indigenous autonomy to the Mexican Congress. But for the EZLN to return to the table, the government would have to offer an olive branch: a gradual withdrawal of military troops from Chiapas. This would be a best-case scenario, and would involve compromises and goodwill by both sides. As of February 1998, however, expectations regarding a negotiated solution remained low.

In addition to the EZLN, a new group—the narco-politicians—became a destabilizing force, particularly in states such as Jalisco, Baja California Norte, Sinaloa, and Guerrero.[23] During the Salinas term, the "success" of the U.S. war on drugs in quelling drug trafficking in Colombia was offset partially by the rerouting of the drug trade through Mexico. The Mexi-

22. See Human Rights Watch/Americas Watch, *Deberes incumplidos: Responsabilidad oficial por la violencia rural en México* (Washington D.C.: Human Rights Watch, 1997).

23. Roberto Zamarripa and Santiago Pérez, "El narco y su espacio," *Enfoque*, August 20, 1995, 3–9; Silvana Paternostro, "Mexico as a Narco-Democracy," *World Policy Journal* 12, no. 1 (1995): 41–47.

can government coexisted uneasily with drug traffickers, in some cases even providing them with political protection. Drug cartels established ties with high-level government officials, state governors, and money-laundering corporations in various sectors of the economy, and cajoled Mexican authorities to assist them when U.S.-Mexican drug-enforcement efforts were tightened.[24] In order to shore up his credibility at home and abroad, Zedillo broke many of the unwritten rules that governed relations between drugs and political power by arresting regional drug lords. As a result, drug-related violence and retribution became a significant feature of Mexico's political landscape.

Other actors, such as the debtors' movement El Barzón (the yoke), emerged as significant challenges given the unpredictable direction of their actions. El Barzón, which began as a union of indebted farmers in the western state of Jalisco, captured headlines after the 1994 economic crisis with its protest marches and bank boycotts and claims to have 4.5 million members in three hundred affiliated groups across the country. The debtors' movement was a spontaneous grassroots uprising that spanned the country's rural and urban sectors; overwhelmingly middle class, it had no apparent ties to political parties. El Barzón lost some momentum with Zedillo's $1 billion plan to restructure private debts;[25] however, given that interest rates remained high and economic recovery was confined to the modernized export sector, the movement continued to hold appeal for those who were disproportionately bearing the burden of adjustment.

Initiatives such as those undertaken by the EZLN and El Barzón illustrate the fact that political activity in Mexico is taking place through a multiplicity of nonparty channels. In addition, this activity is no longer restricted to domestic actors. Mexico now hosts a "democracy network": an extraordinary variety of international election observers, professional associations, foundations, religious and social movements, and NGOs working together to promote democracy in Mexico.[26] The timing of the

24. Jorge Castañeda, "The Underworld Goes Mainstream," *Los Angeles Times*, May 23, 1995.

25. The plan was aimed primarily at Mexico's middle class, saddled with car-loan and mortgage interest rates that average 40 percent and credit-card rates that hover around 79 percent. The government also targeted problems in the agricultural sector, where El Barzón is most influential. Under the plan, banks lowered their rates on all kinds of loans to below-market levels and received a government subsidy to compensate for the lost interest.

26. See Denise Dresser, "Treading Lightly and Without a Stick: International Actors and the Promotion of Democracy in Mexico," in *Beyond Sovereignty: The Collective Defense of Democracy in Latin America*, ed. Tom Farer (Baltimore: Johns Hopkins University Press, 1996).

Chiapas revolt, its impact on international awareness, and the relative cleanliness of the country's first post-NAFTA elections suggest that integration into the world economy has become a catalyst for democracy in Mexico. As globalization proceeds apace, Mexico is increasingly exposed to the influence of an embryonic "transnational civil society."[27] Each successive wave of democratization has contributed to the emergence of formal and informal nongovernmental networks, at home and abroad, devoted to the promotion of human rights, the protection of minorities, the monitoring of elections, the provision of economic advice, and the advancement of governmental accountability.[28]

In the era of post-NAFTA politics, external actors are amplifying the impact of domestic movements for political change in Mexico.[29] Domestic social movements have joined forces with international networks of organizations to press for greater political opening and attention to human and political rights. The success of the Mexican democracy network resides in its capacity to work outside of official government channels and promote democratization in an "indirect" fashion.[30] The activities of the pro-democracy network have led to a slow, important, and permanent redefinition of Mexican sovereignty.

U.S.-Mexican Relations: Stumbling from the Start

In a confidential memo to the State Department leaked to the Mexican press in May 1991, U.S. ambassador to Mexico John Negroponte urged strong support for the Salinas government via free trade, declared that Mexico was changing its attitude toward Washington "dramatically," and argued that NAFTA presented a unique opportunity for expanding

27. I borrow the term "transnational civil society" from Terry Karl, "Democratization Around the Globe: Its Opportunities and Risks," in *World Security: Trends and Challenges at Century's End*, ed. Michael T. Klare and Dan Thomas (London: St. Martin's Press, 1993).

28. Ibid.

29. For an analysis of how pressures from the international system and civil society can contribute to political change within the state, see Alison Brysk, "From Above and Below: Social Movements, the International System, and Human Rights in Argentina," *Comparative Political Studies* 26, no. 3 (1993): 259–85.

30. For a description of forms of "indirect support" that can strengthen democratic institutions in Latin America, see Abraham F. Lowenthal, "The United States and Latin American Democracy: Learning from History," in *Exporting Democracy: The United States and Latin America: Themes and Issues*, ed. Abraham F. Lowenthal (Baltimore: Johns Hopkins University Press, 1991).

U.S. influence in Mexico.[31] The dynamic of U.S.-Mexican relations since the signing of the free-trade agreement proved Negroponte right. The Clinton administration's support of a financial rescue package for Mexico's flailing economy in early 1995 strengthened U.S. leverage over Mexican affairs,[32] including drug and immigration policy. On a number of bilateral issues, Mexico's foreign policy aligned itself increasingly with U.S. interests, demonstrating the importance of bilateral linkage politics. At the same time, on numerous fronts, post-NAFTA interdependence created significant challenges for leaders on both sides of the border.[33]

Over the past century, Mexico and the United States have undergone what has been called a process of "silent integration." However, in contrast with previous inward-looking and protectionist governments, Mexico's technocratic teams under Presidents Salinas and Zedillo deliberately sought to institutionalize and harness that silent integration. Mexico promoted a free-trade agreement with the United States and sought the support of actors abroad to consolidate economic reforms at home. Mexican technocrats strived to ensure the success and sustainability of an ambitious program of economic reform by establishing alliances with international actors. NAFTA, GATT, U.S. investment, binational business alliances, and the financial rescue package of 1995 were marketed by Mexican government elites as a kind of "insurance policy" for maintaining the program of economic liberalization undertaken since the early 1980s.

The logic of Mexico's leaders was that international commitments would assure domestic-policy continuity beyond the Zedillo term and make policy reversal difficult. A frequent complaint on the part of potential investors throughout the 1980s was that Mexico had not fully institutionalized its new neoliberal development model, leaving the ambitious reforms of the Salinas administration open to reinterpretation by future presidents. NAFTA limited the options of the Mexican state by codifying liberal trade and investment policies in an international agreement.[34] By tying the Mexican economy to the international arena, both the Salinas and Zedillo teams hoped to ensure that their economic vision would survive the pendular policy shifts of future *sexenios*.

31. Gerardo Galarza, "Nadie ni nada dervirtía lo que dice Negroponte," *Proceso,* May 20, 1991.

32. For details on the 1995 rescue package, see Ngaire Woods's chapter in this volume.

33. "México-EU," *Enfoque,* October 8, 1995.

34. Nora Lustig, "TLC: A punto de ser socios," *Nexos,* November 1991, and idem, *Mexico: The Remaking of an Economy* (Washington, D.C.: Brookings Institution, 1992).

As part of Mexico's strategy to institutionalize interdependence, the country's economic teams developed strong professional relations with the U.S. financial and business communities and the U.S. government. Mexican bureaucrats traveled abroad frequently to renegotiate debt rescheduling and credit arrangements, to lobby in favor of free trade, and to promote the virtues of Mexico's adjustment program. Salinas and his economic decision makers often surprised International Monetary Fund and World Bank officials by making decisions one step ahead of these institutions—that is, by adopting policies that were in line with the economic model supported by the Bank and the Fund but not on their immediate agenda for Mexico. Considering the emergence of this "Mexico City/Washington consensus," it was not surprising to observe the presence of a strong pro-Salinas constituency in the United States before the Mexican meltdown in December 1994.[35]

During the early 1990s, U.S. investors responded favorably to Mexico's quest for allies in the United States; money managers were attracted to Mexico's higher interest rates, its well-educated policy makers, and the prospect of increased profits under NAFTA. However, the depth of their commitment was uncertain. As the Mexican peso remained overvalued and the Salinas team came to depend on capital inflows to finance the burgeoning current-account deficit, foreign capital arrived primarily in the form of portfolio investment rather than investment in plants and equipment. Between 1989 and 1994 more than two-thirds of capital inflows to Mexico were short-term investments in peso-denominated stocks and bonds, which were attractive by virtue of high current yields and a peso that in real inflation-adjusted terms exceeded 1987 levels.[36]

One of the key symbols of the success of the Salinas government, both at home and abroad, was the stability of the peso. Salinas extended wage and price controls through mid-1994, and the peso's daily devaluation against the dollar was cut in half, from forty to twenty centavos a day, or roughly a 2 percent average. Meanwhile, this volatile, highly speculative form of external financing, together with the peso's appreci-

---

35. For an analysis of the "Washington consensus," see Paul Krugman, "Dutch Tulips and Emerging Markets," *Foreign Affairs* 74, no. 4 (1995): 28–44; Moisés Naím, "Mexico's Larger Story," *Foreign Policy,* July/August 1995, 112–30; and Craig Torres, "Peso Surprise: Mexico's Financial Crisis Ambushed Top Minds in Officialdom and International Investing," *Wall Street Journal,* July 6, 1995.

36. For a fuller explanation of these economic trends, see Manuel Pastor's chapter in this volume.

ation against the dollar, ultimately triggered the financial havoc that surrounded the December 1994 devaluation.

During the last two years of the Salinas term Mexico was trapped in a vicious cycle: real exchange-rate appreciation created a growing imbalance in the current account, which was financed by foreign-capital flows. Capital flows, in turn, provoked even greater appreciation of the currency, thus worsening the current-account deficit. Although economic growth had slowed by 1993, the government did not change course, due to its short-term conviction that price stability was more important than the promotion of competitiveness through a currency devaluation.[37] Retaining the political support of urban voters and key business groups in an election year became one of the primary concerns of government policy.

After the Chiapas rebellion and the Colosio assassination, the election-year temptation to shift from fiscally responsible government spending to massive and politically motivated public expenditures became irresistible. Political and electoral imperatives led to the enactment of contradictory policies, especially during 1994. Nora Lustig has argued that the devaluation was caused primarily by the fiscal and monetary policies adopted during that year.[38] In order to assure the continued influx of foreign capital, the government argued that its main objective was to maintain the existing exchange-rate policy; indeed, as the exchange rate became a symbol of the government's overall policy credibility, any policy deviation would have entailed a collapse in confidence.[39] But in clear opposition to that stated goal, fiscal and monetary policies during 1994 were more expansionary than they should have been, and therefore undermined the goal of exchange-rate stability.[40]

The damage inflicted on the economy by the sudden plunge in for-

37. Nora Lustig, "The Mexican Peso Crisis: The Foreseeable and the Surprise," (Brookings Discussion Paper 114, Brookings Institution, Washington, D.C., 1995), 1.

38. Ibid., 7–9.

39. Jeffry Frieden, "Political Sources and Political Lessons of the 1994–1995 Mexican Crisis" (paper presented at a meeting on the Mexican Crisis, sponsored by the Carnegie Endowment for International Peace and the World Bank, Washington, D.C., October 1995), 15.

40. According to Lustig ("The Mexican Peso Crisis," 14–15), "The monetary authorities decided to 'sterilize' the fall in international reserves by increasing net domestic credit and so keep the monetary base constant. This led to a fall in domestic interest rates beginning in July [1994], a trend contrary to interest rates in the United States. The expansion of net credit exacerbated the pressures on the peso." On the fiscal side the public sector's borrowing requirement had risen by two percentage points due to the development banks' net lending.

eign-investor confidence underscored the extent of Mexico's dependence on foreign-capital flows. The reestablishment of positive political and economic relations with the U.S. government, international financial institutions, and private investors became crucial for the recovery of the Mexican economy. President Clinton's financial rescue package was a response to pressure from U.S. investors, but it also reflected a growing recognition of the structural interdependence of the two economies. As the White House argued, a Mexican default would have spurned an influx of illegal immigration, wreaked havoc on other emerging markets throughout Latin America, and hurt millions of U.S. families with pensions invested in mutual funds.[41]

The rescue package undoubtedly contributed to the short-term stabilization of Mexico's financial system. However, its impact was not limited to the economic realm. As one of the central pillars of growing U.S. influence on Mexico's affairs, the bailout also affected the course of Mexican foreign policy. Mexico's nationalist, independent, and activist foreign policy—one that frequently ran counter to U.S. interests—was largely abandoned. Foremost among the foreign-policy priorities of the Zedillo administration was the avoidance of diplomatic conflicts that might sabotage the economic interests Mexico shared with the United States, whose markets and investments were critical to economic recovery.

Since the approval of the rescue package, the Mexican government has tended to be much more accommodating toward the United States, particularly on drug and immigration issues. The arrest in Mexico and subsequent deportation to the United States of Juan García Abrego, the head of the infamous Gulf Cartel, illustrated how compliant Mexican authorities have become in the face of U.S. pressure. Initially the deportation was justified by the Mexican government based on García Abrego's alleged U.S. citizenship. However, subsequent reports contradicted the government's position. In a private meeting with Mexican legislators, Zedillo admitted that García Abrego had been sent to the United States for "reasons of national security," given that Mexican institutions did not have the resilience to "deal with that kind of power."[42] Zedillo's statements were interpreted as a reluctant admission of the weaknesses

41. "Cabildea la Casa Blanca para evitar que se bloquee el apoyo financiero de EU a México," *La Jornada,* April 5, 1995.

42. Quoted in *Reforma,* January 21, 1996.

of the Mexican judiciary and the lack of progress on judicial reform during his tenure. However, the president's comments also suggested that U.S. pressure led to the decision to extradite. As a result, the arrest did not provide President Zedillo with much political capital, as Mexican public opinion applauded the arrest while protesting García Abrego's deportation to the United States. The capture of García Abrego earned Zedillo praise from the Clinton administration, which was intent on keeping Mexico out of the political debate surrounding Clinton's bid for reelection.

The videotaped beating of Mexican illegal immigrants in Riverside, California, in March 1996 shed light on another potential land mine in U.S.-Mexican relations: immigration. In Mexico the event elicited a general condemnation of the U.S. government and calls for a stronger Mexican stance toward the Clinton administration. Polls revealed that Mexicans felt their government was to blame, first, for failing to provide employment and thus forcing Mexicans to migrate and, second, for failing to adopt a more active role in the protection of the rights of illegal immigrants. In response, Zedillo delivered a speech in which he attempted to minimize the Riverside debacle, thereby refusing to adopt a more critical position regarding U.S. immigration policies. As a result, the Mexican government's reaction was perceived domestically as ineffectual and constrained by Mexico's dependence on U.S. capital.

The incident revealed a continuing source of friction in U.S.-Mexican relations. Despite the passage of California's explicitly anti-immigrant Proposition 187 in 1994, illegal immigration has risen steadily since the onset of the peso crisis.[43] Mexico has been reluctant to press for a bilateral immigration treaty to help control this trend, given that illegal immigrants constitute a useful "safety valve" for the unemployed and provide an important source of capital in the remittances that are sent back across the border. But the growing antimigrant and anti-Mexican sentiment that has swept California—and Washington—could lead to greater U.S. pressure on Mexico to stem the flow. This necessarily would entail the further militarization of the border—a controversial policy with high political costs for the Zedillo administration.

The only issue over which Mexico challenged U.S. foreign policy

---

43. In August 1995 apprehensions of illegal immigrants by U.S. authorities were 26 percent higher than the year before, according to Dianne Solís, "U.S. Stops More Mexicans at Border As Their Economic Opportunities Sink," *Wall Street Journal*, August 8, 1995.

during the first three years of the Zedillo term was the Helms-Burton Act.[44] Since its introduction, the Mexican Ministry of Foreign Affairs has conducted a hemispheric campaign against the bill and condemned U.S. efforts to strengthen the blockade against Cuba. Mexico joined Canada and the European Union in opposing what they considered an unlawful U.S. effort to penalize foreign companies that do business with Cuba.[45] In this instance, the Mexican government could afford to adopt a more confrontational stance against the United States because the bill had been condemned internationally and by other powerful U.S. allies. Mexico joined the rhetorical bandwagon at little cost, simultaneously obtaining the support of Mexican businesses with investments in Cuba.[46]

As Mexico's foreign policy becomes more closely aligned with U.S. interests, and as ties between the two countries grow stronger and more complex, the boundaries that separate U.S. domestic politics from Mexican politics have become increasingly irrelevant.[47] In an era of growing economic interdependence, even political sovereignty is a bilateral affair. Mexico has become a part of domestic battles in the United States, creating new coalitions and reinforcing preexisting cleavages. For example, U.S.-Mexican relations have borne the brunt of three new trends in the U.S. Congress: the weakening of the political center and strengthening of more conservative factions since the 1994 midterm election, the arrival of more isolationist and protectionist members, and increased volatility in foreign-policy issues.[48] When President Clinton sought congressional support for the rescue package at the beginning of 1995, he encountered strong opposition that ultimately required him to bypass Congress and authorize funds without congressional approval.[49] Republican condemnation and questioning of the rescue package, in turn,

44. The U.S. law requires foreign companies to report any property they have in Cuba that was confiscated from U.S. owners by the government of Fidel Castro. It also allows those companies to be sued in U.S. courts for compensation.

45. Jorge I. Domínguez, "La ley Helms-Burton sobre Cuba: Una primera evaluación," *Este País*, no. 61 (April 1996): 54–60.

46. Emilio Zebadúa, "Respuesta a Helms y Burton," *La Jornada*, July 18, 1996.

47. For an analysis of "the new issues of interdependence" between Mexico and the United States, see Robert A. Pastor, *Integration with Mexico: Options for U.S. Policy* (New York: Twentieth Century Fund Press, 1993).

48. Jeremy D. Rosner, "México, el Congreso estadounidense y las nuevas tendencias de la política exterior de Estados Unidos," *Este País*, no. 59 (February 1996): 22–27.

49. See Frederick W. Mayer, "Actitudes estadounidenses hacia México después del TLC," *Este País*, no. 58 (January 1996): 27–31.

forced the U.S. administration to adopt a more aggressive position on immigration control and Mexican financial accountability.

As a result of the financial crisis, corruption scandals, and political turbulence, Mexico's image deteriorated dramatically in the United States. Drug trafficking, corruption scandals south of the border, and increased immigration from Mexico have added to the tide of U.S. resentment. As a result, "even Mexico's friends in Washington would prefer not to be identified as such, especially in an electoral year."[50] Pat Buchanan's bombastic opinions on Mexico pushed his adversary Bob Dole into adopting a more critical position during the 1996 presidential campaign. Responding to political pressure from labor unions that oppose NAFTA, President Clinton delayed an agreement allowing trucks from Mexico to travel freely in U.S. border states. In 1995 Mexican producers shipped so many tomatoes to U.S. markets that Florida growers complained they were being subjected to unfair competition. The outcry focused attention on the U.S.-Mexican trade imbalance and prompted calls for NAFTA's repeal.[51]

Although NAFTA's repeal or renegotiation seems highly unlikely, trade and nontrade issues will continue to generate cycles of confrontation between the two countries. The issue of political change in Mexico, for example, has become a central part of the dynamic of U.S.-Mexican relations. The U.S. press and human-rights organizations are playing a critical role in the discovery and disclosure of corruption, money laundering, and human-rights violations in Mexico. Their activities undoubtedly have contributed to enhanced public scrutiny of the Mexican political system, constraints on corrupt practices, and greater transparency of the political process. U.S. media coverage has also led to the resurgence of calls from U.S. officials for the Clinton administration to use its political and economic clout to democratize Mexico. The demand to condition NAFTA implementation on political opening in Mexico still resonates in Washington. Despite Zedillo's efforts to convince U.S. observers of his commitment to political reform, many congressional leaders remain skeptical. Continued revelations regarding the misconduct of the Salinas family, for example, have exacerbated already negative perceptions.

50. Alan Stoga, "Zedillo en EU: Tiempos difíciles," *Reforma*, October 9, 1995.
51. Diane Lindquist, "Mexico: Flash in the Pan or Export Powerhouse?" *Hemisfile* 7, no. 2 (1996): 3–4.

As U.S. policy toward Mexico becomes more strident and confrontational, U.S. policy makers run the risk of resurrecting Mexico's historical
ambivalence toward its neighbor. Mexican resentment of the United
States has grown in the post-Salinas years and as a result of specific
conditions attached to the rescue package, particularly the use of Mexico's oil revenues as collateral on the loans. The percentage of Mexicans
who support a continuation of NAFTA has declined since 1992, from 51
percent to 34 percent. In 1992, 42 percent of Mexicans believed that
Mexico benefited from NAFTA; in 1995 the number had dropped to 20
percent.[52] Meanwhile, President Clinton had to expend large amounts of
political capital to support Mexican-related causes that are unpopular
among the U.S. electorate (for example, a Times-Mirror poll published in
January 1995 revealed that 79 percent of those interviewed were against
the bailout, while only 18 percent supported it).[53]

Although both governments seem committed to recognizing, enhanc-
ing, and managing interdependence, these data reveal that the future of
U.S.-Mexican relations no longer falls within the exclusive domain of
government-to-government interactions. Relations that once were managed solely by executive branches now involve interactions between the
two societies. Mexican-U.S. relations are increasingly shaped by "fragmented and multiple collective actors."[54] Institutions, organized interests
at the national level, and cross-border coalitions are influencing horizontal relations between the two governments in accordance with specific
interests that are often independent of—or even antagonistic to—the
national interest as it may be construed by national-policy makers.[55] The
future of U.S.-Mexican relations will increasingly be affected by NGO
activity, the media, human-rights organizations, business interests, and
others.[56] According to a survey by the Chicago Council on Foreign Rela-

52. "TLC: Un balance en la opinión pública," *Este País*, no. 58 (January 1996): 29.

53. Mayer, "Actitudes estadounidenses hacia México después del TLC," 30.

54. Alberto Melucci, "Frontierland: Collective Action Between Actors and Systems," cited by
James N. Rosenau, "Coherent Connection or Commonplace Contiguity? Theorizing About the California-Mexico Overlap," in *The California-Mexico Connection*, ed. Abraham F. Lowenthal and Katrina Burgess (Stanford: Stanford University Press, 1993), 5.

55. Stephen P. Mumme, "State Influence in Foreign Policy-Making: Water Related Environmental Disputes Along the U.S.-Mexico Border," *Western Political Quarterly* 38, no. 4 (1985): 620–40.

56. See, for example, Maria Lorena Cook, "Regional Integration and Transnational Politics: Popu-
lar Sector Strategies in the NAFTA Era," in *The New Politics of Inequality in Latin America: Rethinking
Participation and Representation*, ed. Douglas A. Chalmers, Carlos M. Vilas, Katherine Hite, Scott B.
Martin, Kerianne Piester, and Monique Segarra (New York: Oxford University Press, 1997), 516–40.

tions, in 1994 more Americans considered Mexico a "vital interest" for the United States than at any point since such surveys began in 1978.[57] The challenge for leaders on both sides of the border will be to develop and institutionalize that "vital interest" in the most constructive fashion possible.

Conclusion

The perpetual paradoxes and contradictions to which Octavio Paz alluded define Mexican politics in the post-NAFTA era. On January 1, 1994, free trade went into effect, propelling Mexico onto the shining path of North American integration. That same day, armed peasants challenged Mexico's image as a bastion of social peace and political stability in Latin America. Almost a year later, Mexico's first democratically elected president swept into office with promises of *bienestar para la familia* (the well-being of Mexican families). Within just a few weeks, the devaluation had stolen that dream, plunging Mexican incomes to pre-1982 levels.

Among the most dramatic changes in the aftermath of the country's financial debacle was the weakening of Mexican presidentialism. In his efforts to decentralize power and depoliticize the authority of the executive, President Zedillo cut loose lines of control that had long provided the political system its enviable stability.[58] This presidential retreat ultimately led to a decentralization of power favorable to democratic evolution. But it also empowered the leaders of authoritarian enclaves who took advantage of the president's weakness to strengthen their fiefdoms. Zedillo became the first president from the ranks of the PRI willing to sacrifice his party for the sake of economic recovery; the electoral ascent of the PAN together with the twilight of the PRI was a price he was willing to pay.

In the midst of a difficult transition, the critical issue in Mexico after the onset of the crisis became how to sustain prolonged public confidence in the Zedillo team, given that there were no clear indications of

---

57. Rosner, "México, el Congreso estadounidense y las nuevas tendencias de la política exterior de Estados Unidos," 23.

58. Kaufman and Trejo, "Regionalism, Regime Transformation, and PRONASOL."

the quick success of his economic policies.[59] Until economic recovery resumed in 1996, the ruling technocracy survived the impasse by providing institutional outlets for political contestation—that is, by channeling discontent through the ballot box. Democracy became an effective containment policy. The deepening of economic reform under Zedillo entailed the gradual unraveling of the PRI and the electoral ascent of the PAN and the PRD. However, the prevalence of anti-institutional actors—including guerrillas, drug traffickers, and unruly members of the ruling party—underscored insufficiency of the country's institutional arrangements in containing all social and political disaffection.

But beyond granting electoral victories to the opposition, Zedillo was unable to develop a clear strategy for generating political consensus for economic adjustment, or implementing economic policies to relieve broad income disparities. Over 40 percent of Mexico's population continued to live in poverty, and real wages in many sectors remained below pre-1980 levels. Extreme inequalities in income and social well-being prevailed among states and regions and between urban and rural areas. In addition, the benefits of greater integration with the United States were distributed unevenly, deepening regional disparities between a prosperous North increasingly tied to the U.S. economy and a backward South plagued with agricultural stagnation. Mexico increasingly became a "dual society" wherein a growing portion of the population failed to reap the benefits of free trade and economic reform.

Mexican leaders were unable to broaden the coalition of beneficiaries of economic reform and counteract both economic and social polarization. In the process of stabilizing the macroeconomy, the Zedillo government neglected socially beneficial microeconomic intervention by the state and dismantled many of the meager compensatory mechanisms still available. However, it is at the micro level, among extra-institutional actors such as the followers of the EZLN, El Barzón, and disaffected peasant organizations, that the greatest challenges to stability were posed. Social costs wrought by renewed economic austerity continued to place severe strains on Mexico's political and economic system. Although by 1997 the Mexican economy showed signs of renewed growth, that recovery failed to translate into concrete benefits for the majority of the Mexican population.[60] As Jorge Castañeda pointed out, "[A]s long as Mexico

59. Sixty-four percent of those interviewed in a recent poll considered Zedillo's management of the economy "bad" or "very bad." *Reforma,* June 2, 1996, 4A.

60. "Mexico's Surprising Recovery," *Economist,* June 29, 1996, 75–76.

delays the changes that will bring prosperity to all, the country will remain stalled, divided between a minority whose lot depends on the United States and a majority periodically buffeted by economic and political crisis."[61]

As a slew of major and minor conflicts in U.S.-Mexican relations since the enactment of NAFTA reveals, Mexican promotion of greater integration with the United States has become a double-edged sword. The bilateral relationship is riddled with politically sensitive issues—including drug trafficking, immigration, and relations with Cuba—that routinely jeopardize the spirit of North American integration. As a result of NAFTA, the autonomy of Mexico's government elite has been increasingly curtailed. NAFTA solidified and institutionalized Mexico's liberalizing reforms and sharply narrowed the available range of policy options for Zedillo's successors.

Domestic economic policy in Mexico has been influenced heavily by the NAFTA-based economic-integration process. The success of Mexico's economic strategy continues to reside in the willingness of U.S. private investors to channel funds into the country. Dependence on U.S. capital to fund external deficits constrains the government's room to maneuver on many fronts. As a result of NAFTA, future Mexican presidents will not enjoy complete control of all the traditional instruments of foreign and domestic policy, including trade, investment, wage negotiations, and the provision of a viable social safety net. Major policy shifts will prove difficult if not impossible, restricting the government's capacity to respond to changing problems, conditions, and public preferences.[62]

The results of the July 6 midterm election offered one key lesson for actors with a stake in NAFTA: Mexico became more difficult to understand. Those in the United States with an interest in Mexico—government officials, investors, analysts, the media—were suddenly confronted with a country where nothing was written in stone, where the Congress, the provinces, and the PRD mattered. In the past, the U.S. government had one main interlocutor: an omnipotent president and a monolithic disciplined party. For years Americans had the luxury of dealing with a very predictable ruling class. After the election, U.S. officials were forced to learn more about opposition leaders, regional politi-

---

61. Jorge Castañeda, "Mexico's Circle of Misery," *Foreign Affairs* 75, no. 4 (1996): 92.

62. I borrow this point from John Sheahan, *Conflict and Change in Mexican Economic Strategy* (La Jolla: Center for U.S.-Mexican Studies, University of California at San Diego, 1991).

cians, and interparty politics. In the past, the problem with Mexico was its opacity; in the future, the challenge will be its openness—not its undemocratic habits but its uncertainty, not the dead calm of the 1970s but the complexity of the 1990s. Almost overnight Mexico turned into a much more disaggregated, decentralized country, and, in some ways, a more complicated partner.

What can Mexico's NAFTA partners look forward to? More of what the country witnessed in the July 1997 race: more dirty campaigns, more combative elections, more competitive races, but also more transparency and more accountability. In other words, more of the stuff that democracy is made of. As writer Federico Reyes Heroles has argued: "la democracia no es grata" (democracy isn't pleasant). It is a constant tug-of-war, the institutionalization of uncertainty. The country's fundamental problems—poverty and polarization, inequality and unemployment, corruption and drug trafficking, guerrilla warfare and unresolved crimes—will pose as much of a challenge to opposition governments as it did to their PRI predecessors. As the Chiapas uprising underscored, NAFTA, fiscal discipline, surging exports, and external support are no longer sufficient to keep the "other" Mexico at bay. And, as the 1994 devaluation revealed, even economic dream teams can and do make mistakes when they operate without accountability. Post-NAFTA politics in Mexico do not augur the country's arrival in heaven, but they will not condemn Mexico to hell either. Instead, Mexico will finally enjoy the kind of politics that sixty-eight years of PRI purgatory had denied it: a political future—however uneasy, uncertain, and unpredictable—of its own making.

Part III A Free-Trade Agreement
of the Americas?
The Path Ahead

8 The Trade Scenario for Other Latin Reformers in the NAFTA Era

Carol Wise

By the mid-1990s, Latin America as a region had achieved a degree of trade liberalization that was unthinkable as recently as a decade ago. Through a combination of unilateral reductions in tariff and nontariff barriers, increased multilateral participation in the GATT, and the renovation and/or creation of new mini-multilateral schemes such as the Andean Group and

Background research for this chapter was supported by an American Area Republics Fulbright and by the North-South Center at the University of Miami. The author thanks Stephan Haggard and Moisés Naím for their helpful comments on earlier drafts; Manuel Pastor for his comments and assistance in compiling the data base that appears in Table 8.2; and Maria Barboza, Monica Garaitonandia, Julia Holman, and Walter Weaver for their highly capable research assistance. Additional thanks are due to the Latin American institutions and colleagues that hosted this research project: Mauricio Cardenas at FEDESARROLLO in Bogotá, Patricio Meller and Alejandra Mizala at the University of Chile in Santiago, and Adolfo Canitrot at the Instituto Torcuato Di Tella in Buenos Aires.

Mercosur,[1] the region has come a long way toward constructing a more open and transparent trade regime. In terms of the progress that has been made in shifting to a more competitive export-led development model, trade between Latin America and the rest of the world doubled between 1990 and 1995, while trade within the region grew at an annual rate of about 20 percent over the same period.[2] Similarly, both of the subregional groupings just mentioned have seen a 25–30 percent average annual rate of growth in trade among their members since 1991.[3]

While tremendous strides have been made in commercial opening and economic restructuring, today's reformers face three main challenges as these programs enter the medium term. First is the problem of policy efficacy. A comparative analysis of five major reformers (Argentina, Brazil, Chile, Colombia, and Mexico) that are now more than five years into the reform effort reveals the extent to which the somewhat mediocre growth, productivity, and income trends identified for Mexico in Chapter 1 constitute a regional pattern. Apart from the unrealistic expectations that political leaders and policy makers have created regarding the rapidity with which market reforms can deliver concrete economic gains, this chapter suggests that the region's adjustment lag is also related to the fact that commercial opening in the 1980s has mainly been a macroeconomic phenomenon. Although trade liberalization, by definition, implies significant restructuring at the microeconomic level, policy makers have been driven largely by the urgent need to reduce inflation and attract international investment in the wake of the 1982 debt shocks.

A second challenge explored here is the universal need for a "second phase" of strategies, which better link success at the macroeconomic level with the imperatives of dynamic restructuring at the microeconomic level. In hindsight, macroeconomic stabilization has clearly been

---

1. The Andean Group is a renovated integration scheme from the 1960s that has now regrouped into a customs union including Bolivia, Ecuador, Colombia, Peru, and Venezuela; Mercosur, an altogether new arrangement that was implemented on January 1, 1995, is also a customs union and includes Argentina, Brazil, Paraguay, and Uruguay; in June 1996 Chile signed a free-trade agreement with the Mercosur bloc as a whole. For more detail on these mini-multilateral schemes, see Stephan Haggard's chapter in this volume.

2. Miguel Rodrígues and Barbara Kotschwar, "Latin America: Expanding Trade Opportunities," *SAIS Review*, no. 17 (1997): 39–60.

3. See Moisés Naim, "Toward Free Trade in the Americas: Building Blocks, Stumbling Blocks, and Entry Fees," in *Integrating the Americas: Shaping Future Trade Policy*, ed. Sidney Weintraub (Miami, Fla.: North-South Center, University of Miami, 1994), 53–57, and María Beatriz Nofal, "MERCOSUR: Evolution, Opportunities, and Challenges," *MERCOSUR Journal* 1, no. 1 (1995): 9.

a necessary condition for fostering higher growth and investment, but not sufficient for pushing these indicators above the threshold required for more sustainable growth and larger income gains into the next century. The analysis suggests that it is time to put aside the widespread notion that microeconomic innovation will flow naturally from sound macroeconomic management. Rather, a reversal of the region's sluggish productivity rates and dismal distributional record will require a more explicit and coherent set of policies to bridge the gap between macroeconomic success and microeconomic stress.

The third challenge concerns the uncertainty that has surrounded the path forward for Western Hemispheric integration. Although higher levels of fixed investment are essential for spurring economic growth, job expansion, and productivity, the investment boom envisioned by Latin policy makers under an expanded NAFTA and/or a consolidated Western Hemispheric free-trade area has still not materialized.[4] The lag in direct investment is due partly to the need to consolidate the macroeconomic reforms now in place and to rectify remaining microeconomic bottlenecks within labor markets and domestic firms; but it also has to do with the faltering of U.S. leadership in promoting the integration process, particularly in the aftermath of Mexico's 1994 peso crisis. Given the ambiguous path forward for Western Hemispheric integration, this chapter argues a point that had become increasingly clear to such NAFTA hopefuls as Argentina, Chile, and Colombia by early 1995: for some time to come, the most dynamic pull for increased productive investment— both foreign and domestic—lies within the subregional groupings that Stephan Haggard has written about in Chapter 9 of this volume.[5] This chapter is organized around these three themes.

The Political Economic Rationale for Trade Reform in the Region

A range of explanations, which tend to focus on international and/or domestic factors, have been put forth in the political-economy literature

---

4. According to ECLAC, *Strengthening Development: The Interplay of Macro- and Microeconomics* (Washington, D.C.: ECLAC, 1996), 51–52, sustainable growth that renders a systematic rise in per capita GDP "will require an investment of around 28% of GDP, which means a 7% increase in the current average ratio."

5. For more on this point, see Magnus Blomstrom and Ari Kokko, "Regional Integration and Foreign Direct Investment: A Conceptual Framework" (Policy Research Working Paper 1750, World Bank, Washington, D.C., April 1997).

with regard to the causal forces that underpin trade reform.[6] When applying these analyses to Latin America, prominent international-level explanations include the highly disruptive impact of the 1982 debt shocks,[7] and the quiet explosion of intra-industry trade and production that has occurred in the region over the past decade.[8] Domestic-level explanations point to a given country's factors of endowment and chart the ways in which factoral and sectoral preferences get translated into policy by way of interest-group politicking.[9] A final cluster of explanations for trade policy relies on institutional analysis and the ideological biases of those leaders in both the public and the private sectors. Arguments based on the former point to the less-than-democratic nature of the regimes in question and on the post-debt-crisis tendency toward insulating economic technocrats in tight elite-level policy-making cliques in the developing world.[10] Arguments based on the latter suggest that, given the institutional contingencies just described, the president, top government officials, and leaders of public and private peak associations have had significant latitude in instilling their own ideological preferences as national-policy objectives.

While all of the explanations above contribute to our understanding of recent trade-policy reform in Latin America, I would argue that these various international and domestic factors together constitute a more powerful explanation when placed in the following sequence: With respect to the impact of international trends, although increasing levels of intra-industry trade and globally oriented production provided a new structural logic to support commercial opening in some of the cases con-

---

6. Parts of this section borrow from Manuel Pastor Jr. and Carol Wise, "The Origins and Sustainability of Mexico's Free Trade Policy," *International Organization* 48, no. 3 (1994): 459–89.

7. See, for example, Dani Rodrik, "The Rush to Free Trade in the Developing World: Why So Late? Why Now? Will It Last?" in *Voting for Reform: Democracy, Political Liberalization, and Economic Adjustment,* ed. Stephan Haggard and Steven B. Webb (New York: Oxford University Press, 1994), 61–88, and Aaron Tornell, "Are Economic Crises Necessary for Trade Liberalization and Fiscal Reform?" in *Reform, Recovery, and Growth: Latin America and the Middle East,* ed. Rudiger Dornbusch and Sebastian Edwards (Chicago: University of Chicago Press, 1995).

8. On intra-industry trade, and the impetus that it provides for a more open trade regime, see Helen Milner, "Trading Places: Industries for Free Trade," *World Politics* 40, no. 3 (1988): 355–76.

9. See Ronald Rogowski, *Commerce and Coalitions: How Trade Affects Domestic Political Alignments* (Princeton: Princeton University Press, 1989), and Mancur Olson, *The Logic of Collective Action: Public Goods and the Theory of Groups* (New York: Schocken Books, 1968).

10. John Williamson and Stephan Haggard, "The Political Conditions for Economic Reform," in *The Political Economy of Policy Reform,* ed. John Williamson (Washington, D.C.: Institute for International Economics, 1994), 578–81.

sidered here, it was the severe external debt shocks in 1982 that caused existing models of economic management to collapse. On the one hand, the final demise of the import-substitution-industrialization (ISI) model opened up new political and economic spaces for promoting alternative development strategies; on the other hand, an upcoming generation of public and private actors took up this challenge, and in the process stepped outside of traditional state and societal structures and onto a more insulated and exclusive policy-making terrain. Having distanced themselves from former protectionist demands, these new factions aggressively pushed their liberal policy initiatives forward.

Within this general scenario, a second argument concerns the more specific role that trade liberalization has played in stabilizing the macroeconomy in the wake of the debt crisis, as increased import competition became a key instrument for finally bringing inflation down. Why is free trade considered more conducive to macroeconomic stabilization in post-debt-crisis Latin America? It helps to recall that inflation management between 1982 and 1987 was highly unsuccessful throughout the region. Initially, most states responded to the 1982 debt shocks by following the orthodox policy advice of the multilateral institutions, which, among other things, included tight fiscal and monetary policy. Frustrated over the resistance of inflation to these strategies, and by their failure to restore desperately needed foreign-capital flows, countries such as Argentina and Brazil experimented with "heterodox" approaches to stabilization in the mid-1980s. In both cases, this latter strategy actively concealed wages, prices, and the exchange rate, but against the backdrop of loose fiscal policy and high levels of trade protection. The results of these programs were quite disastrous, since each ended with a dramatic outburst of hyperinflation.

As Manuel Pastor points out in Chapter 3 of this volume, it was Mexican policy makers who in 1987 first succeeded in reducing inflation by explicitly linking trade liberalization with macroeconomic stabilization. The Mexican government brought inflation down by negotiating wage and price controls with local business and labor representatives, while simultaneously shrinking the fiscal deficit and liberalizing trade. Quickly, foreign competition, combined with a stable currency, brought inflation under control. At the same time, the Mexican government used free trade as a lure for foreign investment, in hopes that increased capital flows would sustain reserves, further stabilize the currency, and help to preserve the hard-fought macroeconomic victory of reducing inflation from 160 percent in 1987 to 20 percent just two years later. What is unique here is that the desire for free trade on the part of a new cadre of Latin business elites and state policy makers squared well with the need for macroeconomic stabilization in the wake of the debt crisis. Moreover, through this process of linking trade liberalization with macroeconomic stabilization, free trade's traditional opponents have been neutralized.

Four of the five cases reviewed below pursued this similar liberalization-*cum*-stabilization strategy. As can be seen in Table 8.1, Argentina followed in Mexico's footsteps beginning in 1988, and Colombia and Brazil in 1990. Policy makers in all four countries readily admit that trade policy has been driven largely by concerns for macroeconomic stabilization, and that the debate over how best to facilitate microeconomic adjustment has just begun. In contrast, the much earlier liberalization episode in Chile (1975–79) purposefully sought the kind of free-trade shock that microeconomic theory envisions as necessary for fostering higher levels of competition and growth. The following section briefly elaborates on these varying motivations for trade reform, and in the process draws some links between the political economic rationale for commercial opening and the returns thus far with regard to growth, productivity, and income gains.

Disaggregating the Cases

Chile—Trade Liberalization Driven by Microeconomic Concerns

Having liberalized nearly a decade before the debt crisis and with negligible levels of intra-industry trade to spur this commercial reform, the most likely international-level explanation for Chile's opening would be the disproportionate severity with which the 1973–74 oil-price shocks hit the Southern Cone region. While the Southern Cone states generally responded to these earlier external shocks with a combination of harsh market-authoritarian strategies, the Chilean liberalization program was the only one that survived from this period. This is so, even though the launching of the Chilean trade opening was not accompanied by the kinds of institutional innovation or sophisticated state-business relations that characterized the later trade openings, for example, in Mexico and

Colombia.[11] The resilience of Chile's commercial reform is clearly related to the tenacity of the military regime that took control in 1973. By capitalizing on the asymmetries of a highly cohesive and institutionalized base of military power versus a fragmented and polarized civic opposition,[12] the government of General Pinochet (1973–90) easily squelched the kinds of pressure tactics and social protest that have consistently derailed past attempts at trade liberalization in Latin America.

Not unlike the more recent trade openings in the region, this earlier liberalization episode was a reaction both to the shortcomings of ISI over the postwar era and to what military leaders perceived as rampant statism, which in this case had peaked during the preceding Allende government from 1970 to 1973. Yet, it was also prompted by the staunch conviction that abrupt liberalization was the surest means for purging the Chilean economy of cumulative microeconomic distortions.[13] The difficulties that the country experienced in adjusting to that first phase of liberalization have been well documented. Of interest here is the trend displayed in Table 8.2, whereby Chile registered the most dismal performance under the thrust of the 1982–83 external debt shocks, yet quickly rebounded to record the region's highest growth, investment, and total-factor productivity rates over the following decade.[14] Apart from the advantage of launching rigorous stabilization and adjustment measures with little concern for social unrest, the country's rapid recovery was facilitated by the implementation of trade reform before the advent of the debt shocks.[15]

Although the earlier reforms had set the stage for a quick turnaround, there is some debate within the case literature on Chile regarding the specific nature of those post-1983 policy reforms which have

11. What is interesting about this liberalization is that it gave birth to a sizable segment of the state-business coalition that now backs it, rather than the other way around.

12. Stephan Haggard and Robert Kaufman, *The Political Economy of Democratic Transitions* (Princeton: Princeton University Press, 1995), 78–83.

13. Author's interview with Rolf Luders, a member of the economic team under the Pinochet government during this period, July 11, 1996, Santiago, Chile. See also Javier Martínez and Alvaro Díaz, *Chile: The Great Transformation* (Washington, D.C.: Brookings Institution, 1996).

14. According to Sebastian Edwards, *Crisis and Reform in Latin America: From Despair to Hope* (New York: Oxford University Press, 1995), 131, Chile's total-factor productivity increased by 4.96 percent between the 1978–82 period and 1987–91. The comparable figure for Argentina during this same time frame was 1.91 percent, and for Mexico −0.32 percent.

15. Nora Lustig, Introduction to *Coping with Austerity: Poverty and Inequality in Latin America,* ed. Nora Lustig (Washington, D.C.: Brookings Institution, 1995), 21–23.

Table 8.1. Recent commercial policy reforms in Latin America

Country	Reform Period	Pre-Reform Policies	Accomplishments of Trade Reform
Chile	1975–79 1985–88 1996: Signed an FTA[a] with Mercosur[b] bloc as a whole	Multiple exchange rate system; QRs[c] and prohibitions on imports; average tariff 94%, maximum tariff 220%; prior import deposits.	Unified exchange rate; QRs removed; uniform tariff of 10% (excluding automobiles) increased to 35% in response to 1982 debt crisis, but since reduced to a uniform rate of 11%; prior import deposits and most tariff exonerations eliminated.
Mexico	1983–85 (mild) 1985–88 (strong) 1994-Accession to NAFTA	In 1982, QRs covered 100% of tariff positions and 92% of domestic production; average tariff 27%; official reference prices covered 19% of domestic production; export controls covered 60% of total exports.	QR production coverage 20% in 1990; production-weighted average tariff 12.5%; maximum tariff 20%, with most items 10%–20%; most export controls removed; official reference prices removed; joined GATT in 1986; further liberalization of trade under NAFTA with 10–15-year time line.
Argentina	1988–92 1995 Mercosur implemented	Dual exchange rate; QR coverage in manufacturing more than 30%; maximum tariff over 100%; additional specific duties and quasi-tariffs; import prohibitions, advance notice requirements, etc.	Unified exchange rate; QR coverage in manufacturing reduced to approximately 5%; progressive reduction in levels and dispersion of tariffs, with 3 rates and 20% maximum; 12.2% production-weighted average; no specific duties, but some quasi-tariffs remain; some sectoral regimes still in place; further tariff and nontariff reductions scheduled under Mercosur.

Colombia	1984–86 1990–94	QRS covered 61% of tariff positions and 82% of domestic manufacturing; tariff range 0–200%, plus 18% surcharge; average tariff including surcharge 45%.	By end-1990, QRS virtually eliminated, now covering 3% of tariff positions; maximum tariff 100% (excluding luxury automobiles at 300%); tariff surcharge 13%; average tariff including surcharge 33.5%. Targets for 1994: most tariffs 5–15% with automobiles at 100%; tariff surcharge 8%; average tariff including surcharge 12%.
Brazil	Began in 1990 1995 Mercosur implemented	Foreign exchange licensing and negative import lists resulted in discretionary control of virtually all imports; in 1988, maximum tariff 80%.	Foreign exchange licensing virtually eliminated; no negative import lists. Tariff reform initiated in February 1991 sets maximum tariff target of 40% for end-1994; tariff reduction accelerated to 14% in 1993; further tariff and non-tariff reductions under Mercosur.

SOURCES: Kristen Hallberg and Wendy Takacs, "Trade Reform in Colombia: 1990–1994," in *The Colombian Economy: Issues of Trade and Development*, ed. Alvin Cohen and Frank Gunter (Boulder, Colo.: Westview Press, 1992), 286–87; Judith Dean, S. Desai, and James Riedel, "Trade Policy Reform in Developing Countries Since 1985: A Review of the Evidence," World Bank Discussion Papers no. 267 (Washington, D.C., World Bank, 1994); IRELA, "Brazil Under Cardoso: Returning to the Word Stage," dossier no. 52, Instituto de Relaciones Europeo-Latinoamericanas (IRELA) (Madrid: IRELA, 1995); Argentine trade policy information provided by Fernando Flint, Ministry of Economy, Buenos Aires, Argentina.

[a]FTA = Free trade agreement.

[b]Mercosur, or the Southern Cone Common Market, came into effect January 1, 1995, when its four member countries (Argentina, Brazil, Paraguay, and Uruguay) ended tariffs on most of their exports to each other and set a Common External Tariff on imports coming into this free trade area.

[c]QRS = quantitative restrictions.

Table 8.2. Macroeconomic and external indicators for selected Latin American countries

	Argentina							
	1981	1983	1985	1987	1989	1991	1993	1995
Growth of real GDP	−5.9	3.8	−6.6	2.5	−6.3	8.9	6.0	−4.6
Growth of real per capita GNP	−8.6	1.9	−9.1	0.9	−11.6	8.8	5.1	−6.4
Dec.–Dec. inflation	131.3	433.7	385.4	174.8	4,923.3	84.0	7.4	1.6
Total domestic investment as percentage of GDP	22.7	20.9	17.6	19.6	15.5	14.6	18.2	17.5
Private investment as percentage of GDP	16.9	14.8	12.5	15.7	12.2	12.4	15.9	15.2
Public investment as percentage of GDP	5.8	6.1	5.1	3.9	3.3	2.2	2.3	2.4
Real Exchange Rate (1990 = 100)[a]	75.1	157.8	163.8	132.2	202.4	72.1	55.8	54.4
Trade balance (mil$)[b]	712	3,716	4,878	1,017	5,709	4,419	(2,427)	2,238
Current account (mil$)	(4,712)	(2,436)	(952)	(4,235)	(1,305)	(647)	(7,514)	(2,446)
Foreign direct investment (mil$)	730	187	919	(19)	1,028	2,439	2,555	4,336
Foreign portfolio investment (mil$)	1,125	649	(617)	(572)	(1,098)	16,488	24,382	5,005
Total external debt (mil$)	35,657	45,920	50,946	58,458	65,257	65,403	70,576	89,747

	Brazil							
	1981	1983	1985	1987	1989	1991	1993	1995
Growth of real GDP	−4.4	−3.4	7.9	3.3	3.3	0.5	4.5	3.0
Growth of real per capita GNP	−7.3	−6.2	6.2	2.2	2.6	−1.0	1.9	1.5
Dec.–Dec. inflation	100.6	177.9	248.6	432.3	1,759.2	493.8	2,828.7	25.9
Total domestic investment as percentage of GDP	24.3	19.9	18.0	23.2	26.9	19.6	20.4	19.2
Private investment as percentage of GDP	16.6	13.8	12.9	16.8	21.1	14.4	15.5	15.7

	1981	1983	1985	1987	1989	1991	1993	1995
Public investment as percentage of GDP	7.7	6.1	5.1	6.4	5.8	5.2	4.9	3.5
Real Exchange Rate (1990 = 100)[a]	142.3	190.2	214.6	167.4	121.7	110.3	98.2	57.6
Trade balance (mil$)[b]	1,185	6,469	12,466	11,158	16,112	10,578	14,329	(3,157)
Current account (mil$)	(11,764)	(6,834)	(280)	(1,452)	1,002	(1,450)	20	(18,136)
Foreign direct investment (mil$)	2,727	1,796	1,522	1,307	1,654	2,117	1,783	6,243
Foreign portfolio investment (mil$)	4	(270)	(231)	(428)	(361)	3,808	13,534	11,107
Total external debt (mil$)	81,448	98,519	103,601	119,809	114,330	120,701	143,765	159,131

Chile

	1981	1983	1985	1987	1989	1991	1993	1995
Growth of real GDP	4.8	− 3.7	7.0	6.5	9.9	7.2	6.2	8.5
Growth of real per capita GNP	1.8	− 6.0	3.2	7.3	9.7	5.8	6.1	8.2
Dec.–Dec. inflation	9.5	23.1	26.4	21.5	21.4	18.7	12.2	8.2
Total domestic investment as percentage of GDP	18.6	12.0	16.8	19.4	23.0	20.9	25.6	23.2
Private investment as percentage of GDP	13.4	6.3	14.1	13.1	18.2	16.0	19.7	18.2
Public investment as percentage of GDP	5.2	4.7	2.8	6.4	4.8	4.9	5.8	5.0
Real Exchange Rate (1990 = 100)[a]	57.3	85.4	113.4	107.7	106.6	94.3	85.6	73.1
Trade balance (mil$)[b]	(2,677)	986	883	1,309	1,578	1,587	(982)	1,480
Current account (mil$)	(4,733)	(1,117)	(1,414)	(735)	(705)	113	(2,072)	142
Foreign direct investment (mil$)	383	135	146	897	1,299	646	1,241	2,365
Foreign portfolio investment (mil$)	21	3	0	(8)	80	186	910	63
Total external debt (mil$)	15,664	17,928	20,384	21,489	18,032	17,947	20,637	25,562

Table 8.2. (Continued)

	Colombia							
	1981	1983	1985	1987	1989	1991	1993	1995
Growth of real GDP	2.1	1.6	3.3	5.4	3.4	1.8	5.2	5.3
Growth of real per capita GNP	-0.4	-1.0	0.7	3.0	0.5	0.8	3.3	1.5
Dec.–Dec. inflation	26.3	16.6	22.5	24.0	26.1	26.8	23.0	19.5
Total domestic investment as percentage of GDP	17.7	17.2	17.5	17.4	18.1	14.6	18.8	20.0
Private investment as percentage of GDP	10.3	9.7	8.4	10.2	10.2	8.4	11.5	12.9
Public investment as percentage of GDP	7.3	7.5	9.2	7.3	7.8	6.2	7.3	7.1
Real Exchange Rate (1990 = 100)[a]	60.0	60.1	76.7	88.9	95.0	96.9	86.5	64.1
Trade balance (mil$)[b]	(1,572)	(1,494)	(23)	1,868	1,474	2,959	(1,657)	(2,548)
Current account (mil$)	(1,961)	(3,003)	(1,809)	336	(201)	2,349	(2,102)	(4,116)
Foreign direct investment (mil$)	302	722	1,030	345	605	481	1,199	2,785
Foreign portfolio investment (mil$)	(2)	(2)	(1)	48	179	86	498	(21)
Total external debt (mil$)	8,716	11,413	14,245	17,008	16,878	17,334	17,156	20,760

Mexico

	1981	1983	1985	1987	1989	1991	1993	1995
Growth of real GDP	8.7	−4.1	2.7	1.9	3.4	3.6	0.7	−7.2
Growth of real per capita GNP	5.3	−5.2	1.4	0.6	1.4	2.2	−1.5	−10.7
Dec.–Dec. inflation	28.7	80.8	63.7	159.2	19.7	18.8	8.0	52.0
Total domestic investment as percentage of GDP	26.3	17.5	19.2	18.5	18.0	19.2	20.0	17.2
Private investment as percentage of GDP	14.3	11.0	12.5	13.3	13.2	14.7	15.9	14.0
Public investment as percentage of GDP	12.1	6.6	6.7	5.2	4.8	4.5	4.1	3.2
Real Exchange Rate (1990 = 100)[a]	86.5	136.5	113.9	141.1	107.0	87.7	72.9	109.1
Trade balance (mil$)[b]	(3,877)	14,105	8,399	8,786	405	(7,279)	(13,481)	7,089
Current account (mil$)	(16,240)	5,866	800	4,247	(5,825)	(14,888)	(23,400)	(654)
Foreign direct investment (mil$)	3,078	2,192	1,984	1,184	2,785	4,742	4,389	6,963
Foreign portfolio investment (mil$)	831	(385)	(206)	(605)	410	13,344	29,483	(9,477)
Total external debt (mil$)	78,215	92,974	96,867	109,472	93,841	114,067	131,572	165,743

SOURCE: GDP, GNP, and debt taken from World Bank, *World Tables*, CD-ROM, 1997. Inflation, exchange rates, and payments calculated from IMF, *International Financial Statistics* CD-ROM, 09/97. Data on investment from the World Bank's International Financial Corporation.

[a]Calculated using period average exchange rate, US WPI, and domestic CPI.

[b]Trade balance = merchandise exports minus merchandise imports.

been credited for the country's overall economic success.[16] Points of consensus with regard to Chile's post-1983 reform strategy focus on (1) the role that more effective currency management, in particular the shift from a fixed to a flexible exchange rate, has played in setting the country back on course in the throes of the 1982–83 external debt shocks; (2) institutional reforms within the state that occurred gradually over the long period of market-authoritarian rule and that provided the necessary backdrop for these adjustments. These include, for example, the professionalization of key economic policy-making entities like the finance ministry, and the cultivation of an increasingly autonomous central bank through the 1980s; and, finally, there is broad agreement that a post-1983 pattern of collaboration between state elites and private-sector representatives resulted in the more pragmatic and effective set of policies that characterize today's export-led model.

The main points of difference have to do with the extent to which these more sophisticated state financial institutions, their technocratic constituencies, and their backers in the domestic private sector departed from economic orthodoxy in order to rescue what has been so widely touted as an "orthodox" program. There is convincing evidence for such policy divergence, for instance, in the post-1982 restrictions on incoming capital flows, and the temporary hike in tariffs in response to the debt shocks (see Table 8.1). To carry this argument further, one prominent Chilean economist, Patricio Meller,[17] holds that with the reallocation of resources away from manufacturing industry and toward natural-resource exports during the 1970s reform phase, and with the setting of a much more competitive exchange rate in the post-1983 period, the provision of state-sponsored incentives for the promotion and diversification of natural-resource exports quickly began to pay off. Similarly, the state development corporation (CORFO) has granted special subsidies to smaller producers of nontraditional (mainly industrial) exports and played an active role in stimulating small- and medium-sized-enterprise (SME) development since the early 1980s.[18] Although this debate cannot

16. For a comprehensive review of these policy reforms, see Barry Bosworth, Rudiger Dornbusch, and Raúl Labán, eds., *The Chilean Economy: Policy Lessons and Challenges* (Washington, D.C.: Brookings Institution, 1994).

17. Patricio Meller, "Review of the Chilean Trade Liberalization and Export Expansion Process (1974/90)," *Bangladesh Development Studies* 20, no. 2/3 (1992): 155–84.

18. Author's interviews with Carlos Alvarez, Strategic Development Division head, CORFO, July 8, 1996, and Juan Morales, director of Enterprise Development, Confederación Nacional de la Mediana y Pequeña Industria, Servicios, y Artesanado de Chile, July 9, 1996, Santiago, Chile.

be resolved here, this latter group of policies suggests that the medium-term path forward for today's liberalizers may be more flexible, pragmatic, and even dirigiste than has currently been acknowledged.

When judged according to its own goals, there is no taking away from the impressive growth, investment, and productivity gains that Chile has registered under an open-trade regime. As for income gains, although the data on wages and income distribution are considered to be sketchy, the most reliable analyses reflect two trends. First, when compared with the rest of the region, the Chilean track record is one of the most favorable. For example, in stark contrast to Argentina, Brazil, and Mexico, Chile's minimum urban real wage increased by 20 percent from 1987 to 1992;[19] moreover, of the five countries considered here, Chile was the only one that has seen a reduction in urban poverty since 1987.[20] Nevertheless, when wage and distributional trends *within* Chile are compared over time, the data reflect a clear pattern of income stagnation and wealth concentration. On the former, Dagmar Raczynski and Pilar Romaguera note that Chile's current levels of per capita consumption are not much higher than those of the 1970s; on the latter, estimates of the distribution of household expenditures in greater Santiago show that the poorest 20 percent of the population saw its relative share of total expenditures drop from 7.6 percent in 1969 to 4.4 percent by 1988. Conversely, the relative share of the wealthiest 20 percent increased from 44.5 percent to 54.6 percent over this same time period.[21]

Despite a clear commitment to the alleviation of poverty and a substantial improvement in the country's standard of living since the return to civilian rule in 1990, these distributional trends are disappointing, particularly given the long timeline of the Chilean reform process. More recent data for the 1990–93 period still show that the richest 20 percent of the population earned 10.9 times as much as the poorest 20 percent.[22] They also suggest that, even for a trade-reform program inspired largely by the imperatives of microeconomic restructuring, the odds are that more equitable per capita income gains will not flow automatically from higher levels of growth, investment, and productivity, particularly

19. Edwards, Crisis and Reform in Latin America, 279.

20. "Poverty in Latin America and the Caribbean Is Greater Now Than in the 1980's," CEPAL News 16, no. 7 (1996): 1–3.

21. Dagmar Raczynski and Pilar Romaguera, "Chile: Poverty, Adjustment, and Social Policies in the 1980's," in Coping with Austerity, ed. Lustig, 286–90.

22. "Spreading the Benefits of Growth," Latin American Weekly Report, April 11, 1994,351.

when the distributional base is so heavily skewed at the outset of the reforms. Rather, the evidence points to the need for a more aggressive targeting of resources toward achieving this goal, a task that civilian policy makers have now taken up with vigor in the Chilean case.[23]

Mexico and Argentina—Trade Reform Driven by Macropolicy

In both Mexico and Argentina, the combination of severe external shocks in the early 1980s and the structural limitations of ISI rendered obsolete the protectionist government–business–urban-middle-class alliance that had prevailed during most of the post–World War II era. Each case exemplifies the increasing resort to trade liberalization after a prolonged period of frustrated efforts at macroeconomic stabilization following the 1982 debt crisis. These two cases converge in the sense that trade reform was driven by the imperatives of macroeconomic stabilization, and in the extent to which higher levels of intra-industry trade through the 1980s provided the structural impetus for a domestic coalition that supported a more open trade regime.[24] Although the origins and outcomes of these respective reform packages are fairly similar, the policy contexts and institutional settings for reform are markedly different.

As the chapters in Part I of this collection point out, the policy context for Mexico's commercial opening was the Economic Solidarity Pact (or *pacto*) that began in 1987 and was renewed continually up until December 1994. The *pacto* fixed the exchange rate, tightened fiscal and monetary targets, and set wage and price guidelines for stabilizing inflation. Having entered the General Agreement on Tariffs and Trade (GATT) the year before, the Mexican government simultaneously quickened the trade-liberalization timetable that had previously been set, even beyond the GATT guidelines for tariff reductions, as another key component of this inflation-reduction effort. In bringing together all of the main repre-

---

23. Dagmar Raczynski, "Programs, Institutions, and Resources: Chile," in *Strategies to Combat Poverty in Latin America*, ed. Dagmar Raczynski (Washington, D.C.: Inter-American Development Bank, 1995), 207–64.

24. Between 1980 and 1990 Mexico increased its intra-industry trade indices in manufactures from 20 percent to 51 percent, and Argentina from 27 percent to 52 percent. Those producers engaging in intra-industry trade—or the mutual exchange of goods across borders in a certain product category—favor liberalization because it reduces the costs of their imported inputs and because protectionism puts them at an international disadvantage. See Montague J. Lord, "Latin America's Exports of Manufactured Goods," in *Economic and Social Progress in Latin America: 1992 Report* (Washington, D.C.: Inter-American Development Bank, 1992).

sentatives from government, business, and labor, the *pacto* came to symbolize the changing relationship between the public and the private sectors in Mexico, as well as the renovation of the Revolutionary Institutional Party's (PRI's) corporatist ties under a development strategy that departed radically from the heavy statism and patronage of the past.

Within the public sector, the 1980s saw an intentional shift in operational authority and policy influence away from those government ministries that had traditionally housed protectionist sentiments (industry, labor, agriculture), and toward the planning and banking ministries that favored more orthodox policies. As for the Mexican private sector, having survived the various battles for GATT entry, not to mention the 1982 bank nationalization, the country's export-oriented business class quickly found kindred spirits among the widening circle of neoliberal technocrats that began entering government posts in the 1980s. In essence, out of the 1987 Economic Solidarity Pact emerged an alliance between a highly insulated executive, his technocratic corps, and representatives of the country's largest companies and conglomerates. Once the stabilization strategy began to bear the intended results, it was this alliance that sold the trade-liberalization effort at home and forged the domestic constituency that supported Mexico's entry into NAFTA.

In Argentina, the policy context for a similar liberalization-*cum*-stabilization strategy was the passing of the 1991 Convertibility Law, which fixed the exchange rate at one-to-one with the U.S. dollar and drastically reduced the role of the central bank by placing the responsibility for monetary policy in the hands of a currency board.[25] By combining convertibility with major trade and then fiscal reforms, policy makers finally succeeded in halting the chaotic hyperinflation that plagued the country through 1991. Similar to Mexico in its gradual, then rapidly accelerated trade liberalization under the *pacto*, Argentina opened slowly, as part of the bilateral integration thrust with Brazil that began in 1986, and then quickly and more unilaterally escalated its reduction of tariff and nontariff barriers with the implementation of the convertibility-stabilization

25. Alberto F. Ades, "Currency Boards and Its Implications for Argentina" (Economic Research, Goldman Sachs, February 1995). Under a currency board, the monetary base must be fully backed by international reserves. The stabilization mechanism is "automatic": In the event of net capital outflows, the money supply contracts, interest rates increase, economic activity slows, and the current account improves. For further elaboration on Argentina's reform program see Manuel Pastor and Carol Wise, "Stabilization and Its Discontents: Argentina's Economic Restructuring in the 1990's" (Agenda Paper 31, North-South Center, University of Miami, Fla., 1998).

plan in 1991. And, just as Mexican policy makers have sought to bind the country's new liberal-trade-and-investment regime under NAFTA, Argentine officials have committed the country to further liberalization and deregulation within Mercosur.

In terms of the domestic institutional setting in Argentina, the very simplicity of the convertibility plan reflects the low levels of managerial capacity and technical expertise that have traditionally characterized the policy-making apparatus.[26] It is the country's chronic failure to undertake necessary civil-service and administrative reforms, and a profound mistrust of state institutions, that contributed to its comparatively dismal economic performance through the 1980s (see Table 8.2). Although the launching of the 1991 convertibility plan was underpinned by the revamping of the Ministry of Economics into a powerful superministry, the overall reform effort has lacked the far-reaching institutional innovations within the state bureaucracy that have provided a more solid base for market restructuring in Chile and Mexico. Thus, key economic decisions and actual policy implementation have been relegated to an autocratic executive, a handful of elite economic-policy makers, and the representatives of sectoral organizations (e.g., in agriculture, industry, and services) acting on behalf of the country's largest producers.[27]

The results of these respective reform programs thus far reflect the success that each has achieved in pursuing a liberalization-*cum*-stabilization strategy, but also the extent to which ongoing macroeconomic concerns have overshadowed serious debate over the kinds of policies that could better promote microeconomic adjustment. As can be seen in Table 8.2, in varying degrees each country has progressed in the reduction of inflation and in the restoration of growth. Even after the trauma of the peso crisis for Mexico and the related recession, or "tequila effect," for Argentina, each grew by at least 2–3 percent in 1996 and by more than 7 percent in 1997.[28] At the same time, however, neither has managed to boost total investment substantially above the levels realized in the early 1980s; in Argentina foreign direct investment (FDI) has been quite slow to respond to the positive signals that the country has tried so hard to

26. Kathryn Sikkink, *Ideas and Institutions: Developmentalism in Brazil and Argentina* (Ithaca, N.Y.: Cornell University Press, 1991).

27. Luigi Manzetti, *Institutions, Parties, and Coalitions in Argentine Politics* (Pittsburgh, Pa.: University of Pittsburgh Press, 1993), 19.

28. J. P. Morgan, "Global Data Watch" (Morgan Guaranty Trust Company, New York, January 16, 1998).

send, and in Mexico volatile portfolio flows continue to outpace FDI. Finally, while liberalization, privatization, and deregulation have fostered impressive productivity gains within the tradable sectors of the economy, such gains have been offset by historically high unemployment—which in 1996 approached 19 percent in Argentina's major cities—and steep wage compression in both countries.

Underlying these trends is an increasing heterogeneity in the structure of both economies and a worsening of income distribution since the onset of market reforms—neither of which bodes well for maintaining a stable and dynamic pattern of growth over time.[29] As discussed in Chapter 1 of this volume, the Mexican political economy now has two main stories to tell: a success story wherein the top conglomerates in the main tradable sectors have further consolidated their assets and ties with foreign capital and the wealthiest 10 percent of the population has increased its share of national income from 34 percent in 1984 to 41 percent ten years later; and a decidedly unsuccessful scenario wherein those producers and workers within the nontradable sectors have experienced the increasing fragility of small and medium-sized firms, plummeting real wages, and the explosion of activity within the informal economy.

The Argentine scenario has been virtually the same,[30] with the exception that per capita GDP expanded briskly after the implementation of the 1991 stabilization plan—a pattern spurred by the high levels of idle capacity and repressed demand present in the economy at the onset of the convertibility plan—and then slowed after 1995's negative growth rate and the skyrocketing of urban un- and underemployment. As in Mexico, just fifteen to twenty economic groups in Argentina now account for the bulk of exports and 15 percent of GDP, while smaller companies operating in the nontradable sectors continue to struggle against higher interest rates, tight credit, and constricted demand in the domestic market.[31] And, similar to Mexico, the income share of the poorest groups has shifted downward, while the richest 15 percent of the population now accounts for 50 percent of household income.[32] It has, unfor-

29. See, for example, Alberto Alesina and Dani Rodrik, "Distributive Policies and Economic Growth," *Quarterly Journal of Economics* 109, no. 436 (1994): 465–90.

30. Daniel Chudnovsky et al., *Los límites de la apertura: Liberalización, reestructuración productiva y medio ambiente* (Buenos Aires: CENIT/Alianza Editorial, 1996).

31. Author's interviews with Bernardo Kosacoff, CEPAL, Buenos Aires, and Omar Chisari, director, Instituto de Economía, Universidad Argentina de la Empresa, Buenos Aires, August 1, 1996.

32. Author's interview with Luis Beccaria, director, Economics Department, Universidad de Bue-

tunately, taken another set of major external shocks in the form of the 1994 Mexican peso crisis, and a subsequent outbreak of civic protest, to provoke policy makers within both countries seriously to consider the kinds of strategies that could quicken the pace of adjustment for those individuals and firms that have seemingly been excluded from the benefits of trade liberalization and neoliberal reform in general.

Colombia—Commercial Opening in the Absence of Economic Crisis

The political economic rationale for trade reform in Colombia is more subtle than the other cases reviewed thus far. Whereas policy makers in Chile, Mexico, and Argentina shifted to a new economic strategy under the thrust of dramatic external shocks and severe adjustment difficulties, Colombia was able to capitalize on high coffee prices in the mid-1980s and adjusted relatively quickly to the 1982 debt crisis. As Table 8.2 shows, this is the only country that maintained positive growth rates throughout the 1980s, and inflation never surpassed 33 percent. Colombia also differs from these other cases in that the formulation of market reforms was part and parcel of the political process, whereby Congress was a main vehicle for working out the differences between all the various actors that had a stake in the reform process. This is obviously worlds apart from Chile's complete repression of political competition and discourse during the initiation and consolidation of market reforms, or the reliance of Mexico's ruling PRI on tightly circumscribed corporatist control mechanisms, which enabled party leaders to project an image of societal participation in the policy process, when in fact there was very little input.[33]

Although the policy context for trade reform is not as concrete as the launching of Mexico's seven-year *pacto,* or Argentina's passage of the 1991 Convertibility Law, Table 8.1 shows that Colombian policy makers moved just as boldly in reducing tariff and nontariff barriers over the 1990–94 period. Given the weakness of such international explanations as external shocks and/or lobbying pressures from intra-industry traders, and the absence of a precipitating economic crisis on a par with

nos Aires, August 1, 1996. See also "Official Incomes Pattern Is Worse," *Latin American Weekly Report,* February 1, 1996.

33. See Pastor and Wise, "The Origins and Sustainability of Mexico's Free Trade Policy," 478–82, and Haggard and Kaufman, *The Political Economy of Democratic Transitions,* 286–91.

Mexico's and Argentina's struggles against hyperinflation, what prompted domestic coalitions in the public and private sectors to push for an open-trade regime? Moreover, in light of the fact that the current program actually represents Colombia's fourth attempt at commercial liberalization since the mid-1960s, how is it that these subsequent proposals for a liberal trade policy have survived?

According to two frontline policy makers—Rudolf Hommes (finance minister, 1990–94) and Maria Mercedes Cuellar (minister of development, 1989–90)—Colombia's trade reform was driven simultaneously by macro- and microeconomic concerns and by an increasing sense of "peer pressure" to open trade, as Argentina and Brazil forged ahead with liberalization within Mercosur and Mexico moved assertively to negotiate a free-trade agreement with Canada and the United States.[34] At the same time, the early 1990s saw the worsening of an intense political crisis, which continues to plague the country and whose urgency helped to foster a broad consensus around the need for policy reform. Because competitive exchange-rate adjustments in the late 1980s worked against the massive import flows that have plagued Mexico and Argentina in the early 1990s, and because local producers have long had to contend with competition from contraband brought into Colombia by drug traffickers for money-laundering purposes, there was little domestic opposition to trade reform outside of the agricultural sector. Rather, the escalation of ruthless guerrilla conflict during the 1990s, in the form of massacres, bombings, and kidnappings, had the effect of enabling the Gaviria administration (1990–94) to navigate market reforms through the political process, since all sides agreed on the dire need for socioeconomic change in Colombia.

The institutional setting for policy reform is the most sophisticated of the five cases considered here. Since the National Front agreement (1958–76), which put an end to the country's violent civil war, Colombia has been well known for its stable and homogeneous two-party system and for the cultivation of strong economic-planning institutions that have quite successfully avoided the populist excesses that mark the past of most Latin countries.[35] In particular, trade reform was facilitated by

---

34. I am indebted to Rudolf Hommes and Maria Mercedes Cuéllar for the considerable time that each spent discussing Colombia's trade-reform process with me, during two separate interviews conducted in Bogotá on June 13, 1996. See also Miguel Urrutia, "Colombia," in *The Political Economy of Policy Reform*, ed. Williamson.

35. Carlos Juarez, "Politics and Economic Policy in Colombia: Oligarchic Democracy and Techno-

the infiltration of more liberal-minded technocrats into the Ministry of Development, which at the time was the main institutional locus for the formulation of trade policy and traditionally a strong protectionist outback in the state bureaucracy. The alignment of this ministry with those agencies responsible for macroeconomic policy making (e.g., the Ministry of Finance and the Department of Planning) signaled a growing consensus on trade policy, which was mirrored within the government economic team, the office of the executive, and eventually the Congress.

At the macroeconomic level, the domestic debate over trade reform was underpinned by the stalling of growth in 1991 and the leveling-off of FDI; as inflation jumped from 16 percent in 1983 to 32 percent in 1990, the pace of trade liberalization was quickened ahead of plan, since the initial attempt at gradualism had encouraged importers to postpone their purchases until the tariff schedule had been further lowered. Microeconomic concerns centered on the slowing of total-factor productivity, which was partially related to the continued violence and economic stagnation in the rural sector, and on the sluggish pattern of per capita income growth that appears in Table 8.2. Although Colombia is one of the few countries in the region that has improved its distribution of income since 1979–81, having transferred 5.5 percent of national income from the top two deciles to the bottom eight,[36] the growth of per capita GDP has still not improved substantially.

As much as Colombia's trade-policy reform was an appropriate response to these various economic trends, the ability of policy makers fully to address these concerns has been hampered by the same chaotic political dynamics that worked originally to unite producers and politicians in their commitment to liberal policy reform. Despite the state's highly developed economic and planning institutions, the administration of President Ernesto Samper (1994–98) has been entangled from the start in accusations that his electoral campaign was partially funded by the country's drug lords. The stalemate within Congress over Samper's alleged drug ties has prompted the United States to "decertify" Colombia for market preferences that it had enjoyed under the Andean Trade Pref-

---

cratic Reform" (paper presented at the annual meeting of the American Political Science Association, San Francisco, August 29–September 1, 1996).

36. Ariel Fiszbein and George Psacharopoulos, "Income Inequality Trends in Latin America in the 1980's," in *Coping with Austerity*, ed. Lustig, 73.

erence Act,[37] and it has virtually rendered Samper a lame duck for the duration of his term. Unfortunately, although Colombia's two-party system has proved to be competitive enough to raise these volatile charges against the president and to uncover some convincing evidence of their veracity, elite politics have become much too entrenched actually to follow these charges through to their logical conclusion.

This is not to take away from the important macroeconomic gains that Colombia has registered in the 1990s, or from the leadership role it has played in reviving the Andean Group and in initiating a number of other bilateral free-trade accords; however, as the results of economic opening have become more apparent—in particular a jump in growth and productivity in the tradable sector of the economy, while employment, income, and productivity have stagnated in the nontradables sector—political gridlock has limited the kind of analysis and policy debate that will be necessary for the country to make serious improvements in the area of microeconomic adjustment.[38]

Brazil—Trade Liberalization on Its Own Terms

Brazil is surely the most enigmatic of the cases under consideration here. On the one hand, it fell victim to the same 1982 debt shocks that served as a strong catalyst for liberal economic reform in Argentina and Mexico, and Brazil surpasses these countries in its high levels of intra-industry trade in manufacturing. This is to say that the structural conditions that have given rise to outward-oriented trade coalitions in Argentina and Mexico are similar for Brazil. On the other hand, in view of the hyperinflation that persisted in Brazil from 1988 until 1994 (see Table 8.2), it could be argued that the country had even more to gain from the import-competition and liberalization-*cum*-stabilization strategies that have worked to reduce prices in these other countries. Why, then, did policy makers wait until 1993 to deepen their commitment to economic opening, and what accounts for the uneven pace at which liberalization, privatization, and deregulation have proceeded? Predictably, a large part

37. Approved by the U.S. Congress in 1991, the Andean Trade Preference Act was offered as an incentive for the Andean drug-producing countries to cooperate more forcefully with the United States in waging its "war on drugs."

38. Author's interviews with Rafael Herz, Petro Colombia, Bogotá, June 5, 1996; Jesús Duarte, director of social development, National Planning Department, Bogotá, June 6, 1996; and Luis Jorge Garay, Inter-American Development Bank, Bogotá Office, June 13, 1996.

of the answer lies with domestic politics,[39] and in the gradual deterioration of state economic and planning institutions in Brazil.

Since the return to civilian rule in 1985, the Brazilian political system has been plagued by a fragmented and polarized political-party structure, an ineffectual executive, and corruption scandals of such magnitude that impeachment proceedings were initiated against former president Fernando Collor de Mello in 1992. During the second half of the 1980s, Brazil's political economic instability was such that the country saw ten finance ministers and ten central-bank governors, launched five failed anti-inflation shock plans, and underwent four major currency reforms.[40] The extent to which domestic politics have detracted from the economic-reform process is also reflected in the 1988 constitution, which contains explicit "economic-order" clauses that have greatly limited the ability of the executive to implement a comprehensive package of fiscal reforms.[41]

Brazil's economic downslide actually represents the erosion of state capacities that had been developed during an earlier era.[42] In contrast to the conservative central-banking traditions laid down in Colombia and Mexico, economic management in Brazil has been controlled by powerful finance and planning ministries and, since 1985, increasingly by the Congress. These arrangements, while making it more difficult to coordinate macroeconomic policy effectively, were made viable by the initiation of civil-service reforms within key agencies beginning in the 1940s, reforms that harnessed technocratic expertise to strategic sectoral goals. Accounts of the subsequent demise of Brazilian state capacity focus on the encroachment of traditional elites and bureaucratic incompetents into these "pockets of efficiency," a trend that gained force with the thwarting of a number of civil-service reforms by Congress in the 1980s, and with the extremely weak leadership in the executive until the election of President Fernando Henrique Cardoso in 1994.

---

39. See Frances Hagopian, "Traditional Politics and the State in Brazil," in *State Power and Social Forces*, ed. Joel S. Migdal, Atul Kohli, and Vivienne Shue (New York: Cambridge University Press, 1994), 37–64, and Scott Mainwaring, "Brazil: Weak Parties, Feckless Democracy," in *Building Democratic Institutions: Party Systems in Latin America*, ed. Scott Mainwaring and Timothy R. Scully (Stanford: Stanford University Press, 1995), 354–98.

40. See "A Survey of Brazil," *Economist*, December 7–13, 1991, 1–6.

41. Bolivar Lamounier, "Balancing the Short- and Medium-Term: Prospects for Reform and Democratic Development in Brazil" (paper prepared for the Inter-American Dialogue, Tenth Plenary Session, Washington, D.C., October 1996), 2.

42. Sikkink, *Ideas and Institutions*.

It was against this unfavorable political and institutional backdrop that President Collor first moved to liberalize Brazil's trade regime in 1990. However, in contrast to the other cases reviewed here, Brazil's commercial opening was part of an ambitious New Industrial Policy launched by the government in 1990 in an effort to strengthen the country's competitive position in foreign markets.[43] The failure of this first phase of trade liberalization to trigger significant microeconomic restructuring or to exert downward pressure on domestic prices can be attributed to the disarray of those state institutions most responsible for trade policy, and to the series of haphazard stabilization programs that were applied during this period. More to the point, despite the lowering of the average tariff to 14 percent by 1993 (see Table 8.1), Collor's industrial policy dampened price competition by maintaining a wide range of tariffs on some Brazilian durables and capital goods. These barriers were not further reduced until the appointment of Fernando Henrique Cardoso as finance minister and his launching of the Real Plan in July 1994, at which point Brazil joined step with Argentina, Colombia, and Mexico in the use of trade opening as an explicit part of the country's macroeconomic stabilization effort.[44]

By combining trade liberalization with a flexible exchange rate, and by applying greater fiscal and monetary restraint, the Real Plan reduced annual inflation to 26 percent in 1995, its lowest level since 1973, and it set the stage for positive growth (approximately 3 percent of GDP for 1996 and 3.5 percent for 1997).[45] Just as important, Cardoso's reforms have begun to reverse the perverse incentive structure that sustained a seven-year bout of hyperinflation, whereby the government and the private sector had colluded to maintain an inflationary system of price indexing that served both parties extremely well, regardless of the dismal impact on income distribution.[46] Yet, in order to advance his policy re-

43. UNIDO, *Brazil's Industrial Policy: An Assessment in the Light of the International Experience* (Vienna: UNIDO, 1992).

44. Pedro de Motta Veiga, "Brazil's Strategy for Trade Liberalization and Economic Integration in the Western Hemisphere" (paper prepared for the Inter-American Dialogue, Washington, D.C., June 1996), 2, 3.

45. J. P. Morgan, "World Financial Markets: First Quarter 1998" (Morgan Guaranty Trust Company, New York, January 2, 1998), 65.

46. Leslie Elliott Armijo, "Inflation and Insouciance: The Peculiar Brazilian Game," *Latin American Research Review* 31, no. 3 (1996): 7–46. On income distribution, the 1995 data show that the poorest 50 percent of the population holds just 11.6 percent of national wealth, while the richest 20 percent holds 63.3 percent. See "The Real Plan Two Years Later" (Ministry of Finance of Brazil, October 7, 1996).

forms further, Cardoso must finesse the difficult indicators that all of the countries in Table 8.2 have had to grapple with in the process of liberalizing their trade unilaterally: exchange-rate overvaluation, rising trade and current-account deficits, and burgeoning debt. The outbreak of two major international currency crises, in Mexico in late 1994 and the regionwide exchange-rate crisis in Asia during 1997–98, has further complicated the tasks of stabilization and exchange-rate management for Brazil.

As in Colombia, the Brazilian trade-reform effort was subject to prior consultation with Congress, the business sectors, and the trade unions. But unlike actors in Colombia, key political actors in Brazil were more heatedly divided over the nature and extent of the reforms. And, unlike administrations in Chile, Colombia, and Mexico, the Cardoso administration, since the liberalization-*cum*-stabilization program was finally launched, has had relatively limited institutional backup in implementing it. Even Argentine president Carlos Menem's reform strategy—of circumventing an unruly Congress and weak institutional framework through the strong reliance on executive decrees[47]—is less of an option for Cardoso, since the remaining structural reforms (social security, public administration, and the tax system) must be secured via constitutional amendments in order to carry their full impact. Although Cardoso's early victories with the Real Plan facilitated the crafting of a broad congressional coalition that helped push through a first round of constitutional amendments related to the reform package in mid-1995, it is these more comprehensive fiscal measures that are considered to be crucial to the plan's ultimate success.[48] Cardoso must now continue to navigate Brazil's rocky political terrain, including the defense of tough fiscal and monetary initiatives in the midst of his 1998 bid for reelection.

These political and economic challenges help to explain some of Brazil's apparent backtracking on trade liberalization since 1995. As the business sector began to complain of a double squeeze—intensified import competition under an increasingly overvalued exchange rate, plus continued pressures related to volatility in foreign exchange and capital markets—policy makers responded by imposing import quotas on autos

47. Haggard and Kaufman, *The Political Economy of Democratic Transitions*, 206, and Pastor and Wise, "Stabilization and Its Discontents."

48. Lamounier, "Balancing the Short- and Medium-Term," 1–2.

and some consumer durables. Moreover, to the chagrin of Brazil's Mercosur partners, no sooner than had Mercosur's common external tariff (CET) gone into effect than Brazil, by raising tariffs on consumer durables and on some vulnerable nondurables sectors, such as shoes and apparel, breached it.[49] Similarly, as the combination of Brazil's overvalued currency and its large 1997 current-account deficit (nearly 5 percent of GDP) became the target of currency speculators in the wake of the Asian crisis, Brazil colluded with Argentina in raising the CET by as much as 25 percent in some product categories. The government's actions have set off understandable concern from afar that Brazil could be reversing its commitment to trade reform, although it is more likely that these liberalization lapses will prove to be transitory.

The propensity of the Brazilian government to intervene so readily, when most of the states considered here have basically left domestic industry to fend for itself in the face of greater foreign competition, suggests two points about the future direction of Brazilian trade policy. First, as supervisors of the world's ninth largest industrial economy, and as industrializers who perceive themselves as having achieved this status by way of selective protection, Brazilian policy makers have made it clear that at least their version of a trade-liberalization strategy does not preclude the continued resort to sectoral concessions. Second, just as domestic coalitions appear to have settled on a trade opening interspersed with moderate doses of protectionism, public opinion also appears to have converged around the need to move slowly with regard to the deepening of the liberalization commitments that have already been made.[50] In the meantime, as structural adjustment continues to work its way through the economy, policy makers have found themselves increasingly torn between private-sector demands for government assistance and those of a more vociferous mass of poor Brazilians, whose social status continues to deteriorate in spite of the Real Plan's success thus far at stabilizing the economy.

49. María Beatriz Nofal, "MERCOSUR: First Year Balance," *MERCOSUR Journal* 1, no. 2 (1996): 20. The CET has eleven tariff levels, which vary from 0 to 20 percent; however, telecommunications, automobiles, and computer equipment are not covered by the agreement. See also Blomstrom and Kokko, "Regional Integration and Foreign Direct Investment," 31–38.

50. UNIDO, *Industrial Competitiveness in Brazil: Trends and Prospects* (Vienna: UNIDO, 1992), and da Motta Veiga, "Brazil's Strategy for Trade Liberalization," 3–4.

Trends, Lessons, Challenges: The Demand for Public Policy in the Region

There is no denying the tremendous progress that Latin America has made on the reform front since the bleak period following the 1982 debt crisis. Despite continued levels of international financial volatility since Mexico's 1994–95 peso debacle, Latin America's growth projections for 1996–98 are still in the 3 percent range;[51] average inflation for 1996 was estimated at 17 percent, down from an annual average of almost 1,000 percent as recently as 1993; and the average fiscal deficit was just 1.4 percent of GDP in 1997. There is, however, still a downside to these trends. Net capital flows into the region remain unstable (projected at U.S.$68 billion in 1997, down from U.S.$82 billion in 1996), and current growth and investment rates continue to fall short of the levels necessary for sustaining an improvement in employment and equity. Although total-factor productivity gains have been achieved under a more open trade regime, today's high unemployment rates reflect the extent to which productivity improvements have derived from workforce reductions. Most distressing of all has been the persistence of extreme levels of poverty and inequality in the 1990s, as income data show that some 89 million Latin Americans are still left to survive on less than U.S.$1 per day.[52]

Because these trends challenge conventional wisdom concerning a positive relationship between liberalization and enhanced opportunities for wider economic participation, political economists in the 1990s have rigorously set about testing their earlier assumptions. The best of this literature suggests the following:[53] (1) the correlation between high inflation and low growth is indeed significant, since inflation's negative growth effects are felt mostly through the decline in investment;[54] (2)

51. These figures are cited from "Latin America's Backlash," *Economist*, November 30, 1996, 15–21; Shahid Burki and Sebastian Edwards, *Dismantling the Populist State* (Washington, D.C.: World Bank, 1996); and Morgan, "World Financial Markets," 39.

52. Juan Luis Londoño, *Poverty, Inequality, and Human Capital Development in Latin America, 1950–2025*, Latin American and Caribbean Studies, Viewpoints Series (Washington, D.C.: World Bank, 1996), 1.

53. I borrow here from the excellent review by Daniel Lederman, "The Sources of Economic Growth: A Survey from a Latin American Perspective" (paper prepared for the World Bank LAC Economists' Retreat, Annapolis, Md., November 25–26, 1996).

54. Jose De Gregorio, "Inflation, Growth, and Central Banks: Theory and Evidence" (Policy Research Working Paper 1575, World Bank, Washington, D.C., February 1996).

countries with more open and less distorted trade regimes exhibit higher growth, since commercial opening increases comparative advantage, investment, specialization, economies of scale, and total-factor productivity;[55] (3) although all forms of investment are clearly essential for sustained growth, recent analyses show a strong correlation between higher public investment (especially in infrastructure projects) and increases in growth, private investment, and total-factor productivity;[56] (4) finally, while the recent literature suggests that growth can reduce absolute poverty, there is also some evidence that inequality can dampen the prospects for growth.[57] This latter assumption has prompted some to call for a "human-capital shock," or the reduction of poverty and inequality by aggressively stepping up investments in education and efforts at labor-market reform.[58]

What light do these recent political economic findings shed on the Latin American experience, where investment, growth, and greater income gains have all remained somewhat elusive in spite of major advances in liberalization, privatization, and deregulation? At least two lessons stand out. First, in four of the five cases reviewed above, as essential as it was to put an end to high inflation, it appears that the trade-liberalization–*cum*–stabilization strategy has run its course. The risks of relying too heavily on import competition to fight inflation can be seen in Table 8.2, which shows that the combination of trade and current-account deficits has induced policy choices (high interest rates, overvalued exchange rates, and a dependence on portfolio-capital flows) that can detract from growth. The time has come for these countries to broaden and consolidate the macroeconomic-reform effort[59] and to articulate a role for trade policy as part of a larger development strategy. Of the cases reviewed here, only Chile has accomplished the task of

55. Rudiger Dornbusch, "The Case for Trade Liberalization in the Developing Countries," *Journal of Economic Perspectives* 6, no. 1 (1992): 69–86, and Sebastian Edwards, "Openness, Trade Liberalization, and Growth in Developing Countries," *Journal of Economic Literature* 31, no. 3 (1993): 1358–93.

56. Victor J. Elías, *Infrastructure and Growth: The Latin American Case* (Washington, D.C.: World Bank, 1995).

57. Nancy Birdsall, David Ross, and Richard Sabot, "Inequality and Growth Reconsidered: Lessons from East Asia," *World Bank Economic Review* 9, no. 3 (1995): 477–508. The authors argue, for example, that lower inequality can stimulate growth through higher savings and investment rates among the poorest groups, by creating stronger incentives for educational advancement and participation in formal-sector labor markets, and by fostering political and macroeconomic stability.

58. Londoño, *Poverty, Inequality, and Human Capital Development*, 2.

59. For greater detail on this point, see Burki and Edwards, *Dismantling the Populist State*, 14–18.

coordinating trade liberalization with comprehensive macro- and micro-economic reforms, which helps to explain why this case conforms most closely with the political economic findings reviewed in the paragraph above.

A second lesson concerns the almost blind faith that policy makers have placed in the ability of market forces to facilitate economic adjust-ment and thus foster higher rates of growth and income. In fact, this recent political-economy research points to the crucial role that public policy must still play in accelerating per capita income and the accumu-lation of productive investment, for example, by sponsoring public-in-frastructure projects and human-capital development. Again, the Chilean case illustrates the effective use of public policy as a crucial intervening variable for bridging the gap between macro- and micro-level adjustments, which in turn enable policy makers to forge a higher-growth, higher-income development model driven by open trade. The fact that public policy was a main catalyst in the Chilean turnaround in the 1980s, and essential for the "growth-with-equity" campaign imple-mented under civilian rule in the 1990s, suggests that the remainder of the states reviewed here could quicken the pace of reform by formulat-ing an explicit set of public policies to better link macroeconomic stabili-zation with microeconomic adjustment.

At the microeconomic level, today's most obvious adjustment chal-lenges concern the dire need to strengthen human capital and to provide greater backup for domestic firms. On the human-capital front, four of the five cases reviewed here are still in the medium-term phase of eco-nomic restructuring, and political-economy research has increasingly at-tributed the disappointing growth and income patterns to the shortfall in human capital and to remaining distortions in domestic labor mar-kets.[60] A prime drawback to human-capital formation has been the seri-ous lack of an adequate education system to enable the upcoming generation of workers to participate productively in a trade-driven eco-nomic model that demands higher skills. Recent data on educational in-vestments and achievement in the region are telling: although Latin America actually spends more on education than East Asia (3.7 percent

60. The discussion draws on ibid.; Londoño, *Poverty, Inequality, and Human Capital Develop-ment;* and Jeffrey M. Puryear, "Education in Latin America: Problems and Challenges" (paper pre-pared for the Council on Foreign Relations, Working Group on Educational Reform, New York, February 27, 1996).

of GDP versus 3.4 percent), the average Latin worker today is no better educated than the average East Asian worker was in 1970.

As Table 8.3 shows, school-enrollment ratios in Latin America drop quickly at the level of secondary education. Thus, in 1995 the region's average educational level of just 5.2 years placed its adult working population at a startling disadvantage. Underpinning these figures are the generally poor quality of the region's educational strategies, the failure to target resources properly, and the inability thus far to forge a dynamic link between schools and the competitive demands of a market-based development model. The relationship between Latin America's weak human-capital base and poverty/inequality is fairly direct. In Argentina, for example, those with less than five years of schooling have a 69 percent chance of ending up among the poorest 20 percent of the population; conversely, the likelihood that those with sixteen or more years of education would end up in the bottom 20 percent is only 4 percent.

Just as Latin America's workers have had a difficult time finding their place in a rapidly changing labor market, domestic firms are still struggling to adjust to a development model that is now based on competition and market incentives. The analysis of the country cases suggests that liberalization, privatization, and deregulation have thus far failed to reduce long-standing patterns of heterogeneity and asset concentration in the region's industrial structure. In fact, in countries like Argentina and Mexico, the gap seems to be widening between large competitive industrial firms with strong international ties and smaller firms, which tend to be more dependent on domestic markets. For the larger and more globally integrated companies in the region, a dynamic process of microeconomic restructuring is under way, based on intra-industry trade, increasing specialization and economies of scale, rapid productivity gains, and the professionalization of technical and managerial networks.[61] However, the remainder of those firms in the industrial sector, the bulk of which are small and medium-sized companies, still find themselves on the defensive. Although some gains have been made in organizational reform and workforce upgrading, the lack of know-how and financial resources has made it much more difficult for this second group of firms to adapt to today's competitive environment.

It is important to note that these small and medium-sized industrial firms have traditionally been the source of employment expansion in the

---

61. ECLAC, *Strengthening Development*, 36–39.

Table 8.3. Comparative social indicators

Social Indicators		Argentina		Brazil		Chile		Colombia		Mexico	
		1980–85	1989–94	1980–85	1989–94	1980–85	1989–94	1980–85	1989–94	1980–85	1989–94
Housing	Fixed investment (% of GDP)	6.2	5.9	2.6	2.8	4.2	3.3	2.3	2.9	4.4	3.1
Health	Public expenditure (% of GDP)[a]	0.4		1.5		2.9		0.8		0.3	
	Life expectancy	70	72	63	67	71	72	67	70	67	70
	Infant mortality[b]	32	23	71	56	24	12	40	20	49	35
	Access to safe water[c]	55.7	64.3	75.3	96.1	100	100	91.9		80.0	77.5
Education	Public expenditure (% of GDP)[d]	1.7		0.9	3.7	3.6		2.7	2.4	3.0	3.9
	Public expenditure (% of total expenditure)[e]	10.9	12.4	2.8		10.5	12.9	23.8	12.3	13.0	
	Primary gross enrollment ratio[f]	107	107	101	111	105	98	113	119	123	112

Secondary gross enrollment ratio[f]	70	72	36	43	67	70	48	62	56	58
Tertiary gross enrollment ratio[g]		43	11	12		23	11	15	16	14
Illiteracy[h]	5	4	22	17	8	5	15	9	15	10
Pupils reaching grade 4[i]	76	76	46	96	96	95	68	73	83	86

SOURCE: Unless otherwise noted, figures are from *Social Indicators of Development 1996* (Washington, D.C.: Johns Hopkins University Press, for the World Bank, 1996). Figures for 1989–94 are the most recent estimate.

[a]Source for 1980–85 data: *Economic and Social Progress in Latin America, 1988 Report* (Washington, D.C.: Inter-American Development Bank, 1988). Figures in 1989–94 column are for 1990 only and include only public expenditures on health (including social security systems). Source: *Economic and Social Progress in Latin America, 1996 Report* (Washington, D.C.: Inter-American Development Bank, 1996).

[b]Per thousand live births.

[c]Percentage of population.

[d]Source for 1980–85 data: *Economic and Social Progress in Latin America, 1989 Report* (Washington, D.C.: Inter-American Development Bank, 1989). The figures for Brazil are underestimated because they reflect federal government expenditure only. The Brazil and Mexico figures in the 1989–94 column are for 1990 only; the figure cited for Colombia is for 1989 only. Source: *Statistical Yearbook for Latin American and the Caribbean*, UN ECLAC 1994 Edition, 1995.

[e]Again, the figures for Brazil are underestimated because they reflect federal government expenditure only. Latest figures for 1989–94 column vary by country from 1989 to 1993. Sources: *Economic and Social Progress in Latin America, 1989 Report* (Washington, D.C.: Inter-American Development Bank, 1989) and *Economic and Social Progress in Latin America, 1996 Report* (Washington, D.C.: Inter-American Development Bank, 1996).

[f]Percentage of school-age population.

[g]Figures in the 1980–85 column represent an average of 1980 and 1985 data. Source: *Statistical Yearbook for Latin American and the Caribbean*, UN ECLAC 1994 Edition, 1995. Figures in the 1989–94 column represent only 1992 data for Argentina, Brazil, and Chile, 1991 data for Colombia, and 1986 data for Mexico.

[h]Percentage of population over the age of fourteen.

[i]Percentage of cohort.

region, and in other regions, such as East Asia, they have also been an integral part of the production process—from the provision of supply flexibility to the innovation of products and work practices. In Latin America, the guiding assumption has been that, as competition forces formerly protected firms to abandon outdated practices, the necessary transformations will naturally follow. In other words, as prices shift, entrepreneurs will automatically adjust, and the economy will move to a higher-equilibrium growth path.[62] However, this scenario has yet to unfold, which suggests that public policy could be necessary to quicken the pace of adjustment, as it has been in the East Asian context and in Chile since the 1980s.

In Argentina and Mexico, in particular, the unexpectedly long adjustment lag for these weaker industrial firms has hampered job creation, income distribution, and productivity gains. Although Latin policy makers understandably shrink at the idea of "industrial policy" as a throwback to the ISI era, public policy regarding the industrial sector need not fall back on tired remedies. Rather, the role of public policy should be to harness these small and medium-sized industrial firms to the dynamic process of intra-industry trade that is currently driving more intense levels of integration within NAFTA, Mercosur, and to a lesser extent the Andean Group. For example, public policy could facilitate the adjustment process by broadening the access to affordable financing for smaller firms; reducing administrative costs and offering tax incentives that reward productive industrial development; encouraging productive ties across sectors, between large and small firms, and between industry and the educational system; and more aggressively attacking monopolistic business practices.

In hindsight, political leaders more or less sailed through the first phases of market reform in the late 1980s, since the working population in most of these countries was relieved to finally be free of the "inflation tax," and because politicians offered the poorest groups temporary social compensation schemes to help buffer the full impact of structural adjustment.[63] Now, as most of the region enters the more difficult phase of consolidating market reforms, the subsequent rise in poverty-related crime and social violence throughout Latin America suggests that politi-

---

62. See Manuel Pastor Jr. and Carol Wise, "The Politics of Free Trade in the Western Hemisphere" (Agenda Papers 20, North-South Center, University of Miami, Fla., August 1996).

63. Carol Graham, *Safety Nets, Politics, and the Poor: Transitions to Market Economies* (Washington, D.C.: Brookings Institution, 1994).

cians have little choice but to work harder at incorporating the working population into the national political economy on more productive and equitable terms.[64] Contrary to earlier attempts at adjustment in the wake of the debt crisis, when policy makers basically groped in the dark for solutions to extremely difficult adjustment challenges, there is now a rich body of political-economy research to help guide the way.

This recent research affirms that macroeconomic stabilization and trade openness are necessary conditions for growth and income gains, but that the time lag can be long and politically costly; however, public policy—in particular, higher and more qualitative investments in human capital and public infrastructure—can accelerate growth and income gains. Implicitly, this research suggests that it is time for Latin reformers to drop their market blinders, to rehabilitate those state organizations most responsible for social investments, and to formulate a cohesive public-policy framework to quicken the consolidation of market reforms in a more productive and equitable direction.

The Path Forward for Latin Trade Reform: Perceptions Versus Prospects

While the analysis thus far has focused largely on the domestic politics of trade reform, the rapid proliferation of bilateral and mini-multilateral trade accords since 1990 reflects the extent to which Latin trade reform has also become regionalized. By 1997, five major regional groupings had emerged (NAFTA, Mercosur, the Central American Common Market [CACM], the Caribbean Common Market [CARICOM], and the Andean Group), as well as a handful of preferential trade schemes (e.g., the Co-lombia-CARICOM Agreement); at last count, some twenty-six bilateral free-trade agreements had been negotiated, and at least another dozen are in the making.[65] Although intraregional exports doubled to U.S.$32 billion in the five years before 1994,[66] there have been other compelling motives for the regionalization of Latin trade. First, through the negotia-tion of free-trade agreements, policy makers have sought to "lock in"

64. "Latin America's Backlash," *Economist*, November 30, 1996, 20.
65. Richard L. Bernal, "Paths to the Free Trade Area of the Americas" (Policy Papers on the Americas, Center for Strategic and International Studies, Washington, D.C., January 15, 1997), app. 2.
66. "Latin America's Backlash," 19.

trade reforms and thus signal to investors that their commitment to market restructuring is a lasting one; and second, as regionalization has been accompanied by a rapid increase in intra-industry trade in the Western Hemisphere, particularly within NAFTA and Mercosur, policy makers have pursued integration treaties as a way to further expand this more specialized and dynamic form of production.

Throughout Latin America, earlier perceptions of the path forward for regional integration were shaped by President Bush's 1990 Enterprise for the Americas Initiative, which proposed the formation of a free-trade area that would encompass the entire Western Hemisphere. Having secured the NAFTA agreement in late 1993 despite considerable opposition within the United States, the Clinton administration affirmed this earlier hemispheric goal at the 1994 Summit of the Americas, where 2005 was set as the date for completing negotiations for a Free Trade Area of the Americas (FTAA). However, since the 1994 summit, the so-called FTAA process has slowed, as U.S. midterm elections that same year ushered in a majority bloc of freshmen Republicans who were uncharacteristically suspicious of free trade. Mexico's subsequent peso crisis only fueled these suspicions, thus prompting the U.S. Congress to withhold the necessary "fast-track" legislation that would permit President Clinton to proceed credibly with the FTAA negotiations. Although congressional leaders have expressed a willingness to cooperate with Clinton since his reelection in 1996, there are still a number of differences to be ironed out—such as congressional opposition to the future negotiation of labor and environmental side accords of the type that were attached to the NAFTA agreement.

Against this backdrop, the gap has widened between Latin expectations for a U.S.-led integration thrust and the realistic prospects that such leadership will emerge. For example, immediately following the 1993 passage of NAFTA, Argentina, Colombia, and Chile all emerged as plausible candidates for NAFTA accession, a move that would have ostensibly paved the way for the FTAA. Yet, these candidacies quickly faded, as Washington fell into partisan disputes and policy gridlock over how actually to proceed with hemispheric integration. For Argentina, the foreclosing of the NAFTA option came with the official launching of Mercosur on January 1, 1995, and its remarkably rapid trade integration with Brazil; between 1992 and 1996, for example, Brazil accounted for 23.4 percent of Argentine exports, compared with the 9.4 percent that the country sold to the United States during this same time period.[67] The consequences of stalled U.S. leadership in the regional integration process appear to be less benign for FDI flows. As Table 8.2 shows, FDI to Argentina peaked at U.S.$6.3 billion in 1993, but the country has not been able to sustain these flows. In 1996, for example, Argentina's estimated U.S.$2.5 billion in FDI was equal to that of Colombia—a country that, overall, is much less developed.[68]

Colombia's fall from the NAFTA shortlist coincided with the suspension of its preferential access to the U.S. market under the Andean Trade Preference Act, both of which have provoked understandable anxiety within the domestic private sector. Although the Gaviria administration (1990–94) had worked assertively to revamp the Andean Group and to secure a "G-3" FTA with Venezuela and Mexico (effective January 1, 1995)—which was perceived by domestic policy makers as a trial run for Colombia's negotiations with NAFTA[69]—the corruption charges surrounding the Samper administration have considerably reduced the amount of time dedicated to trade policy. Given the acrimonious nature of U.S.-Colombian relations since Samper's election, Colombia has made some halfhearted inquiries about the possibility of negotiating a free-trade agreement with Mercosur. However, the private sector has opposed this idea on the grounds that Colombia's exports to Brazil and Argentina amount to less than 1 percent of its total trade, while total exports to the United States have accounted for around 38 percent.[70] Recent economic trends suggest the potential dynamism that could be unleashed through greater domestic political stability and heightened access to the North American market: despite the country's current malaise, Colombian trade grew by an annual average of 6 percent from 1990 through 1994, and FDI figures for 1996 were nearly double those of 1994.

In principle, Chile was still considered by U.S. trade-policy makers to be a contender for NAFTA entry right up until the definitive failure of the Clinton administration to obtain the necessary fast-track negotiating

67. These figures derive from Morgan, "World Financial Markets," 111.

68. Stephen Fidler, "Latin America Sees Big Investment Flows," *Financial Times*, November 19, 1996.

69. Mauricio Cárdenas and Catalina Crane, "Economic Integration in Colombia: Is There a Strategy?" in *Integrating the Hemisphere*, ed. Ana Julia Jatar and Sidney Weintraub (Washington, D.C.: Inter-American Dialogue, 1997).

70. Ibid., 15–22.

authority in late 1997.[71] Chile's status as the first candidate for NAFTA entry was based on the country's impressive economic performance over the past decade, and this candidacy was supported by the Clinton administration in an effort to maintain credibility concerning its commitment to the FTAA process. The fact that U.S.-Chilean trade is based less on scale and product differentiation (as in intra-industry trade between the United States and Mexico) and more on traditional comparative advantage no doubt also worked in Chile's favor. The perception on all sides was that negotiations with Chile for NAFTA accession would be less likely to set off the numerous sectoral conflicts that emerged during the earlier NAFTA negotiations.

Having waited expectantly in the NAFTA queue since 1993, Chile began making alternative integration plans in 1996. Although the country had signed a number of bilateral free-trade accords in the early 1990s (with Mexico, Bolivia, Colombia, and Venezuela), the Chilean government now moved assertively to forge the kinds of integration ties that held promise for increased trade and investment flows. By late 1996, Chile had secured an FTA with the Mercosur bloc as a whole; it had negotiated an FTA with Canada based largely on the NAFTA text but excluding such NAFTA content issues as intellectual-property rights and financial services; it had renegotiated its 1991 bilateral accord with Mexico, also based on the NAFTA text; and it had pursued a free-trade agreement with the European Union (EU). Chilean policy makers are the first to admit that this roundabout approach to trade integration is a second-best option.[72]

Although the share of Chile's exports to the U.S. market averaged just 16 percent from 1992 to 1996, compared with 32 percent for Asia and 28 percent for Europe,[73] the United States is still Chile's largest single trading partner. And even though Chile's trade and investment ties with Canada and Mexico are just getting under way, estimates of Chile's potential investment gains as a NAFTA member are significant, on the order of 1–2 percent of GDP.[74] Nevertheless, since Chile's exports to neighbor-

71. John F. Harris and Peter Baker, "Clinton Neglected to Sell 'Fast Track' to U.S. Public," *Washington Post*, November 12, 1997, A4.

72. Author's interview with Juan Gabriel Valdes, Chile's lead trade negotiator for the North American bloc, Ministry of Finance, Santiago, July 5, 1996.

73. Morgan, "World Financial Markets," 111.

74. Albert Fishlow, "From NAFTA to a WHFTA? The Summit May Tell," in *Integrating the Americas*, ed. Weintraub, 124–25.

ing countries (Argentina, Bolivia, Peru) have grown by nearly 38 percent a year in the 1989–94 period, and since Chile tops the list of foreign investors in these countries, some have argued that geographical proximity and the forging of closer links with "natural trading partners" should be the main criteria that guide Chile's integration policy.[75]

Whereas the debate over the future of regional integration was cast somewhat narrowly during the early phase of NAFTA implementation (e.g., NAFTA accession versus participation in an alternative subregional scheme), the combination of Washington's trade-policy standoff, the launching of the FTAA process in 1995, and the realization of substantial intraregional trade gains have all helped to create a stronger vision of multilateralism in the region. By late 1997, the FTAA process had resulted in a series of hemisphere-wide meetings of trade and finance ministers, and it had spawned eleven working groups with oversight tasks ranging from sanitary measures to competition policy.[76] While the explicit details and procedures for achieving the FTAA may be some time in the making, at least the Latin focus appears to have shifted to a much broader concern for constructing hemisphere-wide norms to govern trade and investment practices. In other words, as U.S. leadership has faltered, the Latin reference point for trade integration has increasingly converged with the World Trade Organization's (WTO's) notion of a hemisphere-wide adherence to trade-policy norms.

As the entire hemisphere now moves toward a more liberal trading system, differences in size and in levels of development and preparedness have also worked to shape varying preferences for short-term action.[77] The question of how to get from "here" to "there" with regard to the creation of the FTAA has become a main sticking point between the United States and Brazil, in particular. Brazil, for example, has expressed a strong preference to craft hemisphere-wide norms through negotiation within and between the five major subregional trade schemes; the United States, on the other hand, favors an approach that would relegate this responsibility to the eleven FTAA working groups.[78] The fact that these

75. Patricio Meller, "An Overview of Chilean Trade Strategy," in Integrating the Hemisphere, ed. Jatar and Weintraub, 147–49.

76. For an in-depth analysis of the FTAA process, see Stephen Lande, "The FTAA Process: Maintaining the Miami Summit Momentum" (North-South Center, University of Miami, Fla., March 1996), and Stephan Haggard's chapter in this volume.

77. Bernal, "Paths to the Free Trade Area of the Americas," 7.

78. "Brazilian Negotiator Touts MERCOSUR FTAA Proposal," Inside NAFTA, October 2, 1996, 7.

positions, in principle, are not all that far apart suggests that there is more at stake here than meets the eye.

To some extent, Brazil's inclination to construct hemispheric trade norms within a subregional setting reflects the much weaker economic position of the Latin states at the FTAA negotiating table. Whereas the U.S. working-group approach implies less sovereignty and the eventual pursuit of trade liberalization beyond the parameters of the WTO, Latin political leaders—Brazil's President Cardoso foremost among them—still face enormous pressures to consolidate earlier reforms before taking on further commitments. Brazilian reluctance to concede to the U.S. position also reflects long-standing trade tensions between the two countries, especially in the areas of market access and intellectual-property rights.

In the end, perhaps the most divisive factor in the U.S.-Brazilian FTAA dialogue, and a main reason why Brazil never lined up for possible NAFTA accession, is the fundamental differences in each country's approach to political economic management. Although Brazil has now made tremendous strides with trade liberalization and macroeconomic stabilization, it has done so without abandoning its historical affinities for industrial policy and managed trade. Ironically, although domestic politics clearly favor a subregional path to the FTAA that would ostensibly allow Brazil the leeway it prefers for policy maneuvering, numerous studies show that—given its highly developed patterns of intra-industry trade—the country's economic gains would be much greater under a scenario of rapid integration that included the North American market.[79] As Table 8.2 shows, until 1994, flows of FDI into Brazil were on a par with those into Argentina and Colombia; since the implementation of the Real Plan, however, Brazil is now catching up with Mexico: FDI for 1996 is estimated to be U.S.$7.5 billion.[80]

In reality, the sheer economic weight of NAFTA (U.S.$7.4 trillion GDP) and Mercosur (U.S.$1 trillion GDP) in the Western Hemisphere, and the dominant role that the United States and Brazil play, respectively, within each of these blocs, makes it hard to envision a breakthrough in the FTAA process without the collaboration of these two main players. This is so whether a hemisphere-wide approach is advanced by the eleven

79. Da Motta Veiga, "Brazil's Strategy for Trade Liberalization," 2, and Fishlow, "From NAFTA to a WHFTA?" 129–30.

80. Fidler, "Latin America Sees Big Investment Flows."

FTAA working groups or moves forward at the subregional level. As the largest economy in the hemisphere, and the country that is projected to be least affected by trade-related adjustments, the United States has the luxury of placing an offer on the table and waiting until the rest of the region comes around. In contrast, all of the Latin states reviewed here have experienced considerable adjustment stress. Although the subregional approach is perhaps inferior from the standpoint of maximizing trade and investment gains, in the case of MERCOSUR it does afford lead countries, like Brazil and Argentina, extra political space for consolidating domestic reforms and for resolving policy conflicts in the areas of intraregional trade imbalances, exchange-rate differentials, and market access.[81] The procedures for managing these challenging trends are still tentative, but once Brazil is able more firmly to ground itself on both the domestic and the subregional reform fronts, there should be little to stop the United States and Brazil from collaborating constructively in the FTAA process, regardless of the specific venue that is decided upon.

Conclusions

The purpose of this chapter has been to ground the debate over Latin trade reform and Western Hemispheric integration more firmly in the actual experience of several of the region's largest reformers. It has been argued here that a full understanding of the chosen policies and their respective outcomes requires that the post-debt-crisis context for reform be taken into account. The analysis has shown that tariff reductions eventually became an integral part of post-1982 economic stabilization plans across the region. Today's difficulty in resolving some of the medium-term challenges that have accompanied unilateral trade liberalization does not necessarily imply the pre-debt-crisis pattern of returning to high levels of protectionism when the going gets rough. Rather, this recent wave of trade liberalization has advanced to the extent that the distributional logic has been reversed, and thus, going back to protection would be difficult precisely because so much redistribution would be involved.

81. Diana Tussie, "Argentina in the Global Economy: Facing the Dilemmas" (Documentos e Informes de Investigación 202, FLACSO, Buenos Aires, April 1996).

This comparative analysis and the related political-economy literature also suggest that macroeconomic stabilization and trade openness
are necessary conditions for growth and income gains, but that the time
lag can be long and politically costly; however, the research record also
shows that a cohesive public-policy framework—in particular, higher
and more qualitative investments in human capital and public infrastructure—could quicken the pace in resolving the various microeconomic bottlenecks identified here. Implicitly, this research suggests that
it is time for Latin reformers to rehabilitate those state organizations most
responsible for investing in social infrastructure and human capital, and
to work harder at harnessing neoliberal policies to the productive tasks
for which they were originally designed.

When taking into account the wide regional variance in competitive
position and state capacity effectively to manage an open commercial
policy, it becomes clear that the path ahead for Western Hemispheric
free trade is much more complicated than its proponents on either side
of the U.S. border had originally envisioned. While the Clinton administration tried to keep the option of NAFTA accession alive as an interim
step toward achieving an FTAA, that option was foreclosed in late 1997
by the refusal of the U.S. Congress to grant the necessary fast-track negotiating authority to the president. With the distraction of Asia's recent
economic meltdown and the 1998 midterm elections, and with Washington bogged down in a series of apparently interminable scandals, U.S.
trade-policy makers found themselves in the awkward position of heading off to the April 1998 FTAA Summit in Santiago with less focus and
negotiating clout than their Latin counterparts had hoped for.

Apart from the challenge of negotiating a hemispheric accord in the
midst of markedly different policy and procedural preferences, the FTAA
process now faces a larger risk: given the indefinite timeline on the fast-
track impasse, and the financial urgency of the Asian crisis, earlier vi-
sions of Western Hemispheric integration could simply fade in the rear-
view mirror of U.S. policy makers who now find themselves enveloped
by more pressing international economic matters. Nevertheless, bureaucratic gridlock and protectionist inclinations in Washington should not
be mistakenly interpreted as a hemispheric trend. Since the data, on
balance, continue to reflect dynamic trade and investment gains for
those Latin American countries that have pursued subregional integration schemes, U.S. reticence has been met with an increased determination to expand and diversify these trade ties, within and beyond the

Western Hemisphere. In the meantime, mini-multilateral schemes like Mercosur and the Andean Group have provided a forum for participating states to resolve their policy differences and to strengthen their trade position internationally, and these subregional blocs have helped to reinforce the commitment to trade openness and market reform.

9 The Political Economy of Regionalism in the Western Hemisphere

Stephan Haggard

The 1990s have witnessed a revival of regional integration in the Western Hemisphere. Post-debt-crisis stabilization, liberalization, and structural reform laid the foundation for new forms of cooperation. Old agreements, such as the Andean Pact, were renovated, and altogether new accords, like the Southern Cone's Mercosur, came to life. The United States also reassessed the virtues of regionalism. The Canadian-U.S. Free Trade Agreement (CUSFTA) provided a template for the North American Free Trade Agreement (NAFTA), which in turn

I would like to thank Roberto Bouzas, Allen Hicken, Jon E. Huenemann, Homi Kharas, Salvador Lara, Michelle Miller-Adams, Colleen Morton, Daniel Nielson, Kit Panupong, Manuel Pastor, Sarath Rajapatirana, Malcolm Rowat, Jorge Schiavon, Peter Smith, Ricardo Tavares, Diana Tussie, Sidney Weintraub, and Carol Wise for their assistance. Robin King and Antonio Ortiz-Mena provided particularly detailed comments and deserve special thanks.

exercised substantial influence over U.S. thinking about regional integration in the Americas. The Bush administration's Enterprise for the Americas Initiative (EAI), announced in 1990, signaled a willingness to entertain a new hemispheric economic organization; four years later, the United States played a key role in orchestrating the commitment to a Free Trade Area of the Americas (FTAA) at the December 1994 Summit of the Americas in Miami.[1]

Within a year of that summit, the enthusiasm for hemispheric integration had wilted. The 1994–95 Mexican peso crisis raised doubts about the viability of regional accords in the face of continued macroeconomic instability. NAFTA expansion bogged down in the United States in highly polarized debates over the president's negotiating authority; in November 1997, President Clinton's long-delayed fast-track legislation was rejected by a deeply divided Congress. The FTAA process, designed to reconcile an increasingly complex web of crosscutting subregional and bilateral trade agreements, appeared to be falling victim to the divergent interests of the countries in the hemisphere.

Despite the short-term political difficulties facing regional integration in the Americas, the institutional architecture of the hemisphere has in fact been substantially clarified in the years following the Miami Summit. That architecture is best understood in terms of three overlapping regional integration processes. The first is centered on the United States and includes NAFTA, preferential arrangements such as the Caribbean Basin Initiative and the Andean Trade Preference Act, and bilateral agreements emanating not only from the United States but also from Canada and Mexico.

1. On the hemispheric integration process, see Sylvia Saborio et al., *The Premise and the Promise: Free Trade in the Americas* (Washington, D.C.: Overseas Development Council, 1992); Gary C. Hufbauer and Jeffrey J. Schott, *Western Hemisphere Economic Integration* (Washington, D.C.: Institute for International Economics, 1994); Peter Morici, *Free Trade in the Americas* (New York: Twentieth Century Fund Press, 1994); Moisés Naím, "Toward Free Trade in the Americas: Building Blocks, Stumbling Blocks, and Entry Fees," in *Integrating the Americas: Shaping Future Trade Policy*, ed. Sidney Weintraub (Miami, Fla.: North-South Center, University of Miami, 1994); Sidney Weintraub, *NAFTA: What Comes Next?* (Westport, Conn.: Praeger, 1994); Inter-American Development Bank, *Economic Integration in the Americas* (Washington, D.C.: Inter-American Development Bank, July 1995); Ana Julia Jatar and Sidney Weintraub, eds., *Integrating the Hemisphere* (Washington D.C.: Inter-American Dialogue, 1997); Colleen S. Morton, "Progress Toward Free Trade in the Western Hemisphere Since 1994" (Institute of the Americas, San Diego, 1997, mimeo). The best single-volume study of the various regional efforts in English remains Roberto Bouzas and Jaime Ros, eds., *Economic Integration in the Western Hemisphere* (Notre Dame, Ind.: University of Notre Dame Press, 1994). For a comparison of the Latin American and East Asian experiences, see Stephan Haggard, *The Developing Nations and the Politics of Global Integration* (Washington, D.C.: Brookings Institution, 1995).

A second process is an intra–Latin American one and consists of five overlapping subregional integration efforts—the Central American Common Market (CACM), the Caribbean Common Market (CARICOM), the Andean Group, the Southern Cone Common Market (Mercosur), and the Group of Three, or G-3 (encompassing Colombia, Mexico, and Venezuela).[2] Because of the size of the Brazilian and Argentine economies, Mercosur is by far the most important of these undertakings. Like NAFTA, Mercosur has become a magnet for a network of bilateral agreements and was briefly promoted by Brazil as a springboard for the creation of a larger South American Free Trade Agreement (SAFTA).

NAFTA and Mercosur have emerged as the two dynamic poles in the hemispheric integration process. However, overlaying all regional processes are the commitments made at the Miami Summit to negotiate an FTAA for the hemisphere as a whole.

This chapter surveys the political economy of these three regional integration processes and asks how they might be reconciled. The prospects for hemispheric integration are generally positive.[3] Strong pressures for deeper integration in the Americas are rooted in unilateral reform efforts and rapidly increasing intraregional trade and investment. The possibility for reversion to a more protectionist status quo is not altogether absent, but is limited by the growing political consensus on reform, deepening subregional integration processes, and Latin America's commitment to multilateral liberalization through the World Trade Organization (WTO).

However, the countries of the hemisphere also continue to disagree on the scope, speed, and content of the cooperation process. The regionalism of NAFTA reflects a predominantly U.S. conception of deep integration; Latin American initiatives reflect somewhat different policy preoccupations and have been formulated in part as a strategic counterweight to U.S. influence. Domestic political support for deeper integration also remains uncertain. This is no less true for the United States

2. On the new regionalism, see Robert Z. Lawrence, *Regionalism, Multilateralism, and Deeper Integration* (Washington, D.C.: Brookings Institution, 1996); Kym Anderson and Richard Blackhurst, eds., *Regional Integration and the Global Trading System* (London: Harvester Wheatsheaf, 1993); Jaime de Melo and Arvind Panagariya, eds., *New Dimensions in Regional Integration* (Cambridge: Cambridge University Press, 1993); Louise Fawcett and Andrew Hurrell, eds., *Regionalism in World Politics* (Oxford: Oxford University Press, 1995); and Edward Mansfield and Helen Milner, eds., *The Political Economy of Regionalism* (New York: Columbia University Press, 1997).

3. See Roberto Bouzas and Jaime Ros, "The North-South Variety of Economic Integration: Issues and Prospects for Latin America," in *Economic Integration in the Western Hemisphere*, ed. Bouzas and Ros, 21–28.

than it is for other countries in the hemisphere. Although American officials sought to decouple progress toward an FTAA from fast-track authority, the long delays in the Clinton administration's quest for fast-track authority and its ultimate defeat in late 1997 naturally raised doubts about U.S. commitment to the process. The return of populism to Venezuela and continued Brazilian reticence about further liberalization are reminders that the broader political support for deeper integration in Latin America's new democracies remains equivocal.

An increasingly important element of path dependence is also at work. The very existence of different regional processes makes their ultimate reconciliation more, rather than less, difficult. In theory, a strong core scheme could provide a focal point for negotiations, in part by generating fears of exclusion. Yet at present there are at least two cores—NAFTA and Mercosur—each of which represents different substantive norms and institutional arrangements. The five other subregional agreements are seeking to maintain or define their identities, and each of these agreements, in turn, is conducting its own "foreign policy" by striking bilateral agreements with outsiders.

The key to hemispheric integration rests on how the North American and South American complexes will be reconciled. Latin America's commitment to the WTO process will play an important role in this regard. Those obligations—rather than either NAFTA or Mercosur norms— ultimately will serve as both the starting point and model for hemispheric negotiations. However, functional negotiations cannot provide the pathway to a hemispheric agreement, which requires linkages and trade-offs across issues. Only a high-level political initiative on the part of the two most important regional groupings, NAFTA and Mercosur, can make the FTAA a reality.

The North-American Complex

North American Trade Policies of the United States, Canada, and Mexico

Beginning in the 1970s, the United States was rightly accused of periodic lapses into protectionism.[4] But the picture of a protectionist United States

4. The following draws on Haggard, *The Developing Nations and the Politics of Global Integration*, chap. 2. See also I. M. Destler, *American Trade Politics* (Washington, D.C.: Institute for International Economics, 1992), chap. 6, and Thomas O. Bayard and Kimberly Ann Elliott, *Reciprocity and Retaliation in U.S. Trade Policy* (Washington, D.C.: Institute for International Economics, 1994).

no longer captures the complexity of American trade politics. By the mid-1980s, the Reagan administration had devised a new trade policy that emphasized the reduction of unfair trade practices abroad, building a coalition of exporters and multinational corporations to offset the political pressure coming from Congress and import-competing sectors. The issues of interest to this coalition centered on the rules affecting foreign investors; indeed, much of U.S. trade policy is not concerned with trade but with national treatment and regulatory reforms that favor American multinationals. This is true of the U.S. interest in liberalizing services and expanding the protection of intellectual property, as well as the more straightforward discussion of trade-related investment measures (TRIMS); these issues figured prominently in the Uruguay Round and NAFTA negotiations and remain central to the U.S. agenda for the FTAA.

Pursuing multilateral negotiations was one component of the U.S. strategy of market opening. Nonetheless, the power the United States wields over its trading partners and the well-rehearsed features of American government that generate highly particularistic trade policies made bilateralism an attractive option. Even while the United States pressed strongly for the completion of the Uruguay Round, it pursued issues such as services and intellectual property on a bilateral basis. On occasion, the United States had recourse to what Jagdish Bhagwati and Hugh Patrick have called "aggressive unilateralism," of which Super 301 was emblematic.[5] Renewed interest in regionalism is unlikely to eliminate the temptation to bilateralism. Not only does the negotiation of regional arrangements ultimately hinge on key bilateral deals, but the size, power, and politics of the United States make it unlikely that this option will be abandoned altogether.

Despite recurrent efforts to diversify their foreign economic relations, Mexican and Canadian trade policies are shaped profoundly by the two countries' inordinate and apparently inescapable dependence on the United States, a dependence that differentiates them from all other coun-

---

5. The initial 301 legislation, introduced in 1974, was designed to enforce trade rights conferred under the GATT or bilateral treaties by giving the executive the right to initiate retaliatory action. However, section 301 also contained a second category of offenses: "unreasonable" barriers to U.S. trade and investment that were *not* covered by the GATT. So-called Special 301 provisions were directed at intellectual-property protection. It was this broadened category of offenses that became the source of contention. See Jagdish Bhagwati and Hugh Patrick, eds., *Aggressive Unilateralism: America's 301 Trade Policy and the World Trading System* (Ann Arbor: University of Michigan Press, 1990).

tries in the hemisphere. Tight integration with the U.S. economy has been a long-standing and constant feature of both countries' foreign economic relations; however, some conditions must have changed for a regional agreement with the United States to gain appeal. Three factors were central: the growth of protectionist actions in the United States, the fear of being disadvantaged by the conclusion of separate bilateral pacts, and more fundamental changes in Mexican and Canadian economic policy.

When Prime Minister Brian Mulroney announced his intention to negotiate the CUSFTA in 1985, a major justification was the need to reduce the risk of congressional and administrative actions by establishing a regional-dispute-settlement mechanism.[6] The creation of the Canada-U.S. Trade Commission and Chapter 19 oversight procedures were a major objective of the Canadians and arguably the political linchpin of the agreement. Similar motives operated in Mexico's case. Refik Erzan and Alexander Yeats show that of all the Latin American countries, Mexico has the largest amount of total trade adversely affected by U.S. nontariff barriers; reining these in was clearly an objective of the bilateral discussions that preceded NAFTA and of the agreement itself.[7]

A second factor that influenced Canadian interests in the design of NAFTA was the fear of a "hub-and-spoke" approach to regional integration in which the United States would sign separate bilateral agreements with its trading partners. Influential analyses by Michael Hart, Richard Lipsey, and Ronald Wonnacott argued that such a structure would enhance U.S. bargaining power, disadvantage Canada in the Mexican market, and favor the United States with respect to investment-location decisions.[8] Similar fears have been voiced in Latin America and have played an important role in stimulating interest in NAFTA accession.[9]

---

6. See Gilbert R. Winham, "Why Canada Acted," in *Bilateralism, Multilateralism, and Canada in U.S. Trade Policy,* ed. William Diebold Jr. (Cambridge: Ballinger Publishing, 1988), 45.

7. Refik Erzan and Alexander Yeats, "U.S.–Latin America Free Trade Areas: Some Empirical Evidence," in *The Premise and the Promise: Free Trade in the Americas,* by Sylvia Saborio et al. (Washington, D.C.: Overseas Development Council, 1992), 136, table 5.

8. See Michael M. Hart, *A North American Free Trade Agreement: Strategic Implications for Canada* (Ottawa: Centre for Trade Policy and Law and the Institute for Research on Public Policy, 1990); Richard Lipsey, "Canada at the U.S.-Mexico Free Trade Dance: Wallflower or Partner?" (C. D. Howe Institute Commentary 20, 1990); and Ronald J. Wonnacott, "U.S. Hub and Spoke Bilaterals and the Multilateral Trading System" (C. D. Howe Institute Commentary 23, 1990).

9. See United Nations Economic Commission for Latin America and the Caribbean, "Open Regionalism in Latin America and the Caribbean" (LC/L.808 [CEG.19/3], January 14, 1994), 76–78.

Finally, the ability to reach these agreements rested on fundamental coalitional and policy shifts in Canada and Mexico that took place *prior to* the regional initiative. In Canada, the move toward a bilateral agreement grew out of a larger reassessment of domestic policy by the Macdonald Royal Commission that called into question both the government's relatively high tariff policy (for the OECD) and the newly emergent penchant for restrictions on foreign direct investment. The Conservative Mulroney government embraced the Macdonald Commission report calling for a bilateral free-trade agreement (FTA) with the United States because it would support the Conservatives' domestic reform efforts; a regional agreement was part of a domestic political effort to reorient policy. Because of developments within the Liberal Party, the change of government did not spell a fundamental departure from the Conservatives on issues of regional integration.[10]

The move toward freer trade in Mexico that set the stage for NAFTA unfolded in the wake of the debt crisis.[11] The government initially held the view that stabilization should precede structural adjustment, but the stabilization efforts of 1985–86 were accompanied by the initiation of trade reform and the negotiations that led to Mexican accession to the GATT. The growth of an internationalized Mexican business sector provided support for NAFTA,[12] but the initiative itself rested on President Salinas's preoccupation with securing foreign investment to support his domestic adjustments efforts.[13] Salinas was particularly discouraged by a trip to Europe that revealed a preoccupation with developments in the

10. . See Alan S. Alexandroff, "The Federal and Provincial Liberal Parties and NAFTA," in *Beyond NAFTA: An Economic, Political, and Sociological Perspective,* ed. A. R. Riggs and Tom Velk (Vancouver: Fraser Institute, 1993).

11. See Robert R. Kaufman, Carlos Bazdresch, and Blanca Herredia, "Mexico: Radical Reform in a Dominant Party System," in *Voting for Reform: Democracy, Political Liberalization, and Economic Adjustment,* ed. Stephan Haggard and Steven B. Webb (New York: Oxford University Press, 1994); Manuel Pastor Jr. and Carol Wise, "The Origins and Sustainability of Mexico's Free Trade Policy," *International Organization* 48, no. 3 (1994): 459–89; and Nora Lustig, *Mexico: The Remaking of an Economy* (Washington, D.C.: Brookings Institution, 1992), 114–20.

12. See Pastor and Wise, "The Origins and Sustainability of Mexico's Free Trade Policy," and Strom Thacker, "From Silent to Active Partner: Big Business, the State, and Free Trade in Mexico" (Ph.D. diss., University of North Carolina, 1995), chap. 6.

13. The reforms in the investment regime began soon after the debt crisis, but were extended in 1989. Changes in intellectual-property law began in 1987, and between 1989 and 1990 the government independently launched a series of deregulation initiatives, some of which were accompanied by privatization that provided new opportunities for foreign investment in finance, road transport, petrochemicals, telecommunications, sugar, mining, and fishing.

former Soviet bloc and a lack of interest in, or knowledge about, the depth of the Mexican reforms.[14] Salinas's commitment to NAFTA thus served two purposes: it signaled foreign investors of Mexico's commitment to the reform process while also locking in those reforms against possible domestic detractors.

The Mexican crisis of 1994–95 naturally called these commitments into question. Critics faulted NAFTA for its limited scope, including a neglect of macroeconomic policy and social issues.[15] As the contributions to this volume make clear, there were a variety of political challenges that could be linked, if not directly to NAFTA, at least to the liberalizing reformism of which it was symptomatic: the strong showing of the opposition party led by Cuauhtémoc Cárdenas in the 1988 presidential election; the Chiapas revolt, timed explicitly to coincide with NAFTA's inauguration on January 1, 1994; and the increasing disaffection with neoliberalism within the traditional wing of the Revolutionary Institutional Party (PRI) that became manifest beginning in 1995.

Despite predictions that the crisis would prove NAFTA politically unsustainable, the opposite occurred; the Zedillo administration's dedication to the agreement grew even more firm. Mexico made some upward tariff adjustments for third parties, resisted U.S. pressure to negotiate an acceleration of liberalization commitments, and came under fire over several implementation issues.[16] But precisely because of the unsettled conditions in financial markets, and the centrality of foreign savings to the success of the government's reform plans, it was even more important that the politically weakened Zedillo administration demonstrate its continued commitment to reform.

NAFTA Expansion and the Hemispheric Agenda

Before the Miami summit, there were three contending models of how hemispheric cooperation might be achieved. The first, and most steeply

14. Robert A. Pastor, "Salinas Takes a Gamble," *New Republic*, September 10 and 17, 1990, 27–32.

15. In addition to the contributions to this volume, see Rudiger Dornbusch and Alejandro Werner, "Mexico: Stabilization, Reform, and No Growth," *Brookings Papers on Economic Activity*, no. 1 (1994): 253–315; Jaime Ros, "Mexico in the 1990s: A New Economic Miracle?" in *The Politics of Economic Restructuring: State-Society Relations and Regime Change in Mexico*, ed. Maria Lorena Cook, Kevin J. Middlebrook, and Juan Molinar Horcasitas (La Jolla: Center for U.S.-Mexican Studies, University of California at San Diego, 1994); and Manuel Pastor Jr. and Carol Wise, "Challenges to Western Hemispheric Integration: Free Trade Is Not Enough," *SAIS Review* 15, no. 2 (1995): 1–16.

16. On Mexico's trade-policy response to the crisis, see *Inside NAFTA*, March 8, 1995, 1, 20.

discounted, was the type of hemisphere-wide negotiation process that the summit ultimately launched. The more plausible routes to hemispheric integration were held to lie in an expansion of the North American bloc, through either the enlargement of NAFTA or the negotiation of bilateral FTAs between the United States and interested Latin American countries. By late 1995, it had become clear that NAFTA would not serve as the vehicle for achieving a hemispheric pact. However, three problems with the NAFTA accession model shed light on the problems facing the hemispheric integration process: NAFTA's focus on issues primarily of interest to the United States, its dispute-settlement procedures, and complications arising out of its organizational form as a free-trade area.

The NAFTA Agenda. NAFTA is frequently assumed to constitute a "deeper" agreement than any of its South American counterparts. Under this interpretation, the problem for hemispheric integration lies in the fact that other countries are unable to comply with NAFTA's tough standards.[17] Many Latin American countries *are* unwilling to adopt NAFTA standards, but it is misleading to think that intricate, multi-issue accords can be measured along a single dimension of "depth." The text of Mercosur outlines an integration process that is in some ways deeper than that of NAFTA—for example, in its ultimate commitment to a common market and in the explicit mention of macroeconomic-policy coordination, infrastructure integration, and industrial-policy harmonization. The difference among agreements in the hemisphere is not simply their "depth," but the variation in national-policy interests that undergird them.

Given NAFTA's close reflection of U.S. policy interests, is the NAFTA agenda sufficiently appealing to other countries in the hemisphere that they are likely to accept it in its entirety, as either accession or a NAFTA-like FTAA implies? Even if we limit our attention to the trade-liberalization component of NAFTA, the political and economic logic for other countries to reach such an agreement with the United States is far from clear.

The dramatic trade liberalization that has occurred in Latin America should not be confused with a willingness to take the politically more difficult step of freeing substantially all trade with the United States. Only in Chile, Peru, and Bolivia have governments been able to impose

17. Sidney Weintraub has built on this observation to argue *against* an overly rapid expansion of NAFTA, on the grounds that it would weaken the agreement. Sidney Weintraub, *NAFTA: What Comes Next?* (Westport, Conn.: Praeger, with the Center for Strategic and International Studies, 1994), 7, 64–65.

low, uniform tariff structures, and even in these countries average tariffs remain substantially higher than in the United States.[18] In ten Latin American countries, the average tariff in 1994 was between 9 percent and 12 percent and in five other counties between 15 percent and 18 percent. The dispersion across product categories has fallen dramatically, but substantial variations continue in sectoral levels of protection across countries and in the common external tariffs negotiated by new common markets—variations that reflect both strategic industrial-policy interests and straightforward protection (to the extent that the two can be distinguished). New subregional agreements also have adopted different transition processes with respect to the politically delicate issue of the phasing out of tariffs on intrabloc trade and the granting of intrabloc preferences in the form of exceptions lists.

The problem is not simply one of political "will"; it is not clear that the trade structures of the countries in the hemisphere, either in terms of geography or composition, make an agreement with the United States compelling.[19] No Latin American country, including even the small Caribbean and Central American countries, approaches Mexico's reliance on the U.S. market.[20] Dependence on the United States falls almost linearly with distance. After Mexico, the Central American and Caribbean countries are most dependent on the North American market, with an export share for CACM as a whole of 56 percent and for CARICOM of 51 percent. Venezuela approaches this level. Colombia and Ecuador come next, with North American shares in the low 40s. When we turn to the Southern Cone, the ratios fall precipitously: 23 percent for Brazil, 21 percent for Argentina, and only 18 percent for Chile. For these countries, reaching agreements with South American, European, and even Asian

18. The following draws on the compendium by Luis Jorge Garay and Antonio Estevadeordal, "Protection, Preferential Tariff Elimination, and Rules of Origin in the Americas" (Inter-American Development Bank, Washington, D.C., June 1995).

19. In the absence of any theory of why regional clusters have the membership they do, analysts have developed a variety of economic and policy indicators that seek to measure the costs, benefits, and likelihood of closer association. See Hufbauer and Schott, *Western Hemisphere Economic Integration*, chaps. 2 and 5; Bouzas and Ros, "The North-South Variety of Economic Integration," 13–21; Jeffrey Frankel, Ernesto Stein, and Shang-jin Wei, "Trading Blocs and the Americas: The Natural, the Unnatural, and the Super-Natural," *Journal of Development Economics* 47, no. 1 (1995): 61–95; and Alan Deardorff, Drusilla K. Brown, and Robert M. Stern, "Expanding NAFTA: Economic Effects of Accession of Chile and Other Major South American Nations," *North American Journal of Economics and Finance*, no. 6 (fall 1995): 149–70.

20. The following draws on Hufbauer and Schott, *Western Hemisphere Economic Integration*, 38–39, table 3.6.

partners should be of equal importance to striking a bargain with the United States.

Turning to the composition of trade, Latin America's exports are still dominated by natural resources and agricultural products. Despite relatively high tariffs or import quotas in some sectors—meat, wheat, rice, dairy products, peanuts, and sugar—these products generally face relatively low barriers in the U.S. market. Erzan and Yeats calculate that 18 percent of all Latin American exports encounter tariffs of 5 percent or higher in the U.S. market.[21] Even if we factor in nontariff barriers—a nontrivial impediment to the growth of certain labor-intensive manufactures—only 8 percent of exports face such barriers. As a result, even if the North American market were to be opened completely—a highly unlikely prospect—the boost to Latin American exports would be relatively small; Erzan and Yeats suggest a figure of 8 percent.

If the cost-benefit calculus of signing onto a preferential trade arrangement with the United States is unclear, the prospects are even more uncertain that Latin American states will embrace the remainder of the NAFTA agenda, which centers as much on investment as on trade. Chapter 11 spells out the general commitment to extend national treatment and MFN status to foreign investors from NAFTA partners with respect to establishment, acquisition and sale of assets, management, and conduct, and extends that coverage to include minority shareholders. Specific protections include an unrestricted right to repatriation of profits, capital, and royalty payments; the guarantee of fair compensation for expropriation; and a dispute-settlement process that allows investors the opportunity for binding international arbitration.

These general protections are extended to services in Chapter 12 and are buttressed further by even more detailed sectoral agreements in automobiles, energy, financial services, and telecommunications that go beyond market access to the nature of the national regulatory regime.

The interest of Latin American countries in attracting investment has led them to gravitate toward NAFTA standards to a substantial extent, granting investors national treatment and reducing restrictions on business behavior, such as sectoral prohibitions, performance requirements, and exchange controls. However, these policy changes are not the same

---

21. Refik Erzan and Alexander Yeats, "Free Trade Agreements with the United States: What's in It for Latin America?" (World Bank Policy Research Working Paper 827, World Bank, Washington, D.C., 1992), 13.

as NAFTA standards.[22] A compendium of bilateral investment accords compiled by the Organization of American States (OAS) is revealing with respect to Latin American policy preferences in this area; it shows substantial differences in the terms, conditions, and exceptions, even among those signed between the United States and individual Latin American countries.[23]

A more important piece of evidence concerns the rules governing foreign investment in the major regional accords and in individual countries. Mercosur's Protocol of Colonia for the Promotion and Reciprocal Protection of Investments (January 1994) set out terms similar to those in Chapter 11 of NAFTA, but the exceptions lists are much longer, services are not addressed explicitly, and key sectors targeted by NAFTA either have not been addressed (particularly financial services) or have involved specific national reservations (telecommunications and energy).[24] Argentina has launched a wide-ranging liberalization of its investment regime for outsiders, but Brazil continues to maintain a variety of restrictions on foreign direct investment (FDI): constitutional limits on private-sector participation in particular sectors, statutory limits on profit and capital repatriation, performance requirements, and restricted access to local capital markets. The Andean countries moved a long way toward liberalization of foreign investment in the repeal of the notorious Decision 24 in April 1991, but individual countries continue to maintain barriers when measured against NAFTA norms. Elsewhere, interest in the issue remains weak. CACM does not address investment questions at all, and although CARICOM has called for the development of a regionwide investment regime, it is yet to be developed.

Similar doubts can be raised about the "entry fees" that Latin American signatories would have to pay in areas such as government procurement and intellectual-property protection, where NAFTA standards go substantially beyond WTO commitments. The very existence of NAFTA

22. As Alan Rugman has argued most insistently, the investment provisions of NAFTA are somewhat less far-reaching than they look, because of the various exceptions contained in a series of annexes. The annexes permit numerous exclusions, and bargaining over those exclusions would undoubtedly be a part of any accession negotiation. See Alan M. Rugman and Michael Gestrin, "NAFTA's Treatment of Foreign Investment," in *Foreign Investment and NAFTA,* ed. Alan M. Rugman (Columbia: University of South Carolina Press, 1994), 53–60.

23. Organization of American States, "Compendio de acuerdos bilaterales de inversión del Hemisferio Occidental" (Organization of American States, Washington, D.C., 1996).

24. Thomas Andrew O'Keefe, "The Prospects for Mercosur's Inclusion into the North American Free Trade Agreement (NAFTA)," *International Law Practicum* 8, no. 1 (1995): 8.

and the quest to attract investment may over time create incentives to mirror NAFTA provisions in these areas.[25] To date, however, these incentives have been weakened by the fact that the region received substantial capital inflows before the Mexican crisis and appeared to recover relatively quickly from the "tequila effect." The pressing need to court investors, which was a crucial factor in the initial willingness to contemplate NAFTA standards, has waned, and difficult areas like government procurement and intellectual property have remained contentious issues.

Dispute-Settlement Procedures. If the substantive agenda of NAFTA is not altogether palatable to other Latin American countries, dispute-settlement procedures constitute one of its drawing cards. Strengthened dispute-settlement mechanisms promise to limit the discretionary excesses of U.S. trade policy and could constitute the core quid pro quo of an expanded NAFTA or NAFTA-like FTAA. But the entry fees in this area could constitute a serious political barrier to an extension of NAFTA norms as well.

Chapter 20 of NAFTA established a trilateral Trade Commission of cabinet-level representatives to oversee implementation of the agreement, adjudicate disputes, and supervise the work of NAFTA's eight committees, five subcommittees, and seven working groups. There is no particular problem in expanding these bodies to include new members, beyond the costs of accommodating larger numbers. It is, however, the provisions of Chapter 19, which establish a dispute-settlement procedure for antidumping (AD) and countervailing-duty (CVD) actions, that constitute NAFTA's most novel institutional innovation.[26] In the CUSFTA negotiations, the Canadian preference was to eliminate national AD and CVD laws altogether in favor of a regional competition policy that would be enforced through binding dispute settlement. When that failed, the fallback was to create a supranational review process that would reduce the cost and time associated with judicial review in the United States and guarantee that the process was shielded to some extent from political

25. This point is made by Colleen Morton, "Outlook for Free Trade in the Americas" (paper prepared for the American Business Forum, Cartagena, Colombia, March 19–20, 1996).

26. The following draws on Gilbert R. Winham, "Moving WTO Dispute Settlement Toward the Model of Administrative Review" (Dalhousie University, October 1995, unpublished manuscript), and Beatriz Leycegui, William B. P. Robson, and S. Dahlia Stein, eds., *Trading Punches: Trade Remedy Law and Disputes Under NAFTA* (Washington, D.C.: National Planning Association, 1995), particularly Leycegui, "A Legal Analysis of Mexico's Antidumping and Countervailing Regulatory Framework."

interference. Under Chapter 19, each country retained its own AD and CVD laws. Ad hoc binational panels superseded national judicial review of final determinations by domestic courts, but ruled only on whether the administrative action was broadly supported by the evidence and in line with *domestic* law. The panels would not act on—nor would they create—common rules.[27]

This solution was acceptable to the United States only because Canadian law already resembled U.S. law not only in its substance but in its underlying approach to administrative law, due process, and legal procedure. Mexico's interest in gaining access to Chapter 19 protections, by contrast, posed serious problems; not only were there substantive differences in Mexico's AD/CVD laws, but Mexico's civil-law tradition diverged fundamentally from Anglo-Saxon common law. Contrasts extended to administrative procedure, including the absence in Mexico of strict requirements with respect to notification procedures, the precise definition of "interested parties," and the compilation of an administrative record. Only with explicit commitments by Mexico to change its administrative-law procedures were the United States and Canada willing to permit the extension of Chapter 19.

Ironically, other Latin American countries that are rewriting their trade-remedy laws are converging on an American practice that is flawed in important respects. However, differences in fundamental legal norms remain, decreasing the probability of natural convergence. For example, the Brasilia Protocol of December 1991, which governs dispute settlement in Mercosur, differs in fundamental respects from the NAFTA process, particularly in limiting the ability of private parties to seek redress without the support of their governments.[28] In the area of competition policy, U.S. law is based on an Anglo-Saxon model of general prohibitions coupled with a reliance on courts, precedent, and rule of reason, while most Latin American countries have turned to European models rooted in the civil-law tradition. A NAFTA-like dispute-settlement mechanism thus requires either that fundamental differences in national legal systems be reconciled or that the agreement recognize a wider spectrum

27. Chapter 19 of the CUSFTA called on the parties to negotiate a new policy framework within seven years, and required the parties to submit changes in national laws to binational review. But the aspiration of a common regional policy was dropped when Chapter 19 was extended to Mexico in NAFTA.

28. "U.S. Embassy Cable on Mercosur Dispute Procedures," *Inside NAFTA*, February 22, 1995, 8–9.

of national legal norms; the latter would make the Chapter 19 process unwieldy, if not altogether unworkable.[29]

Strategic Issues in the Expansion of an FTA. A third set of barriers to an extension of the NAFTA model have to do with the political economy of free-trade areas more generally.[30] The choice of an FTA over a customs union was a necessary concession to pragmatism: given higher tariffs in Mexico, it would have been impossible for the NAFTA partners to negotiate a customs union.[31] The same observations certainly hold for the rest of the hemisphere. The choice of the FTA form allows new entrants to NAFTA to maintain tariff autonomy vis-à-vis third parties and avoids the difficult fights over a common external tariff (CET) that have plagued Mercosur, the Andean Pact, and CACM. Participation in the multilateral system would, over time, produce pressures for a downward adjustment of tariffs toward U.S. levels, and even incentives to move toward the formation of a customs union.

The very formation of an FTA that includes a large country like the United States naturally has far-reaching implications for the trade strategies of other countries in the region. The key question is whether strategic calculations lead countries to "bandwagon" onto NAFTA or to balance against it. On the one hand, the investment and trade expansion offered by NAFTA provide strong incentives for other countries to avoid exclusion.[32] Defensive calculations are evident among the "Northern Tier" of Andean, Central American, and Caribbean countries that have a high level of dependence on the U.S. market. The negotiation of the G-3—in fact two bilateral agreements between Mexico and Venezuela, and Mexico and Colombia—and the Mexico–Costa Rica and Mexico-Chile FTAS mirrored the NAFTA in important respects, including its investment provisions. Because of rules of origin, the G-3 does not in fact position Colombia and Venezuela in the U.S. market. Nonetheless, it signaled their ability and willingness to contemplate NAFTA standards.

However, these tendencies to bandwagon onto NAFTA are partly off-

29. I am thankful to Ana Julia Jatar for these points.

30. See Anne Krueger, "Free Trade Areas vs. Customs Unions" (NBER Working Paper 5084, National Bureau of Economic Research, Cambridge, Mass., 1995).

31. A common external tariff (CET) was negotiated on particular products, most importantly, computers.

32. Richard Baldwin has built on this observation to construct a "domino" theory of regionalism in which exporters harmed by trade diversion become strong lobbyists for entry. Richard Baldwin, "A Domino Theory of Regionalism" (NBER Working Paper 4465, National Bureau of Economic Research, Cambridge, Mass., September 1993).

set by two political economic considerations that push in the opposite direction. First, the expansion of a preferential agreement has the effect of eroding the preference margin enjoyed by the high-tariff country as a result of membership in the agreement. Mexico's official position has been that those meeting NAFTA standards are welcome to join, but it has shown no particular enthusiasm for expansion. In the negotiation of a hemispheric FTAA, Mexican industries are likely to seek delay of concessions that imply increased competition and the erosion of preferences.

A second, more complex problem is that FTAS require rules of origin to establish that goods shipped between partners in fact originate in the partner country. As demonstrated by the automobile and textiles and apparel sectors during the NAFTA negotiations, rules of origin can become the locus of protectionist lobbying and create a number of strategic problems.[33] On straightforward welfare grounds, an extension of NAFTA's complex and restrictive rules-of-origins regime is undesirable; in fact, other WTO members already have challenged them.[34] But there are also political interests in the rules already negotiated that are likely to pose a challenge quite apart from the tremendous complication of how existing rules-of-origin regimes would be reconciled in a new agreement.

The Accession Process: Chile as an Example. Were these factors not enough to demonstrate the difficulties of the expansion of a NAFTA-like accord, the NAFTA accession process certainly would be. Chile is the country in South America that has moved the farthest toward NAFTA norms. The Chilean negotiations reveal that the political barriers to a wider hemispheric agreement lie not only on the Latin American side but also in the United States. As early as the middle of 1995, the four countries had worked through a series of preparatory sessions, and, by September, Chile had submitted formal proposals on a number of the NAFTA chapters.

The main stumbling block to accession has proved to be the vagaries of American politics. The implementing legislation of NAFTA did not

33. Douglas Karmin, "Rules of Origin and the North American Free Trade Agreement" (Congressional Research Service, 1992), 7–11. Rules of origin can have the effect of exporting protection from one country to another, for example, by making it profitable to import from a high-cost partner in order to gain duty-free access, or by generating protectionist pressures from industries that rely on tradable inputs but do not face common prices in the FTA due to differences in tariffs toward third parties. See Krueger, "Free Trade Areas vs. Customs Unions," and the discussion by Sylvia Maxfield and Adam Shapiro in Chapter 2 of this volume.

34. A working group in the WTO has been established to study the issue, and it is on the agenda of the FTAA process as well. See *Inside NAFTA*, July 26, 1995, 1.

authorize fast-track procedures for accession negotiations, forcing the Clinton administration to bargain with a Republican Congress over fast-track terms. That quest immediately became mired in an executive-legislative battle, fueled by business opposition to the NAFTA side agreements, over whether labor and environmental issues should be explicitly included or excluded from the legislation. The opportunity for a compromise on neutral wording was missed, and, by the end of 1995, the issue had fallen victim to the budget battle and Patrick Buchanan's insertion of protectionist trade politics into the 1996 presidential race.

Chile had long insisted that it would not negotiate without fast-track authority, fearing rightly that such an effort would require a second negotiation to meet congressional objections.[35] The diversified structure of Chilean trade, the limited gains to Chile from NAFTA, and the high adjustment costs it implied, particularly in import-competing agricultural segments, should have signaled clearly that this position was not a bluff. Though Chile negotiated through most of 1995 on the assumption that fast-track authority would eventually be obtained, Santiago already had begun to explore a Mercosur option in mid-1994, as well as an affiliation with the European Union; agreements with each were reached by mid-1996.[36] When the NAFTA negotiations ground to a halt, Chilean advocates of expanding ties with the Southern Cone gained ground.[37] Chile kept the NAFTA option alive by initiating a bilateral negotiation with Canada. But by the end of 1997, Clinton's fast-track efforts had once again foundered, and Chilean trade officials began downplaying the significance of NAFTA accession in favor of concluding a satisfactory FTAA.

Alternatives to NAFTA Expansion: Bilateralism

North American trade policy toward the hemisphere is not limited to NAFTA expansion or a hemispheric agreement. The North American bloc has also expanded through bilateral agreements. The first U.S. step to institutionalize economic ties with the Americas—the Reagan adminis-

---

35. On Chilean strategy, see Andrea Butelman, "Elements of Chilean Trade Strategy: The United States or Mercosur?" in *Economic Integration in the Western Hemisphere*, ed. Bouzas and Ros, and Alberto Valdes, "Joining an Existing Regional Trade Agreement from the Perspective of a Small Open Economy: Chile's Accession to NAFTA and MERCOSUR," *American Journal of Agricultural Economics* 77, no. 5 (1995): 243–50.

36. "Hemos cantelado los interés nacionales," *El Diario* (Santiago, Chile), June 24, 1996, 24.

37. See *Latin American Regional Reports: Southern Cone*, RS-95-09, November 23, 1995, 6.

tration's Caribbean Basin Initiative (CBI) of 1982—was motivated not by economic calculations but by security interests.[38] The Andean Trade Preference Act, proposed by Bush in November 1989 and passed by Congress two years later, also was motivated by a strategic calculation—the war on drugs—and took a broadly similar form.[39]

A more important precedent for the bilateral line of thinking was the Enterprise for the Americas Initiative (EAI) announced on June 27, 1990. Unlike the exceptionalism inherent in the CBI and the Andean agreement, the EAI held out the promise of a hemispheric FTA "from Alaska to Tierra del Fuego."[40] Like the CBI, the EAI rested on the three pillars of investment promotion, U.S. aid (via debt reduction), and the elimination of trade barriers, but the investment and debt-reduction components of the package were relatively modest; the centerpiece was its provisions concerning trade. Bush announced that the United States stood ready to enter into free-trade agreements either with individual countries or with groups of countries. Given that such a step was likely to be too dramatic for some countries to consider, Bush also offered the negotiation of bilateral "framework" agreements that would permit more incremental negotiations covering particular issues of relevance. By the end of 1990, seven countries had negotiated bilateral framework agreements with the United States; by the end of 1992, only three countries—Cuba, Surinam, and Haiti—had not signed such an agreement.[41]

The EAI is now rightly seen as an artifact of the Bush administration that was overtaken by subsequent events, even before Bush left office. The EAI assumed that the United States would sign separate agreements with different regional groupings, which would constitute "stepping stones" to a larger hemispheric free-trade area. This vision was super-

38. For an overview of the CBI's history, see the *Annual Report on the Impact of the Caribbean Basin Economic Recovery Act on U.S. Industries and Consumers* (U.S. International Trade Commission), various issues.

39. For an overview of the context for U.S. Andean policy, see Raphael F. Perl, "United States Andean Drug Policy: Background and Issues for Decisionmakers," *Journal of Interamerican Studies and World Affairs* 34, no. 3 (1992): 13–36.

40. See Sidney Weintraub, "The New U.S. Economic Initiative Toward Latin America," *Journal of Interamerican Studies and World Affairs* 33, no. 1 (1991): 1–18, and Joseph S. Tulchin's excellent interpretive history, "The Enterprise for the Americas Initiative: Empty Gesture, Shrewd Gambit, or Remarkable Shift in Hemispheric Relations?" in *The Enterprise for the Americas Initiative,* ed. Roy Green (Westport, Conn.: Praeger, 1993).

41. Among the agreements reached was the Rose Garden Agreement with Mercosur. See Rebecca Dandeker, "The Rose Garden Agreement: Is Mercosur the Next Step to a Hemispheric Free Trade Zone?" *Law and Policy in International Business* 24, no. 1 (1992): 157–80.

seded by NAFTA, which came to be seen as the favored route to hemispheric integration. Bill Clinton was completely silent on the EAI during his presidential campaign and did nothing to revive it once elected.

But if the EAI itself is dead, the Clinton administration has taken actions and sent signals that bilateral arrangements will continue to matter. Unlike the ambition of NAFTA expansion or the "single undertaking" of the FTAA, the EAI prudently recognized that hemispheric integration would be a multitrack affair; similar ideas have been voiced by a number of Clinton-administration trade-policy officials.[42] In 1995, the Clinton administration announced its interest in negotiating a new round of bilateral investment treaties (BITS) with Latin America in advance of any free-trade negotiations that might ensue. Given that U.S. policy interests center to a substantial degree on investment questions in any case, and that commercial negotiations are stalled, BITS and framework agreements are not merely preparatory; they constitute significant agreements in their own right.[43] Nor has the United States forgone its right to pressure Latin American countries bilaterally on other issues through variations on the 301 process; ongoing intellectual-property-rights disputes with Argentina provide a clear example.

Whatever the outcome of broader hemispheric processes, it is unlikely that this propensity for bilateralism will disappear altogether. If the course of multilateral negotiations provides any indication, key bilateral deals also will play an important role in cementing a hemispheric agreement. But before examining the Miami process, it is first important to balance the picture by looking at the Latin American complex.

The Latin American Complex

There are currently five major intra–Latin American trade groupings: Mercosur, the Andean Pact, the G-3, CACM, and CARICOM, the last of which organized thirteen English-language Caribbean countries. Among them, these agreements cover all countries outside NAFTA except Cuba,

---

42. See, for example, Jeffrey Garten, "A Defining Moment for the Western Hemisphere" (remarks before the Consejo Profesional de Ciencias Económicas, Buenos Aires, March 25, 1994), 20ff.

43. For an overview of the BIT strategy, see *Inside NAFTA*, March 8, 1995, 4–5.

the Dominican Republic, Haiti, Panama, and Surinam.[44] In addition, at least twenty bilateral free-trade agreements have been reached under the aegis of the Latin American Integration Association, as well as a number of additional "bilateral" negotiations between subregional agreements and individual countries, such as those between Mercosur and Bolivia and between Mercosur and Chile.

A thorough review of these intra–Latin American trade agreements is impossible here, but two points are germane to an analysis of the hemispheric integration process. First, the norms governing these agreements by no means naturally converge with those of NAFTA or even toward a more minimal free-trade-area standard. Not only have agreements been built on different principles, but divergent political and economic interests and macroeconomic imbalances have created barriers to the full implementation of those commitments that have been made. Second, all Latin American agreements have been subject to strong external pulls, creating a complex network of bilateral deals that ultimately complicates rather than eases the hemispheric coordination problem.

The Smaller Countries: CARICOM and the CACM

The conclusion of NAFTA was a spur to CARICOM and CACM to hasten the pace of their own integration efforts. Although the prospect that the countries of either grouping would enter NAFTA have dimmed, the United States had signaled that it was more likely to negotiate Central American access to NAFTA as a bloc. As late as mid-1995, a Commonwealth Secretariat report had concluded cynically that "the most important function of CARICOM may be as a single regional organisation for negotiating membership of an expanded NAFTA."[45] The Miami commitments added an additional incentive to accelerate intrabloc discussions.

Until the 1990s, CARICOM made little progress toward the common market that its name implies; between the organization's formation and the early 1990s levels of intraregional trade actually fell. An ambitious work program announced at the July 1989 CARICOM meeting in Grenada, including completion of the common market, was only partly imple-

---

44. In 1995, Surinam joined CARICOM, and a more comprehensive Association of Caribbean States (ACS) was launched that included not only all of the Caribbean and Central American countries, Mexico, Venezuela, and Colombia, but (much to the chagrin of the United States) Cuba as well. However, the ACS does not have pretensions to develop into a regional integration agreement.

45. As cited in the *Financial Times* (International Edition), June 21, 1995, 7.

mented despite "firm" deadlines.[46] An influential 1992 report by the West Indian Commission, entitled *A Time for Action,* issued a thoughtful warning that if progress were not forthcoming, CARICOM could suffer the disintegration of the West Indian Federation that preceded it.[47] By 1996, there were signs of life. After five years of negotiations, the community established a customs union with a top tariff rate of 30 percent and finally agreed to eliminate all licensing of imports from within the community.

Despite the high top tariff rate and the relatively modest concession of eliminating intra-union licensing, substantial concerns about both internal and external tariff reductions emerged from protected industries in the larger countries. Yet this is hardly surprising given that the rationale behind the CET and the so-called Common Protective Policy was a regional industrial policy.[48] Beyond the finalization of the CET, CARICOM also has a "deep-integration" agenda. However, it differs fundamentally from that outlined in NAFTA and centers on regional development policy, migration issues, and trade and investment facilitation through such measures as cooperation on transport and a Caribbean Investment Fund.

CACM also reflects both the political difficulties and differences in priorities that have characterized customs unions in Latin America.[49] The end of the Central American wars and the common adoption of wide-ranging economic-reform programs provided the political basis for relaunching the common market. At the Antigua Summit of June 1990, a "Plan of Economic Action for Central America" was developed, and in following summits, agreement was struck on a new common external tariff with a tariff range of 5 percent to 20 percent. The San Salvador Summit of March 1995 reasserted the region's commitment to integration.

Signs of divergence quickly reemerged, however. Honduras and Costa Rica developed major fiscal and external imbalances that contributed to intraregional trade deficits. Trade policies also diverged. The

---

46. Richard L. Bernal, "CARICOM: Externally Vulnerable Regional Integration," in *Economic Integration in the Western Hemisphere,* ed. Bouzas and Ros, 179–80.

47. *Time for Action: The Report of the West Indian Commission* (Barbados: West Indian Commission, 1992).

48. *Financial Times,* July 14, 1995, 4, and Bernal, "CARICOM," 181.

49. See Florencio Ballestro and Ennio Rodríguez, "Central America: Towards a Harmonized Economic Area," *Integration and Trade* 1, no. 1 (1997): 2–36, and Hubert Escaith, "The Countries of the Central American Common Market and the Challenges of a Hemispheric Free Trade Area: The Extent of Macroeconomic Preparedness," ibid., 37–59.

Salvadoran government launched a more aggressive liberalization, while Honduras and Nicaragua, with less competitive industrial structures, were reluctant to liberalize further. A large chunk of regional production—notably agricultural products and services—has been off the political agenda altogether. The continuing dependence of all countries in the region on tariff revenues constitutes a further barrier both to completing the common market and to reducing the CET.

Beyond commercial issues, the CACM has a rich institutional structure, including a secretariat, a regional development bank, and a plethora of committees and working groups. There are also more overt links to high politics in Central America than there are in other regional integration schemes through the mechanism of the Organization of Central American States. Yet institutions should not be equated with the depth of integration; CACM remains one of the thinnest of the intra–Latin American accords, with very limited commitments beyond those in the commercial area and a handful of trade facilitation and infrastructure measures.

Even if strong internal agreements were reached in CARICOM and CACM, the small size of the two groupings and their trade dependence on the United States and (in the case of the Caribbean countries) the European Union would make external relations more important than internal ones. The Caribbean countries retain links both to their formal colonial metropoles and to the European Union as a whole through the Lomé Conventions. These relations with Europe themselves create complex divisions within the region: between English-, French-, Dutch-, and Spanish-speaking countries, between the officially designated more developed and least developed countries, and particularly between those countries that rely heavily on postcolonial trade patterns and those that have established a presence in the North American market. Countries with strong ties to former colonial powers generally have not diversified their economies to the same extent; indeed, reliance on Europe probably has discouraged such diversification. As a result, these countries have less interest in making the concessions required to reach an agreement with North America or with the hemisphere more generally.[50]

---

50. The Lomé Convention protocols on sugar, rum, rice, and particularly bananas also have proved divisive, since they pit formerly colonial exporters that rely heavily on the protocols against the more efficient "dollar" banana producers of Central America. See Mark Rosenberg and Jonathan T. Hiskey, "Changing Trading Patterns of the Caribbean Basin," *Annals of the American Academy of Political Science* 533 (May 1994): 100–111.

In contrast to the Lomé Convention's focus on agricultural trade, the CBI is based on nonreciprocal trade concessions and tax and tariff provisions that have encouraged the development of offshore assembly operations. NAFTA, however, threatens to reduce substantially the advantages the region has enjoyed vis-à-vis Mexico.[51] Roughly one-third of Caribbean exports face no competition from Canada and Mexico, and half of the remaining goods (ores, petroleum, agricultural products) face no trade restrictions. However, preferential access to the U.S. market under the CBI was limited in important respects, and remaining exports faced protection, particularly in the textiles and clothing sector. Because the WTO phaseout of the Multifibre Accord is slow and involves a high degree of product selectivity, the more rapid NAFTA phaseout will give Mexico a temporary advantage that could become more enduring. Caribbean countries will also suffer from the diversion of component outsourcing that falls under the 807 tariff protocols, which subject goods to duty only on value added; such trade will now be altogether duty-free between Mexico and the United States.

The high level of dependence on the United States makes "NAFTA parity" a primary goal of the Caribbean and Central American countries. But the history of the CBI suggests that NAFTA parity is likely to prove an uphill political battle. During the 1992 presidential campaign, the program came under sharp political attack for exporting jobs, and Congress subsequently placed limits on the executive branch's ability to promote foreign investment abroad or to finance export-processing zones as part of its aid program. An Interim Trade Program for the Caribbean basin would have lowered duties on a range of goods excluded from the CBI, but over the course of 1995 it foundered on pressure from U.S. labor unions and textile manufacturers and on fears of Asian transshipment, and finally fell victim to the budget wrangle; efforts to revive it in 1997 also failed. Even if the political impasse is resolved, the United States will expect further policy adjustments whether as part of a NAFTA association agreement or part of the FTAA itself.

Given these difficulties, CACM, CARICOM, and their individual coun-

---

51. See Stephen Lande and Nellis Crigler, "The Caribbean and NAFTA: Opportunities and Challenges" (IDB-ECLAC Working Papers on Trade in the Western Hemisphere 51, Washington, D.C., July 1993), 21–23, and Sarath Rajapatirana, "Global Competitiveness and Regional Integration: Implications for the Caribbean" (World Bank, Washington, D.C., September 5, 1995). The region also enjoys the benefit of the Canadian CARIBCAN program.

try members have been aggressive in pursuing bilateral options;[52] however, as the internal histories of CARICOM and CACM suggest, these new agreements generally have taken a "least-common-denominator" form, with substantial exceptions, long phaseouts, and limited commitment to deep-integration issues. As the ultimate negotiation of the FTAA came closer, the smaller countries increasingly devoted their efforts to assuring that they would receive special attention, including additional aid, in any agreement reached.

The Andean Group and the G-3

In size, the Andean Group stands between the smaller trade groupings of the Caribbean and the much larger Mercosur. The Group has a long and well-documented history as one of the more ambitious integration schemes in the developing world, though one based on the idea of regional import substitution and tight controls on foreign investment. At the outset of the 1980s, intra–Andean trade was almost as low as that among the CARICOM countries. The crises of the 1980s led to the de facto breakdown of the old agreement. Fundamental policy shifts in member countries—Bolivia in 1985, Venezuela in 1989, Colombia in 1990, and Peru in 1992—opened the door to a revival. A presidential summit in the Galapagos in December 1989 set the target of a free-trade area by the end of 1993 (1995 for Bolivia and Ecuador) and a customs union by December 1997. Most important, the Galapagos meeting initiated a series of productive presidential summits. The November 1990 summit accelerated the 1989 timetables, and the presidential meeting in Cartagena in December 1991 resulted in the Acta De Barahona, which launched the common market; the internal free-trade area has been in force since 1993 among all countries except Peru, and a common external tariff was put in place between 1995 and 1997. Intraregional trade rose sharply after 1989, buttressed by growing intraregional investment and the forging of intraregional corporate alliances.

Nor were political initiatives limited to commercial questions narrowly construed; unilateral reforms provided the basis for progress on

---

52. For example, CARICOM negotiated preferential access to Venezuela's markets in 1991 and took the initiative in creating the Association of Caribbean States. Central American countries, both individually and collectively, also have pursued active bilateral diplomacy. Costa Rica was the first to sign an FTA with Mexico; the so-called Northern Triangle of Guatemala, Honduras, and El Salvador has had a strong incentive to follow suit; and Colombia and Venezuela signed an FTA with five Central American countries in 1993.

several deep-integration issues as well. The Andean Group repealed the notorious Decision 24, which previously had governed foreign investment in the region, replacing it with a new statute that equalized tax and fiscal incentives, reduced restrictions on capital gains and profit remittances, and eliminated the burdensome requirement that foreign firms form joint ventures with domestic firms. In 1992 and 1993, the Andean Group countries adopted new standards with respect to intellectual-property rights and have made efforts to coordinate investment policies.

Nonetheless, like its neighbors to the north, the Andean Group has faced both substantial internal difficulties as well as crosscutting external pressures. The decision to launch a common market immediately created divisions within the group. Colombia and Venezuela wanted an escalated, though simple, common external tariff. Peru and Bolivia pursued a more radical flat-tariff-rate approach. Ecuador complained that liberalization was too abrupt. The initial launching of an FTA in January 1992 included only Colombia, Venezuela, and Bolivia. The negotiation of the CET proved even more contentious, with only Colombia and Venezuela initially reaching agreement. Venezuelan subsidies became an issue of contention with Colombia and Peru, and the design of a variable-levy scheme for sensitive agricultural products became a source of conflict in 1993–94, one resolved by maintaining a highly protectionist stance vis-à-vis the outside (with a top tariff rate of 35 percent). In a pattern also visible in Mercosur, the smaller, less industrialized countries—Bolivia and particularly Ecuador—demanded preferential treatment. As in other agreements, these various conflicts were resolved by institutionalizing extensive exceptions and special deals, including sectoral arrangements that effectively managed trade in several sensitive sectors.

But commercial disagreements were not the only ones dividing the community; more fundamental political issues also intervened. Peruvian president Alberto Fujimori's *autogolpe* created political tensions with Venezuela and led to Peru's temporary withdrawal from the grouping in 1992; after the December 1991 meeting, the presidents did not meet again until late 1995. The change in government in Venezuela in 1994 represented the first time since the Latin American reform process began in the mid-1980s that openly populist forces enjoyed an electoral triumph; the Venezuelan government's reversal of previous reforms under President Caldera naturally called into question the future of the Andean project. The tragicomic border skirmishes between Peru and Ecuador in 1995 also slowed regional progress.

In the meantime, the Andean effort faced a variety of external pulls not dissimilar from those faced by CARICOM and CACM. The single most divisive issue among the parties in the early 1990s was the question of how to handle free-trade negotiations with third parties. Bolivia reached an agreement with Mercosur, and over the course of 1997 the Andean Group as a whole sought to reach an agreement with the Southern Cone countries. An equally important pull came from the north. As internal divisions within the Andean Group mounted and the trade diverting effects of NAFTA became more apparent, Colombia and Venezuela turned to external negotiations as a way of forcing the pace of Andean integration. This tactic quickly generated an independent initiative—the G-3 between Mexico, Colombia, and Venezuela—that proved more important than the Andean Group itself.[53] The G-3 mirrored the overall structure of NAFTA, and was thus far more comprehensive than the Andean Group design.

The Andean process is thus increasingly pulled between NAFTA and Mercosur. Andean integration did not get back on track until late 1995, when a presidential summit created a new organizational structure that formally mirrored the European Union in important respects. Given the prior political problems that the Andean countries have faced in completing the common market, however, such institutional initiatives must be viewed with some skepticism.

Mercosur

Mercosur represents a more significant undertaking than the other regional agreements in Latin America.[54] Like NAFTA, it is an altogether

53. The Colombian-Venezuelan axis had always been central to the Andean Group in any case; the two countries were, in January 1992, the first to eliminate their tariffs toward others in the region, and a bilateral agreement in August 1993 included important sectoral agreements in agriculture, oil, electrical-power cooperation, and autos.

54. The literature on Mercosur is vast. For general introductions, see Winston Fritsch and Alexandre A. Tombini, "The Mercosur: An Overview," in *Economic Integration in the Western Hemisphere*, ed. Bouzas and Ros; Roberto Bouzas, "La agenda económica del Mercosur: Desafíos de política a corto y mediano plazo" (FLACSO Serie de Documentos e Informes de Invesitgación, Buenos Aires, November 1995); Sam Laird, "Mercosur Trade Policy: Toward Greater Integration" (World Trade Organization, Geneva, August 1995, mimeo); O'Keefe, "The Prospects for Mercosur's Inclusion."

new agreement rather than a revival or merger of preexisting ones. Unlike NAFTA, the two core members—Argentina and Brazil—are large, inward-looking developing countries that historically have traded relatively little with one another, appeared to have few complementarities, and were even geopolitical rivals.

The Mercosur agreement is best seen as the outcome of a gradual political and military rapprochement that had its roots in the late military period.[55] The two military governments signed a series of political agreements in 1980 and created a binational commission in 1982 that laid the groundwork for the Argentina-Brazil Economic Integration and Cooperation Program (PICE) launched in 1986, following the transition to democracy in both countries. The PICE was rooted in a series of sector-level "complementarity" agreements that are now viewed as anachronisms of the import-substitution era.[56] However, industry protocols in capital goods, iron and steel, and wheat provided crucial business support for the liberalization process, particularly in Argentina, where fears of being swamped by its larger neighbor remain powerful. The PICE thus had an explicit industrial-policy component that included eliminating quantitative restrictions (QRs) while retaining tariff protection, providing subsidies to exporters, and cooperative ventures between Argentine and Brazilian firms. Finally, as with a number of other integration efforts, the agreement had a strong trade-facilitation component, including trade financing, development of the land and maritime transport networks, and coordination of telecommunications research and services.

Mercosur is typically interpreted as constituting a dramatic break from the "old" bilateralism of the PICE. The root cause of this change was a new structural adjustment strategy spurred by the hyperinflations that plagued both countries in the late 1980s.[57] The initiation of these trade

55. This interpretation follows Andrew Hurrell, "Regionalism in the Americas," in *Regionalism in World Politics*, ed. Fawcett and Hurrell.

56. See, for example, Fritsch and Tombini, "Mercosur," 82–83.

57. Argentine trade reforms in 1990–91 were the more radical of the two, and included the removal of all QRs and the adoption of a highly simplified tariff structure in April 1991. In March 1990, the new Brazilian government initiated a reform that affected export subsidies, QRs, and tariffs. For further detail on the Argentine and Brazilian trade reforms, see Table 8.1 in Carol Wise's chapter in this volume. On the link between macroeconomic instability and trade policy in the two countries, see Adolfo Canitrot and Silvia Junco, "Macroeconomic Conditions and Trade Liberalization: The Case of Argentina," and Regis Bonelli, Gustavo B. Franco, and Winston Fritsch, "Macroeconomic Instability and Trade Liberalization in Brazil," both in *Macroeconomic Conditions and Trade Liberalization*, ed. Adolfo Canitrot and Silvia Junco (Washington, D.C.: Inter-American Development Bank, 1993).

reforms set the stage, first, for the bilateral commitment to a common market in the Ata de Buenos Aires (June 6, 1990), to be implemented through an ambitious program of linear and automatic tariff cuts. Following President Bush's announcement of the Enterprise for the Americas Initiative in June 1990, Uruguay called for a summit of all the Southern Cone countries, including Chile, that led ultimately to the Treaty of Asuncion, which launched Mercosur (March 26, 1991, entering into force on November 29, 1991).

As a customs union, the objectives of the treaty included the free movement of goods, services, and factors of production by January 1, 1995. Despite an ambitious agenda, the signatories focused initially on implementing the common market. As elsewhere in Latin America, this did not prove to be an easy task.[58] Elimination of residual nontariff barriers, harmonization of customs procedures, and even convergence on AD/CVD procedures were easily accomplished. The more difficult issues were the completion of the internal market and the design of the CET. As elsewhere, conflicts between smaller and larger countries and industry resistance generated a zigzagging pattern of negotiation that led ultimately to a hybrid customs union and FTA, which allowed countries to retain tariff autonomy on some products and to claim exemptions to internal free trade. The smaller countries opted for lower tariffs than those favored by Brazil in a number of strategic industries, including capital goods, telecommunications equipment, informatics, and particularly autos, which tariffs have become an ongoing source of tension with the United States.

In addition, both Argentina and Brazil have temporarily reversed trade-policy commitments in order to shore up domestic stabilization efforts. Differences in the macroeconomic adjustment strategies of the two major countries—Argentina's virtual gold standard, or "Convertibility Law," and Brazil's more flexible exchange-rate management—constitute an ongoing concern for the viability of the accord because of the sharp swings in competitiveness that have occurred.

There is no question that Mercosur constitutes a major liberalizing achievement, one that has spawned a substantial surge in intra-Mercosur trade. Yet, when the exceptions to the CET are coupled with the excep-

---

58. On the politics of negotiating the common market, see Luigi Manzetti, "The Political Economy of MERCOSUR," *Journal of Interamerican Studies and World Affairs* 35, no. 4 (1993/94): 101–41, as well as *Latin American Regional Reports: Southern Cone Report,* October 15, 1992, February 4, 1993, July 1, 1993, August 5, 1993, November 18, 1993, February 10, 1994, and December 29, 1994.

tions to the common market—explicit sectoral arrangements in autos and sugar, and Brazilian promises to offset its trade surplus by buying crude oil and wheat—it becomes clear that the distance between the bilateralism of the PICE and the regionalism of Mercosur is somewhat less than is often thought. Intra-industry trade, increased intraregional investment, and protection for key sectors constitute the political glue of the new agreement just as they did with the old.[59]

However, the work plan of the group went substantially beyond the common market and the CET. Though the secretariat remains small, the agreement is institutionally ambitious. The Protocol of Ouro Preto (December 17, 1994) established a hierarchy of consultative structures from a minister-level Council of the Common Market to a subministerial Common Market Group (CMG) and a Trade Commission; even though formal macroeconomic-policy coordination remains in the future, this structure has provided the venue for informal exchanges of information. A series of working groups established under the CMG and the Trade Commission indicates the scope of envisioned integration. In addition to trade, there are groups on customs, technical standards, fiscal and monetary matters related to trade, inland transport, maritime transport, industrial and technology policy, agricultural policy, energy, macroeconomic-policy coordination, and labor policy; each of these committees, in turn, has a detailed work program, and progress has been made in a number of important areas, such as financial regulation. Mercosur differs from NAFTA in several respects, but there can be little doubt that it constitutes a deep-integration agreement.

The roughly concomitant completion of the common market and the Miami Summit pushed Mercosur into a flurry of external activity in 1995. Because of its size—Mercosur countries account for 40 percent of Latin American exports—and the geographic diversity of Southern Cone trade, the "foreign policy" of Mercosur differed substantially from the external relations of CACM, CARICOM, and the Andean Group. Argentina differed from Brazil in its preference to keep open the NAFTA option and in its attempts to maintain a balancing role between Brazil and the United States. Nonetheless, the two large Mercosur partners did not face any particular urgency in coming to terms with the United States, partic-

---

59. See, for example, Jose Carlos Vidal, "Economic Relations Between Brazil and Argentina: The Shift in the Eighties" (Ph.D. diss., University of Illinois at Champagne-Urbana, 1993), chap. 6 on intra-industry trade.

ularly as it became clear after 1994 that Argentina was unlikely to enter NAFTA. Mercosur could therefore credibly represent itself as the core of a Latin American alternative to the NAFTA model.

The Brazilian idea of a South American Free Trade Area, put forth in the fall of 1994, rose and fell rapidly in the year after it was proposed. Negotiations with the Andean Group quickly bogged down in conflicts over the preferences that the smaller countries would be allowed to retain, and the (surprising) Andean quest for negotiations on services, investment, and intellectual property. Mercosur's negotiations with Chile waxed and waned with the fate of Chile's negotiations with NAFTA. However, by early 1996 the idea of a SAFTA appeared less and less farfetched. Both Chile and Bolivia had reached associate agreements with Mercosur, leaving only the remaining Andean countries outside the South American bloc, and at the end of 1997 it appeared that some agreement would be reached on that score. By 1996, there were also signs of a Mexico-Brazil rapprochement, embedded in the first tentative signs of U.S.-Brazilian and NAFTA-Mercosur initiatives and Mexico's decision to negotiate a "transitional" trade agreement with the Mercosur.

Building Blocks or Stumbling Blocks?

The proliferation of regional initiatives reflects the profound unilateral reforms in the hemisphere and the continuing interest in liberalization and deeper policy coordination. However, the nature of these agreements makes it difficult to see them as building blocks for a hemispheric accord. First, despite their stated ambitions, regional initiatives have quite defensibly focused on the implementation of commercial commitments: negotiating and implementing FTAs and common markets. Yet a combination of domestic political resistance, differences among the interests of larger and smaller countries, and continuing difficulties in sustaining macroeconomic and exchange-rate stability have slowed implementation and given rise to regimes containing numerous exceptions. Moreover, the interest in freeing trade among the countries in these subregional agreements should not be misinterpreted as reflecting a commitment to free trade vis-à-vis the rest of the world. To the contrary, such agreements either reflect a stated interest in *retaining* protection or have in fact institutionalized numerous protectionist exceptions.

Second, while all of these agreements move beyond commercial policy, the conception of deepening in the Latin American context differs substantially from the North American conception. For example, migration and the coordination of agricultural policy are important in CARICOM, while coordination of industrial policy is of particular interest in Mercosur. In all cases, much more attention is given to trade facilitation through transport, communication, and infrastructure integration than is visible in North America.

Finally, there are problems that arise from the sheer complexity of proliferating interregional agreements. The economic and political forces for subregional integration are typically offset by strong centrifugal pressures to reach agreements with extraregional actors. For the smaller countries, these pressures arise from the natural limitations of regionalism. The less important the trade within the region, the greater the incentive to negotiate with major partners; the more important the trade within the region, the less the interest in discriminatory arrangements. The signing of bilateral accords also appears to contain a strategic dimension, since regional groupings seek to position themselves vis-à-vis other regional agreements, countries, and even extrahemispheric actors like the European Union.

In principle, the proliferation of crosscutting bilateral deals could constitute the very process through which these regional agreements dissolve and hemispheric convergence occurs. However, a review of these initiatives reveals no such tendency; "external" agreements tend to gravitate toward least-common-denominator principles. The fact that such initiatives are unlikely to converge naturally constitutes one of the key reasons for bypassing the regional level altogether and moving directly to a hemisphere-wide negotiation strategy.

The FTAA Process

Before Miami, an inclusive agreement among all countries in the Americas was discounted as the least likely way for hemispheric integration to occur. Nonetheless, the model did have a number of recognized benefits. Such an organization would begin with all parties "present at the creation" and would thus avoid the invidious distinctions between insiders and outsiders that would accompany either an expansion of NAFTA or the negotiation of bilateral FTAs. Inclusiveness would mitigate the concerns of countries with diversified trade and investment relations about overly close association with the United States. Such an organization also would serve to enhance the voice of the Latin American countries in their dealings with the United States and thus could serve as a check on American unilateralism. Above all, such an agreement promised to reconcile the welter of emerging subregional accords.

The Clinton administration's postponement of the quest for fast-track authority in September 1994 severely dampened hopes that the Miami Summit would yield a meaningful trade agreement; early U.S. statements downplayed the economic dimension of the summit in favor of a host of other environmental and social issues. Nonetheless, the Plan of Action ratified by the summit opted for the negotiation of a Free Trade Area of the Americas (FTAA) by no later than 2005, with "concrete progress toward the attainment of this objective" to be made before the end of the century. The precise means through which the FTAA was to be achieved remained ambiguous in the summit declaration. Substantial concessions were made to existing regional agreements by calling for their expansion and for discussions among them. Stephen Lande and Nellis Crigler have labeled this the "accretion" model and note that the flurry of regional activity that occurred in 1995 could be interpreted in part as a response to the summit.[60]

However, the most important innovations were a wide definition of the substantive agenda and the initiation of a number of hemisphere-wide political processes that implied a more overarching "harmonization" model. The coverage of the prospective accord encompasses the main areas of NAFTA (though NAFTA is not mentioned), as well as new issues such as competition policy and workers rights. The summit leaders established a Committee on Hemispheric Financial Issues to promote the liberalization of capital movements and the progressive integration of capital markets. Nor were the more concrete trade-facilitation interests of the Latin American states ignored. The summit committed countries in the hemisphere to work with the private sector and international financial institutions on joint ventures to develop regional energy and transportation networks and directed the Inter-American Telecommunications Commission (CITEL) of the OAS to work toward liberalization and common standards in telecommunications.

The political process launched by the summit pushed strongly in the direction of functional negotiating bodies. This was not apparent at first;

60. Stephen Lande and Nellis Crigler, "Trade Aspects of the Miami Summit of the Americas: The First Ninety Days" (North-South Center, University of Miami, Fla., May 1995).

indeed the institutional machinery appeared quite thin and the accomplishments of the first two ministerials limited. Unlike the Asia Pacific
Economic Cooperation (APEC), the Miami Summit did not create a secretariat. Rather, ministerial meetings were to be the main political venue,
with administrative and analytic support provided by the Tripartite
Committee of the OAS (supported by a newly created trade unit), the
Inter-American Development Bank (IDB), and the United Nations Economic Commission on Latin America and the Caribbean (ECLAC). The
Immediate Action Plan called on these bodies to systematize data on the
region, to compare the obligations of existing agreements, and to examine a number of areas that might be ripe for "immediate action"; over
the course of the next year, it became clear that this work would be
conducted by a series of technical working groups, the definition and
mandate of which, however, proved highly political.

The role of the United States as host of the first ministerial meeting
in June 1995 appeared to give it substantial agenda-setting powers.
Drawing on procedures developed in connection with the EAI, the staff
of the Office of the United States Trade Representative used the Trade
and Investment Framework consultations as the vehicle for exploring
ideas for "immediate action" with major groups of countries (Mercosur,
Andean Pact, CARICOM, and CACM). The U.S. approach at the outset was
maximalist: the FTAA should "improve" on WTO commitments by getting
Latin America to sign on to ten sectoral "zero-for-zero" accords; accelerate commitments made in the Uruguay Round negotiations with respect
to government procurement and intellectual-property rights; and expand service offers in telecommunications, finance, and entertainment.
The United States called for the elimination of all product exceptions in
existing regional agreements by 1999 and outlined a broad range of issues on which it sought the establishment of working groups, including
worker rights and the environment.[61]

The Latin American countries argued that WTO commitments were
part of a "balanced" outcome in the Uruguay Round and should not be
touched unless the United States was willing to make similar concessions, such as accelerating the phaseout of the Multifibre Agreement or
committing to WTO-plus disciplines to limit the use of antidumping and
countervailing duties. Individual Latin American countries advanced

---

61. See the discussions and leaked documents in *Inside NAFTA*, April 19, May 3, May 17, May
31, and June 14, 1995. The following paragraphs draw on these sources.

counterproposals, such as technical support for tariff reforms, facilitating trade by small and medium-sized firms, infrastructure financing, and, above all, special consideration of the problems facing smaller economies.

The Denver Trade Ministerial of June 1995 was a disappointment. The U.S. strategy of advancing a long list of demands without any apparent reciprocity wore thin, and Brazil appeared successful in its effort to challenge the United States on both substance and process. Any acceleration of WTO commitments was firmly rejected, as was U.S. insistence on controversial issues such as the environment and labor rights. The final list of seven substantive working groups was closer to the Brazilian preference for five than the U.S. request for eleven.[62] The meeting also established a working group on the smaller economies, opening the door to consideration of a two-track FTAA. The initial tasks undertaken by the working groups were limited to the compilation of information, and Brazil openly rebuffed the new OAS trade unit for seeking to play a more active agenda-setting role.

Behind this early jousting was a more fundamental difference between the United States and Brazil on how the FTAA would emerge. The United States and Canada sought a multilateral agreement that would constitute a "single undertaking"—meaning countries would commit to all of its components—and would build on the achievements of the WTO and NAFTA. Brazil favored a process in which existing regional agreements would constitute the building blocks, first through a process of deepening, and then ultimately through interbloc negotiation.[63] The Brazilian initiative for a SAFTA must be seen in this light: as a strategic move to increase Latin American bargaining power in the bloc-to-bloc negotiations that ultimately would ensue.

For this strategy to succeed, however, it was imperative that the momentum toward functional negotiations through the emerging working groups be slowed; this objective was apparent throughout the ministerial and working-group meetings in 1996 and 1997 and in particular in the Brazilian proposal that the negotiations be staged so that the most

62. The seven working groups cover market access, customs procedures and rules of origin, investment, standards and technical barriers to trade, sanitary and phytosanitary standards, subsidies, antidumping and countervailing duties.

63. See Jose Botafogo Goncalves, "The Challenges of Hemispheric Integration: A Brazilian View," *Brazil File* 5, no. 1 (1996): 7–8.

difficult market-access issues be held off to the very end of the negotiation process, in 2003–5.

The Brazilian strategy served to slow the integration process and gave rise to extremely complex diplomatic posturing in 1996 and 1997. However, it became increasingly clear that the Brazilian approach of building blocs, limited commitments, and a gradual and phased negotiation presented a viable alternative. If the FTAA did not go beyond WTO commitments, there was little point in having a hemispheric dialogue; the whole purpose of regionalism is to strike bargains that cannot be reached at the WTO level. If the FTAA does go beyond the WTO, however, it necessarily must consider the baseline established by NAFTA and any new issues that are not on the WTO or NAFTA agendas.

Latin American countries blocked the formation of working groups on a number of sensitive items in Denver, but governments committed themselves at that meeting to form working groups on the more contentious issues of government procurement, intellectual-property rights, services, and competition policy at the Cartagena Summit in March 1996. The task of the working groups in the early stages may have been limited to information gathering, but the tripartite mechanism proved extremely effective at collating data.[64] By 1997, the relevant information had largely been gathered, the working groups had explored a number of technical issues in depth, and pressure mounted to turn the working groups into negotiating bodies. By the end of 1997, Brazil had become increasingly isolated. Consensus had been reached—or it had become apparent—that negotiations would be launched at the Santiago Summit in March 1998, that the FTAA would be a single undertaking, and that all of the issues discussed in the working groups would be on the table at once, even if actual negotiations might transpire at different speeds.

In one sense, however, the Brazilian position contains an important element of political truth. The fate of hemispheric cooperation ultimately will hinge on bringing together the two most important groupings in the region—NAFTA and Mercosur. To speculate on how that might occur requires a brief overview of these findings.

---

64. This point is developed in Morton, "Outlook for Free Trade in the Americas." Over the second half of 1995 all of the working groups met at least once and began the process of collecting information and considering possible proposals for immediate action. See OAS Trade Unit, "Free Trade Area of the Americas: Working Groups" (Organization of American States, Washington, D.C., 1995, mimeo).

Conclusion

Because of divergent interests, regional integration efforts have developed quite differently throughout the hemisphere. The North American complex represents a particular form of deep integration that reflects U.S. corporate interests and the high levels of trade and investment dependence of Mexico and Canada on the United States. Viewed over the longer run, Latin American convergence around these ideas appears striking; nonetheless, what I have called the Latin American complex is substantially more diverse. Differences in levels of development, policy regimes, and underlying political forces eliminated the possibility that NAFTA accession could serve as the vehicle for hemispheric integration.

The assumption that a hemispheric accord could emerge either from convergence or from negotiation among existing agreements has also fallen by the wayside. This view wrongly assumed either a "natural" deepening process that is similar across highly dissimilar regional efforts or a "perfection" process disciplined by an overarching set of multilateral or hemispheric commitments—commitments that differ substantially from revealed policy preferences.

Yet an unstructured negotiation among blocs also proved a nonstarter; there must be some agenda, some focal points that will shape the negotiation process. Those focal points were given by the functional committees that constituted the heart of the FTAA process between 1995 and 1997 and that will now be converted into negotiating bodies.

The task at the time of this writing in late 1997 is to look ahead to how the divergent interests in the hemisphere, and particularly differences between NAFTA and Mercosur, might be reconciled through these negotiations. The basis for such a grand pact is much too complex to foresee with any clarity, but it would likely involve a trade-off between the North American interest in services and intellectual property and the Latin American interest in market access, dispute settlement, and trade facilitation; as well as growing convergence around issues such as standards and investment.

Such trade-offs cannot be achieved without high-level political initiative that permits cross-issue linkage. The future, therefore, hinges centrally on domestic politics, particularly in the United States, where the defeat of fast track in late 1997 showed a renewed skepticism with respect to international trade and trade policy. In the absence of a "big push" by NAFTA and Mercosur—and thus ultimately by the United States and Brazil—hemispheric integration will continue to encompass a complicated patchwork of multilateral, regional, subregional, and bilateral commitments, a patchwork that necessarily implies a more diluted vision of the FTAA than that articulated at Miami.

Selected Bibliography

Aguirre, Pedro, Ricardo Becerra, Lorenzo Córdova, and José Woldenberg. *Una reforma electoral para la democracia.* Mexico City: Instituto de Estudios para la Transición Democrática, 1995.

Alba Vega, Carlos. "La microindustria ante la liberalización económica y el Tratado de Libre Comercio." *Foro Internacional* 23, no. 3 (1993): 453–83.

Alesina, Alberto, and Dani Rodrik. "Distributive Policies and Economic Growth." *Quarterly Journal of Economics* 109, no. 436 (1994): 465–90.

Alexandroff, Alan S. "The Federal and Provincial Liberal Parties and NAFTA." In *Beyond NAFTA: An Economic, Political, and Sociological Perspective,* ed. A. R. Riggs and Tom Velk. Vancouver: Fraser Institute, 1993.

Anderson, Kym, and Richard Blackhurst, eds. *Regional Integration and the Global Trading System.* London: Harvester Wheatsheaf, 1993.

Andreas, Peter, Eva Bertram, Morris Blachman, and Kenneth Sharpe. "Dead End Drug Wars." *Foreign Policy,* no. 85 (winter 1991–92): 106–28.

Appendini, Kirsten. "Agriculture and Farmers Within NAFTA: A Mexican Perspective." In *Mexico and the North American Free Trade Agreement: Who Will Benefit?* ed. Victor Bulmer-Thomas, Nikki Craske, and Mónica Serrano. New York: St. Martin's Press, 1994.

———. "Transforming Food Policy over a Decade." In *Economic Restructuring and Rural Subsistence in Mexico: Corn and the Crisis of the 1980s,* ed. Cynthia Hewitt de Alcántara. La Jolla: Center for U.S.-Mexican Studies, University of California at San Diego, 1994.

Aspe, Pedro. *El camino mexicano de la transformación económica.* Mexico City: Fondo de Cultura Económica, 1993.

Atkeson, Andrew, and José-Víctor Ríos-Rull. "How Mexico Lost Its Foreign Exchange Reserves." NBER Working Paper 5329. National Bureau of Economic Research, Cambridge, Mass., 1995.

Bach, Robert. "Processes of Migration." In *The Challenge of Integration: Europe and the Americas,* ed. Peter Smith. New Brunswick, N.J.: Transaction Publishers, 1993.

Bagley, Bruce M., and William O. Walker III. *Drug Trafficking in the Americas*. New Brunswick, N.J.: Transaction Publishers, 1994.

Balassa, Bela, et al. *Development Strategies in Semi-Industrial Economies*. Baltimore: Johns Hopkins University Press, 1982.

Baldwin, Richard. "A Domino Theory of Regionalism." NBER Working Paper 4465. National Bureau of Economic Research, Cambridge, Mass., 1993.

Ballestro, Florencio, and Ennio Rodríguez. "Central America: Towards a Harmonized Economic Area." *Integration and Trade* 1, no. 1 (1997): 2–36.

Barkin, David. *Distorted Development: Mexico in the World Economy*. Boulder, Colo.: Westview Press, 1990.

Barry, Donald. "The Road to NAFTA." In *Toward a North American Community? Canada, the United States, and Mexico*, ed. Donald Barry. Boulder, Colo.: Westview Press, 1995.

Barry, T., H. Browne, and B. Sims. *Crossing the Line: Immigrants, Economic Integration, and Drug Enforcement on the U.S. Mexican Border*. Albuquerque, N.Mex.: Resource Center Press, 1994.

Bauer, Raymond, Ithiel de Sola Pool, and Lewis Dexter. *American Business and Public Policy*. Chicago: Aldine, 1972.

Bayard, Thomas O., and Kimberly Ann Elliott. *Reciprocity and Retaliation in U.S. Trade Policy*. Washington, D.C.: Institute for International Economics, 1994.

Becerra, Ricardo, Pedro Salazar, and José Woldenberg. *La reforma electoral de 1996: Una descripción general*. Mexico City: Fondo de Cultura Económica, 1997.

Bernal, Richard L. "CARICOM: Externally Vulnerable Regional Integration." In *Economic Integration in the Western Hemisphere*, ed. Roberto Bouzas and Jaime Ros. Notre Dame, Ind.: University of Notre Dame Press, 1994.

———. "Paths to the Free Trade Area of the Americas." Policy Papers on the Americas. Center for Strategic and International Studies, Washington, D.C., 1997.

Bhagwati, Jagdish. "Incentives and Disincentives: International Migration." *Weltwirtschaftliches Archiv* 120, no. 4 (1984): 678–701.

Bhagwati, Jagdish, and Arvind Panagariya. "The Theory of Preferential Trade Agreements: Historical Evolution and Current Trends." *American Economic Review* 86, no. 2 (1996): 82–87.

Bhagwati, Jagdish, and Hugh Patrick, eds. *Aggressive Unilateralism:*

America's 301 Trade Policy and the World Trading System. Ann Arbor: University of Michigan Press, 1990.

Birdsall, Nancy, David Ross, and Richard Sabot. "Inequality and Growth Reconsidered: Lessons from East Asia." *World Bank Economic Review* 9, no. 3 (1995): 477–508.

Blomstrom, Magnus, and Ari Kokko. "Regional Integration and Foreign Direct Investment: A Conceptual Framework." Policy Research Working Paper 1750. World Bank, Washington, D.C., 1997.

Bonelli, Regis, Gustavo B. Franco, and Winston Fritsch. "Macroeconomic Instability and Trade Liberalization in Brazil." In *Macroeconomic Conditions and Trade Liberalization,* ed. Adolfo Canitrot and Silvia Junco. Washington, D.C.: Inter-American Development Bank, 1993.

Bosworth, Barry, Rudiger Dornbusch, and Raúl Labán, eds. *The Chilean Economy: Policy Lessons and Challenges*. Washington, D.C.: Brookings Institution, 1994.

Bouzas Roberto, and Jaime Ros. "The North-South Variety of Economic Integration: Issues and Prospects for Latin America." In *Economic Integration in the Western Hemisphere,* ed. Roberto Bouzas and Jaime Ros. Notre Dame, Ind.: University of Notre Dame Press, 1994.

———, eds. *Economic Integration in the Western Hemisphere*. Notre Dame, Ind.: University of Notre Dame Press, 1994.

Brown, Drusilla K. "The Impact of a North American Free Trade Area: Applied General Equilibrium Models." In *North American Free Trade: Assessing the Impact,* ed. Nora Lustig et al. Washington D.C.: Brookings Institution, 1992.

Bruhn, Kathleen M. "Social Spending and Political Support: The 'Lessons' of the National Solidarity Program in Mexico." *Comparative Politics* 28, no. 2 (1996): 151–77.

———. *Taking on Goliath: The Emergence of a New Left Party and the Struggle for Democracy in Mexico*. University Park: Pennsylvania State University Press, 1997.

Bruno, Michael. "Opening Up: Liberalization with Stabilization." In *The Open Economy: Tools for Policymakers in Developing Countries,* ed. Rudiger Dornbusch and Leslie Helmers. EDI Series in Economic Development. Washington, D.C.: Oxford University Press for the World Bank, 1988.

Brysk, Alison. "From Above and Below: Social Movements, the International System, and Human Rights in Argentina." *Comparative Political Studies* 26, no. 3 (1993): 259–85.

Bulmer-Thomas, Victor. "Mexico and NAFTA: Who Will Benefit?" In *Mexico and the North American Free Trade Agreement: Who Will Benefit?* ed. Victor Bulmer-Thomas, Nikki Craske, and Mónica Serrano. New York: St. Martin's Press, 1994.

Burki, Shahid, and Sebastian Edwards. *Dismantling the Populist State.* Washington, D.C.: World Bank, 1996.

Busch, Marc L., and Helen V. Milner. "The Future of the International Trading System." In *Political Economy and the Changing Global Order,* ed. Richard Stubbs and Geoffrey Underhill. Toronto: McClelland & Stewart, 1994.

Bustelo, Pedro. "Neoliberalismo y nuevos países industriales." *Revista de Economía* (Madrid), no. 727 (1994): 77–93.

Butelman, Andrea. "Elements of Chilean Trade Strategy: The United States or Mercosur?" In *Economic Integration in the Western Hemisphere,* ed. Roberto Bouzas and Jaime Ros. Notre Dame, Ind.: University of Notre Dame Press, 1994.

Calvo, Guillermo A., and Enrique G. Mendoza. "Petty Crime and Cruel Punishment: Lessons from the Mexican Debacle." *American Economic Review* 86, no. 2 (1996): 170–75.

Camacho Solís, Manuel. *Cambio sin ruptura.* Mexico City: Alianza Editorial, 1994.

Cameron, Maxwell A., and Brian W. Tomlin. "Canada and Latin America in the Shadow of U.S. Power." In *Toward a North American Community? Canada, the United States, and Mexico,* ed. Donald Barry. Boulder, Colo.: Westview Press, 1995.

Campodónico, Humberto. "La política del avestruz." In *Coca, cocaína y narcotráfico,* ed. Diego García Sayan. Lima: Comisión Andina de Juristas, 1989.

Canitrot, Adolfo, and Silvia Junco. "Macroeconomic Conditions and Trade Liberalization: The Case of Argentina." In *Macroeconomic Conditions and Trade Liberalization,* ed. Adolfo Canitrot and Silvia Junco. Washington, D.C.: Inter-American Development Bank, 1993.

Cárdenas, Mauricio, and Catalina Crane. "Economic Integration in Colombia: Is There a Strategy?" In *Integrating the Hemisphere,* ed. Ana Julia Jatar and Sidney Weintraub. Washington, D.C.: Inter-American Dialogue, 1997.

Carrillo, Mario Alejandro, and Rigoberto Ramírez. "El Partido Acción Nacional en el primer año de gobierno de Ernesto Zedillo." *El Cotidiano* 75 (March–April 1996): 12–18.

Cartwright, Dorwin, and Alvin Zander, eds. *Group Dynamics: Research and Theory*. Evanston, Ill.: Row, Peterson, 1953.

Castañeda, Jorge. "Mexico's Circle of Misery." *Foreign Affairs* 75, no. 4 (1996): 92–105.

Centeno, Miguel. *Democracy Within Reason: Technobureaucratic Revolution in Mexico*. University Park: Pennsylvania State University Press, 1994.

Centro de Estudios Económicos del Sector Privado (CEESP). *La economía subterránea en México*. Mexico: CEESP, 1987.

———. "Evolución y problemática de las empresas en 1994." *Actividad Económica*, no. 183 (1995).

Chudnovsky, Daniel, et al. *Los límites de la apertura: Liberalización, reestructuración productiva y medio ambiente*. Buenos Aires: CENIT/Alianza Editorial, 1996.

Clark, Ian. "Should the IMF Become More Adaptive?" IMF Working Paper. Washington, D.C., 1996.

Clavijo, Fernando, and S. Valdivieso. "La política industrial de México, 1988–1994." In *La industria mexicana en el mercado mundial: Elementos para una política industrial*, ed. Fernando Clavijo and J. Casar, vol. 1. Mexico City: Lecturas de El Trimestre Económico, FCE, 1994.

Cockcroft, James D. *Mexico: Class Formation, Capital Accumulation, and the State*. New York: Monthly Review Press, 1983.

Cook, Maria Lorena. "Regional Integration and Transnational Politics: Popular Sector Strategies in the NAFTA Era." In *The New Politics of Inequality in Latin America: Rethinking Participation and Representation*, ed. Douglas A. Chalmers, Carlos M. Vilas, Katherine Hite, Scott B. Martin, Kerianne Piester, and Monique Segarra. New York: Oxford University Press, 1997.

Cornelius, Wayne A., Ann L. Craig, and Jonathan Fox, eds. *Transforming State-Society Relations in Mexico: The National Solidarity Strategy*. La Jolla.: Center for U.S.-Mexican Studies, University of California at San Diego, 1994.

Council on Foreign Relations. *Lessons of the Mexican Peso Crisis: Report of an Independent Task Force*. New York: Council on Foreign Relations, 1996.

Cox, Robert. *Production, Power, and World Order*. New York: Columbia University Press, 1987.

Crespo, José Antonio. "El rol de la presidencia en el cambio político." In *Jaque al Rey: Hacia un nuevo presidencialismo en México*. Mexico City: Joaquín Mortiz, 1995.

Cruz Rivero, Carlos, et al. "The Impact of Economic Crisis and Adjustment on Health Care in Mexico." Innocenti Occasional Papers 13. Italy, February 1991.

Dandeker, Rebecca. "The Rose Garden Agreement: Is Mercosur the Next Step to a Hemispheric Free Trade Zone?" *Law and Policy in International Business* 24, no. 1 (1992): 57–180.

Deardorff, Alan, Drusilla K. Brown, and Robert M. Stern. "Expanding NAFTA: Economic Effects of Accession of Chile and Other Major South American Nations." *North American Journal of Economics and Finance*, no. 6 (fall 1995): 149–70.

De Gregorio, Jose. "Inflation, Growth, and Central Banks: Theory and Evidence." Policy Research Working Paper 1575. World Bank, Washington, D.C., February 1996.

de Janvry, Alain, et al. "NAFTA and Mexico's Maize Producers." *World Development* 23, no. 8 (1995): 1349–62.

———. "Ejido Sector Reforms: From Land Reform to Rural Development." In *Reforming Mexico's Agrarian Reform*, ed. Laura Randall. New York: Sharpe, 1996.

de la Madrid, Miguel. "Doce años de cambios en México." *Este País*, no. 53 (August 1995).

De Long, Bradford, Christopher De Long, and Sherman Robinson. "The Case for Mexico's Rescue: The Peso Package Looks Even Better Now." *Foreign Affairs* 75, no. 3 (1996): 8–14.

de Melo, Jaime, and Arvind Panagariya, eds. *New Dimensions in Regional Integration.* Cambridge: Cambridge University Press, 1993.

Destler, I. M. *American Trade Politics.* Washington, D.C.: Institute for International Economics, 1992.

———. "American Trade Politics in the Wake of the Uruguay Round." In *The World Trading System: Challenges Ahead,* ed. Jeffrey J. Schott. Washington, D.C.: Institute for International Economics, 1996.

———. "Renewing Fast-Track Legislation." Policy Analyses in International Economics. Institute for International Economics, Washington, D.C., September 1997.

Doeringer, Peter, and David Terka. "Business Strategy and Cross-Industry Clusters." *Economic Development Quarterly* 9, no. 3 (1995): 225–37.

Domínguez, Jorge I. "Immigration as Foreign Policy in U.S.–Latin American Relations." In *Immigration and United States Foreign Policy,* ed.

Robert W. Tucker, Charles B. Keely, and Linda Wrigley. Boulder, Colo.: Westview Press, 1990.

Dornbusch, Rudiger. "The Case for Trade Liberalization in the Developing Countries." *Journal of Economic Perspectives* 6, no. 1 (1992): 69–86.

Dornbusch, Rudiger, Ilan Goldfajn, and Rodrigo O. Valdés. "Currency Crises and Collapses." *Brookings Papers on Economic Activity*, no. 2 (1995): 219–93.

Dornbusch, Rudiger, and Alejandro Werner. "Mexico: Stabilization, Reform, and No Growth." *Brookings Papers on Economic Activity*, no. 1 (1994): 253–315.

Dresser, Denise. "Mexico: The Decline of Dominant Party Rule." In *Challenges to Democratic Governance in Latin America*, ed. Abraham F. Lowenthal and Jorge I. Domínguez. Baltimore: Johns Hopkins University Press, 1991.

———. *Neopopulist Solutions to Neoliberal Problems: Mexico's National Solidarity Program*. La Jolla: Center for U.S.-Mexican Studies, University of California at San Diego, 1991.

———. "Treading Lightly and Without a Stick: International Actors and the Promotion of Democracy in Mexico." In *Beyond Sovereignty: The Collective Defense of Democracy in Latin America*, ed. Tom Farer. Baltimore: Johns Hopkins University Press, 1996.

———. "Conflicting Imperatives: The Political Economy of the Crisis." In *Mexico 1994: Anatomy of an Emerging Market Crash*, ed. Sebastian Edwards and Moisés Naím. Washington D.C.: Carnegie Endowment for International Peace, 1998.

Dunn, Timothy J. *The Militarization of the U.S.-Mexico Border, 1978–1992: Low Intensity Conflict Doctrine Comes Home*. Austin, Tex.: Center for Mexican-American Studies, 1996.

Edwards, Sebastian. "Openness, Trade Liberalization, and Growth in Developing Countries." *Journal of Economic Literature* 31, no. 3 (1993): 1358–93.

———. *Crisis and Reform in Latin America: From Despair to Hope*. New York: Oxford University Press, 1995.

———. "Exchange-Rate Anchors, Credibility, and Inertia: A Tale of Two Crises, Chile and Mexico." *American Economic Review* 86, no. 2 (1996): 176–80.

Eichengreen, Barry, and Albert Fishlow. *Contending with Capital Flows:*

What Is Different About the 1990s? New York: Council on Foreign Relations, 1996.

Elías, Victor J. *Infrastructure and Growth: The Latin American Case.* Washington, D.C.: World Bank, 1995.

Elliott Armijo, Leslie. "Inflation and Insouciance: The Peculiar Brazilian Game." *Latin American Research Review* 31, no. 3 (1996): 7–46.

Erzan, Refik, and Alexander Yeats. "Free Trade Agreements with the United States: What's in It for Latin America?" World Bank Policy Research Working Paper 827. World Bank, Washington, D.C., 1992.

———. "U.S.–Latin America Free Trade Areas: Some Empirical Evidence." In *The Premise and the Promise: Free Trade in the Americas,* by Sylvia Saborio et al. Washington, D.C.: Overseas Development Council, 1992.

Escaith, Hubert. "The Countries of the Central American Common Market and the Challenges of a Hemispheric Free Trade Area: The Extent of Macroeconomic Preparedness." *Integration and Trade* 1, no. 1 (1997): 37–59.

Fawcett, Louise, and Andrew Hurrell, eds. *Regionalism in World Politics.* Oxford: Oxford University Press, 1995.

Fishlow, Albert. "From NAFTA to a WHFTA? The Summit May Tell." In *Integrating the Americas: Shaping Future Trade Policy,* ed. Sidney Weintraub. Miami, Fla.: North-South Center, University of Miami, 1994.

Fishlow, Albert, et al., eds. *Miracle or Design? Lessons from the East Asian Experience.* Washington, D.C.: Overseas Development Council, 1994.

Fiszbein, Ariel, and George Psacharopoulos. "Income Inequality Trends in Latin America in the 1980's." In *Coping with Austerity: Poverty and Inequality in Latin America,* ed. Nora Lustig. Washington, D.C.: Brookings Institution, 1995.

Fitzgerald, E.V.K. *Intervention Versus Regulation: The Role of the IMF in Crisis Prevention and Management.* Oxford: Queen Elizabeth House, 1995.

Flynn, Stephen E. "Worldwide Drug Scourge." *Brookings Review,* winter 1993.

Foley, Michael. "Privatizing the Countryside: The Mexican Peasant Movement and Neoliberal Reform." *Latin American Perspectives* 22, no. 1 (1995): 59–76.

Foweraker, Joe. "From NAFTA to WHFTA? Prospects for Hemispheric Free Trade." In *Cooperation or Rivalry? Regional Integration in the Ameri-*

cas and the Pacific Rim, ed. Shoji Nishijima and Peter H. Smith. Boulder, Colo.: Westview Press, 1996.

Fox, Jonathan. "Political Change in Mexico's New Peasant Economy." In *The Politics of Economic Restructuring: State-Society Relations and Regime Change in Mexico,* ed. Maria Lorena Cook, Kevin J. Middlebrook, and Juan Molinar Horcasitas. La Jolla: Center for U.S.-Mexican Studies, University of California at San Diego, 1994.

Frankel, Jeffrey, Ernesto Stein, and Shang-jin Wei. "Trading Blocs and the Americas: The Natural, the Unnatural, and the Super-Natural." *Journal of Development Economics* 47, no. 1 (1995): 61–95.

Frieden, Jeffry. "Political Sources and Political Lessons of the 1994–1995 Mexican Crisis." Paper presented at a meeting on the Mexican Crisis, sponsored by the Carnegie Endowment for International Peace and the World Bank, Washington, D.C., October 1995.

Fritsch, Winston, and Alexandre A. Tombini. "The Mercosur: An Overview." In *Economic Integration in the Western Hemisphere,* ed. Roberto Bouzas and Jaime Ros. Notre Dame, Ind.: University of Notre Dame Press, 1994.

Garay, Luis Jorge, and Antonio Estevadeordal. "Protection, Preferential Tariff Elimination, and Rules of Origin in the Americas." Inter-American Development Bank, Washington, D.C., 1995.

Gates, Marilyn. "The Debt Crisis and Economic Restructuring: Prospects for Mexican Agriculture." In *Neoliberalism Revisited: Economic Restructuring and Mexico's Political Future,* ed. Gerardo Otero. Boulder, Colo.: Westview Press, 1996.

Gil-Díaz, Francisco, and Agustin Carstens. "One Year of Solitude: Some Pilgrim Tales About Mexico's 1994–1995 Crisis." *American Economic Review* 86, no. 2 (1996): 164–69.

Golub, Stephanie R. " 'Making Possible What Is Necessary': Pedro Aspe, the Salinas Team, and the Next Mexican 'Miracle.' " In *Technopols: Freeing Politics and Markets in Latin America in the 1990s,* ed. Jorge Domínguez. University Park: Pennsylvania State University Press, 1997.

Gonzalez-Block, Rene, et al. "Health Services Decentralization in Mexico." *Health Policy and Planning* 4, no. 4 (1989): 301–14.

Graham, Carol. *Safety Nets, Politics, and the Poor: Transitions to Market Economies.* Washington, D.C.: Brookings Institution, 1994.

Griffith-Jones, Stephany. *Managing World Debt.* London: Harvester Wheatsheaf, 1988.

Haggard, Stephan. *The Developing Nations and the Politics of Global Integration.* Washington, D.C.: Brookings Institution, 1995.

Haggard, Stephan, and Robert Kaufman. *The Political Economy of Democratic Transitions.* Princeton: Princeton University Press, 1995.

Hagopian, Frances. "Traditional Politics and the State in Brazil." In *State Power and Social Forces,* ed. Joel S. Migdal, Atul Kohli, and Vivienne Shue. New York: Cambridge University Press, 1994.

Hart, Michael M. *A North American Free Trade Agreement: Strategic Implications for Canada.* Ottawa: Centre for Trade Policy and Law and the Institute for Research on Public Policy, 1990.

Harvey, Neil. "Rural Reforms and the Zapatista Rebellion: Chiapas, 1988–1995." In *Neoliberalism Revisited: Economic Restructuring and Mexico's Political Future,* ed. Gerardo Otero. Boulder, Colo.: Westview Press, 1996.

Heath, Jonathan E. "The Devaluation of the Mexican Peso in 1994: Economic Policy and Institutions." Policy Papers on the Americas VI, Study 5. Center for Strategic and International Studies, Washington, D.C., 1995.

Heath, Jonathan R. "Evaluating the Impact of Mexico's Land Reform on Agricultural Productivity." *World Development* 20, no. 5 (1992): 695–712.

Herzog, Lawrence A. "Changing Boundaries in the Americas: An Overview." In *Changing Boundaries in the Americas,* ed. Lawrence A. Herzog. U.S.-Mexican Contemporary Perspective Series 3. La Jolla: Center for U.S.-Mexican Studies, University of California at San Diego, 1992.

Hewitt de Alcántara, Cynthia, ed. *Economic Restructuring and Rural Subsistence in Mexico: Corn and the Crisis of the 1980s.* La Jolla: Center for U.S.-Mexican Studies, University of California at San Diego, 1994.

Hinojosa-Ojeda, Raul, and Sherman Robinson. "Labor Issues in a North American Free Trade Area." In *North American Free Trade: Assessing the Impact,* ed. Nora Lustig et al. Washington, D.C.: Brookings Institution, 1992.

Hoskins, W. Lee, and James W. Coons. "Mexico: Policy Failure, Moral Hazard, and Market Solutions." Policy Analysis 243. CATO Institute, Washington, D.C., 1995.

Hufbauer, Gary C., and Jeffrey J. Schott. *North American Free Trade: Issues and Recommendations.* Washington, D.C.: Institute for International Economics, 1992.

————. *NAFTA: An Assessment*. Rev. ed. Washington, D.C.: Institute for International Economics, 1993.

————. *Western Hemisphere Economic Integration*. Washington, D.C.: Institute for International Economics, 1994.

Hurrell, Andrew. "Latin America in the New World Order: A Regional Bloc of the Americas?" *International Affairs* 68, no. 1 (1992): 121–39.

Janis, Irving. *Groupthink*. Boston: Houghton Mifflin, 1982.

Jatar, Ana Julia, and Sidney Weintraub, eds. *Integrating the Hemisphere*. Washington, D.C.: Inter-American Dialogue, 1997.

Jha, Raghbendra. *Macroeconomics for Developing Countries*. London: Routledge, 1994.

Kahler, Miles. "The United States and the International Monetary Fund: Declining Influence or Declining Interest?" In *The United States and Multilateral Institutions*, ed. Margaret Karns and Karen Mingst. Boston: Unwin Hyman, 1990.

Karl, Terry. "Democratization Around the Globe: Its Opportunities and Risks." In *World Security: Trends and Challenges at Century's End*, ed. Michael T. Klare and Dan Thomas. London: St. Martin's Press, 1993.

Karmin, Douglas. "Rules of Origin and the North American Free Trade Agreement." Congressional Research Service, Washington, D.C., 1992.

Kaufman, Robert R., Carlos Bazdresch, and Blanca Heredia. "Mexico: Radical Reform in a Dominant Party System." In *Voting for Reform: Democracy, Political Liberalization, and Economic Adjustment*, ed. Stephan Haggard and Steven B. Webb. New York: Oxford University Press, 1994.

Kaufman, Robert R., and Guillermo Trejo. "Regionalism, Regime Transformation, and PRONASOL: The Politics of the National Solidarity Program in Four Mexican States." Columbia University, October 1995, unpublished paper.

Keohane, Robert O., ed. *Neorealism and Its Critics*. New York: Columbia University Press, 1986.

Klepak, Hal. "What's in It for Us? Canada's Relationship with Latin America." FOCAL Papers. Canadian Foundation for the Americas, Ottawa, 1994.

Krasner, Stephen D., ed. *International Regimes*. Ithaca, N.Y.: Cornell University Press, 1983.

Krauze, Enrique. "La presidencia imperial." In *Tiempo contado*. Mexico City: Editorial Océano, 1996.

Krueger, Anne. "Free Trade Areas vs. Customs Unions." NBER Working Paper 5084. National Bureau of Economic Research, Cambridge, Mass., 1995.

Krugman, Paul. "Dutch Tulips and Emerging Markets." *Foreign Affairs* 74, no. 4 (1995): 28–44.

Kuczynski, Pedro-Pablo. *Latin American Debt.* Baltimore: Johns Hopkins University Press, 1988.

Laird, Sam. "Mercosur Trade Policy: Toward Greater Integration." World Trade Organization, August 1995. Mimeo.

Lande, Stephen, and Nellis Crigler. "The Caribbean and NAFTA: Opportunities and Challenges." IDB-ECLAC Working Papers on Trade in the Western Hemisphere 51. Washington, D.C., July 1993.

———. "Trade Aspects of the Miami Summit of the Americas: The First Ninety Days." North-South Center, University of Miami, Fla., 1995.

Lawrence, Robert Z. *Regionalism, Multilateralism, and Deeper Integration.* Washington, D.C.: Brookings Institution, 1996.

Leamer, Edward. " Wage Effects of a US-Mexican Free Trade Agreement." NBER Working Paper 3391. National Bureau of Economic Research, Cambridge, Mass., 1992.

Levy, Santiago, and Sweder van Wijnbergen. "Transition Problems in Economic Reform: Agriculture in the Mexico-U.S. Free Trade Agreement." Policy Research Working Papers. World Bank, Washington, D.C., August 1992.

Leycegui, Beatriz, William B. P. Robson, and S. Dahlia Stein, eds. *Trading Punches: Trade Remedy Law and Disputes Under NAFTA.* Washington, D.C.: National Planning Association, 1995.

Londoño, Juan Luis. *Poverty, Inequality, and Human Capital Development in Latin America, 1950–2025.* Latin American and Caribbean Studies, Viewpoints Series. Washington, D.C.: World Bank, 1996.

López Obrador, Andrés Manuel. *Entre la historia y la esperanza.* Mexico City: Editorial Grijalbo, 1995.

Lord, Montague J. "Latin America's Exports of Manufactured Goods." In *Economic and Social Progress in Latin America: 1992 Report.* Washington, D.C.: Inter-American Development Bank, 1992.

Lowenthal, Abraham F. "The United States and Latin American Democracy: Learning from History." In *Exporting Democracy: The United States and Latin America: Themes and Issues,* ed. Abraham F. Lowenthal. Baltimore: Johns Hopkins University Press, 1991.

Lowenthal, Abraham F., and Katrina Burgess, eds. *The California-Mexico Connection.* Stanford: Stanford University Press, 1993.

Lujambio, Alonso. *Federalismo y congreso en el cambio político de México.* Mexico City: Universidad Nacional Autónoma de México, 1995.

Lustig, Nora. *Mexico: The Remaking of an Economy.* Washington, D.C.: Brookings Institution, 1992.

———. "NAFTA: Potential Impact on Mexico's Economy and Beyond." In *Economic Integration in the Western Hemisphere,* ed. Roberto Bouzas and Jaime Ros. Notre Dame, Ind.: University of Notre Dame Press, 1994.

———. Introduction to *Coping with Austerity: Poverty and Inequality in Latin America,* ed. Nora Lustig. Washington, D.C.: Brookings Institution, 1995.

———. "The Mexican Peso Crisis: The Foreseeable and the Surprise." Brookings Discussion Papers 114. Brookings Institution, Washington, D.C., 1995.

———. "Mexico in Crisis, the U.S. to the Rescue: The Financial Assistance Packages of 1982 and 1995." Brookings Discussion Papers. Brookings Institution, Washington, D.C., July 1996.

Mainwaring, Scott. "Brazil: Weak Parties, Feckless Democracy." In *Building Democratic Institutions: Party Systems in Latin America,* ed. Scott Mainwaring and Timothy R. Scully. Stanford: Stanford University Press, 1995.

Mainwaring, Scott, and Matthew Schugart, eds. *Presidentialism and Democracy in Latin America.* Cambridge: Cambridge University Press, 1996.

Mansfield, Edward, and Helen Milner, eds. *The Political Economy of Regionalism.* New York: Columbia University Press, 1997.

Manzetti, Luigi. *Institutions, Parties, and Coalitions in Argentine Politics.* Pittsburgh, Pa.: University of Pittsburgh Press, 1993.

———. "The Political Economy of MERCOSUR." *Journal of Interamerican Studies and World Affairs* 35, no. 4 (1993/94): 101–41.

Martin, Philip. *Trade and Migration: NAFTA and Agriculture.* Washington, D.C.: Institute for International Economics, 1993.

———. "Mexican-U.S. Migration: Policies and Economic Impacts." *Challenge,* March 1995, 56–62.

Martínez, Javier, and Alvaro Díaz. *Chile: The Great Transformation.* Washington, D.C.: Brookings Institution, 1996.

Mayer, Frederick W. *Interpreting NAFTA: The Art and Science of Political Analysis.* New York: Columbia University Press, forthcoming.

McKeown, Timothy. "Firms and Tariff Regime Change: Exploring the Demand for Protection." *World Politics* 36, no. 2 (1984): 215–33.

Meller, Patricio. "Review of the Chilean Trade Liberalization and Export

Expansion Process (1974/90)." *Bangladesh Development Studies* 20, no. 2/3 (1992): 155–84.

———. "An Overview of Chilean Trade Strategy." In *Integrating the Hemisphere*, ed. Ana Julia Jatar and Sidney Weintraub. Washington, D.C.: Inter-American Dialogue, 1997.

Meyer, Lorenzo. *Liberalismo autoritario*. Mexico City: Editorial Océano, 1995.

Milner, Helen. "Trading Places: Industries for Free Trade." *World Politics* 40, no. 3 (1988): 355–76.

———. "Industries, Governments, and the Creation of Regional Trade Blocs." In *The Political Economy of Regionalism*, ed. Edward Mansfield and Helen Milner. New York: Columbia University Press, 1997.

Morici, Peter. *Free Trade in the Americas*. New York: Twentieth Century Fund Press, 1994.

Mumme, Stephen P. "State Influence in Foreign Policy-Making: Water Related Environmental Disputes Along the U.S.-Mexico Border." *Western Political Quarterly* 38, no. 4 (1985): 620–40.

Nadelmann, Ethan. *Cops Across Borders: The Internationalization of U.S. Law Enforcement*. University Park: Pennsylvania State University Press, 1993.

Naím, Moisés. "Toward Free Trade in the Americas: Building Blocks, Stumbling Blocks, and Entry Fees." In *Integrating the Americas: Shaping Future Trade Policy*, ed. Sidney Weintraub. Miami, Fla.: North-South Center, University of Miami, 1994.

———. "Mexico's Larger Story." *Foreign Policy*, July/August 1995, 112–30.

O'Donnell, Guillermo. "Do Economists Know Best?" *Journal of Democracy* 6, no. 1 (1995): 23–28.

Office of Technology Assessment. *U.S.-Mexico Trade: Pulling Together or Pulling Apart?* Washington, D.C.: U.S. Congress, 1992.

O'Keefe, Thomas Andrew. "The Prospects for Mercosur's Inclusion into the North American Free Trade Agreement (NAFTA)." *International Law Practicum* 8, no. 1 (1995): 5–13.

Oks, Daniel, and Sweder van Wijnbergen. "Mexico After the Debt Crisis: Is Growth Sustainable?" *Journal of Development Economics* 47, no. 1 (1995): 155–78.

Olson, Mancur. *The Logic of Collective Action: Public Goods and the Theory of Groups*. New York: Schocken Books, 1968.

Orme, William A. *Understanding NAFTA*. Austin: University of Texas Press, 1996.

Ozorio, Anna Luiza, Scott Graham, and Leandro Alves. "Poverty, Dereg- ulation, and Informal Employment in Mexico." World Bank, Wash- ington, D.C., 1994. Mimeo.

Pastor, Manuel, Jr. *Inflation, Stabilization, and Debt: Macroeconomic Ex- periments in Peru and Bolivia.* Boulder, Colo.: Westview Press, 1992.

———. "Mexican Trade Liberalization and NAFTA." *Latin American Re- search Review* 29, no. 3 (1994): 153–73.

Pastor, Manuel, Jr., and Carol Wise. "The Origins and Sustainability of Mexico's Free Trade Policy." *International Organization* 48, no. 3 (1994): 459–89.

———. "Challenges to Western Hemispheric Integration: Free Trade Is Not Enough." *SAIS Review* 15, no. 2 (1995): 1–16.

———. "The Politics of Free Trade in the Western Hemisphere." Agenda Papers 20. North-South Center, University of Miami, Fla., 1996.

———. "State Policy, Distribution, and Neoliberal Reform in Mexico." *Journal of Latin American Studies* 29, no. 2 (1997): 419–56.

———. "Stabilization and Its Discontents: Argentina's Economic Re- structuring in the 1990's." Agenda Papers. North-South Center, Uni- versity of Miami, Fla., 1998.

Pastor, Robert A. "NAFTA as the Center of the Integration Process: The Nontrade Issues." In *North American Free Trade: Assessing the Im- pact,* ed. Nora Lustig et al. Washington, D.C.: Brookings Institution, 1992.

———. *Integration with Mexico: Options for U.S. Policy.* New York: Twentieth Century Fund Press, 1993.

Paternostro, Silvana. "Mexico as a Narco-Democracy." *World Policy Journal* 12, no. 1 (1995): 41–47.

Perez-Lopez, Jorge. "The Automotive Sector in the NAFTA: Negotiating Issues from a U.S. Perspective." In *Sectoral Labor Effects of North American Free Trade,* ed. Rafael Fernandez de Castro, Monica Verea Campos, and Sidney Weintraub. Austin: University of Texas Press, 1993.

Perl, Raphael F. "United States Andean Drug Policy: Background and Issues for Decisionmakers." *Journal of Interamerican Studies and World Affairs* 34, no. 3 (1992): 13–36.

Peschard-Sverdrup, Armand B. "The 1997 Mexican Midterm Elections: Post-Election Report." Western Hemisphere Election Study Series. Center for Strategic and International Studies, Washington, D.C., Au- gust 30, 1997.

Peters, Enrique Dussel. "From Export-Oriented to Import-Oriented Industrialization: Changes in Mexico's Manufacturing Sector, 1988–1994." In *Neoliberalism Revisited: Economic Restructuring and Mexico's Political Future,* ed. Gerardo Otero. Boulder, Colo.: Westview Press, 1996.

Portes, Alejandro, Manuel Castells, and Lauren Benton, eds. *The Informal Economy: Studies in Advanced and Less Advanced Countries.* Baltimore: Johns Hopkins University Press, 1989.

Pozas, Maria de los Angeles. *Industrial Restructuring in Mexico.* La Jolla: Center for U.S.-Mexican Studies, University of California at San Diego, 1993.

Psacharopoulos, George. "Time Trends of the Returns to Education: Cross National Evidence." *Economics of Education Review* 8, no. 3 (1989): 225–31.

Puryear, Jeffrey M. "Education in Latin America: Problems and Challenges." Paper prepared for the Council on Foreign Relations, Working Group on Educational Reform, New York, February 27, 1996.

Raczynski, Dagmar. "Programs, Institutions, and Resources: Chile." In *Strategies to Combat Poverty in Latin America,* ed. Dagmar Raczynski. Washington, D.C.: Inter-American Development Bank, 1995.

Raczynski, Dagmar, and Pilar Romaguera. "Chile: Poverty, Adjustment, and Social Policies in the 1980's." In *Coping with Austerity: Poverty and Inequality in Latin America,* ed. Nora Lustig. Washington, D.C.: Brookings Institution, 1995.

Ramos, Joseph. *Neoconservative Economics in the Southern Cone of Latin America, 1973–1983.* Baltimore: Johns Hopkins University Press, 1986.

Robinson, Sherman, et al. "Agricultural Policies and Migration in a United States–Mexico Free Trade Area." Working Paper 617. Department of Agricultural and Resource Economics, University of California at Berkeley, 1991.

Rodrígues, Miguel, and Barbara Kotschwar. "Latin America: Expanding Trade Opportunities." *SAIS Review* 17 (1997): 39–60.

Rodríguez, Victoria E. *Decentralization in Mexico: From Reforma Municipal to Solidaridad to Nuevo Federalismo.* Boulder, Colo.: Westview Press, 1997.

Rodríguez, Victoria E., and Peter Ward. *Political Change in Baja California: Democracy in the Making.* La Jolla: Center for U.S.-Mexican Studies, University of California at San Diego, 1994.

Rodrik, Dani. "Promises, Promises: Credible Policy via Signalling." *Economic Journal* 99, no. 397 (1989): 756–72.

———. "The Rush to Free Trade in the Developing World: Why So Late? Why Now? Will It Last?" In *Voting for Reform: Democracy, Political Liberalization, and Economic Adjustment,* ed. Stephan Haggard and Steven B. Webb. New York: Oxford University Press, 1994.

———. "Understanding Economic Policy Reform." *Journal of Economic Literature* 34, no. 1 (1996): 9–41.

———. *Has Globalization Gone Too Far?* Washington, D.C.: Institute for International Economics, 1997.

Roett, Riordan. "The Mexican Devaluation and the U.S. Response: Potomac Politics, 1995-Style." In *The Mexican Peso Crisis: International Perspectives,* ed. Riordan Roett. Boulder, Colo.: Lynne Rienner, 1996.

Rogowski, Ronald. *Commerce and Coalitions: How Trade Affects Domestic Political Alignments.* Princeton: Princeton University Press, 1989.

Ros, Jaime. "Mexico and NAFTA: Economic Effects and the Bargaining Process." In *Mexico and NAFTA: Who Will Benefit?* ed. Victor Bulmer-Thomas, Nikki Craske, and Mónica Serrano. London: Macmillan & Institute for Latin American Studies, 1994.

———. "Mexico in the 1990s: A New Economic Miracle?" In *The Politics of Economic Restructuring: State-Society Relations and Regime Change in Mexico,* ed. Maria Lorena Cook, Kevin J. Middlebrook, and Juan Molinar Horcasitas. La Jolla: Center for U.S.-Mexican Studies, University of California at San Diego, 1994.

Ros, Jaime, et al. "Prospects for Growth and the Environment in Mexico in the 1990s." *World Development* 24, no. 2 (1996): 307–24.

Rosenau, James N. "Coherent Connection or Commonplace Contiguity? Theorizing About the California-Mexico Overlap." In *The California-Mexico Connection,* ed. Abraham F. Lowenthal and Katrina Burgess. Stanford: Stanford University Press, 1993.

Rosenberg, Mark, and Jonathan T. Hiskey. "Changing Trading Patterns of the Caribbean Basin." *Annals of the American Academy of Political Science* 533 (1994): 100–111.

Rubio, Luis. "Mexico, NAFTA, and the Pacific Basin." In *Cooperation or Rivalry? Regional Integration in the Americas and the Pacific Rim,* ed. Shoji Nishijima and Peter H. Smith. Boulder, Colo.: Westview Press, 1996.

Rugman, Alan M., and Michael Gestrin. "NAFTA's Treatment of Foreign Investment." In *Foreign Investment and NAFTA,* ed. Alan M. Rugman. Columbia: University of South Carolina Press, 1994.

Ruiz Durán, Clemente. "México: Crecimiento e innovación en las micro y pequeñas empresas." *Comercio Exterior* 43, no. 6 (1993): 525–29.

Saborio, Sylvia, et al. *The Premise and the Promise: Free Trade in the Americas*. Washington, D.C.: Overseas Development Council, 1992.

Sachs, Jeffrey, Aaron Tornell, and Andrés Velasco. "The Collapse of the Mexican Peso: What Have We Learned?" NBER Working Paper 5142. National Bureau of Economic Research, Cambridge, Mass., June 1995.

Sassen, Saskia. "Why Migration?" *NACLA Report on the Americas*, July 1992.

Schattschneider, E. E. *Politics, Pressures, and the Tariff*. Englewood Cliffs, N.J.: Prentice Hall, 1935.

Secretaría de Desarrollo Social (SEDESOL). *Solidarity in National Development: New Relations Between Society and Government*. Mexico City: SEDESOL, 1993.

Serra, Jaime, et al. *Reflections on Regionalism: Report of the Study Group on International Trade*. Washington, D.C.: Carnegie Endowment for International Peace, 1997.

Sheahan, John. *Conflict and Change in Mexican Economic Strategy*. La Jolla: Center for U.S.-Mexican Studies, University of California at San Diego, 1991.

Sherk, Donald R. "Emerging Markets and the Multilateral Development Banks." *Columbia Journal of World Business* 29, no. 2 (1994): 44–52.

Shifter, Michael. "United States–Latin American Relations: Shunted to the Slow Track." *Current History* 97, no. 616 (1998): 49–54.

Shwedel, Kurt. "La competitividad del sector agroindustrial." In *La industria mexicana en el mercado mundial: Elementos para una política industrial*, ed. Fernando Clavijo and J. Casar, vol. 2. Mexico City: Lecturas de El Trimestre Económico, FCE, 1994.

Sikkink, Kathryn. *Ideas and Institutions: Developmentalism in Brazil and Argentina*. Ithaca, N.Y.: Cornell University Press, 1991.

Sklair, Leslie. *Assembling for Development: The Maquila Industry in Mexico and the United States*. La Jolla: Center for U.S.-Mexican Studies, University of California at San Diego, 1993.

Smith, Peter. "The United States, Regional Integration, and the Reshaping of the International Order." In *Cooperation or Rivalry? Regional Integration in the Americas and the Pacific Rim*, ed. Shoji Nishijima and Peter H. Smith. Boulder, Colo.: Westview Press, 1996.

———, ed. *The Challenge of Integration: Europe and the Americas*. New Brunswick, N.J.: Transaction Books, 1993.

Southard, Frank. "The Evolution of the International Monetary Fund." Essays in International Finance 135. Department of Economics, Princeton University, 1979.

Springer, Gary L., and Jorge L. Molina. "The Mexican Financial Crisis: Genesis, Impact, and Implications." *Journal of Interamerican Studies and World Affairs* 37, no. 2 (1995): 57–81.

Stairs, Denis. "Change in the Management of Canada–United States Relations in the Post-War Era." In *Toward a North American Community? Canada, the United States, and Mexico,* ed. Donald Barry. Boulder, Colo.: Westview Press, 1995.

―――. "The Canadian Dilemma in North America." In *NAFTA and Sovereignty: Trade-offs for Canada, Mexico, and the United States,* ed. Joyce Hoebing et al. Washington, D.C.: Center for Strategic and International Studies, 1996.

Stanford, Lois. "The 'Organization' of Mexican Agriculture: Conflicts and Compromises." *Latin American Research Review* 28, no. 1 (1993): 188–201.

Stern, Nicholas (with Francisco Ferreira). "The World Bank as 'Intellectual Actor.'" Development Economics Research Programme Discussion Paper, DEP/50. London School of Economics, 1993.

Tanzi, Vito. *The Underground Economy in the United States and Abroad.* New York: Lexington Books, 1982.

Thacker, Strom. "From Silent to Active Partner: Big Business, the State, and Free Trade in Mexico." Ph.D. diss., University of North Carolina, 1995.

Thompson, Gary D., and Paul N. Wilson. "Ejido Reforms in Mexico: Conceptual Issues and Potential Outcomes." *Land Economics* 70, no. 4 (1994): 448–65.

Tornell, Aaron. "Are Economic Crises Necessary for Trade Liberalization and Fiscal Reform?" In *Reform, Recovery, and Growth: Latin America and the Middle East,* ed. Rudiger Dornbusch and Sebastian Edwards. Chicago: University of Chicago Press, 1995.

Trigueros, Ignacio. "The Mexican Financial System and NAFTA." In *Mexico and the North American Free Trade Agreement: Who Will Benefit?* ed. Victor Bulmer-Thomas, Nikki Craske, and Mónica Serrano. New York: St. Martin's Press, 1994.

Tulchin, Joseph S. "The Enterprise for the Americas Initiative: Empty Gesture, Shrewd Gambit, or Remarkable Shift in Hemispheric Relations?" In *The Enterprise for the Americas Initiative,* ed. Roy Green. Westport, Conn.: Praeger, 1993.

Tussie, Diana. "Argentina in the Global Economy: Facing the Dilemmas." Documentos e Informes de Investigación 202. FLACSO, Buenos Aires, April 1996.

United Nations Economic Commission for Latin America and the Caribbean (ECLAC). *NAFTA Implementation in the United States: The First
Two Years*. Santiago: ECLAC, 1996.

————. *Strengthening Development: The Interplay of Macro- and Microeconomics*. Washington, D.C.: ECLAC, 1996.

United Nations Industrial Development Organization (UNIDO). *Brazil's
Industrial Policy: An Assessment in the Light of the International Experience*. Vienna: UNIDO, 1992.

————. *Industrial Competitiveness in Brazil: Trends and Prospects*. Vienna: UNIDO, 1992.

————. *Mexico: The Promise of NAFTA*. Vienna: UNIDO, 1994.

U.S. Department of State. Bureau of International Narcotics Matters. *International Narcotics Control Strategy Report*. Washington, D.C.: U.S.
Government Printing Office, 1991.

Valdes, Alberto. "Joining an Existing Regional Trade Agreement from
the Perspective of a Small Open Economy: Chile's Accession to NAFTA
and MERCOSUR." *American Journal of Agricultural Economics* 77, no. 5
(1995): 243–50.

Vaubel, Roland. "The Political Economy of the International Monetary
Fund." In *The Political Economy of International Organizations*, ed.
Roland Vaubel and Thomas Willett. Boulder, Colo.: Westview Press,
1991.

Vidal, Jose Carlos. "Economic Relations Between Brazil and Argentina:
The Shift in the Eighties." Ph.D. diss., University of Illinois at Champagne-Urbana, 1993.

Waverman, Leonard. "The NAFTA Agreement: A Canadian Perspective."
In *Assessing NAFTA: A Trilateral Analysis*, ed. Steven Globerman and
Michael Walker. Vancouver: Fraser Institute, 1992.

Weintraub, Sidney. "The New U.S. Economic Initiative Toward Latin
America." *Journal of Interamerican Studies and World Affairs* 33, no.
1 (1991): 1–18.

————. "U.S.-Mexico Trade: Implications for the United States." In *Assessments of the North American Free Trade Agreement*, ed. Ambler H.
Moss. Miami, Fla.: North-South Center, University of Miami, 1993.

————. *NAFTA: What Comes Next?* Westport, Conn.: Praeger, 1994.

————. *NAFTA at Three: A Progress Report*. Washington, D.C.: Center
for Strategic and International Studies, 1997.

Weldon, Jeffrey. "The Political Sources of Presidentialism in Mexico."
In *Presidentialism and Democracy in Latin America*, ed. Scott Main-

waring and Matthew Schugart. New York: Cambridge University Press, 1996.

Wiarda, Howard J. "After Miami: The Summit, the Peso Crisis, and the Future of U.S.– Latin American Relations." *Journal of Interamerican Studies and World Affairs* 37, no. 1 (1995): 43–68.

Williams, Heather. *Planting Trouble: The Barzón Debtors' Movement in Mexico.* La Jolla: Center for U.S.-Mexican Studies, University of California at San Diego, 1996.

Williams, Phil. "Transnational Criminal Organizations: Strategic Alliances." *Washington Quarterly* (winter 1995): 57–72.

Williamson, John, and Stephan Haggard. "The Political Conditions for Economic Reform." In *The Political Economy of Policy Reform,* ed. John Williamson. Washington, D.C.: Institute for International Economics, 1994.

Winham, Gilbert R. "Why Canada Acted." In *Bilateralism, Multilateralism, and Canada in U.S. Trade Policy,* ed. William Diebold Jr. Cambridge: Ballinger Publishing, 1988.

Wonnacott, Ronald. "Free-Trade Agreements: For Better or Worse?" *American Economic Review* 86, no. 2 (1996): 62–65.

Woods, Ngaire. "Ethics and Interests in the International Political Economy: The Management of the Mexican Debt, 1982–1989." Ph.D. thesis, Oxford University, 1992.

Zabludovsky, Jaime. "Trade and Industrial Policy for Structural Adjustment in Mexico." In *Perspectives on the Pacific Basin Economy,* ed. Takao Fukuchi and Mitsuhiro Kagami. Tokyo: Asia Club Foundation, 1989.

Zangari, B. J., ed. *NAFTA: Issues, Industry Sector Profiles, and Bibliography.* Commack, N.Y.: Nova Science Publishers, 1994.

Zearley, Thomas. "Creating an Enabling Environment for Housing: Recent Reforms in Mexico." *Housing Policy Debate* 4, no. 2 (1993): 239–49.

Zínser, Adolfo Aquilar. *Vamos a ganar: La pugna de Cuauhtémoc Cárdenas por el poder.* Mexico City: Editorial Océano, 1995.

Contributors

Peter Andreas is an SSRC-MacArthur Foundation Fellow on Peace and Security in a Changing World and is completing his Ph.D. in government at Cornell University. He is a co-author of *Drug War Politics: The Price of Denial* (Berkeley and Los Angeles: University of California Press, 1996).

Denise Dresser is professor of political science at the Instituto Tecnológico Autónomo de México (ITAM). She has been a visiting research fellow at the Center for U.S.-Mexican Studies, University of California, San Diego; a postdoctoral fellow at the Center of International Studies, University of Southern California; and a senior visiting fellow at the Inter-American Dialogue. She is the author of *Neopopulist Solutions to Neoliberal Problems: Mexico's National Solidarity Program* (La Jolla: Center for U.S.-Mexican Studies, University of California at San Diego, 1991) and of numerous articles on Mexican politics and U.S.-Mexican relations. She is currently at work on a book dealing with the politics of economic reform in Mexico. She is on the advisory board of *Este País* and writes a political column for the Mexican newspaper *Reforma*.

Stephan Haggard is professor at the Graduate School of International Relations and Pacific Studies at the University of California, San Diego. He is the author of *Pathways from the Periphery: The Political Economy of Growth in the Newly Industrializing Countries* (Ithaca, N.Y.: Cornell University Press, 1990) and *The Developing Nations and the Politics of Global Integration* (Washington, D.C.: Brookings Institution, 1995) and co-author, with Robert Kaufman, of *The Political Economy of Democratic Transitions* (Princeton: Princeton University Press, 1995). He has been a consultant to the U.S. Agency for International Development, the World Bank, the United Nations Conference on Trade and Development, and the OECD and is a member of the Council on Foreign Relations.

Jonathan Heath is an independent economist specializing in Mexico's economic outlook. He writes for the Mexico City newspapers *Reforma* and *Mexico City Times*. His most recent articles are "The Devaluation of the Mexican Peso in 1994," published by the Center for Strategic and

International Studies (CSIS); "El Empleo en México," published by IMEF; and "The Sustainability of Political and Economic Reform in Mexico," to be published by the Americas Society.

Sylvia Maxfield is associate professor of political science at Yale University, where she has been a full-time faculty member since 1987. She is the author of numerous books and articles on the political economy of emerging market countries, with emphasis on finance; her most recent book, *Gatekeepers of Growth* (Princeton; Princeton University Press, 1997), is about the politics of central banking in Latin America and Asia. Maxfield has received numerous grants and awards for academic achievement, including, most recently, an International Affairs Fellowship from the Council on Foreign Relations and a Pew Faculty Fellowship. Maxfield's consulting experience includes the public and private sectors.

Manuel Pastor Jr. is professor and chair of Latin American and Latino Studies at the University of California, Santa Cruz. A former Kellogg and Guggenheim Fellow, he has published articles on Latin American macroeconomic stabilization in *Latin American Research Review, International Organization, Journal of Development Economics, World Development,* and elsewhere. Sponsored by the U.S. Institute of Peace and the Social Science Research Council, he is currently conducting research comparing Argentina and Mexico in the postliberalization era.

Adam Shapiro is a graduate of Yale University with a B.A. in ethics, politics, and economics. Upon graduation from Yale, he spent a year researching economic liberalization in Argentina on a Fulbright Scholarship, and is currently an investment analyst at Darby Overseas Investment Fund in Washington, D.C.

Carol Wise is assistant professor at Johns Hopkins University's School of Advanced International Studies (SAIS). Before joining SAIS in 1994, she conducted a project titled "The Political Economy of North American Trade" at the Carnegie Endowment for International Peace in Washington, D.C. She has published articles on Latin American political economy in the *Latin American Research Review, International Organization, International Economy, Journal of Interamerican Studies and World Affairs, SAIS Review, Journal of Latin American Studies,* and *Studies in Compara-*

tive International Development. This edited collection is part of a larger research agenda on the politics of free trade in the Western Hemisphere, which has been funded by the John D. and Catherine T. MacArthur Foundation, the North-South Center at the University of Miami, and the U.S. Institute of Peace.

Ngaire Woods is lecturer and fellow in politics at University College, Oxford University. She is presently working on a book about international financial institutions and has published articles on issues in international political economy in *International Studies Quarterly* and *Millennium*. Most recently she edited the volume *Explaining International Relations Since 1945* (Oxford: Oxford University Press, 1996).

Index

accession to NAFTA, hemispheric initiatives and, 317–18

Accords of San Andrés Larráinzar, 242

"accretion" model for free-trade agreements, 333

Acta De Barahona, 325

administered protection, NAFTA's provisions for, 23

adult-education programs, job skills training and, 62

"aggressive unilateralism," North American trade policies and, 306–9

agricultural measures in NAFTA (Chapter 7), U.S.-Mexican negotiations on, 101–6

agricultural policy in Mexico: drug trafficking increases and, 211; government initiatives, 68–70; illegal immigration and, 212–15; market basis for, 63–68

agricultural products: CACM formation and, 323–24; Latin American exports in, 312

Allende, Salvador, 130

Alliance for National Welfare program, expansion of, 76

Alliance for the Recovery of Economic Growth, 78n.79

alternative open unemployment rate (TDAA), 198

American Farm Bureau, export subsidies in NAFTA and, 105–6

Andean Group: CARICOM formation and, 322–25; Colombian trade liberalization and, 280–81, 295; common external tariff (CET) and, 316; economic integration and, 304; investment provisions, 313; Latin American trade liberalization and, 259–60, 293–301, 320, 325–27; provisions of, 35, 260n.1; public policy development and, 292–93

Andean Trade Preference Act, 280–81, 295, 303, 319

antidumping measures: Mercosur provisions, 329–31; NAFTA negotiations on, 116–17, 314–16

Antigua Summit, CACM formation and, 322–23

arbitration procedures, investment provisions in NAFTA and, 110–11

Argentina: business-government coalitions in, 36; commercial policy reforms, 266; educational policies in, 289; industrial restructuring in, 292; inflation management in, 178; investment regime in, 313; macroeconomic and external indicators, 268; Mercosur and, 328–31; NAFTA membership proposed, 294; North American markets and, 311; trade liberalization in, 264, 274–79, 328n.57

Argentina-Brazil Economic Integration and Cooperation Program (PICE), 328–31

Argentina-Ecuador agreement, 2

Asian currency crises: Brazilian trade liberalization and, 284; hemispheric trade initiatives and, 300–301; impact on Mexico of, 34–35, 77

Asia Pacific Economic Cooperation (APEC), 334

Aspe, Pedro, 160

asset concentration: agricultural policy in Mexico and, 65–70; concentration of, in Mexican industrial sector, 57–58; Latin American economic development and, 289–93; in Mexico, NAFTA's impact on, 25–28

Association of Caribbean States, 321n.44

Ata de Buenos Aires, 329

Atlacomulco group of PRI, 234

Auto Decrees, NAFTA negotiations and, 89–93

autogolpe, 326

automotive trade and investment, NAFTA provision (Annex 300-A) negotiations, 88–93

Bach, Robert, 204, 216

"bandwagon" effect, strategic expansion issues, 316–17

Bank for International Settlements (BIS): peso